THE ROMAN EMPIRE IN LATE ANTIQUITY

In this volume, Hugh Elton offers a detailed and up-to-date history of the last centuries of the Roman Empire. Beginning with the crisis of the third century, he covers the rise of Christianity, the key Church Councils, the fall of the West to the barbarians, and the Justinianic reconquest, and concludes with the twin wars against Persians and Arabs in the seventh century AD. Elton isolates two major themes that emerge in this period. He notes that a new form of decision-making was created, whereby committees debated civil, military, and religious matters before the emperor, who was the final arbiter. Elton also highlights the evolution of the relationship between aristocrats and the Empire and provides new insights into the mechanics of administering the Empire, as well as frontier and military policies. Supported by comments on primary sources and anecdotes, *The Roman Empire in Late Antiquity* is designed for use in undergraduate courses on late antiquity and early medieval history.

Hugh Elton is Professor and Program Coordinator in the Program of Greek and Roman Studies at Trent University. A scholar of Late Roman political and military history, he has directed two archaeological projects in Turkey. He is the author of *Warfare in Roman Europe, AD 350–425* and *Frontiers of the Roman Empire*.

THE ROMAN EMPIRE IN LATE ANTIQUITY

A POLITICAL AND MILITARY HISTORY

HUGH ELTON

Trent University

CAMBRIDGE
UNIVERSITY PRESS

CAMBRIDGE
UNIVERSITY PRESS

University Printing House, Cambridge CB2 8BS, United Kingdom

One Liberty Plaza, 20th Floor, New York, NY 10006, USA

477 Williamstown Road, Port Melbourne, VIC 3207, Australia

314–321, 3rd Floor, Plot 3, Splendor Forum, Jasola District Centre, New Delhi – 110025, India

79 Anson Road, #06-04/06, Singapore 079906

Cambridge University Press is part of the University of Cambridge.

It furthers the University's mission by disseminating knowledge in the pursuit of education, learning, and research at the highest international levels of excellence.

www.cambridge.org
Information on this title: www.cambridge.org/9781108456319
DOI: 10.1017/9781139030236

First published 2018

Printed in the United States of America by Sheridan Books, Inc.

A catalogue record for this publication is available from the British Library.

ISBN 978-0-521-89931-4 Hardback
ISBN 978-1-108-45631-9 Paperback

CONTENTS

ILLUSTRATIONS

MAPS

ABBREVIATIONS

AE	*L'Année Epigraphique*
CJ	*Codex Justinianus*
CT	*Codex Theodosianus*
Ep.	*Epistula* = Letter
fr.	fragment
HE	*Historia Ecclesiastica* = Ecclesiastical History
IG	*Inscriptiones Graecae*
IGLS	*Inscriptions grecques et latines de la Syrie*
IGRR	*Inscriptiones Graecae ad Res Romanas Pertinentes*
ILS	*Inscriptiones Latinae Selectae*
OGIS	*Orientis Graecae inscriptiones selectae*
Or.	*Oratio* = Speech
P.Ital.	*Die nichtliterarischen lateinischen Papyri italiens aus der Zeit 445–700*, ed. Tjäder, J.O. (Lund, 1955)
SEG	*Supplementum Epigraphicum Graecarum*
Select Papyri	Hunt, A. S. and Edgar, C. C., *Select Papyri II: Non-Literary Papyri, Public Documents* (Cambridge, MA, 1927)

NOTES ON NAMES, PLACES, AND TITLES

Names of individuals have normally been presented in the Latin form, following the spelling used in the *Prosopography of the Late Roman Empire* (Cambridge, 1970–1992), though some well-known names like Constantine, Julian, and Justinian have been left in their English forms. Referencing to primary sources is generally restricted to quotations, though with the intent that consulting the *Prosopography* will lead those interested directly to primary sources. City names follow the format of Jones, A. H. M., *Cities of the Eastern Roman Provinces²* (Oxford, 1971). Technical terms are kept as far as possible, though usually in Latin rather than Greek. For ease of reading, the bishop of Rome is used in the fourth century; pope thereafter; the bishops of Constantinople, Antioch, and Alexandria as patriarchs; and the bishop of Jerusalem as patriarch after 451.

Much of the scholarship on the Later Roman Empire depends on Jones, A. H. M., *The Later Roman Empire* (Oxford, 1964). This is explicitly a social, economic, and administrative study of the Empire, though it does contain a history covering 284–602. In its focus on the primary source material for these areas, it is unsurpassed as a single work and is indispensable to serious study of the Late Empire. Equally indispensable are the three volumes of *The Prosopography of the Later Roman Empire* (Cambridge, 1970, 1980, 1992), covering 260–395, 395–527, and 527–641. These provide biographical entries with primary source references for the majority of secular figures. There are numerous addenda, as would be expected for such a project, as well as the gradual publication of similar volumes dealing with Christian prosopography, currently covering Africa (303–533), Italy (313–604), and the diocese of Asia Minor (313–641). For topography, *The Barrington Atlas of the Greek and Roman World* (Princeton, 2000) is invaluable.

Much of our understanding of the events of these centuries depends on coins, laws, and inscriptions. For the evidence of the coins, the series of *Roman Imperial Coinage* provides a detailed catalogue. For the laws of the *Codex Theodosianus*, Matthews, J. F. *Laying Down the Law* (New Haven, 2000) provides an excellent introduction, while Honoré, A., *Tribonian* (London, 1978) is very good on the reign of Justinian. For the whole topic of how the law worked in the Late Empire, see Harries, J., *Law and Empire in Late Antiquity* (Cambridge, 1999).

Excellent introductions to the events are available in *The Cambridge Ancient History*, Volume 12, eds. Bowman, A., Cameron, A. and Garnsey, P. (Cambridge, 2005) covering 193–337, Volume 13, eds. Bowman, A. and Garnsey, P. (Cambridge, 1998) covering 337–425, and Volume 14, eds. Bowman, A., Ward-Perkins, B. and Whitby, M. (Cambridge, 2000) covering 425–600. Similar broad approaches are provided by Johnson, S., ed., *The Oxford Handbook to Late Antiquity* (Oxford, 2012), Rousseau, P., ed., *A Companion to Late Antiquity* (London, 2009), and Bowersock, G., Brown, P. and Grabar, O., *Late Antiquity: A Guide to the Post-Classical World* (Princeton, 1999). Finally, the three recently published Cambridge Companions provide coverage at a more detailed level. Lenski, N., ed., *Cambridge Companion to the Age of Constantine*[2] (Cambridge, 2011), Maas, M., ed., *Cambridge Companion to the Age of Attila* (Cambridge, 2014), and Maas, M., ed., *Cambridge Companion to the Age of Justinian* (Cambridge, 2005). In all cases, although the coverage is often similar in depth to the approach followed here, the team-driven approach and the long time periods between the first commissioning of the chapters and the volumes' final publication sometimes means that there is no single interpretive framework.

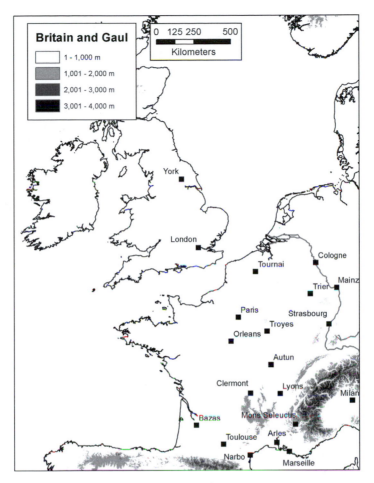

Map 1. Gaul and Britain

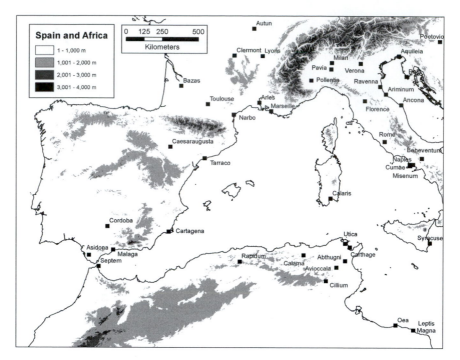

Map 2. Spain and Africa

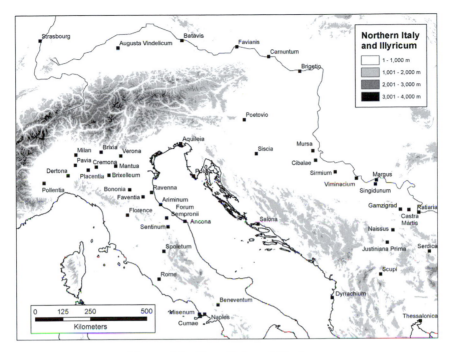

Map 3. Northern Italy and Illyricum

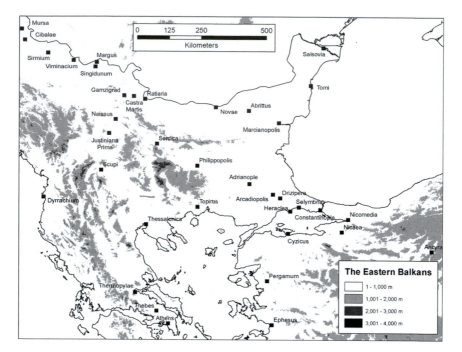

Map 4. The Eastern Balkans

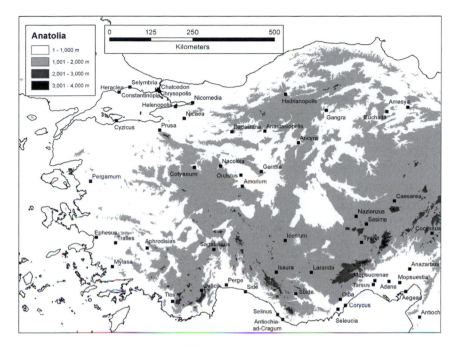

Map 5. Anatolia

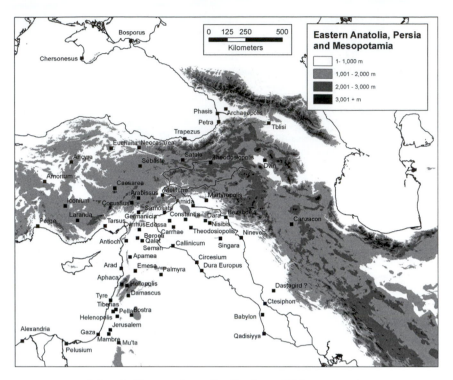

Map 6. Eastern Anatolia, Persia, and Mesopotamia

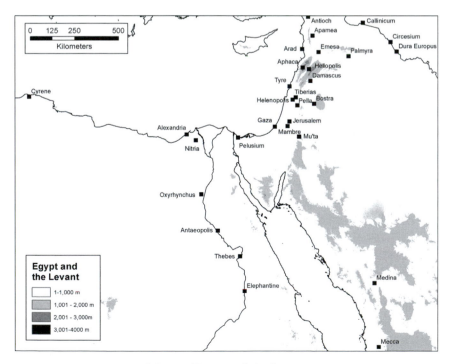

Map 7. Egypt and the Levant

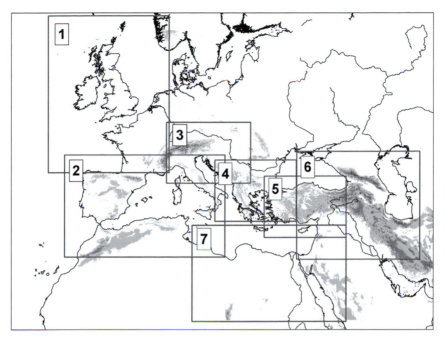

Map 8. Location map

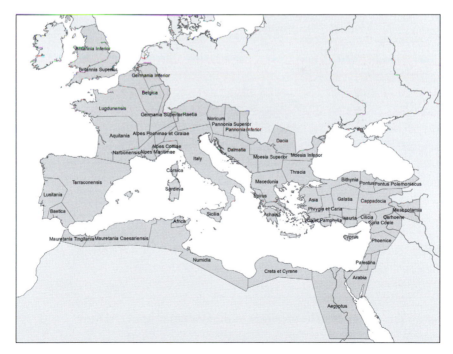

Map 9. The provinces of the Roman Empire, AD 260

Map 10. The provinces of the Roman Empire, AD 395

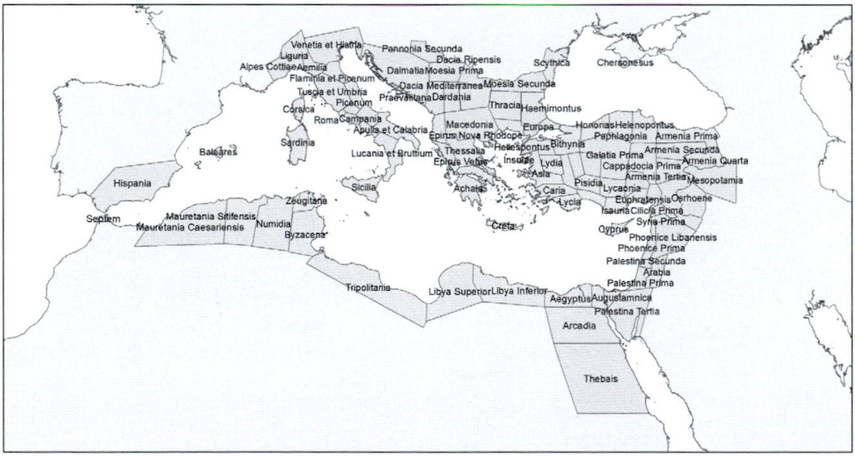

Map 11. The provinces of the Roman Empire, AD 565

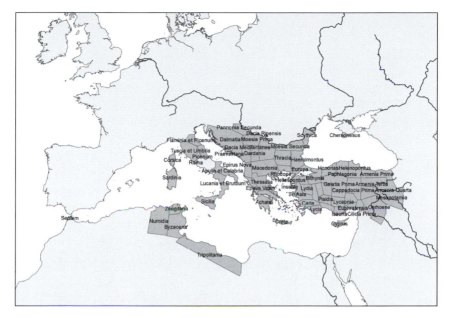

Map 12. The provinces of the Roman Empire, AD 641

Map 13. The dioceses of the Roman Empire

INTRODUCTION

There are many ways to look at the Late Roman Empire. This book presents one version of Roman imperial history between AD 260 and 641. At its heart lies my feeling that much of the current study of late antiquity fails to understand the Empire itself. Too often, the complexity and reality of the Empire have been masked by the writing of simplified history, both by moderns and by ancients. It is easier to tell the story of Rome in this fashion, but it creates an image of the ancient world as somehow simpler than our own. Since we have only a few glimpses into the feelings of contemporaries about government, understanding the Empire from the point of view of the emperor himself is difficult. When one of the Empire's first rulers, Tiberius I (14–37), said that running the Empire involved "holding a wolf by the ears" (Suetonius, *Tiberius* 25), it poses significant questions about what the emperor did and about the Empire itself.

In writing any sort of history, compromises have to be made. This book is written in the belief that the period between 260 and 641 forms a unity and that events in this period relate more closely to each other than to the period before or after. This period is not defined by Christianity, though this was a large part of what made the Empire different from the first or second centuries. Rather, it was defined by an aristocracy created through service to the emperor and the existence of centralized field armies. It is a long period, and to cover the major events and processes and yet keep the book short enough to be readable requires avoiding deep discussion of many points that would be considered more fully if space were not an issue. As Ammianus Marcellinus wrote in the fourth century, "Besides these battles, many others less worthy of mention were fought in various parts of Gaul, which it would be superfluous to describe, both because their results led to nothing worthwhile, and because it is not fitting to spin out a history with insignificant details" (Ammianus 27.2.11). Nonetheless, I remain uneasy about the necessary compression of complex matters, though attempt to comfort myself by taking Plutarch's view that "the careers of these men embrace such a multitude of events that my preamble shall consist of nothing more than this plea: if I do not record all their most celebrated achievements or describe any of them exhaustively, but merely summarize for the most part what they accomplished, I ask my reader not to regard this as a fault" (*Alexander* 1)

This work is a history of the Late Roman Empire and thus not a history of late antiquity. There is something that justifies the broadly defined study of culture that at its widest covers an area between Ireland and the Indian Ocean between 200 and 800. This work might be seen as traditional or old-fashioned, closely following the approach of J. B. Bury's 1923 *History of the Later Roman Empire*, though covering a longer time span (Bury covered 395–565). However, the explosion of scholarly interest and the changes in society make it impossible to write a history in the early twenty-first century that could compare to Bury in depth. Religion, for example, plays a much larger role in this work than in his. I feel that this work also benefits considerably from the Brownian approach to late antiquity, since we now have a much more nuanced view of the cultural world of the Roman Empire, i.e., the climate in which decisions were made and the various influences to which Late Roman officials were exposed. In this respect, Jill Harries' *Law and Empire* has been particularly inspiring for its exposition of a culture of criticism, as well as the concept that repeated laws were those which worked. I also feel that this work owes much to the approaches taken by John Matthews and Fergus Millar to the Empire.

This work is directed toward undergraduate students. In my experiences of teaching this period, I have felt a lack of a modern work that is short enough to be readable but also tells enough of the history of the Roman Empire to facilitate writing assignments and classroom discussion. I have tried to make it clear how our story is written from the primary sources. At the same time, I have restricted suggestions of secondary material to English language works that my students might read, though potential graduate students should not take this to mean that other languages are unnecessary

Three themes run through this history, linking Gallienus in 260 to Heraclius in 641. The first is that the Empire always remained centered on the person of the Roman emperor, who ran the state through meetings. These meetings generated paperwork that was disseminated to officials, and the officials then communicated back to the emperor. For the vast majority of the issues discussed at meetings, there were choices that could be made. Although our source material is imperfect, it frequently allows us to see the political process at work, with factions putting forward differing proposals that were decided on by the emperor. This interpretation thus rejects the model (often poorly defined) of an emperor at the mercy of various advisers, such as his wife, eunuchs, or generals. There were periods when such individuals had an influence on policy, but the structure of the Empire was such that these influences were always challenged by other participants in the political process. The second theme is that ruling the Empire required the consensus of the ruled. In the short term, it might be possible to dominate subjects by fear, but in the longer term different methods were likely to be more effective. The Empire was most vulnerable at moments when this consensus broke down and imperial unity was fractured. By the mid-third century, all emperors were aware of the fate of Gaius, Nero, and Commodus and generally avoided their excesses. This brings out a third theme, that there was little that was new about the problems of the late Empire, dominated as it was by issues of extracting resources (whether money, goods, or manpower) to provide security for its inhabitants. Although the means and methods of confronting internal and external problems changed greatly, it was still a continuation of the early Roman Empire, not an entirely new Empire. This did not change with Christianity, though the new religion provided a new way of confronting these sorts of issues. Nonetheless, there are two features that distinguish the study of the Roman Empire in late antiquity from that of the first two centuries AD, even as they do not define it. One is the presence of Christianity, a religion that eventually penetrated into every village of the Roman imperial state. And the other is the volume of primary evidence, itself in part the result of Christianity. We thus have far more details, far more complaints about taxation, etc., but know little about earlier situations where the evidence for the state, driven by epigraphy, is often different. The way that this evidence is read has changed dramatically over the past half-century, as modern scholars have a growing awareness of the tendency of our sources to select and edit their work, both as they were arguing their cases, and then subsequently as they made these cases to posterity.

The continuity of the Empire and its administration was part of its success. The repetition of the same events, of campaigns against the Franks and the Persians, of struggles with bishops, and of complaints and petitions to the emperors, can occasionally become tedious to read. But this repetition is the fabric of the Empire, even as it crumbled in the west in the fifth century. This history also takes a positive view of emperors and their administration. The majority of Romans involved in imperial administration worked long hours and tried to be fair. Many of them also made mistakes, and some would have been corrupt, others lazy. But to judge their performance from the writings of petitioners arguing cases, and in particular from the participants in ecclesiastical disputes, would be a poor methodology. Imperial records make a far better case for how the emperors wished to run the state, though we have so few of these and so many complaints. We find the bishop Theodoret in 448 writing two letters to imperial officials, questioning whether the emperor really had sent a letter to him. Since this letter had been delivered personally by the *comes* Rufus, and Theodoret had acknowledged its receipt in writing, it is probably better to see a man resisting authority rather than seriously doubting that the letter had actually been sent by the emperor (*Ep.* 79, 80). This sort of criticism of government is similar to that of sports fans of their team's managers; nonstop, negative, blessed by hindsight, and commenting on things about which they know little and can't do for themselves. This optimistic point of view may sometimes have led me to view events through rose-tinted glasses. The Late Roman Empire was often, if not always, a violent, corrupt, prejudiced state, but it was also one where imperial clemency was a virtue, and one often practiced.

Writing this book would not have been possible without others. First are my fellow ancient historians, whom I find constantly stimulating on paper and in person; these dialogues have increased my understanding enormously. A second group is my colleagues (other teachers, librarians, and support staff) at the various institutions at which I have worked, whose constant interest in what I do both surprises and humbles me. And third are the students I've been privileged to teach. The staff at Cambridge University Press and the anonymous referees have also been outstanding. My thanks to you all.

I

———

THE LATE THIRD CENTURY, 260–313

In the second half of the third century, the Roman ship of state was a battered vessel. The emperor Gordian III had died on campaign against the Persians in Mesopotamia in 244, the emperor Decius had died in the Balkan marshes near Abrittus at the hands of a Gothic army in 251, and the emperor Valerian had been captured by the Persians and dragged off to captivity in early 260. The Empire would survive, but it needed to change dramatically if it was to harness its resources to deal with these storms.

At the moment that Valerian was captured by the Persians, there were two other Roman emperors. One was his son Publius Licinius Egnatius Gallienus, already a full partner in power with the status of Augustus, and the other was his grandson Saloninus, with the lesser imperial status of Caesar. These men ruled over an Empire that stretched from north Britain to the Red Sea, from Mauritania to the Black Sea, inhabited by about 60 million subjects, the majority of whom were Roman citizens. The emperor was the chief magistrate of the Roman state whose power was absolute. Thus, according to the legal theorist Ulpian in the early third century, "What is pleasing to the emperor has the force of law" (*Digest* 1.4.1). This statement was later included in the *Digest*, a compilation of laws issued in the reign of the sixth-century emperor Justinian, and was just as valid then as when written by Ulpian.

A theory of absolutism, however, did not make an emperor. There was no body that sanctioned his acclamation, and though emperors often appealed to the support of the Senate, the people, or the army, in practice the only qualification required for the position of emperor was acceptance by others. Any Roman could claim to be emperor, and by the middle of the third century this had become a common phenomenon. Since the theory of imperial power was built around a single emperor (or an emperor sharing his power with his sons), acclamation while there was another emperor was a challenge to the current ruler. Emperors usually described a rival for imperial power as a *tyrannus*, a Latin term usually translated as "usurper." This understandable tendency makes more sense for contemporaries than for modern historians; to draw distinctions between imperial rivals based on their eventual success is a poor methodology for understanding imperial power. Until the final defeat of any claimant to imperial power, he could and did issue laws and coins, raise legions and taxes, and appoint officials. This legitimacy was, however, tempered by the amount of support that an imperial claimant had, and many emperors saw their imperial dreams rapidly crushed.

Although with enough support any claimant could become emperor, this does not mean that they could remain emperor. Acceptance by others was critical for running the Empire, and an emperor had to be seen to obey the law. Thus a law of Valentinian III from 429 included in the *Codex Justinianus* in the sixth century referenced the proverb that "for an emperor to be bound by the laws himself is profitable for the majesty of the ruler" (*CJ* 1.14.4). A certain amount of arbitrary behavior by an emperor might be acceptable, but only so much. In this respect, the lack of an accession process made contemplation of removing an objectionable emperor relatively easy.

Despite the lack of any formal need for qualifications, Romans of all sorts, not just lawyers, spent some time thinking about the role of the emperor. The orator Mamertinus, when addressing the emperor Maximian at Trier in Gaul in 289, described what he thought the emperor had to do:

> To admit into your heart the care of so great a state and take on the fate of the whole world and, having forgotten yourself, as it were, to live for the people; to stand on such a lofty summit of human affairs from which it is as if you are looking down on every land and sea, and in turn with your eyes and mind you look to where peace is assured, where a storm is threatening, which governors are emulating your justice, which generals maintain the glory of your courage, to receive innumerable messengers from every direction and to send out as many orders, to think about so many cities and nations and provinces, to pass all nights and days in perpetual care for the safety of all (*Latin Panegyrics* 10.3.3–4).

It was a daunting job description, but there was no shortage of candidates. Some, perhaps most, were driven by desire for power. But for many, the chance to show that they could do the job better and to help more people would have been a powerful motivator. After all, the hours were long, the work was frequently uncomfortable and dusty, and there was a high risk of failure resulting in death. Mamertinus' list of cares, however, does not tell us how the Empire was actually ruled. Although the emperor was the final arbiter, imperial decision-making and the creation of policy normally took place through a consultative process. The emperor's advisory council (known as the *consilium* until the end of the third century, thereafter as the *consistorium*, the *sacrarium*, or the *silentium*) always remained a consultative body carrying out meaningful discussions. The consistory was originally a body that received imperial visitors and received its name from the fact that only the emperor sat, while the rest of the council met standing. The debate took place in front of the emperor, but he made the final decisions in all cases. On many occasions, contemporaries or later historians claimed that individuals had an undue influence on the emperor, particularly those described as weak or young, but this does not mean that such individuals actually controlled the government; council meetings were not normally attended by the emperor's wife or sister. The tone of discussions may have varied from emperor to emperor, but the commitment to presenting points of view and the logistical realities of running the state meant that it was difficult for dogma to overrule budgets. Membership of the advisory council was never statutory, but consisted of senior officials at court as well as friends and trusted advisers of the emperor; though there may have been some informality, the meetings were minuted. There are no detailed descriptions of the working of the imperial council in the mid-third century, but an anecdote from Porphyry's *Life of Plotinus*, a philosopher, is suggestive:

> The Emperor Gallienus and his wife Salonina greatly honoured and venerated Plotinus. He thought to turn their friendship to some good purpose, saying that there had been a certain city of philosophers in Campania, now in ruins; he asked for the city to be rebuilt and to make over the surrounding district to the city when it was founded; those intending to live there would live under Plato's laws: the city was to be called Platonopolis; and he himself promised to withdraw there with his companions. The philosopher's intent would have happened most easily, if some of those around the emperor, either by jealousy, by resentment, or some other wretched reason obstructed the opportunity (Porphyry, *Life of Plotinus* 12).

Porphyry was presumably making the most of the relationship between Plotinus and the emperor, but the way that he explains the rejection of Plotinus' plan suggests a consciousness of conciliar decision-making. Despite the emperor's friendship for Plotinus, Porphyry does not paint a picture of the philosopher attending the council. Not every matter would have been discussed by a large collection of imperial officials. On some occasions, the council was bypassed, either by individuals going to the emperor directly or by the emperor himself going directly to an individual. Thus in 269, a

Herul exile, Andonnoballus, approached the emperor Claudius II at dinner, "and said 'I wish to ask a favour of you'. The emperor, thinking that he would ask for something substantial, gave him permission to make his request. And Andonnoballus said 'Give me some good wine'" (Peter the Patrician *Claudius* fr. 4). This was in public, but even when a petitioner might be able to speak relatively privately, the emperor was never truly alone. He was always accompanied by his bodyguards and by various personal attendants (*cubicularii*) who looked after his private space, known as the imperial bedroom (*sacrum cubiculum*), though in palaces this was a series of apartments rather than a single room. There were also various retainers to look after the imperial vestments and to deal with immediate demands for money. Traditionally, the *cubicularii* were eunuchs whose lack of families meant they were thought less likely to be corrupted while also being safe to keep around the imperial women. Often perceived as gatekeepers, eunuchs were usually treated in a negative fashion by contemporaries. There were perpetual tensions between the need to protect the body and time of the emperor and the need for him to be accessible to his officials and subjects. Emperors, as well as subjects, were also well aware of the danger of isolation.

IMPERIAL ADMINISTRATION

Open speech at the consistory was one way for the emperor to remain in touch with his Empire. Another way, not mentioned in Mamertinus' list of cares, was to receive petitions from his subjects and respond to them. The right to petition was universal for imperial subjects, even for slaves, as well as for cities, while emperors were supposed to be generous givers. Some of these petitions could be dealt with by simple gifts of cash or land. Around 258, Lollianus Homoeus, a publicly funded teacher of grammar from Oxyrhynchus in Egypt, sent a petition to Valerian and Gallienus, requesting the emperor assign him the income from a local orchard worth 600 Attic drachmae instead of the civic salary of 500 Attic drachmae that had been paid unreliably. He explained that rather than continually asking for payment from the city, he preferred to ask the emperor to intervene. Lollianus also wrote a covering letter to a friend that reveals he had sent an earlier petition to the emperor about this via another friend (*Oxyrhynchus Papyri* 47.3366). Lollianus' request was typical. Was he the victim of an inept civic administration as he claimed or a manipulator going over the head of the city to increase his income by 20 percent? Much of our evidence for petitions comes from the cities in the Greek-speaking part of the Empire, though this may reflect a tendency to erect inscriptions rather than a greater tendency to appeal to the emperor. Replies to petitions such as Lollianus', usually known as rescripts, were drafted by an official known as the *a libellis*, but by the end of the third century were known as the *magister libellorum*. There was a standard format for imperial rescripts that were dictated by the emperor in Latin and were then posted publicly. They tended to state the relevant law briefly, rather than making a judgment regarding the case, often followed by a request to a local official to investigate. Other imperial correspondence was handled by the *ab epistulis* (later *magister epistularum*), usually one each for Greek and Latin correspondence, while imperial laws, usually known as edicts, were drafted by the *magister memoriae* and then discussed in the consistory.

These imperial officials produced a lot of paperwork. We know little about how these records were stored, and the mobile nature of third-century Roman government meant that there were practical limits on how much documentation could be kept; much of the paperwork was probably sent to Rome, stored in imperial estates, or discarded. Even when the relevant paperwork was accessible, much depended on the quality of indexing and filing. Emperors were accustomed to rule on matters directly and then correcting themselves or overruling precedent where necessary.

These offices were in theory tightly organized, but reality varied enormously. The number of administrative officials was small and the emperor absolute, so there was often a tendency to get things done rather than to follow slavishly previous practices. This would have worried some, infuriated others, and been seen as an opportunity by yet others. Titles too were treated casually, with numerous variations even in documents produced by imperial officials. The bureaucracy could be very intimate. The plot that led to Aurelian's murder in 275 was incited by Eros, an official of one of these offices who, imitating the emperor's handwriting, created a list of names slated for execution and then showed it to the supposed victims. The claim that his officials knew the emperor's hand when they saw it says much about the size of government and the emperor's prominent role in it.

The imperial administration was relatively small, but it had to run a large empire that was constantly in touch with the emperor. There were rhythms to this contact, with cities sending delegations at the accession of a new emperor, a process that would have involved around two thousand embassies every time a new emperor was acclaimed, every celebration of five years of rule (*quinquennalia*), and for imperial triumphs. The embassies that brought the voluntary but expected gold crowns for the emperor added to the logistical strain imposed by the court on cities as it moved. For the ambassadors, this may have been a high point of their lives, and though not every ambassador had the chance to speak before the emperor, many did. Menander the

Rhetor advised keeping these speeches down to 150 to 200 lines, perhaps ten minutes of speaking, but even so, the majority of these carefully prepared speeches would have gone undelivered.

These crowns were brought to the emperor from all parts of the world because he, and not the city of Rome, was the capital of the Empire. Foreigners were struck by the diversity of the Empire. When the Persian king Sapur I (240–272) recorded his defeat of Valerian on his great inscription from Naqsh-i Rustam, he listed the peoples accompanying the emperor, men from "Germania, Raetia, Noricum, Dacia, Pannonia, Moesia, Istria, Hispania, Mauritania, Thracia, Bithynia, Asia, Pamphylia, Isauria, Lycaonia, Galatia, Lycia, Cilicia, Cappadocia, Phrygia, Syria, Phoenicia, Judaea, Arabia, Mauritania [again], Germania [again], Lydia, and Mesopotamia." Regional identities were not entirely submerged within a Roman identity, but being Roman was expressed in numerous ways. Thus court and government could always be subdivided into groups, some based on origins, but others formed by links created in education or government service. Illyrian soldiers were particularly common, with their characteristically shaven heads, but were not an undifferentiated group; men from Thrace spoke Greek as a first language, those from Pannonia Latin. Dalmatians lived on the coast of the Mediterranean and preferred wine, but Pannonians lived in temperate Europe and drank beer. This taste for beer might unite the Pannonians with Egyptians and Britons, but their language, dominant skin color, clothing, and food tastes could divide them (see Figure 1).

As well as soldiers there were numerous civil officials, poets, and other entertainers in the *comitatus*, and even a few intellectuals, such as the philosopher Plotinus, known to both Gallienus and his wife. Like the soldiers, the courtiers came from all over the Empire and even beyond. They included Pipa, daughter of a Marcomannic king and the mistress of Gallienus, though how she interacted with his wife, the Augusta Cornelia Salonina Chrysogone, is unknown. Some of the visitors had the prestigious title of companion of the emperor (*comes Augusti*), such as the Italian senator Pomponius Bassus, consul for 259 and a decade later the first man in the senate (*princeps senatus*) under Claudius II.

THE TRAVELING EMPEROR

In the middle of the third century, the emperor was constantly on the move. Although modern writers often describe the environment around the emperor as a court, third-century writers often used the Latin *comitatus*,

Figure 1. Mosaic showing an Imperial official wearing a *chlamys*, from an early fourth-century villa at Piazza Armerina, Sicily. (Luigi Nifosi/Shutterstock.com)

meaning the imperial entourage, or even the Greek *stratopedon*, a military camp. As well as the emperor, bodyguards, soldiers, administrative officials, imperial records, and a traveling mint, there would also have been cooks, slaves, baggage carts, and pack animals, totaling thousands, if not tens of thousands, of men and animals. The *comitatus* stretched out for kilometers, a long train of men, animals, and carts. A generation later, Constantine wrote to Acilius Severus, urban prefect of Rome, about the *palatini*, who "are not strangers to the dust and work of the camp, who follow our standards, who are always performing their tasks, who the length of the marches and the difficulty of the campaign bothers as they are intent on their learned duties" (*CT* 6.36.1). The mobility would have been a challenge to petitioners and ambassadors who sometimes had to catch up with a moving emperor, but it brought him to more places in person.

Every time the emperor entered a city, he was officially welcomed with an arrival ceremony (*adventus*) by the city's dignitaries (see Figure 2). Although routine for the emperor, this procedure was not well practiced in many parts of the Empire and could be a great strain on small cities. When Constantine I arrived at Autun in Gaul in 311, an orator claimed that

> we decorated the roads by which he might come into the palace with modest ornamentation, but brought out the standards of all our *collegia* (guilds),

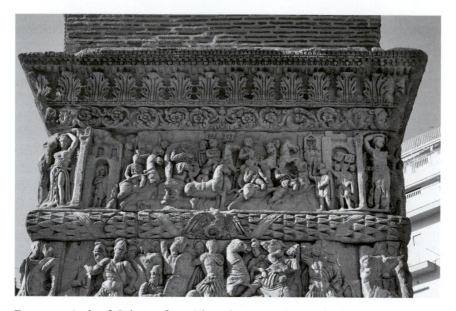

Figure 2. Arch of Galerius from Thessalonica in Greece, built in 296, showing an *adventus*. The emperor rides in a wagon with a military escort.

the statues of all our gods, and a very small number of loud instruments which, in short bursts, we brought round to you often, by running (*Latin Panegyrics* 5.8.4).

There was then a speech of welcome from a local orator, terrifying for the orator, probably boring for the emperor, but like all such ceremonial occasions, sometimes surprising, amusing, or challenging. Billeting the visitors would involve temporary accommodation, with the emperor either staying on imperial estates or requisitioning one of the larger houses in the city to the simultaneous joy and horror of its owner. The cost of these imperial visits was high, though the financial strain was less on the larger cities on the imperial arteries such as Trier, Sirmium, or Antioch, where there were palaces and facilities. If the emperor kept moving, problems were lessened, but costs could be considerable if he and his *comitatus* stayed in one place for several days. But strain for some meant economic opportunity for others, with the chance to profit from hungry and thirsty soldiers and courtiers. For smaller cities, however, lying on the military route meant problems, sometimes documented when they appealed to the emperor. In 246, Philip wrote in Latin to the Aragueni, living on an imperial estate in Phrygia, in response to a Greek petition that claimed that "those sent to the district of the Appiani leave the road, the soldiers and the masters of the leading men in the city.

And they come to us as they leave the road, taking us from our work and requisitioning our plough oxen" (*OGIS* 519).

IMPERIAL RESOURCES

Feeding the men and animals of the imperial household and the *comitatus* lay in the hands of the praetorian prefect. With the exception of the emperor's personal possessions, all aspects of the Roman state ran through his office. The most critical of his duties was the extraction of resources from the Empire in the form of money, goods, and manpower and then redistributing these to support the army and other state agencies. But like all other imperial officials, the prefect received petitions and acted as a judge. The prefect could also lead military expeditions, as Heraclianus did against Palmyra in 267, although Gallienus' creation of a separate cavalry army under its own commander provided some relief from these duties. Providing figures for imperial income and expenditure or for changes is impossible, but some generalizations can be made. The emperor was deeply concerned about finance, but the Empire was not well equipped to maximize its income. Most taxation was nonprogressive, based on holdings of land rather than of income. The same applied to trade, which was usually taxed on the movement of goods rather than on their manufacture and sale. Tax concessions were one of the privileges of the aristocracy, so there were numerous exemptions. This attitude militated against using the power of the state to increase the rate of collection, while the custom for new emperors to remit uncollected arrears further reduced income. The largest single item of imperial expenditure was the army, perhaps a third of state income. Compared to this, all other items of expenditure were small, even when involving large sums of money. There are frequent comments by contemporaries on imperial finances, but much of it was by men who were poorly informed. Although we hear of difficulties in collection and complaints about being taxed, such complaints cannot be used to assess the weight of taxation, even when producing splendid rhetoric. Thus Lactantius' claim that under Diocletian the number of beneficiaries of taxation exceeded the number of taxpayers (7.3) is of little use in understanding the amount of wealth available to the Empire and how this changed over time.

In the middle of the third century, the income of the Empire was theoretically divided between the personal possessions of the emperor (known as the *ratio privata* or the *res privata*) and the possessions of the Roman state (*res summa*), but in practice these distinctions were technical. The *res privata* was administered by the *rationalis rei privatae* (later the *comes rei privatae*), the *res summa* by the *rationalis rei summae* (later the *comes sacrarum largitionum*), and the other income streams came under the authority of the praetorian prefect. With some changes, all three offices continued to function into the seventh century. Below these political appointments was a complicated secretariat of professional bureaucrats in both the *comitatus* and in the provinces.

The emperor's possessions were huge, the result of the accumulation of the properties of three centuries of earlier emperors, with holdings in every province. How much of the Empire's land was owned by the emperor himself is, of course, unknowable, but an estimate of 5 to 10 percent of the land in the Empire might be plausible, though varying by region. In the mid-fifth century, the city territory of Cyrrhus in the province of Eufratensis contained 60,000 *iugera*, of which 10,000 belonged to the emperor. There was a core of estates in Africa and in Cappadocia known as the *domus divina* that served to support imperial household expenses. Many imperial estates were rented out, often on perpetual (emphyteutic) leases. The *res privata* also included the properties of individual emperors, bequests in wills (which often included the emperor as a co-heir), estates that were intestate, and confiscated estates. The largest source of confiscations was from those condemned, including the lands of unsuccessful challengers for imperial power. Soon after the death of Valerian, Gallienus defeated Regalianus and Ingenuus in the Balkans and added their estates to the *res privata*. He did the same with the properties of Macrianus and Callistus in 261. But as quickly as lands were added, they could be given away. The emperor was regularly approached with requests for money or favors and frequently granted them. Emperors were supposed to be generous, and Porphyry's narrative regarding Plotinus' request is built on the assumption that the emperor was only prevented from being generous by his counselors.

The second stream of imperial income, the *res summa*, included taxes on land (*tributum soli*) and on people (*tributum capitis*), as well as the *aurum coronarium* and the *aurum oblaticum*, which was paid by the Senate on the same occasions as the *aurum coronarium*. There were also numerous other minor streams of income, including sales taxes, fines, legacies, and customs duties, as well as income from mines. From the reign of Aurelian, devaluations sparked a period of major inflation of prices began, and the value of taxes paid in coin thus declined drastically.

The third stream of imperial income was of various goods in kind levied directly by the praetorian prefect. These were usually used to supply the *comitatus* and campaigning armies, issued as ration (*annona*) and fodder allowances (*capitus*). In the provinces, these taxes were handled by various procurators or *rationales* who reported directly to the prefect. These officials often had loosely defined roles, so the *a rationibus* Macrianus ended up in charge of the supplies for Valerian's fateful campaign. Thus a papyrus from Oxyrhynchus records the despatch of thirty-six oxen and their drivers from Egypt to Syria in 253–256 for one of Valerian's campaigns in response to the orders from the prefect of Egypt, Titus Magnius Felix Crescentillianus (*Oxyrhynchus Papyri* 42.3109). Other responsibilities of the prefect included the physical infrastructure of the Empire, in particular roads and post stations for the *cursus publicus*.

IMPERIAL SPENDING

Most of the resources collected went to meet the emperor's two major financial responsibilities, feeding the city of Rome and paying the army that protected the Empire. Rome in the third century was a huge city with a population that some scholars are prepared to estimate as a million. Even at a very conservative half a million, this was a huge concentration of population. It was not equaled in Europe until the eighteenth century and as a premodern city Rome was rivaled only by medieval Baghdad and Chang'an. Water was critical for drinking, but also for bathing, and Rome was well equipped with aqueducts, maintained by imperial officials. There was also a free distribution of bread for 120,000 recipients, each of whom regularly received 50 ounces of bread to 369, 36 ounces of better-quality bread thereafter. This involved the state in shipping grain from Egypt and North Africa, the responsibility of the *praefectus annonae*, and in managing bakeries in Rome. The emperor also subsidized public entertainments at Rome, mostly gladiatorial combats and animal hunts in the Flavian Amphitheater (now better known as the Colosseum) and chariot races in the Circus Maximus. There were also displays for other reasons, such as Gallienus' celebration of ten years of rule (*decennalia*) in 262. These made the emperor accessible to his subjects, and at all of these events various chants allowed the population to express their feelings. The emperor might choose to listen, but we should not mistake this for democracy.

Most of the spending on the army came from the accounts of the *res summa*, including issues of clothing for imperial officials and soldiers, salaries, and donatives. Salaries had by the mid-third century been heavily eroded by inflation and from the 270s were little more than pocket money. They were replaced by the direct issues of food and fodder (previously deducted from salaries) and by donatives. In the third century, donatives were annual gifts for imperial birthdays and consulates that by the fourth century had become standardized to five gold *solidi* and a pound of silver per man, paid at imperial accessions and five *solidi* on five-year anniversaries (*quinquennalia*). Donatives were the biggest payment at one time issued by the state. To make these payments, the Empire had a number of mints. There was a single imperial currency, though for small change this was often supplemented by locally minted coins in the third century. Most coins minted were in gold and in bronze, though there were occasional issues of silver. During the early third century, most imperial coinage was produced at Rome, Antioch, and Viminacium, though emperors during the late third century increased their numbers. Valerian moved the Viminacium mint to Milan and opened a new mint at Lyons in Gaul, while Gallienus created additional mints at Siscia and Cyzicus, and Aurelian moved the Milan mint to Ticinum. The third century did see major inflation although the large-scale use of in-kind payments reduced the impact of inflation. Moreover, since most imperial cash payments were in gold, not in silver or bronze, and the relationship between the metals was not fixed, the state was further isolated from inflationary effects. However, the continued minting of bronze coinage for donatives and military pay, none of which was withdrawn from circulation by taxation, tended to fuel inflation.

THE ARISTOCRACY

The manpower to run the Empire was drawn mostly from the Roman aristocracy. This was traditionally divided into two orders, the wealthier and more prestigious senate and the equestrians. Both orders were wealthy enough to live and to serve, or not serve, the emperor as they pleased. Italy was well represented, but most provinces had at least one senator and several equestrians. Although many inherited their status, the majority of senators and equestrians were appointed to these orders by the emperor, either as a result of petitions or so that they had the status required to hold imperial office. Augustus' achievement at the end of the first century BC of breaking the link between military and political success had by the third century led to a disassociation of the interests of the landed aristocracy and those of the Empire. This was not of great significance when things were going well, but if territory was not well defended, or even lost, then the attachments to Rome failed rapidly. Although senatorial status was still important, the Empire was ruled from where the emperor was. For most imperial purposes, therefore, the Senate of Rome had become a historical curiosity, and even when the emperor was in Italy, he was usually in the north, at Milan, not at Rome.

Successful service as a magistrate or general could be rewarded by the emperor with the consulate, of which there were two per year and used to date all events within the Empire until the sixth century. Holding it with the emperor was a particular honor, though imperial consulates also had the effect of reducing the number of rewards for the aristocracy. Emperors usually held the consulate in their first full year in office. In 260, the consuls were Publius Cornelius Saecularis, urban prefect between 258 and 260, and Caius Iunius Donatus, urban prefect in 257. Similarly, in 261 Lucius Petronius Taurus Volusianus shared the consulate with Gallienus. Volusianus had had an almost exclusively military career, including service at the court of Valerian, before being promoted to praetorian prefect and becoming consul. After this, he went on to serve as Gallienus' urban prefect in 267–268.

In the mid-third century, the Empire was divided into about fifty provinces (in addition to Italy, not a province at this point), most of which were administered by two officials, a governor, and a procurator. The provincial governor, usually a senatorial *legatus Augusti pro praetore*, was concerned with law and order, which included commanding any troops stationed in the region. Almost all provincial governors and legionary commanders were imperially appointed, although the Senate assigned governors for Achaea, Asia, and Africa from a list of candidates provided by the emperor. The procurator, usually from the equestrian order, was concerned with collecting taxes. Smaller provinces were administered by equestrian prefects who combined both roles. Governors were often referred to as *praesides*, *iudices*, or *hegemones*.

The nominal senate membership of six hundred had never been sufficient to provide enough talented and willing individuals to serve as governors or legionary commanders. Moreover, from the early third century, many senatorial families ceased to hold government positions, and by the middle of the century limited themselves to offices such as urban prefect or the proconsulates of Asia, Achaea, or Africa. The emperor would have known many of these officials personally, though the more time he spent away from Rome, the less well he knew them. Emperors were thus forced to turn either to their own staffs or to the aristocrats of the much larger equestrian order to carry out an increasing number of administrative and military functions. The supposed exclusion of Senators from military command by Gallienus (according to Aurelius Victor) reflects the reality that by this point, unlike the early third century, few legions were commanded by senators. Senatorial governors of provinces were also a dying breed, and by the 280s almost every provincial governor (except in Asia, Africa, and Achaea) was an equestrian *praeses*, not a senatorial legate. Thus Lucius Artorius Pius Maximus in Syria Phoenice under Diocletian was one of the last senatorial legates known, but far more typical was the first known governor of the province of Isauria, an equestrian *hegemon*, Aulus Voconius Zeno, under Gallienus.

The provinces ruled by these governors varied enormously in size and responsibility. Provinces were made up of the territories of a number of cities. Cities were defined by status, not by size, and were administered by a city council known as the *curia* and made up of local aristocrats (*curiales* or decurions), and most had city walls, baths, a temple to the imperial cult, several other temples, a bishop for the Christians, and a marketplace. Within each city's territory were a number of villages as well as the rural residences (often described by modern writers as villas) of the local aristocracy. As we saw with Gallienus, it was possible for emperors to create new cities, though these were usually named after themselves or their wives, not after philosophers. The provinces in Britain, on the Rhine and the Danube and in Syria, were of great military importance, and their governors were in charge of forces as large as twenty thousand men. In Syria Phoenice, Artorius commanded *Legio III Gallica* and a number of auxiliary regiments, perhaps ten thousand men. On the other hand, smaller provinces such as Aquitania in Gaul had only a minimal garrison. Any provincial force under a single commander was far smaller than the field army at the disposal of the emperor.

Although heavily concerned with the extraction of surpluses of men and money, in other ways Roman government tended to sit loosely on a complicated set of previous administrative structures, especially in the East. The village of Baetocaece in the territory of the city of Arad in Syria Phoenice erected an inscription in 258/260 that contained a rescript of Valerian, Gallienus, and Saloninus in response to a petition delivered by Aurelius Marea and others. This petition concerned temple privileges that had been originally granted by a Seleucid monarch named Antiochus, probably Antiochus I (281–261 BC). Valerian's subscription confirmed that "whoever rules the province will keep intact for you the ancient privileges from the kings, confirmed by the custom of later time" (*IGLS* 7.4028). The rescript, as well as much of the documentation, was then inscribed on the temple wall.

The story of Baetocaece is that of a typical Roman village, a story of a community with a complex history of its own, unknown to much of the Empire, yet feeling intimately connected to the emperor. The Roman state in 260 had suffered some significant military defeats in recent years, and some of these rippled through to Baetocaece. Despite these defeats, there were no great problems to be solved, simply the day-to-day business of running a huge Empire. This Empire was large and complicated; the details that often overwhelm us would often have been as baffling to contemporaries. There is plentiful evidence for events and processes, though not as much as we would like or as is available to historians of later eras. Most of this evidence reflects a point of view, and most of the evidence we have for individual Romans does not reflect the point of view of either the state or the emperor. What follows is an attempt to tell the story of the Empire from the perspective of the emperor.

GALLIENUS (260–268)

The Roman Empire was surrounded by enemies on all sides, habitually known to the Romans as barbarians. This term is used here because it was what the Romans called their enemies, carrying with it the Roman belief in their cultural superiority. Eusebius, in a speech delivered to Constantine in 336, described how Romans felt when "barbarians, like the wild nomad tribes, no better than savage beasts, assail the nations of civilized men, ravage their country, and enslave their cities, rushing on those who inhabit them like ruthless wolves of the desert, and destroying all who fall under their power" (*Tricennial Oration* 7.2). In the Levant and along the imperial frontier in Africa, the Romans were faced by numerous barbarian tribes, mostly illiterate and living in villages or as nomads. These were small-scale threats as the steppes and deserts had difficulty in supporting large populations. In Europe, the northern Rhineland was inhabited by Frankish tribes, the southern Rhineland by Alamannic tribes, while on the Danube there were Sarmatians in the west and Goths in the east; there were also many other smaller tribes on both frontiers. They too were mostly illiterate villagers who rarely posed significant threats to the Empire. Typical was a Roman victory altar erected on September 11, 260, at Augusta Vindelicum in Raetia to record a victory over the Alamannic Iuthungi:

> In honour of the divine house and to the blessed goddess Victoria, because the barbarians of the people of the Semnones or of the Iuthungi on the eighth and seventh days before the Kalends of May were slaughtered and put to flight by soldiers of the province of Raetia, by troops from Germania, and by the people, after releasing many thousands of Italian prisoners, and in realisation of his vows, Marcus Simplicinius Genialis, *vir perfectissimus*, acting in place of the governor, with the same army, with proper gratitude, placed this memorial and dedicated it on the third day before the Ides of September when the conusls were our lord emperor Postumus Augustus and Honoratianus (*AE* 1993.1231).

However, there were numerous moments when the Romans lost their superiority. Some were from bad luck, but there were occasions when Roman power was weakened by the absence of troops, detached to deal with other

Figure 3. Persian relief from Naqsh-i Rustam showing the emperors Valerian (standing) and Philip (kneeling) being held captive by Sapur. (M. Khebra/Shutterstock.com)

frontier areas, to fight civil wars, or when talented barbarian leaders were able to create temporary alliances with their neighbors. It was such a grouping of Goths led by Cniva that had defeated and killed the emperor Decius in 251 at Abrittus, south of the Danube and close to Marcianopolis. Frontier defense was thus a constant requirement, and Roman emperors had had to work hard to keep the population safe.

Rome faced a very different enemy on its eastern frontier in the form of Persia. The Persians were a literate city-based society ruled by the Sasanid dynasty, but were still called barbarians by the Romans. The Persian king had the title "King of the Kings of Iran and non-Iran" and an aspiration to reconquer all territory held by Persia in earlier centuries, an area that included Egypt, Syria, and Anatolia. Following the death of Gordian III in Mesopotamia in 244, in 253 the Romans lost control of Syria to the Persians, Antioch was sacked, and Sapur I won a victory at the battle of Barbalissus. A new Persian offensive in 256 captured Dura Europus, then in early 260 the Sasanids laid siege to Edessa and Carrhae. Marching to relieve them, both Valerian and his praetorian prefect were captured by the Persians after a battle east of these cities (see Figure 3). By the end of the third century, Lactantius would claim that Valerian was used as a mounting block by Sapur while alive and that after his death the emperor was flayed and his skin dyed red and displayed in a temple. Whether this really happened, and Lactantius was writing to show how persecutors of Christians such as Valerian came to bad ends, the Roman emperor had been taken alive by barbarians.

Sapur now led his armies west into Syria and Anatolia and boasted of his achievements in the great trilingual inscription at Naqsh-i Rustam, which listed the Roman cities sacked during this campaign. After sacking Antioch, Sapur first occupied Cilicia, including Tarsus, Anazarbus, and Seleucia, then some troops followed the Isaurian coast as far west as Selinus and Antiochia ad Cragum, while others crossed the Cilician Gates and reached Laranda and Iconium and into southern Cappadocia. Several of Gallienus' subordinates, Callistus, Macrianus, and Odenathus, began a series of counterattacks against the Persians. Callistus was Valerian's praetorian prefect, Macrianus was responsible for the supplies of Valerian's expedition, and Odenathus was a soldier from Palmyra in Syria.

At the same time as Valerian was fighting his final campaign against the Persians, Gallienus was faced with an imperial challenge from Postumus, governor of Germania Inferior, a province with a large garrison. In Gaul, Postumus had murdered Gallienus' son and imperial colleague Saloninus at Cologne in summer 260 and was proclaimed emperor, with his authority being accepted in Gaul, Britain, and Spain. There was an uneasy accommodation with Gallienus in Italy, though no formal recognition, and both administrations nominated their own consuls. Roman territory across the Rhine between Germania Superior and Raetia, known as the Agri Decumates, was evacuated at this point.

The capture of Valerian and murder of Saloninus left Gallienus as sole emperor (260–268). Although he had a brother, from that point on Gallienus ruled alone. As the first few years of his sole reign show, the problem of rival emperors was significant and the author of the *Historia Augusta* claimed that there were thirty (though this number was chosen because of its historical echoes). Superficially, men claimed the Empire when they felt the emperor to be inadequate, but this alone cannot explain the frequency of these challenges. The frequency and our lack of information may make them seem trivial, but the defeated were executed, usually along with their family and many of their closest supporters, and their lands confiscated. In addition to Postumus' Gallic Empire, Gallienus was challenged by several men who would be emperor, including Ingenuus, governor of Pannonia, defeated at Mursa in 260 by Aureolus, and Regalianus, killed by Sarmatians in the Balkans. In the east, after some successes against the Persians, Callistus and Macrianus declared Macrianus' two sons Macrianus and Quietus as *Augusti* in Syria in 261. Macrianus led his homonymous son into Europe, where they were defeated by Aureolus in Illyricum, while Callistus and Quietus were defeated by Odenathus at Emesa in 261. With their fall, Aemilianus, prefect of Egypt, was acclaimed as emperor before falling to Gallienus' men in 262. This all reflects a sudden lack of confidence in Gallienus at a time of great crisis. Once Gallienus had seen off these challengers in 260–261, he was able to concentrate on external enemies for several years.

As the death of Regalianus at the hands of the Sarmatians also shows, throughout the 260s there were constant attacks by barbarians on the northern frontiers of the Empire, crossing the Rhine or Danube, and in some cases sailing into the Black Sea or even into the Mediterranean. These sorts of events were background noise, a consequence of having an Empire. The usual rhythm was of raids into Roman territory followed by Roman counteroffensives and peace. The scale of these varied, and at moments of perceived Roman weakness, or talented barbarian leadership, the raids were larger. In the third century, order was always restored, even if it took a while. In some cases, such as that of Regalianus, local initiative moved to do this before imperial initiatives could. Although frontier districts were accustomed to these incursions, the appearance deeper within the Empire of Goths taking prisoners in Pontus in the 250s, raiding in Greece near Thermopylae in 262 or Heruls at Athens in 267, was still shocking, particularly to those who were not familiar with the frontiers. In many cases, the population was able to defend themselves, and we possess a rousing speech by Dexippus that he may have given when he led the Athenians against the Heruls. But often they failed and chaos ensued. Athens was sacked, while in Anatolia the *Canonical Letter* of Gregory Thaumaturgus, bishop of Neocaesarea in Pontus in the 250s, concerns those "who by force hold as those who escaped from the barbarians," "who have been counted as barbarians and have done what should not be dared against their own race [*homophylōn*]," and "those who dared to attack the houses of others during the barbarian invasion" (*Canons* 6, 7, 8).

The early years of Gallienus' sole reign also saw Roman victories as well as defeats. In 260, Genialis defeated the Iuthungi in Raetia, Decianus won victories in North Africa, Aureolus defeated Ingenuus in the Balkans, and three generals, Odenathus, Callistus, and Macrianus, expelled the forces of Sapur in the east. Meanwhile, Gallienus himself defeated some Alamanni near Milan. The need for a defensive system able to act in numerous parts of the Empire simultaneously was clear, but the lesson of the imperial challengers was that giving too many troops to subordinates ran the risk of an attempt to seize power in their own name. In the east, Gallienus was lucky with Odenathus, who was very loyal to him, holding the powerful but vague office of governor of the entire east (*corrector totius Orientis*), in control of Syria and the Persian frontier down to his death in 267. Gallienus, once the Balkans had been restored to some sort of order, spent 262–264 in Rome when he came into contact with Plotinus. In 265, he crossed the Alps against Postumus, but this expedition was abandoned when he was wounded by an arrow and the uneasy peace with the Gallic Empire continued. Gallienus now chose to focus on Gothic raids from the Danube and Black Sea regions, which led to the sack of Athens by the Heruls in 267. And then the murder of Odenathus and a rebellion in Palmyra required another eastern expedition led by the praetorian prefect Heraclianus.

In 267–268, in addition to the troops in the *comitatus* with Gallienus, there were Roman field armies in the east under Heraclianus, in Greece under Marcianus, and in north Italy under Aureolus. In 268, Aureolus revolted in Milan and declared himself emperor. Gallienus left the Balkans and laid siege to Aureolus, but during the siege he was murdered by a group of his officers on March 22. The responsibility for his death is variously reported as belonging to Heraclianus, Marcianus, or Aurelian, though conspicuously not to his successor Claudius. Gallienus was fifty at his death and had ruled since 253. He was buried in a tomb on the Via Appia near Rome and, like many of his predecessors, was deified, i.e., given the same honors as the gods. Despite the numerous enemies he faced, Gallienus' reign had shown that the Empire had the resources to overcome the challenges arrayed against it, though the emperor had to travel extensively to get close to the problems faced. What was necessary was a way of keeping Roman energies focused on external problems rather than dividing among themselves.

CLAUDIUS II (268–270) AND QUINTILLUS (270)

The new emperor acclaimed at Milan in the autumn was Marcus Aurelius Claudius, a soldier from the Balkans. Aureolus surrendered and was executed, freeing Claudius to win victories against some Alamanni and Iuthungi in northern Italy in 269 and against some Goths at the battle of Naissus in the Balkans. Some of the Gothic prisoners were settled as farmers, others were enrolled in the army. He also resumed hostilities with the Gallic Empire and sent troops into southern Gaul under command of the *praefectus vigilum* Placidianus. When Claudius died from plague at Sirmium in early 270, he was succeeded by his brother Quintillus. Nothing is known of Quintillus' career, and subsequent events suggest that he had few military credentials. Within a month, another soldier of Balkan origins, Aurelian, aged about fifty-five, had declared himself emperor. Aurelian, who claimed that Claudius had named him as heir, led the army to Aquileia, where Quintillus, with few troops who would stand by him, committed suicide.

AURELIAN (270–275)

After Lucius Domitius Aurelianus was acclaimed at Aquileia in May 270, he was forced to campaign in northern Italy against more raiding groups of Iuthungi, then against the Vandals in Pannonia. At the end of the year, he suppressed a revolt of mint workers in Rome led by Felicissimus. After successfully campaigning against the Goths and Carpi in 271, Aurelian took advantage of his victories to withdraw troops and most of the population from Dacia north of the Danube. This significantly reduced the length of the border to be defended. At the same time, some of the Carpi were settled in Thrace. He then returned to Rome late in 271 when he ordered the construction of a new defensive wall. Rome had long outgrown its earlier defenses, which dated from the fifth century BC. Even though Rome itself had not been attacked, for the past century, barbarian attacks on northern Italy had occurred repeatedly. Aurelian's plans were for a wall circuit 19 kilometers long with sixteen gates and 381 towers. Unlike the earlier wall, this protected parts of the city on the west bank of the Tibur, as well as incorporating some existing structures, such as the camp of the praetorians in the northeast of the city and the pyramid of Gaius Cestius on the south side.

In early 272, Aurelian turned to the east. Following the murder of Odenathus in 267, his wife Zenobia appeared to believe that her husband's position was hereditary, a view that was not shared by the emperor. She thus acclaimed her son Vaballathus Augustus and took the title of Augusta for herself. Zenobia's title was the same as that of Gallienus' wife Salonina, also honored with coins. Since Vaballathus was about a year old, Zenobia also ruled in his name. Both Odenathus and Zenobia were from Palmyra, a Syrian city on the western edge of the Syrian steppe. It had long profited from the import of goods from India and China, which were shipped into the Persian Gulf and then moved up the Euphrates Valley and transported in caravans across the desert to Palmyra. From Palmyra, these goods were moved on to the Syrian coast. For defense of these caravans against raiders outside the Empire, Palmyra had its own troops, independent of the Roman army, though Roman troops were also based in the city and Palmyrans served in Roman regiments. The city was also distinguished by its art and the use of the Palmyran language in inscriptions. All of this may have helped give Zenobia a sense of entitlement to Roman power. If so, she had read the situation wrongly.

Before his death, Gallienus had sent his praetorian prefect Heraclianus against the city, but he was defeated, while Claudius had little time to pay attention to the east. From 270, Vaballathus professed loyalty to Aurelian, minting coins in both their names. At the same time, his troops occupied

Arabia and Egypt in 270 and parts of Anatolia as far as Ancyra in 271. As they advanced, Roman officials and troops were forced to choose between an emperor in the West and one in the East. Many of Vaballathus' soldiers were thus Romans professing loyalty to Vaballathus rather than to Aurelian. One of these was Statilius Aemilianus, who was appointed as *praefectus Aegypti* by Vaballathus; when he later abandoned Vaballathus, he was left in his post by Aurelian. For a victorious emperor in a civil war, there was a delicate balance between clemency and harshness. If he were too aggressive about punishing the defeated, he could easily find a conspiracy rising against him, but it was not good to be seen as soft either. The dilemma can be seen in Peter the Patrician's account of the capture of Tyana in Cappadocia. To fire up his troops for the assault, Aurelian told his men not to leave even a dog alive. However, after the city fell, he forbade the troops from plundering, and then, when challenged, told the men to kill all the dogs. "Afterwards, he called them together and said: 'We are fighting to liberate the cities and if we prefer to pillage them, they will no longer have faith in us'" (Peter the Patrician, *Aurelian* fr. 4).

Aurelian arrived in Syria in 272 and defeated Vaballathus at Immae near Antioch and at Emesa before capturing Palmyra itself. As a defeated rebel, Zenobia made a wonderful character around whom to write history, but we know little about her own actions or motivations. Aurelian treated the Palmyrans as if they were barbarians, sending the prisoners (including Zenobia) to Rome for a triumphal parade and assuming the victory title "Palmyrenicus." Vaballathus was not heard of again, and though Zosimus claimed he died on the way to Rome, he said the same thing about Zenobia. Once Vaballathus had been defeated, Aurelian marched back to Byzantium for the winter. He was forced to return to Palmyra when a revolt broke out and this time sacked the city in summer 273. A new Roman garrison, *Legio I Illyricorum*, was placed in the city. Its culture lost its distinctiveness; there were no more Palmyran troops, no more Palmyran language inscriptions, while the gradual cessation of the caravan inscriptions, the latest being datable to 279/280, also suggests a changing city. From the reign of Diocletian trade with Persia was limited to Nisibis ensuring that Palmyra could never regain the position she had held. After a visit to Egypt, Aurelian then returned to the west.

Here, between 260 and 274, there was a separatist Roman Empire composed of Gaul, Spain, and Britain. Unlike Vaballathus, who was riding the edge of calling himself an emperor, there was no doubt that Gaul had an emperor and even consuls were appointed. Following the death of Postumus at the hands of his own troops in 268, other emperors carried on ruling this Empire: Marius (268), Victorinus (268–270), and Tetricus (270–274). After

Postumus' death, however, there was less confidence, and during the reign of Claudius II (268–270), Spain and parts of Narbonensis and Aquitania had already returned their allegiance to the central Empire. Aurelian now entered Gaul in early 274, defeating Tetricus in a battle on the Catalaunian Plains. Tetricus and his son, the Caesar Tetricus II, surrendered. Tetricus himself was not seen as much of a threat. Most defeated imperial challengers were executed and their heads sent round the Empire, but Aurelian appointed Tetricus as *corrector Lucaniae* and allowed his son to sit in the Senate. This was compassionate, but it shows the lack of relevance of the Senate to imperial politics.

Aurelian had thus restored the unity of the Roman Empire with two campaigns in a period of three years. The outward manifestation of this unity was the holding of a single triumphal parade in Rome in 274, displaying both Zenobia and Tetricus, as well as inscriptions referring to Aurelian as the "restorer of the world" (*restitutor orbis*). Like Tetricus, Zenobia was well treated and she retired to a villa at Tivoli given to her by Aurelian. He increased the scale of free distribution of bread to the city, as well as adding distributions of pork. Aurelian now built a large temple to the Sun in Rome, as well as establishing a quadrennial series of athletic games. The religious significance of these actions is unclear, but there is a vast amount of speculation, fueled by the replacement of Jupiter by the "Unconquered Sun" (*Sol Invictus*) as the dominant figure on his coins from 273.

Aurelian made other and more dramatic changes to the Roman coinage, probably as a consequence of the revolt of the mint workers in 270. In 274, he minted a new gold coin, at fifty to the pound, heavier than the earlier *aurei*. His new silver coins had a much higher silver content than previous issues. However, the critical innovation was in breaking the previous rigid link between the value of silver and gold coins. This abandonment of the gold standard led to rapid inflation for prices expressed in bronze, so that in Egypt in 246 it cost 24 drachmas to buy an *artaba* of wheat (perhaps double the rate of a century earlier). By 293/4, rates of 220 and 300 drachmas per *artaba* are recorded. At the same time, the imperial gold coinage was stable, and for those whose transactions were carried out in gold, this was a great advantage. Why Aurelian took these measures is unclear, though he may have been motivated by a desire to take all his predecessors' coinage out of circulation and leave himself as the sole authority figure on all imperial coinage.

Aurelian's campaigns show the continued power of the Roman state, provided it was not diffused in civil war. The triumphal parade of 274, like Aurelian's construction of a new wall, shows that Rome was still the center of the Empire. However, the way that Aurelian had won his

victories, campaigning in Syria and in Gaul with an army and administration led by men who were not senatorial aristocrats, shows that it was
the emperor who was at the center of the Empire, and not the city. At the
same time, the repeated fracturing of imperial unity showed the need to
have effective regional leadership. The success of Valerian and Gallienus
and the uneasy balance between Postumus and Gallienus showed that the
Empire could be ruled by more than one emperor, even though Aurelian
married but without children seemed to have no choice but to rule alone.
Following his triumph in 274, Aurelian did not stay in Rome for long and
any thought of the succession was subordinated to taking revenge for the
defeat of Valerian. But as he began making preparations for a Persian war,
Aurelian was murdered at Heraclea in Thrace in late 275. The conspiracy
was designed to eliminate Aurelian, not to make anyone emperor, and no
one with the army seemed ready to claim power.

TACITUS (275–276) AND PROBUS (276–282)

Eventually, after a six-week interregnum, Marcus Claudius Tacitus was
acclaimed emperor at Rome at the end of the year. He had been consul in
273 and was acceptable to the army. Tacitus hastened east to Aurelian's army
in Thrace where he executed as many of the assassins as he could find. He
then continued to march east, spending the winter at Perge in Pamphylia
to campaign against groups of Goths from the Black Sea who were raiding
southern Anatolia. His presence here is attested by a remarkable inscription
located on a monument on one of the city's main streets (*SEG* 34.1306).

> Up with Perge, which alone has the right of asylum
> Up with Perge, which Tacitus…
> Up with Perge, *neokoros* since Vespasian
> Up with Perge, honored with a sacred *vexillum*
> Up with Perge, honored with silver coinage
> Diana of Ephesus, Diana Perasia
> Up with Perge, Imperial Treasury
> Up with Perge, four time *neokoros*
> Up with Perge, first among the assize centers
> Up with Perge, where consulars seek honor
> Up with Perge, where consulars sponsor athletic competitions
> Up with Perge, the head of Pamphylia
> Up with Perge, which is not false in anything
> All the rights by a decree of the Senate

The presence of the emperor at Perge was thus marked by the acclamations to the army and silver coinage, which was not normally minted by cities. Indeed, the minting of bronze civic coinage in Anatolia had generally ceased under Gallienus, but Perge even minted a series of bronze coins to commemorate Tacitus' visit, the last bronze coinage issued by a city in Anatolia. From Pamphylia, Tacitus moved northeast to Cappadocia, making further preparations for the Persian war. However, he was murdered in June 276, supposedly because he had been pursuing the assassins of Aurelian too aggressively. This time there was no interregnum, as his half-brother and praetorian prefect, Marcus Annius Florianus (276), claimed the purple in Bithynia. But at the same time, the Syrian army acclaimed its commander, Probus, as emperor (276–282). Florianus responded aggressively by rapidly crossing the Taurus Mountains to Tarsus. Although he was strong militarily, commanding the field army that Aurelian had assembled for the Persian war, after some skirmishes with Probus he was deposed by his own troops in early September 276 and executed.

Like other recent emperors, Marcus Aurelius Probus (276–282) was a soldier of Balkan origins, born in Sirmium in 232, who had served under Gallienus and Aurelian. The confusion after Aurelian's death was still leading to the emergence of other emperors, similar to the challenges Gallienus had faced after Valerian's capture in 260, and Probus was faced with a rash of men declaring themselves emperor. These included revolts by Saturninus in Egypt in 280; by Lydius at Cremna in Pisidia, where the remains of his siege works are still visible; in Britain; and by Proculus and Bonosus in Gaul. Probus first continued Tacitus' attacks on the assassins of Aurelian, then marched to the Rhine, where in 277–278 he fought against the Franks and Alamanni. Some of the prisoners taken were settled in the Roman Empire, including Burgundians and Vandals being given land in Britain. In 281, he visited Rome, after which he planned a campaign against the Persians, i.e., continuing the plans made by Aurelian and Tacitus. When he reached Sirmium, the news that his praetorian prefect Carus had been declared emperor by some soldiers in Raetia and Noricum led immediately to his murder.

CARUS (282–283), CARINUS (283–285), AND NUMERIANUS (283–284)

M. Aurelius Numerius Carus was acclaimed emperor in September 282. He was a Gaul, though little else is known about him. Like Valerian, Carus was able to share power with his two sons, Carinus and Numerianus, who were both swiftly proclaimed as Caesars. Carus first fought on the Danube in early 283 against the Sarmatians and Quadi. Then he sent Carinus to Gaul while Numerianus accompanied him in the long-planned war against the Persians. Carus marched through Mesopotamia and reached, or even captured, Ctesiphon, where he died in July 283 after being struck by a bolt of lightning. It was a remarkably short reign, and like that of Claudius II, ended by chance. Following Carus' death, his sons both became *Augusti*, Marcus Aurelius Carinus in the west, Marcus Aurelius Numerius Numerianus in the east. Despite the death of Carus on campaign, there was no immediate crisis, only a calm transfer of power. Numerianus led the army out of Persia, spending the winter in the east, and made plans to return to Europe. As the army marched through Anatolia, however, he developed an eye illness and was confined to his litter. Then Numerianus' dead body was discovered at Chalcedon, the result of his murder by father-in-law and praetorian prefect Aper. This was the version of Diocletian, who, following a meeting of an army council, was acclaimed emperor himself at Nicomedia and executed Aper in November 284. How much of this is true is now unknowable, given Diocletian's subsequent influence on the historical tradition. Thus for the author of the *Historia Augusta*, both Carus and Numerianus were good men, but Carinus was "the most contaminated of all men," guilty of a series of crimes, including having nine wives (16.1). The detail that it was Diocletian himself who cut down Aper in front of the army could not be excised from the tradition, a reminder of the martial nature of Roman society. Carinus marched east from Gaul, where he was faced with Marcus Aurelius Julianus (284–285), who had been acclaimed emperor in northern Italy after the death of Carus. Carinus defeated Julianus in battle at Verona and then moved farther east to Moesia Superior, where he clashed with Diocletian at the Battle of Margus in spring 285. He would have won a victory, we are told, but was murdered by one of his own men; the claim that his murderer was the disgruntled husband of a woman he had seduced, however, sounds like more Diocletianic propaganda.

DIOCLETIAN (284–305) AND THE ESTABLISHMENT OF THE TETRARCHY

Once Carinus was dead, Caius Valerius Diocletianus was the sole ruler of the Roman state. He was still faced with the same problems as his predecessors: continued border warfare, an unresolved conflict with Persia, and the likelihood of more imperial challengers. Both Valerian and Carus had tackled the problem by appointing family members as co-emperors, but Diocletian had no son. He had, however, seen the success of Carus' appointing Caesars. Inspired by this, Diocletian in summer 285, only a year after his accession, shared his imperial power with a nonrelative, Maximian, a soldier from Sirmium who had served under Aurelian and Probus. They divided power so that Diocletian usually managed the eastern parts of the Empire, Maximian the western. Maximian was at first appointed as Caesar by Diocletian himself on July 21, 285, in Milan. Then on April 1, 286, he was promoted to Augustus, equal in rank to Diocletian though second in seniority. Like Diocletian, he had a court, an army, his own praetorian prefect and cohorts, and the ability to appoint governors, issue coinage, and make laws. There were precedents for similar power-sharing arrangements with nonrelatives: Augustus and Agrippa in the first century, and Marcus Aurelius and Lucius Verus in the second century. Much of the arrangement's success comes from Maximian's loyalty to Diocletian; he was content to share power, perhaps able to look back to the relative stability of Valerian and Gallienus' rule compared with the political whirlwind that followed.

The creation of a second emperor addressed many problems by spreading imperial power more widely, but it was soon clear that a more drastic solution was needed. In 293, Diocletian added two Caesars (*Caesares*), Constantius in the West and Galerius in the East, to create a college of four emperors known to modern historians as the Tetrarchy. The two new Tetrarchs were joined to their senior colleagues by marriage alliances. Galerius married Diocletian's daughter Valeria, while Constantius, who had been Maximian's praetorian prefect since 288, divorced his wife Helena to marry Maximian's stepdaughter Theodora. Although Constantius and Galerius as *Caesares* did not have their own praetorian prefects, but shared those of the *Augusti*, they did have their own courts and armies, and issued their own laws.

Even with four emperors, restoring order was not easy, and Diocletian and his new team had to fight hard to reestablish Roman strategic control over the frontier zones. The major enemy was the Persians, though Carus' successful campaign had led to peace with Vararanes III (276–293). After Narse I (293–302) had become Persian king, he expelled Trdat III in 296, thus starting war again with the Romans. Diocletian fought against the Persians in 296, and then Galerius took over. He was badly defeated in a battle between Callinicum and Carrhae, after which Diocletian was so angry that he made Galerius run in front of his chariot in his purple robes for several miles. Galerius may have been humiliated, but by 298 won a victory in Greater Armenia where he captured the Persian camp, including the wives and children of the Persian king Narse. This victory allowed a peace to be made that was favorable to Rome. Trdat III was restored to Armenia and the regions of Intelene, Sophene, Arzanene, Corduene, and Zabdicene, lying north of the Tigris, became Roman, though administered by Armenian satraps rather than by Roman officials. Nisibis was now defined as the center for commercial exchange between Persia and Rome, an act that meant the battered Palmyra would never rise above the status of just another city. And it was agreed that the Iberian king would be appointed by the Romans. While Galerius was concentrating on the Persians, Diocletian in 297 went to Egypt to deal with Lucius Domitius Domitianus, who had claimed imperial power at Alexandria. There are numerous letters preserved regarding local arrangements for this visit, including a confirmation from the administrator of the territory around Panopolis to Hermias, son of Paniscus, that he had been assigned as "overseer of vegetables in preparation for the auspiciously impeding visit of our ruler, the ever victorious Diocletian, the Senior Augustus" (*P.Beatty Panop.* I.249–251). Alexandria had to be besieged for eight months. When the city finally fell, Malalas recorded a story that Diocletian ordered his troops not to stop slaughtering the population until the blood reached his horse's knees. When the horse stumbled, the slaughter was stopped and the relieved Alexandrians then erected a statue to honor of the emperor's horse (12.41). Diocletian's own monument was a column 26 meters high, topped by a statue of himself (now known as Pompey's Pillar), dominating the skyline of the city.

Events in the Balkans are particularly hard to untangle, depending for the most part on imperial victory titles rather than detailed historical accounts. These wars can be divided into campaigns against Sarmatians and Quadi on the Middle Danube and campaigns against Carpi and Goths on the lower Danube. Diocletian possibly fought against the Sarmatians in 285, was in Raetia in 288, fought against the Sarmatians in 289, against the Carpi in 296, and again in 304. Galerius fought the Marcomanni in 299/300, the Carpi in 301, the Carpi and the Sarmatians in 302, the Carpi in 303, the Sarmatians in 306/307, and the Carpi again in 308.

The defense of the Rhine frontier was turned over immediately to Maximian, who in 285 defeated the emperor Amandus. In 286, Marcus Aurelius Carausius seized power in northern Gaul and Britain. Carausius had been sent by Maximian against pirates in the English Channel but was accused of keeping booty for himself. When Maximian ordered his arrest and execution, Carausius rebelled. His forces included the North Sea fleet and hired forces of Franks. Carausius' Empire was much like the Gallic Empire less than two decades earlier, with its own consuls, though some of his coinage claimed that he was the brother of Diocletian and Maximian. Maximian's initial expedition against Carausius in 289 was unsuccessful, but four years later Carausius was expelled from Gaul by the newly appointed Caesar Constantius. After Carausius was murdered and replaced as emperor by his *rationalis summae rei* Allectus, Constantius built a new fleet and with

Figure 4. Gold medallion of Constantius I minted in Trier to commemorate his victory over Allectus in 296. A mounted Constantius is greeted by the personification of London (British Museum).

his praetorian prefect Asclepiodotus invaded Britain in 296. A spectacular medallion commemorating the victory over Allectus was soon issued (see Figure 4). While Constantius was attacking Britain, Maximian fought on the Rhine in summer 296 against the Franks. He then moved to Spain in the autumn, making preparations for the war in Mauritania against the Quinquegentiani. By 297, he was in Mauritania, in 298 at Carthage and maybe in Tripolitania, and then crossed the Mediterranean to Rome in 299. Prisoners taken in all of these wars were settled in Roman territory, particularly Franks in Gaul, Carpi in Pannonia, and large numbers of Sarmatians. The results of this flurry of imperial activity were well publicized. The Gallic orator and ex-*magister memoriae* Eumenius, speaking in Gaul in 298 to the governor of Lugdunensis, referred to "the messengers that keep on arriving, sweating, and announcing victories," and inviting his audience

> to imagine either Egypt, her anger calmed [the revolt of Domitianus] and quiescent under your clemency, Diocletian Augustus, or else you, invincible Maximian, striking the columns of defeated Moors like lightning, or, under your right hand, lord Constantius, Batavia and Britain bringing out their shabby heads from the woods and waves, or you, Maximian Caesar [= Galerius] trampling the bows and quivers of the Persians (*Latin Panegyrics* 9.21.1–3).

TETRARCHIC IDEOLOGY

It was not just the system of four emperors that allowed the restoration of order. It also required four men who were good soldiers who trusted each other. Persuading contemporaries that the emperors were a team was obviously difficult since the unity of the Tetrarchy was continuously reinforced. Every emperor thus acted as part of the imperial college and its "undivided authority" (*indivisum patrimonium*), so a standard iconography showed all four emperors at once, whether in the form of statuary such as the Venice Tetrarchs, the reliefs on the Arch of Galerius in Thessalonica, or the wall paintings of the Temple of Ammon at Egyptian Thebes (see Figures 2 and 5). Thus at Rapidum in Mauritania Caesariensis, the equestrian *praeses* Ulpius Apollonius erected an inscription praising the new world:

> In their most fortunate and blessed times, the Imperator Caesar Caius Valerius Diocletianus *invictus pius felix* Augustus and Imperator Caesar Marcus Aurelius Valerius Maximianus *invictus pius felix* Augustus and Flavius Valerius Constantius and Galerius Valerius Maximianus, most noble Caesars restored from the foundations to a pristine condition the *municipium* of Rapidum which for a long time had been captured and overthrown by an incursion of rebels (*ILS* 638).

The remote representation of this ideology of unity was critical since the Tetrarchs were rarely able to demonstrate it in person. After the acclamation of Maximian in 285, he only met with Diocletian in 288, 290, and 303, while the Tetrarchy as a whole never met as four men in the same city.

With multiple emperors who rarely met, the city of Rome might have regained a central position in the Empire. However, the personal nature of imperial rule meant that all of the institutions of the Roman state were attached to emperors, not to Rome. The increased imperial presence on the

Figure 5. The Venice Tetrarchs. Carved from porphyry, with one arm clasped round each other's shoulders to show unity, but with the other hand on their sword hilts. (ansharphoto/Shutterstock.com)

northern edges of the Empire resulted in the creation or enlarging of imperial centers to support emperors and their retinues in London, Trier, Milan, Aquileia, Sirmium, Serdica, Thessalonica, Nicaea, Nicomedia, and Antioch. These cities were provided with an imperial palace, a hippodrome used both for public appearances and for chariot races, a treasury, and warehouses. A panegyrist described what this looked like at Trier in 310: "I see a Circus Maximus rivalling, I believe, the one in Rome, I see basilicas and a forum, imperial works, and a seat of justice raised to such a height that they promise to be worthy neighbours of the stars and the sky" (*Latin Panegyrics* 6.22.5). They lay on the main military routes connecting the eastern, Danube, and Rhine frontiers, with sea access where possible. Milan and Aquileia were thus much better suited than Rome for moving either to the Rhine or Danube.

As well as centers for government, the Tetrarchs also built personal palaces. Galerius built a spectacular residence at his birthplace of Felix Romuliana (Gamzigrad) in Dacia Ripensis, while Diocletian built a monumental complex at Salona in Dalmatia for his retirement. This creation of these new palace complexes increased the marginalization of Rome. Gallienus had lived in Rome between 262 and 265, but had spent 260–261 and 265–268 on campaign. Although Aurelian erected new walls for the city, built the Temple of the Sun, and held his triumphal parade there, he spent only a few months in Rome. Many other emperors in the late third century never reached Rome: Maximian, based in the west, visited four times, but Diocletian only visited for his *vicennalia* in 303 and Constantius I never went. Although Maximian was not a frequent visitor, he did initiate a huge new bath complex in the northeast of the city dedicated to Diocletian.

When Diocletian visited Rome, Lactantius reports that Diocletian, "unable to bear the Roman freedom of speech, peevishly and impatiently burst away from the city" (Lactantius, *dmp* 17). Although the emperor lived at the center of an armed camp, surrounded by an elaborate protocol and by armed guards, he was still expected to be accessible to his subjects. Public appearances might be scripted, but there were numerous opportunities to express one's opinions to the emperor, though usually more formal than the population of Rome's outcries. It was both an expectation and a reality that that all private petitioners could reach the emperor, whether in writing or in person. Of the fourteen rescripts known to have been issued by Maximian, six were to women, including one issued by him as Caesar to Calpurnia Aristaeneta regarding a son who was immoderately overspending his inheritance at Milan in February 286 (*CJ* 3.29.4). Despite the formality and the difficulty of approaching the emperor, it was possible for many. Diocletian and the *comitatus* arrived at Byzantium on April 2, 293, having been at Heraclea in Thrace the day before. They stayed for about two weeks, but by April 15 had moved to Melantias in Thrace and by April 17 were back at Heraclea. While at Byzantium, on April 13 at least eight rescripts were issued covering topics from the correct procedure in disputes over slave ownership to instructing Marciana, who claimed to be a minor, to make her case in front of the provincial governor. Only one of these rescripts was addressed to a government official, the praetorian prefect Asclepiodotus; the remainder of the recipients, including two women, were private citizens.

As emperors were increasingly absent from the ceremonial and senatorial traditions of the city of Rome, the imperial courts began to develop new rituals of their own. The Republican heritage of the Senate and an emperor who claimed to be the first among equals had always kept elements of informality in the court. With the Tetrarchy, the last vestiges of this heritage were lost as new officials attached to the imperial household (*sacrum cubiculum*, literally the imperial bedroom) began to play an important role in controlling access to the emperor. As in many other aristocratic households, many of these attendants were eunuchs. The *primicerius sacri cubiculi* may be attested as early as 312, and there was a *praepositus sacri cubiculi* (officer in charge of the imperial bedroom) in 326. These men often attracted the hatred of their contemporaries who claimed that they controlled the emperor. Controlling access to the emperor gave many eunuchs influence, but they were always dependent on the emperor's favor. Moreover, since emperors still met with petitioners and discussed many matters in council, no eunuch was able to isolate the emperor. After the eunuchs and the guards, Diocletian required a formal process of kneeling and kissing the corner of the imperial robe, a ritual known as *adoratio*. This made the emperor more remote, and may have contributed to the change in the way being emperor was treated in the fourth century. Certainly, the ease of being accepted as emperor that characterized the second half of the third century had gone, even if imperial insignia was confined to a diadem and scepter (see Figure 6).

DIOCLETIANIC REFORMS

There had been about fifty provinces in the reign of Gallienus, but an early fourth-century document, the Verona List, lists almost one hundred provinces. The greatest increase was in the reign of Diocletian so that, according to Lactantius, "the provinces were chopped into slices; many *praesides* and many officials lay upon on every region territory and almost every city" (*dmp* 7.4). Thus in Anatolia, the province of Caria and Phrygia had been created out of Asia in the 250s, but it was split again into two separate provinces in 301/305 while Italy was now divided into eight provinces.

Figure 6. Scepter ascribed to the Imperial insignia of Maxentius, discovered on the Palatine Hill in Rome in 2006 (National Museum of Rome).

Many of the smaller provinces, however, such as Cyprus, Germania Secunda, and Lusitania, continued unchanged, though the proconsular provinces of Asia and Africa were drastically reduced in size. With the increase in the number of provinces, Diocletian created an intermediate layer of administration, grouping provinces into dioceses under a new official, the *vicarius*, with judicial and financial duties who acted a deputy for the praetorian prefect (*vicarii agens vices praefectorum praetorio*). Each of the twelve *vicarii* was responsible for a diocese of between six and eighteen provinces. The dioceses were initially Britain, Gaul, Viennensis (also known as the Seven Provinces), Spain, Africa, Italy (subdivided into southern and central Italy, though technically under a *vicarius* of the urban prefect, and northern Italy), Pannonia, Moesia, Thrace, Asiana, Pontica, and lastly Oriens, a huge area including both Syria and Egypt, whose *vicarius* was called the *Comes Orientis*. The establishment of the vicariates still respected the proconsuls of Asia and Africa (though not Achaea), who continued to be outside the control of praetorian prefects and reported directly to the emperor.

The *vicarii* helped ease the burden on the overloaded praetorian prefects. These were now more numerous, with each Augustus having his own acting as part of a college of prefects, though *vicarii* closer to an emperor probably reported to him rather than to a more distant prefect. As under Gallienus, prefects remained responsible for recruiting troops and providing supplies to the army and the imperial staff, as well as acting as judges; taking care of public works, roads, and the *cursus publicus*; and often serving as generals. In background they were not always soldiers; some, like Hermogenianus under Diocletian, were lawyers. From 297, the levying of goods, especially food, animals, and clothing, by the praetorian prefect to support the army and *comitatus* was regularized as the *annona militaris*. Henceforth, annual contributions were based on a combination of land units (*iuga*) and head counts (*capita*), assessed for every village and city. With minor modifications, and frequent commutations of goods for money, this was the basis of imperial taxation into the seventh century AD. This reorganization of the imperial tax system was accompanied by an empire-wide census of land, people, and animals carried out by professional surveyors (*censitores*). Almost all of our evidence is eastern, though similar parties were working throughout the Empire. In Syria Palestina, the survey was led by Aelius Statutus, and in Syria Coele and Egypt by Iulius Septimius Sabinus. Near Qalat Seman in Syria Coele in the territory of Beroea, an inscription read as follows:

> For the safety and victory of our lords Diocletian and Maximian Augusti and Constantius and Maximian [=Galerius] most noble Caesares the boundaries of the Kaprokeroi were established under the supervision of

Iulius Sabinus, *lamprotatos censitor* in the year 345 [of the era of Antioch], Panemos [= July 297] (*SEG* 20.335).

This enormous process mapped the territory of every village throughout the Empire. At the same time as the survey teams were working on village boundaries, registers of individual estates and landholdings were also being created. These were then submitted to each city to coordinate tax collection. Each holding was described in terms of a combination of units of land (*iuga*) and head counts of people and animals (*capita*) though the amount and type of land that made up a *iugum* varied from region to region. In Syria, for example, a fifth-century document known as the Syro-Roman Lawbook recorded

> the *iugum* was measured in the days of the Emperor Diocletian and became fixed. Five *iugera* which make 10 *plethra* [another Roman unit of land measurement] of vineyard were established as 1 *iugum*; 20 *iugera* of seed land which make 40 *plethra* provide *annonas* of 1 *iugum*. ... So too land which is of poorer quality and is reckoned as second quality: 40 *iugera* which make 80 *plethra* pay 1 *iugum*.

Although paying tax was a universal obligation, the age at which tax began to be levied varied regionally. For head count purposes, two women could be counted the same as one man, though this too could vary; a law of 386 reassigned a *caput* from one man or two women to two or three men or to four women, at least for some provinces in Anatolia (*CT* 13.11.2). Since *iuga* and *capita* were of equal value, the two categories were often combined into a single category. The state's estimates were calculated in both terms of goods (wheat and barley, meat, oil, and wine) and money. Many assessments were commuted, the choice of cash or kind probably also varied regionally according to the number of state employees (military and civilian) to be fed and the ability of the taxed area to transport goods. Regional variations in the way in which the assessments were calculated did not affect the calculations of the praetorian prefect that simply divided the required totals by the number of *iuga* and *capita*. Since the prefects in theory calculated their requirements annually, it was possible to adjust taxation rates year by year.

As well as impacting social groups and types of land in differing ways, the taxation system focused heavily on agricultural areas. Italy too was now treated differently. Although its nonprovincial status under earlier emperors meant that it had been exempt from some taxes, it had always been subject to the *annona*. Since the *annona* now formed the largest part of state resource extraction, Italy seemed less special. This change was not popular; when Severus attempted to impose the *capitatio* on cities in Italy in 306, it drove some to support Maxentius' seizure of power. At the end of the fourth century, the *Historia Augusta* describes an idealized prefect, which gives a sense of what the complaints about the system:

> Do you see how he does not oppress the provincials, how he keeps the horses where there is fodder and orders rations for soldiers where there is grain, how he never compels a provincial or a land-holder to provide grain where he has none or horses where he has no pasture? There is no arrangement better than to order in each place what is produced there so that the state may not be oppressed by transport or other costs (*Triginti Tyranni* 18.6–7).

Prefects who had actually done the job would probably be dumbstruck by the simplemindedness of the criticism; on the other hand, there probably were cases where there really was no fodder to be had, and yet the prefect had to feed his master's mounts and continued to make demands on the locals.

The diocesan structure was also used to reorganize the imperial mints. By the end of Diocletian's reign, a mint had been established in most dioceses, usually at cities frequented by emperors such as Nicomedia or Trier. In a change to Aurelian's minting practices, gold *aurei* were at first at minted at 70 to the pound, though by 290 their weight had been increased and they were minted at 60 to the pound. Another financial reform in 301 had less success, an edict stipulating the maximum prices for goods and services throughout the Empire. Though widely promulgated, it soon lapsed.

Diocletian also made major changes to imperial service. The earlier and sometimes nominal separation of posts into equestrian and senatorial hierarchies had by the end of the third century evolved into a single hierarchy of imperial service. In ascending order, this was *vir perfectissimus, vir eminentissimus, vir clarissimus* (which brought with it senatorial rank), *vir spectabilis*, and, from Constantine's reign in the fourth century, *vir illustris*. Instead of senatorial status coming from holding various magistracies, as it had since the early days of the Roman Republic, it was now derived from participating in an imperial hierarchy. Military responsibilities were removed from the majority of provincial governors, almost all of whom now came from nonmilitary backgrounds. This process was gradual and even at the end of the reign governors are sometimes found with military duties, e.g., Verinus, *praeses* of Syria in 305 who led troops into Armenia or Aurelius Asclepiades, *praeses* of Arabia under the First Tetrarchy, who built a fort at Qasr Bishr. The existing senatorial careers remained in place, so serving as praetor and quaestor was still important for an Italian aristocrat who wished to enter the senate. However, the senatorial aristocracy had generally ceased to hold military posts, and by the end of the third century the only imperial posts left to the senatorial aristocracy were the proconsulates of Achaea,

Asia, Africa (the latter both reduced in size), provincial governorships in Italy (about nine posts), and the urban prefecture of Rome. And even among these posts, Diocletian sometimes installed his own men, such as the *vir perfectissimus* Lucius Sul(picius?) Paulus.

The late third century thus saw the rise of an imperial aristocracy based on holding offices rather than land. The lack of wealth requirements and a separation of military and civil hierarchies led to the development of a class of professional soldiers who were imperial officials. This also allowed the promotion of non-Romans as officers, a process often described as "barbarization." Thus Crocus, the Alamannic king present at Constantine's accession in 306, was probably in command of troops. The separation of civil and military hierarchies and the creation of a true imperial service also created a new aristocracy. By allowing these aristocrats into the Senate, it was no longer dominated by men defined by landholding and hereditary blood and wealth, but by imperial service. This new aristocracy took time to develop, and it was not until the mid-fourth century that its form began to become clear.

Removing military responsibilities and reducing the size of provinces gave governors more time to devote to a smaller number of cities. For some, this would have been seen as an increase in efficiency, for others an increase in workload or in imperial interference in their business. At the same time, the restructuring of tax collection around the *annona militaris* put a greater burden on city councils, so that role of provincial governors was mostly limited to hearing legal cases and enforcing the imperial will. These duties became easier from the 290s with the publication of two collections of law, the *Codex Gregorianus* (first edition ca. 292) and the *Codex Hermogenianus* (first edition 295). In many cases, governors did not need such aids but simply returned appeals to lower officials. When in 260 the prefect of Egypt received a petition from Aurelia Artemis claiming that a neighbor had rustled her sheep, he recorded its existence and then forwarded it to the *epistrategus* with an order to investigate. We have both the petition and a copy of the subsequent proceedings at the *epistrategus'* court (*Select Papyri* 2.262, 293). Governors also wrote to emperors, filing regular reports and requesting investigation of problems and guidance on legal matters. Governors were also responsible for the enactment of the imperial will, either in response to an edict or as a result of a direct order delivered by letter.

CHRISTIANITY AND OTHER RELIGIONS

Carrying out some orders like organizing imperial supplies was simple, but other situations, in particular the persecution of Christians, were more complex. For Gallienus as emperor, religious affairs took up very little of his time. This is not to say that religion was ignored or unimportant in the mid-third century. Roman emperors had always had a clear relationship with the divine powers, with each emperor holding the office of *Pontifex Maximus*, i.e., the chief priest of the Roman state. He was also given divine honors by the imperial cult, which had a temple and priests in most cities of the Empire. On the death of an emperor, he was often given divine honors by the Senate, as happened to Gallienus, Claudius II, Aurelian, Diocletian, Maximian, Galerius, Constantius I, Constantine I, and Constantius II. This layer of state religion lay on top of many forms of local religion, most of which were polytheistic and tolerant of the beliefs of others. This attitude was not shared by Christianity, which was monotheistic and nontolerant. The monotheism was of little concern to the emperor, but any unwilling-ness of Christians to participate in the imperial cult was of great concern since imperial well-being was strongly associated with respect for the gods. Sometimes this led to persecution, although in the third century Roman per-secution was as unsystematic as Christian protest. When Valerian launched a program of persecution in 259, his *rationalis rei summae* Macrianus was blamed for this by Dionysius, bishop of Alexandria. When Dionysius was brought before Aemilianus, Prefect of Egypt, he declared the following:

> We both honour and worship the One God and creator of all things, who handed over the Empire to the most highly beloved of God, Valerian and Gallienus, *Augusti*; and to Him we continuously pray for their Empire so that it may stay calm (Eusebius, *HE* 7.11.8).

It was not enough. Dionysius was exiled, and like other Christians, banned from assembling, while the property of those executed was added to the imperial treasury. Valerian's persecution was abandoned by Gallienus, who issued an edict of toleration. Christians were then ignored by the Empire for the next forty years, to the extent that Christian opponents of the Antiochene bishop Paul of Samosata even appealed to Aurelian. They had excommunicated Paul for heresy, but now he refused to leave his church. Aurelian ordered the church to belong "to those to whom the bishops of the dogma of Italy and the City of the Romans should write" (Eusebius, *HE* 7.30.19). For Aurelian, this was no different from any other appeal, and his orders to the bishops were the same as those to other imperial officials: inves-tigate and decide. This worked when Christianity was a small cult, but relationships began to be strained as Christianity grew in strength, from being a minority group at the beginning of the third century to being a wide-spread group with established churches in most cities at its end. Conflict was not, however, inevitable and the frequent sacrifices on behalf of the emperor did not stop many Roman Christians from serving as soldiers in the third century. When the *proconsul Africae* Cassius Dio interrogated a reluctant Christian conscript by the name of Maximilianus in 295, he claimed that "in the sacred *comitatus* of our lords Diocletian, Maximian, Constantius, and Galerius there are Christian soldiers and they serve" (*acta Maximiliani* 2.9).

Non-Christian attitudes also changed over this period. Both Aurelian and Carus described themselves as Lord and God (*dominus et deus*), and Aurelian made much of the Sun God, especially at Rome where he built a new temple. Diocletian also added a divine component, and from 286 the new ideology of the Tetrarchy included the association of Diocletian with Jupiter and Maximian with Hercules. Each emperor was thus associated with his own elite legion, the Ioviani for Diocletian and the Herculiani for Maximian. The same structure was found on coins, with the legend Jupiter the Preserver (IOVI CONSERVATORI) being placed on the reverse of many of Diocletian's issues, Hercules the Preserver (HERCULI CONSERVATORI) on those of Maximian, a pattern also used on the coins of the Caesars Constantius and Galerius.

THE GREAT PERSECUTION, 303

The tolerant environment then suddenly changed in 303, when Diocletian launched what is often known as the Great Persecution. This followed earlier purges of Christians from court and the army, one of whom Aurelius Gaius, a soldier who had served in the *comitatus* all over the Empire and who was buried at Cotiaeum in Phrygia. His epitaph was established "as a memorial until the Resurrection" (*SEG* 31.1116). However, sacrifices continued to turn out poorly, and this was blamed by some on the presence of Christians. Before Diocletian began the persecution, the decision was discussed in the consistory. The imperial word was law, but few emperors acted in anger or made decisions without consultation. At least, they were supposed not to, and it would not have taken even the most egotistical emperor long to realize that it was just less trouble this way. Following oral presentations, there was a discussion in front of the emperor, who then made his decision. Some of the work of the consistory took place in public, as shown by a fragment of the consistory minutes preserved in the *Codex Justinianus*. Diocletian ruled as follows:

> The sons of decurions should not be sent to the beasts. And when there was an exclamation from the people, the emperor also said: the vain voices of the people should not be heard; for it is not appropriate for their voices to

be believed when they wish that either the guilty be absolved of an accusation or the innocent be condemned (*CJ* 9.47.12).

Lactantius describes these discussions that led to the persecution. He was a professor of rhetoric at Nicomedia who had arrived in the city while Christians were being purged from the court and the army. As such, Lactantius would have occasionally been at court functions and certainly mixed socially with members of the consistory, such as Sossianus Hierocles, *praeses* of Bithynia in 303 and thus normally resident in Nicomedia. From a refutation written by Eusebius, we know Hierocles wrote two books attacking Christianity and comparing Jesus to Apollonius of Tyana. He describes Diocletian, who

> summoned many to the *consilium*, so that whatever fault he committed might be ascribed to others. There a few magistrates and a few officers, were admitted and, proceeding by rank, questioned. Some, because of their hatred of the Christians, thought they should be destroyed, as hostile to the gods and as enemies of public religion; others felt differently but, having understood the will of that man [Galerius], either from fear or wishing to gratify him they agreed in the same opinion (Lactantius, *dmp* 11.5–6).

There were, according to Eusebius, two edicts. The first ordered the destruction of churches and of holy writings, while church property was confiscated and assigned to the imperial *fiscus*; the second imprisoned church leaders and required them to sacrifice. Those who handed over sacred materials, such as Mensurius, bishop of Carthage, were despised by their colleagues and known as *traditores*. However, enforcement of the persecution varied, and Constantius I was famously restrained in the areas he ruled.

CONSTANTIUS I (305–306), GALERIUS (305–311), AND THE SECOND TETRARCHY

In 305, Diocletian and Maximian laid down the purple and retired. The long reign of Diocletian had seen major change. The greatest achievement was political, breaking the cycle of civil war, by assembling a team of co-emperors who trusted each other. This allowed the restoration of order. The long reign also allowed the introduction of numerous changes in government, particularly a new system of taxation and a new structure of service. Both these changes were, however, the result of existing trends, and their association with Diocletian may appear strongly to us because the primary sources are better for this period than for the preceding half-century. Nonetheless, the achievement was real.

These imperial retirements were unprecedented. Aurelius Victor's mid-fourth-century account includes two different explanations, though one need not accept his feeling that, "by nature an excellent man, [Diocletian] spurned ambition and returned to life in the community" (*de Caesaribus* 39.48). Writers in the early fourth century offered two interpretations. For some panegyrists, the retirements were the result of a planned scheme, an interpretation that is also suggested by adjustments to Maximian's regnal years following a meeting of Maximian and Diocletian in Rome in 303. For the Christian Lactantius, it was a result of the urging of an ambitious Galerius. A serious illness in 304 probably has much to do with Diocletian's decision. Constantius was now the senior Augustus (in control of Gaul, Spain, and Britain) in partnership with Galerius (Moesia and Thracia). The new Caesar in the west was Flavius Valerius Severus (Italy and Africa), in the east Galerius Valerius Maximinus (usually known as Maximinus Daia) (Asia, Pontica, and Oriens). Twin ceremonies were organized on May 1, 305, with Diocletian acclaiming Galerius and Maximinus at Nicomedia, while Maximian acclaimed Constantius and Severus at Milan. Maximinus was Galerius' nephew, another Balkan soldier, while Severus was a friend of Galerius' from Illyricum. After the ceremonies, the two original Tetrarchs then retired, Maximian to Italy, and Diocletian to Salona in Dalmatia to grow cabbages.

Both the promoted Constantius and the retired Maximian had adult sons, neither of whom was honored. The easiest explanation of their marginalization is the influence that Galerius had on Diocletian, who was his father-in-law. Moreover, Galerius was with Diocletian in 305, whereas Maximian and Constantius were not. It was easy not to promote them, but harder to make them happy. Galerius was concerned enough about Constantine to keep him as a hostage in his *comitatus* at Serdica. When Constantine left the court, he rode to Gaul as fast as possible to join his father at Boulogne, killing the post horses on the way lest he be recalled – a wonderful story, but told only after Galerius was unable to refute it.

Constantius died at York in Britain on July 25, 306, and Flavius Valerius Constantinus was acclaimed as Augustus by the army on the same day. He was Constantius' son by his first wife Helena, born in 272, a soldier who had served in Mesopotamia, Egypt, and the Balkans. After his acclamation, Constantine wrote to Galerius, who accepted him as Caesar, a status with which Constantine was content. Although Galerius' acceptance was realistic, it pushed Maximian's son Maxentius to claim imperial power in Rome on October 28, 306. Although his authority was soon accepted in Africa and southern and central Italy, northern Italy remained under the control of Severus at Milan. Severus soon marched against Maxentius, but at Ravenna was abandoned by his troops, many of whom had campaigned with Maxentius' father, and captured. Maxentius now took control of the northern parts of Italy and restored his father as Augustus in spring 307. The rapid abandonment by Maximian of his retirement suggests he was not entirely happy with the way it had developed. Maximian also arranged an alliance with Constantine, appointing him as Augustus and giving him his daughter Fausta in marriage. There followed a brief and unsuccessful campaign in Italy by Galerius in September 307 during which Severus was executed by Maxentius. Maximian then attempted to depose his son Maxentius in spring 308 (perhaps in the hope of coming to terms with Galerius) but when the attempt failed, he fled to Constantine. Maxentius' control of Africa was lost temporarily to Lucius Domitius Alexander, who was *vicarius Africae* before he seized power there in 308.

The Tetrarchic system was clearly not working well in the west, now split among Domitius Alexander, Constantine, and Maxentius, all of whom had been made emperor without reference to Galerius. Galerius therefore arranged an imperial conference at Carnuntum in Pannonia Prima in November 308, drawing Diocletian, probably reluctantly, out of Salona. The result of the conference was that another of Galerius' protégés, Licinius, a Dacian, was acclaimed as Augustus to replace Severus in the west, while Maximinus and Constantine were left as Caesars. Constantine ignored Galerius' attempt to demote him, rejected the offered title of "son of Augustus," and continued to style himself Augustus. Maxentius in Italy and Domitius Alexander in Africa also held imperial power, though it was not accepted by the others. Despite the problems, the ideal of the Tetrarchy continued to exist. In 310, an imperial communication was posted at Tlos in Lycia, which, though heavily fragmentary, clearly lists four emperors (*CIL* 3.12133). The special relationship with Jupiter and Hercules continued with an inscription from Aquincum showing Galerius as Iovius (*ILS* 658).

After Carnuntum, Maximian returned to Gaul. At Arles, he is said to have again seized power, then to have committed suicide in summer 310. His death made Constantine's relations with Galerius easier, and the information that we have about his fate was certainly processed by Constantine's propaganda managers. These managers were also active in creating a particular image for Constantine. In 310, we first hear of his descent from Claudius II, though authors writing about his father in the reign of Diocletian knew nothing about the claim. It was widely reported, however, in panegyrics of Constantine, in inscriptions, and in some historians. But one can only have sympathy for the orator making a speech on Constantine in this year forced to open with "I shall begin with the first divinity who is your ancestor, of whom most people are still, perhaps, ignorant, although those who love you know it very well" (*Latin Panegyrics* 6.2.1).

Although Maxentius was excluded from the settlement at Carnuntum, he was still emperor in Italy. In 309, he sent an expedition to Africa under his praetorian prefect, Rufius Volusianus, which defeated Domitius Alexander and regained control of this region. In Rome, he began a series of projects aimed at transforming the city. In the Forum, he started the huge Basilica of Maxentius; in the northeast part of the city, he completed the Baths of Diocletian, another enormous project; and three kilometers to the south of the city, he built a new circus, complete with a villa and mausoleum.

The peace that had been reestablished by the Conference at Carnuntum did not last long. Diocletian appears to have died in 311, but the date is uncertain, and there are different versions of his death in the contemporary writers Lactantius and Eusebius, suggesting real obscurity. Galerius died from a wasting disease in May 311, a fate recorded with great joy by Christian writers who saw this as divine punishment for the Great Persecution. With all four members of the original Tetrarchy now dead, there was no way to restrain the ambitious. Licinius claimed the dioceses of Pannonia, Thrace, and Moesia in his own name, having previously shared them with Galerius. He then made an alliance with Constantine, in which Constantine would deal with Maxentius, while Licinius would deal with Maximinus.

In spring 312, Constantine crossed the Alps against Maxentius, capturing Verona by siege, then marching on Rome. Here, he defeated the forces of Maxentius at the Battle of the Milvian Bridge on October 28. Maxentius drowned in the Tibur as he attempted to retreat from the battle; his body was then recovered and his head sent first round the city, then later to Africa. This left Constantine as sole emperor in the west. Licinius came to Milan to marry Constantine's sister Constantia. The two emperors also issued a decree of universal toleration at Milan in spring 313. The unity of imperial approach to persecution was fractured after 305. For each emperor, the benefits from the persecution of Christians had to be weighed against the costs. In the west, Constantine was tolerant of all religions from 306 and Maxentius even returned some confiscated property to Christians. In the east, Galerius canceled his persecution in 311, although Maximinus continued to persecute. In Palestina,

> edicts of the tyrant were issued for the first time, commanding that the rulers of the cities should diligently and speedily see to it that all the people offered sacrifices. Throughout the city of Caesarea, by command of the governor, the heralds were summoning men, women, and children to the temples of the idols, and besides this, the regimental commanders were calling out each one by name from a roll, and an immense crowd of the wicked were rushing together from all quarters (Eusebius, *Martyrs of Palestina* 4).

Some of those Christians were condemned to fight as gladiators, but refused to eat or train, even when dragged in front of Maximinus himself. Others were condemned to the mines, so 130 mutilated Egyptian Christians arrived in Cilicia in 308; once liberated under Licinius, the survivors founded the Laura of the Egyptians near Anazarbus, still there in the early sixth century. Later, in January 312, the theologian Lucian of Antioch was brought to Nicomedia, interrogated by Maximinus in person, then executed.

Most of our source material focuses on the wars between the Tetrarchs, but there were continued foreign wars. In particular, Maximinus fought against the Persians in Armenia in 312. This war was soon abandoned, and in early 313, while Licinius was in Italy, Maximinus force-marched his army from Syria to the Hellespont. It was a difficult march and casualties were high, Licinius was taken by surprise, and Maximinus occupied Byzantium. Licinius meanwhile marched east hastily, declaring Maximinus a public enemy:

> As to the portraits which were set up in every city for the honour [of Maximinus] and of his children, some were thrown down from a height to the ground and broken up, others had the faces ruined by being blackened with dark paint; his statues, as many as had been set up in his honour, were similarly thrown down and broken up, lying out as a joke and entertainment to those who wished to insult and abuse them (Eusebius, *HE* 9.11.2).

The two armies met at Adrianople on April 30, 313, and Licinius was victorious. Crossing into Anatolia, he pursued Maximinus' tired forces back to the Taurus and then stormed the Cilician Gates. Maximinus retreated to Tarsus, where he was besieged by Licinius' forces, committed suicide in July, and was buried outside the city. Licinius proceeded to execute Maximinus' son, Maximus, as well as the sons of Severus and Galerius, who were at Maximinus' court. The Roman Empire was now ruled by two Christian emperors, Constantine and Licinius.

The half-century between the capture of Valerian and the suicide of Maximinus is a challenging period to analyze, a period of rapid, if not bewildering, political change. But throughout it all, there was never any doubt of Roman success, and all of the political struggles were over who was to be master of the Roman world. The sense of crisis brought about by the Persian successes in midcentury was now over, and fighting in Mesopotamia was a struggle for dominance rather than for elimination. But in addition to the struggles for mastery of the Empire, it was also a time of major administrative change. At the beginning of the period, the Empire was still related administratively to that of Augustus, but by the reign of Constantine, it was a different sort of state. The process of transitions to the late Roman Empire was not complete, but with the exception of Christianity, all of the major elements were now in place.

FURTHER READING

The source material for constructing a narrative for the third-century Roman Empire is complex. There is no detailed connected narrative that survives between the works of Herodian (covering 180–238) and Ammianus Marcellinus (354–378). This absence is particularly significant for the reigns of Diocletian and Constantine. Although no detailed narrative survives, several sources provide a narrative of sorts, including Zosimus, Eutropius, Aurelius Victor, and the *Historia Augusta*. Zosimus wrote a work in a Hellenizing style in Constantinople in the late fifth century, covering the early third century to his own day. The sections on the third century relied on the now lost histories of Dexippus and Eunapius. Dexippus was an Athenian whose history covered events down to 272, Eunapius of Sardis' history covered 270–404; both are now preserved only in fragments. Zosimus' pagan sympathies meant that his work was subsequently damaged, with the entire chapter on Diocletian removed at a later date; we also lack the final sections. Festus, Eutropius, and Aurelius Victor wrote short histories of the Roman Empire during the 370s, all based on a common source, a now lost work usually referred to as the *Kaisergeschichte* (History of the Emperors), a short imperial history covering the period from the reign of Augustus to either 337 or 357. Down to 284, they occasionally can be supplemented by the *Historia Augusta*. This consists of biographies claiming to be written by six historians in the late third and early fourth centuries but is actually the work of a single unknown individual writing at the end of the fourth century and also based on the *Kaisergeschichte*. Alongside the secular histories was the first *Ecclesiastical History*, written by Eusebius in the early fourth century, which, unlike the classicizing historians, cited large numbers of documents. Eusebius' history can be supplemented by some of his other works, as well as Lactantius, who wrote earlier in the fourth century. Also useful are the various Latin panegyrics and the *Origo Constantini*.

For a general overview, there are good introductions in Cameron, A., *Later Roman Empire, AD 284–430* (Cambridge, MA, 1993), Harries, J., *Imperial Rome, AD 284–363: The New Empire* (Edinburgh, 2012), Hekster, O., *Rome and Its Empire, AD 193–284* (Edinburgh, 2008), Kulikowski, M., *The Triumph of Empire: The Roman World from Hadrian to Constantine* (Boston, 2016), and Potter, D. S., *The Roman Empire at Bay*[2] (London, 2014). Important for chronology are Peachin, M., *Roman Imperial Titulature and Chronology, AD 235–284* (Amsterdam, 1990), Corcoran, S., *Empire of the Tetrarchs*[2] (Oxford, 2000), and Barnes, T. D., *The New Empire of Diocletian and Constantine* (Cambridge, MA, 1982).

The emperors before Diocletian have not been well studied, a testament to the problems with the source material. De Blois, L., *The Policy of the Emperor Gallienus* (Leiden, 1976) remains the best introduction to his reign. See also Drinkwater, J. F., *The Gallic Empire* (Stuttgart, 1987) and Watson, A., *Aurelian and the Third Century* (London, 2004). For Lollianus' letter, Parsons, P. J., "Petitions and a Letter: The Grammarian's Complaint," in Hanson, A. E., ed., *Collectanea Papyrologica* (Bonn, 1976), 409–446. For

Tacitus at Perge, Roueché, C., "Floreat Perge," in Mackenzie, M. M. and Roueché, C., eds., *Images of Authority* (Cambridge, 1989), 206–228.

From the Tetrarchy onward, there is an abundance of work. The best starting point is Lenski, N., *Cambridge Companion to the Age of Constantine*[2] (Cambridge, 2011). See also Rees, R., *Diocletian and the Tetrarchy* (Edinburgh, 2004) and Leadbetter, W., *Galerius and the Will of Diocletian* (London, 2010). On Constantine, see Bardill, J., *Constantine, Divine Emperor of the Christian Golden Age* (Cambridge, 2011) and Lieu, S. N. C. and Montserrat, D., *Constantine: History, Historiography and Legend* (London, 1998).

2

THE EARLY FOURTH CENTURY, 313–363

Following the death of Maximinus in 313, the Roman Empire was split between two rulers, Constantine in the west and Licinius in the east. The recent collapse of the Tetrarchy suggested that any sharing of power between the two imperial colleagues was likely to be short-lived, despite their wedding alliance. Indeed, Constantine, married to Maxentius' sister, would be well aware of the tenuousness of such alliances. Initially, however, the two emperors seemed to trust each other. Constantine campaigned on the Rhine against some Franks in 314, while Licinius fought in Persia in 314. There was certainly plenty to do, and both emperors faced the challenge of healing the scars from the civil wars, rewarding their supporters, but at the same time not alienating the defeated. It was this concern that led Constantine to keep Maxentius' urban prefect Anullinus in office for a while after the Battle of the Milvian Bridge.

More important, however, was the adoption of Christianity by Constantine and Licinius. This set the Roman Empire on a new course, somewhat different from the opposition to the faith of Diocletian, Galerius, and Maximinus and also different from the toleration offered by other Tetrarchs. Both emperors supported Christianity actively, though most of Licinius' acts were later claimed by Constantine. Although imperial support for Christianity was new, the support was granted in traditional fashion. The emperor was the chief priest of Rome, the *Pontifex Maximus*, a post held by Constantine throughout his reign, as by all his heirs. The success of the Empire depended on treating the gods or God correctly. Thus Maximinus Daia asked in 312, "who can be found who is so stupid or lacking of all intelligence that he does not perceive that it is by the benevolent care of the gods that the Earth does not refuse the seeds given to it?" (Eusebius, *HE* 9.7.8). The only disagreement from Christians would have been over who was to provide the care.

A law granting universal toleration was issued by Licinius and Constantine in February 313 (a document often called the Edict of Milan, because it followed discussion between the two emperors in that city). This promised toleration to all religions, i.e., both pagans and Christians, because

> the reverence paid to divinity deserves to be treated in first place, so that we give both to Christians and to all others freedom to follow whatever religion they wish; so that whatever divinity who is seated in heaven might be pleasant and propitious to us and to everyone who is controlled by our power (Lactantius, *dmp* 48.2).

It made it clear that all religions were to be given freedom of worship and confiscated church property was to be restored, with provisions for compensation for those who had been given such property by earlier emperors. As the first Christian emperors, Licinius and Constantine acted to establish the basis for all future interactions between the Empire and the church. Christians could now have government careers in ways that had not been open to them before. Thus Ablabius rose from obscure origins in Crete to become *vicarius* of Asiana in 324/326, praetorian prefect in 329–337, and even consul in 331. But being pagan was not an impediment to a successful career, and Constantine appointed Sopater, a pagan sophist from Syria, as an assessor because he was "captivated" by him. When Sopater was executed, the fifth-century pagan writers Eunapius and Zosimus claimed that Ablabius was responsible for his death. Although there were still many pagans, imperial favor for Christianity was sufficiently clear that when the Phrygian town of Orcistus appealed to Constantine in 331 to be given the status of a city, it stressed that all of its population were "followers of the most holy religion" (*ILS* 6091). Other contemporaries drew the same conclusions, like the poet Palladas, whose epigrams describe the emperor as beloved by God and bronze statues of the gods being melted down.

For all the imperial support of Christianity, both emperors also made efforts to show pagans that they were emperors for all Romans. Thus under Licinius, the *dux* Romulus consecrated a statue (*simulacrum*) of the Sun-god ca. 323 (*ILS* 8940) in Scythia. Coins struck by Constantine and Licinius both commemorated the Unconquered Sun and Jupiter the Preserver (SOL INVICTUS, IOVI CONSERVATORI), but there were no coins struck that praised the Christian god. And Constantine supported the travel of Nicagoras, torchbearer of the Eleusinian Mysteries, from Athens to Egypt in 326. At the same time, the imperial cult was still celebrated by Christian emperors. Most famously, in the last decade of his reign, Constantine allowed the construction of a temple dedicated to his family at Hispellum in Italy, though he did stipulate that no sacrifices should take place. Similarly, non-Christian priests still erected inscriptions, as at Ovacık in Lycia, claiming that they had performed all "public services," which would have included sacrifices (*SEG* 41.1390). In Rome, the cult of the Vestal Virgins continued and sacrifices were regularly made at the Altar of Victory by the Senate. At the same time, there were some antipagan measures, including the banning of sacrifice and forbidding of new cult statues. A few temples in the east were destroyed, at Aegeae in Cilicia, at Aphaca and Heliopolis in Phoenice Libanensis, and at Mambre in Palestina Prima, though these famous sites seem to have been chosen as examples. Otherwise, the majority of pagan temples were ignored, though their estates were confiscated and transferred to the *res privata*. Finally, the condemnation of prisoners as gladiators was replaced with condemnation to the mines. The effectiveness of these laws is difficult to assess, but they were a clear statement that the state was now in favor of Christianity and opposed to paganism.

These minor measures paled in comparison to the direct support for the infrastructure of Christianity. In 313, Constantine granted exemption from municipal administrative duties and taxes to clergy and in 319 extended the exemption from all public duties to all clerics. Then in 321 he legitimized bequests to the church. Further laws granted the property of intestate clerics to the church, while most bishops, being unmarried and dying in office, had a tendency to leave their property to the church. In the early fourth century, the church was not a wealthy organization, but by these means had acquired large quantities of wealth by the fifth century. The emperor also authorized annual grants from city incomes to support virgins, widows, and clergy, and Constantine gave bishops the power to hear some civil suits. In 333, he ruled that any party in a case before a verdict was given could appeal to a bishop and that the bishop's judgment was inappealable and would be executed by the state. When Ablabius, in his capacity of praetorian prefect, questioned this, Constantine explicitly reaffirmed it. As Ablabius saw, this ruling could have been very disruptive to justice, though in practice the law seems to have been ignored.

Constantine also gave numerous gifts to the church, in particular allowing bishops to draw on imperial resources for church construction, first in the west and from 324 in the east. Many of these foundations were built on and supported by estates transferred from imperial property, though the confiscation of civic temple estates meant that this generosity cost the emperor little. Other donations were of lands that the imperial treasury had received in earlier confiscations, like the estate of a certain Cyriaca given to the church of St. Laurentius in Rome. Many of Constantine's donations were recorded in the *Liber Pontificalis*, which itemizes 10.5 tons of silver, 2,335 pounds of gold, and 34,255 *solidi* (= 475 pounds of gold) from estates scattered across the Empire. Perhaps as early as 313, construction began on the church of St. John in Lateran at the southern side of the city on the site of the barracks of the recently disbanded *equites singulares*. This was a very large building, with a nave 100 meters long and 53 meters wide, decorated with marble revetment and columns of red and green granite, holding a congregation of perhaps three thousand. This structure brought Christians in Rome out of their house-churches and gave them a huge cathedral, similar to the audience halls of the aristocracy and radically different from pagan temples. In 313, Constantine made a gift of Fausta's palace, close to the Lateran, to the church, perhaps for use as a bishop's residence. A second major construction project was Santa Croce in Gerusalemme in the same area of the city, later used to house the fragment of the True Cross that Helena brought from the Holy Land in 327. Although large amounts of imperial resources were assigned to these buildings, they were kept out of the core of the city, avoiding a direct challenge to tradition and a mostly pagan aristocracy. Constantine's philanthropy was not, however, confined to churches, and Rome also acquired the Arch of Constantine commemorating his victory over Maxentius, a large bath complex, and a restored and enlarged Circus Maximus (see Figures 7 and 8). He also completed the Basilica Nova in the Forum, a project that had been started by Maxentius but was now modified to include a 12-meter-tall statue of Constantine himself. His also generosity reached other cities and at Naples, the *Liber Pontificalis* records the construction of a basilica supported by 490 pounds of silver, estates with an income of 673 *solidi*, as well as an aqueduct and a forum for the city. After his victory over Licinius, Constantine was also able to build churches in the east. The emperor's construction of churches in the Holy Land included the Church of the Holy Sepulchre at Golgotha and another on the Mount of Olives in Jerusalem, as well as other churches at Bethlehem.

Assessing the cost of these donations is difficult. Although lavish by the standards of individuals, they were relatively small compared to overall imperial income. Probably more significant than the donations of land were the ability to receive bequests and the immunities from taxation and civic duties that were granted. In the long term, these mechanics drained men and income from the state, as well as reinforcing an institution whose survival was not dependent on the survival of the Roman Empire. This new imperial support for their religion was probably pleasing to the majority of Christians, but it came at the price of an emperor who would intervene in church affairs. This intervention could easily be seen as a positive result when applied outside the Empire. In 314, a council of bishops at Caesarea in Cappadocia appointed Gregory the Illuminator as Catholicos of Armenia,

Figure 7. Arch of Constantine in Rome, dedicated in 315, showing the emperor (with his head missing) addressing the People from the Rostra in the Forum. (Alinari Archives)

who then baptized King Trdat III of Armenia, creating another Christian kingdom on the borders of the Persian Empire.

CONSTANTINE AND THE DONATISTS

But within the Empire, as the appeal of Paul to Aurelian had shown, Christians could also petition the emperor. When Christians were a persecuted minority, there was no need to listen, but as Christianity became a tolerated religion, the emperor had a duty to listen to these appeals. However, some Christians had a world view that did not accept the earthly authority of the emperor, at least as far as religious matters were concerned. It became rapidly apparent that these two perspectives would prove hard to reconcile. In late 312 or early 313, soon after defeating Maxentius, Constantine sent three letters to Carthage. Two were addressed to Anullinus, proconsul of Africa, and a relative of Maxentius' urban prefect; the other was addressed to Caecilian, bishop of Carthage. We do not know what led to Constantine writing these letters, though he did so having "learnt that certain men,

Figure 8. Arch of Constantine, in Rome, dedicated in 315, showing Constantine's army on the march. (Tupungato/Shutterstock.com)

not having settled minds, wish to turn aside the laity of the most holy and Catholic church by some low means of corruption" (Eusebius, *HE* 10.6.4). The letters show what Christians would describe as the involvement of the emperor in church affairs, though Constantine would have seen only the business of ruling the Empire. These letters show clear support for Caecilian, not least by insisting that Anullinus make sure that Caecilian's clergy were exempt from public office. The emperor was also giving bishops direct orders as if they were imperial officials, giving him money and telling him how to distribute it. But as with persecutions of Christians, settling intra-Christian disputes would prove to be difficult.

Constantine's intervention was required because of disputes between the rural African clergy and those of the city of Carthage. These two groups had different views on those who gave up books or sacrificed during Diocletian's persecution, often described as *traditores*. The rural clergy took a much harder line on this than did the urban clergy. Following the death of bishop Mensurius of Carthage in 307/308, vilified by the rural clergy as a *traditor*, a hurried election in the city acclaimed Caecilian, who was then consecrated by Felix, bishop of Aptunga. Concern about the election led to a council of seventy Numidian bishops declaring the election invalid and appointing Majorinus as bishop of Carthage. It was soon after this that

Constantine wrote to Anullinus and Caecilianus. He may have hoped that the affair was settled, but in 313 the Numidian bishops, now led by Donatus (who had succeeded Majorinus as one bishop of Carthage), approached Constantine directly. In response to the Donatist appeal, Constantine created a commission at Rome of three Gallic bishops under Miltiades, bishop of Rome. Miltiades added fifteen Italian bishops. This was the first Church Council, taking place at the behest of the emperor and meeting in the palace of Constantine's wife Fausta on the Lateran. The council declared Caecilian innocent of charges and condemned Donatus for rebaptizing *traditores*. The Donatists refused to accept the judgment of the council, arguing that Miltiades himself had attended sacrifices made by a *traditor*. Miltiades could appeal to the authority of St. Peter, but his authority depended on the support of the emperor and on the willingness of the clergy to accept his judgments.

The Donatists then appealed again to Constantine, claiming that Miltiades' decision had been made in secret and that the Council at Rome had not heard the entire case. Constantine left the Rhine in the summer of 314 and went to Arles, where he called another Church Council in August. The thirty-three bishops considered matters other than the Donatist problem. One of the council's canons concerned Christian soldiers, addressing the commandment "thou shalt not kill." At Arles, the bishops agreed to excommunicate soldiers who put down their arms even in peacetime, making the church support the military authority of the state. The council also heard the case made by the Donatists and found against them. Constantine described the verdict as the Judgment of Christ. "For I say – and it is the truth – that the judgment of priests ought to be regarded thus, as if the Lord himself sat in judgment" (Optatus, Appendix 5). Persuading a committee and implementing the decision were two separate matters; the Donatists refused to accept the judgment of this council too. They appealed to Constantine again, claiming that both Felix and Caecilianus were *traditores*. Constantine was now forced to investigate further, though by 315 he had decided that the supposedly incriminating letter written by Caecilianus to Felix was partially forged and that not only were Felix and Caecilian not *traditores*, but that some Donatist bishops were. When the results of Constantine's investigation were announced in Carthage, rioting ensued. A further hearing took place in Milan in October 315, with the same result, and rioting continued. Constantine finally decided to go to Africa himself. The commitment of the emperor to a process of investigation and public hearings is noteworthy. Distracted by the looming conflict with Licinius, Constantine abandoned his plans to deal with the Donatist situation personally and in 316 Eumelius, *vicarius* in Africa was ordered to confiscate Donatist churches. This was not always carried out peacefully, and we hear of a tribune Marcellinus, whose troops massacred a congregation in the church of Avioccala. The imperial persecution of Christians and the creation of martyrs was difficult to defend, and persecution ceased rapidly. By 321, the Donatist exiles had been recalled, and Constantine wrote to the Catholic bishops, saying that revenge would be left to God. The Donatists remained a strong movement in North Africa, and in 336 270 bishops assembled for a council. The large numbers were impressive, though African rural bishoprics tended to be small.

CIVIL WAR BETWEEN CONSTANTINE AND LICINIUS

Relations between Constantine and Licinius now collapsed. We are told that Constantine proposed making his brother-in-law Bassianus Caesar, and when Licinius refused, Bassianus revolted against Constantine, who then had him executed. Constantine then used Licinius' involvement as a justification for war. Other sources tell a simpler story of Constantine's ambition. Constantine marched into the Balkans and defeated Licinius at Cibalae in Pannonia in October and again at Campus Ardiensis near Adrianople in January 317 (where Licinius' troops were led by a short-lived imperial colleague, Valens). Peace was then made with the transfer of the dioceses of Pannonia and Moesia to Constantine, although Licinius continued to control Thrace and campaigned against some Sarmatians in 318. The two emperors also shared the consulate for 319. Constantine, however, kept a close eye on Licinius, mostly remaining in the Balkans and never moving farther west than Milan. It was probably at this period that Constantine formed the close attachment to Serdica that led him to describe it as "my Rome" (Peter the Patrician, Constantine fr 15.1). Managing Gaul was left in the hands of his son Crispus, who had been appointed Caesar at Serdica in March 317. In the same ceremony, Constantine's eldest son from his second marriage, Constantine, and Licinius' son, Licinius, were both promoted to the rank of Caesar, even though Constantine was perhaps a year old at this point and Licinius less than two. Coins were struck for both of the sons in both parts of the Empire immediately.

The peace made between Licinius and Constantine in 318 seemed unlikely to last, though both emperors continued to strike coins in the name of their imperial colleagues and Licinius celebrated his *decennalia* in 317 (see Figure 9). War started again in 324. Licinius' persecution of Christians may have provided a pretext. Licinius according to an inscription preserved at Salsovia in the province of Scythia, required troops based there to make

Figure 9. Silver bowl minted at Naissus in 317 to commemorate the *decennalia* of Licinius. The center inscription, loosely translated, means, "May the next ten years be like the first ten" (Boston, Museum of Fine Arts, 1970.568).

annual sacrifices to the Sun (*ILS* 8940). However, Constantine's ambition was probably the real driver. Constantine attacked by land and sea. On land, Licinius was defeated at Adrianople in July, though Constantine was slightly wounded in the battle. Then a large fleet commanded by Crispus defeated Licinius' naval forces in the Hellespont. Constantine now crossed into Anatolia and defeated Licinius in a third battle at Chrysopolis in September. When Licinius surrendered, Constantia successfully begged her brother for the life of her husband; the deposed Licinius was sent to Thessalonica along with his son (and Constantine's nephew) Licinius Caesar. As Maximian had shown, emperors could come back from retirement. The defeated emperors were too dangerous to let live for long, and in spring 325 they were executed.

THE FOUNDATION OF CONSTANTINOPLE, 324

Only six weeks after his victory over Licinius at the battle of Chrysopolis, Constantine founded a new city on the site of Byzantium (Istanbul) on November 8, 324. The choice was a rejection of Diocletian and Licinius' use of nearby Nicomedia as their capital. Both Byzantium and Nicomedia were sites with good communications, to the west with the Via Egnatia, north to the Danube, and to the east; also, both offered good sea access. However, unlike Nicomedia, Byzantium was highly defensible (as Constantine knew after besieging the city during the campaign against Licinius), had an excellent port, and did not have associations with earlier Tetrarchs. The core of the city was on the promontory, but there were suburbs to the north at Sycae, linked by a bridge from Blachernae and a ferry from the city. Between Sycae and the city lay the main port area of the Golden Horn. Later constructions were two harbors on the south side of the promontory, of Julian and Eleutherias, close to the imperial grain warehouses. The city walls, running for 2.5 kilometers from the Golden Horn to the Sea of Marmara and enclosing an area of ca. 600 hectares, were completed by 328, and the city was formally consecrated on May 11, 330 with the celebrations taking place in the Hippodrome.

Despite the large size, the city was rapidly occupied. Constantine encouraged settlement by attaching imperial estates in Anatolia and Thrace to villas in the city. From 332 there was a bread dole attached to eighty thousand houses (unlike Rome, where the dole was attached to individuals). This rapidly growing population was fed by transferring the grain shipments from Egypt that had previously been sent to Rome. The city became so big that it could only be fed as part of a state-managed process, and we are told that in the sixth century the annual shipments from Egypt to Constantinople totaled eight million *artabae*, enough to feed six hundred thousand people for a year (Justinian, *Edict* 13.8), and that the Romans "shipped the wealth of Egypt in the summer season to the Roman cities and with merchantmen turned the sea into dry land" (Theophylact 2.14.7).

Constantinople was founded not just as a new city, but as an imperial city, a second Rome. There were many similarities to the Tetrarchic capitals, including the creation of a palace area in the southeast part of the promontory, as well as warehouses and a Hippodrome, begun under Septimius Severus, with a capacity of perhaps seventy thousand to eighty thousand and an imperial box, the *kathisma*, which led directly to the imperial palace. There was a mint from 326, the huge Baths of Constantine (though not begun until 345), aqueducts, and even an imperial zoo inherited from Licinius. Seven Roman miles outside the city was the Hebdomon, the base for Constantine's army, a port, and it soon acquired an imperial palace. But unlike the Tetrarchic cities, Constantinople had its own Senate, though at first the senators only had the rank of *clari*, not *clarissimi* as in Rome, and no urban prefect is attested until 359.

The new city was ornamented with artworks (often of figures from pagan mythology) brought from all over the Empire, many used to decorate the Baths of Zeuxippus. Other areas benefiting from Constantine's collecting including the porphyry Tetrarchs in the Philadelphion (now in Venice) (see Figure 5) and the serpent column commemorating the battle of Plataea in the Hippodrome (still there today). And there were claims that Constantine moved the Palladion, a wooden image of Athena supposedly brought from Troy to Rome by Aeneas, to his new city. The religious buildings mixed Christian and non-Christian structures. The first cathedral was an existing Christian center, Hagia Eirene, supplemented by a Hagia Sophia built by Constantine, both close to the imperial palace. There was also the Church of the Holy Apostles built on the Mese close to the walls. This served as a church and a mausoleum for Constantine, and from 336 housed the relics of the apostles Andrew and Luke. To go between these churches involved traveling down the Mese and passing through the Forum of Constantine with its huge column topped with a statue of Constantine. However, existing pagan sites in the city were not disturbed. Constantine not only restored a temple to Cybele, but he also built a temple to Fortuna (Tyche). The same mixture of old and new is shown by the banning of condemning prisoners to fight in the arena, although the emperor continued to support other gladiatorial displays, beast hunts, and chariot races.

The generous imperial grants to encourage settlement fostered the growth of the new aristocracy of service. Many of these senators were initially drawn from court and army circles. There were attempts to recruit wealthy individuals, but this resulted in them leaving their own cities, and thus to complaints such as that of Libanius, who at the end of the fourth century claimed that it "lived luxuriously on the sweat of other cities" (*Or.* 1.279). His contemporary Eunapius was similarly scathing about Constantine's encouraging settlers "because he loved to be applauded in the theatres by men so drunk that they could not hold their liquor" (*Lives of the Sophists* 462). The emperor may have told a different story, of a need to have talented individuals serving the whole Empire, not just their city.

CONSTANTINE AND ARIANISM

Following his defeat of Licinius, Constantine inherited another intra-Christian dispute, though this was about theology, very different from the

Donatist controversies. The original dispute had started between Alexander, bishop of Alexandria, and Arius, one of his presbyters. Arius argued that God was unbegotten, eternal, and without beginning. From this, it followed for Arius that Christ as the Son of God must be later than the Father and that therefore there was a time when Christ did not exist. For many, believing that all parts of the Trinity were coeval, this was heresy. When Arius was excommunicated by Alexander, he appealed to Bishop Eusebius of Nicomedia, Licinius' capital, for support. Eusebius and many eastern bishops found Arius' thought acceptable, though many did not. Alexander, meanwhile, wrote to other bishops, detailing his actions against Arius but also stirring up further debate. Even if there had been mechanics within the church to manage such issues, the ability and willingness of Christians to appeal to the emperor would have made them moot. And from an imperial perspective, the combination of a willingness to appeal for imperial resolution combined with an unwillingness to accept an unwelcome verdict was highly frustrating. Emperors, usually self-confessed as not being theological experts, were concerned mostly with unity, often with a highly pragmatic perspective. After his defeat of Licinius in September 324, Constantine was soon caught up in this controversy. Initially, he tried to dismiss the theological question in favor of church unity and in October sent a letter to both Arius and Alexander (carried by Ossius of Cordoba, who continued to act as Constantine's adviser on Christian matters) asking whether they could agree to differ (Eusebius, *Life of Constantine* 2.64–72). When this proved impossible, Constantine attempted to resolve the problem by summoning a council of bishops of the entire church, representing both east and west. This first ecumenical council gave an opportunity to address many issues of concern to the church besides Arius' theology, including the date of Easter and how to deal with the Melitians, a group of Egyptian Christians who, like the Donatists, were rigorous in their treatment of *traditores*.

Constantine played an active part in the meeting at Nicaea in May 325, even though Ossius of Cordoba actually presided over the council. There were supposedly 318 delegates, the majority from the eastern Empire, though there were a few from the west, including Ossius and Caecilian of Carthage. However, neither the bishop of Rome nor anyone tasked specifically to represent him was present. The attendance of all the bishops was facilitated by the imperial postal service. Many of the bishops had come with petitions, though Constantine's burning of them suggests that he saw many of their requests as unimportant. Unlike most later church councils, the proceedings were not recorded at the time, though twenty canons are preserved, so there is no record of the debates about Arius. Constantine's desire for unity led to the formulation of a single creed, and the approach settled on was a desire to exclude Arius. The creed thus stressed the unbegotten nature of Christ. It did so by using a term that Arius and Eusebius of Nicomedia found unacceptable, describing Christ as "of the same nature" as God, *homoousios* in Greek, *consubstantialis* in Latin. The Novatian bishop Acesius also attended the council, though he was considered nonorthodox because of the Novatian belief that any sin after baptism could only be forgiven by God. When he refused to accept the creed, Constantine replied, "Set up a ladder, Acesius, and climb into heaven alone" (Socrates 1.10.4). By the end of the council, only three of the delegates, Arius and two of his Libyan supporters, had refused to sign the creed and were exiled. Eusebius of Nicomedia and Theognis of Nicaea accepted the creed but not the anathemas against Arius; Constantine unilaterally exiled them three months later. According to Constantine, "what pleased 300 bishops is nothing other than the judgement of God" (Socrates 1.9.24). Given a little more time, Arius, Eusebius, and Theognis also accepted the use of the term *homoousios* and were restored following another council at Nicaea in December 327 attended by 250 bishops. Constantine probably felt satisfied, even though Alexander refused to attend and refused to reinstate Arius, defying the command of the emperor. Despite later interpretations, it should not be thought that the council reflected a near-universal commitment to the Nicene Creed.

After the council, Constantine wrote "other letters that were rather like panegyrics against Arius and those of like mind, making fun of him and attacking him in an ironic fashion, and sent them round everywhere to be posted in the cities" (Socrates 1.9.64). The emperor had summoned the council, created unity, then imposed punishment, and announced his verdict. Constantine's creation of unity at Nicaea meant that all bishops were in agreement with each other. For almost all of Roman history up to this point, this sort of imposition of the imperial will had resulted in imperial victory; at worst, those who disagreed could blacken the emperor's name after his death. Nor did pagan priests disagree in the way that Christian bishops did. For the next three centuries, the same problems were to recur. The emperor wished only for a united church. The bishops fought passionately among themselves over theology, refusing to accept the will of the majority and refusing to accept imperial authority even though they appealed to it constantly. Contemporaries were sometimes mystified at the passion for debate shown by bishops. Yet, frustrating as they undoubtedly were to emperors, their passionate engagement shows their commitment. They were committed because it mattered, both in the long term and for day-to-day matters.

Between 312 and 324, Constantine had fought and won five battles against his imperial rivals. It was a formidable achievement, though won at a terrible cost in Roman blood. After this, he was still left with the same problems of ruling the Empire as had faced Diocletian. It was clear that one man could not rule the Empire alone, but instead of turning to trusted colleagues, Constantine turned to his family. Crispus, his son from his first marriage, was appointed Caesar on March 1, 317, along with Constantine II, from his second marriage (born in February 316). Constantine II's brothers were also soon promoted, Constantius II (born August 7, 317, appointed Caesar on November 8, 324) and Constans (born ca. 323, Caesar on December 25, 333). Crispus, however, was suddenly executed at Pola in Italy in 326; ancient rumors suggested an affair between Crispus and Constantine's second wife Fausta, who died in obscure circumstances in the same year. After Crispus' death, Constantine kept imperial power within his own family. Thus his half-brother Dalmatius did not receive imperial dignity, despite his loyalty and efficiency. When Calocaerus, in charge of the emperor's camels, declared himself emperor in Cyprus in 334, Dalmatius defeated him on Cyprus, brought him to Tarsus, and burned him alive. However, one of Dalmatius' sons, also called Dalmatius, was appointed Caesar on September 18, 335, and the other, Hannibalianus, was married to Constantine's daughter Constantina and appointed *Rex Regum et Ponticarum Gentium* (King of Kings and of the Pontic Peoples). The final version of Constantine's family tetrarchy had Constantine as Augustus supervising four Caesars: Constantine II based in Gaul; Constantius II on the eastern frontier; Constans in Italy, Africa, and Pannonia; and Dalmatius in Thrace, Dacia, and Macedonia. The youth of some of the Caesars meant that the system was only beginning to become effective when Constantine died in 337.

CONSTANTINE'S ADMINISTRATIVE REFORMS

The most significant of the changes in governmental structure under Constantine was the removal of military command functions from the praetorian prefects, although the creation of more emperors under the Tetrarchy had meant that this role was already becoming less common. However, the portfolios of praetorian prefects were still enormous, including military recruitment, the supply of armies, the imperial *comitatus*, and arms production. In addition, they acted as judges, served as the emperor's chief of staff, and were responsible for public works, roads, and the *cursus publicus*. Like emperors, they acted collegially. Until Constantine's sole rule, prefects were attached to emperors, but with the assignment of territory to Constantine's sons in the late 330s, they gradually became attached instead to territory. The first region to acquire its own prefect was Africa, though this appears to have been an anomalous case, probably because of the problems with the Donatists. By 335, there were five prefects who probably represented prefectures in the east, Italy (including Pannonia), Africa, Illyricum (Dacia, Macedonia, Thrace), and Gaul (including Spain and Britain). In the 320s, Constantine split the diocese of Moesia into two parts, Dacia in the north and Macedonia in the south.

During the Tetrarchic wars, Constantine had created a single field army around himself. The troops in this army, often known as the *comitatus*, now had a separate status as *comitatenses*. The command roles removed from praetorian prefects were now held by two new officers, the *magister peditum* (master of infantry) and *magister equitum* (master of cavalry), who between them led the imperial field army. These titles were nominal rather than literal, and both officers commanded infantry and cavalry, often being referred as *magistri militum* (masters of soldiers). The single imperial field army was soon divided as Constantine assigned military responsibilities to his family, thus as early as 318 or 319, Crispus led his own army in Gaul, where he won several victories against Franks and Alamanni. There is no sign at this point that any of the sons had their own *magister equitum* and *magister peditum*. Then with the establishment of four Caesars in 335, each had his own field army. The troops on the borders remained under the command of *duces* with the status of *limitanei* or *ripenses*. Although civil and military duties were mostly separated, as in all periods of Roman administration there was overlap as when Constantine wrote to Ursinus, the *dux* of Mesopotamia, banning the creation of eunuchs in the Empire (*CJ* 4.42.1). This separation of civil and military hierarchies facilitated promotion for men whose talents were best suited to war, in particular men from outside the Empire. Thus Bonitus, of Frankish origin, is first heard of fighting against Licinius while his son Silvanus became a *magister militum* under Constantius II.

Another change in the upper levels of government was the appearance of the *magister officiorum* (master of the offices), an official who oversaw the various *magistri scriniarum* (masters of the book-boxes), as well as the corps of *agentes in rebus* (a vague term meaning "acting on imperial business"), the guard regiments of the *scholae*, the imperial arms factories, and the *cursus publicus*. When first heard of in 320, this office was held by a *tribunus et magister officiorum*, but by 324 the tribune had disappeared and it was ranked as an *illustris* position in its own right. By the fifth century, he was often known simply as the *magister*. Both Licinius and Constantine had *magistri officiorum*, so its origin may have been earlier than 320. Constantine also created a *quaestor* who drafted imperial constitutions, taking this role from the *magister libellorum*, who was now concerned mostly with appeals.

The distinction between the equestrian and senatorial order, of such significance under the early empire, began to be more and more obscured by the frequent promotion of equestrians into positions usually held by senators. Even when attempts were made to maintain a distinction, as when Constantine created a new senatorial rank of *consularis* for governors of some provinces (mostly in Italy), some of the holders had recent equestrian antecedents. Perhaps as a response to this blurring, Constantine developed the position of *comes*, a companion of the emperor. During the third century, this was a description of a relationship to the emperor, but Constantine formalized the title as both an honor and a rank. As an honor, it was attached to positions close to the emperor, such as *comes et magister militum*. As a rank, it was usually given to senators, though was subdivided into three grades. Many of the older offices were now renamed, so that the *a rationalis* became the *comes sacrarum largitionum* and the *rationalis rei privatae* became the *comes rei privatae*. There soon appeared military *comites rei militaris*.

The reign of Constantine saw a new concept of the senatorial order. While it had traditionally been based on a combination of wealth and holding civic magistracies, Constantine made numerous grants of senatorial rank to officials holding imperial posts. The result was the transformation of the Senate from a body of limited size representing the Empire's past to a status that reflected the servants of the emperor. Within the Senate of Rome there was still a core of senators who claimed to represent the old ways, but the new Senate of Constantinople was composed mostly of imperial officials. Senators had always been referred to as *viri clarissimi* (most renowned men). Now a new rank was introduced, that of *vir illustris* (illustrious man), held by *magistri militum*, the *magister officiorum*, and urban and praetorian prefects. This was the highest rank that could be held by an official until the late fifth century. Constantine created an additional honor, that of patrician (*patricius*). The first attested holder of the office was Optatus in 334, who was also consul in that year.

Imperial women come into greater prominence from the early fourth century onward. Imperial wives had often had the title of Augusta, coinage was frequently issued in their name, and their statues were often displayed alongside those of the emperor. Occasionally, they were honored in other ways, with Diocletian naming a province after his daughter Valeria. Christianity brought new opportunities for women, and Constantine's family were in the forefront of church patronage. His mother Helena, visited the Holy Land, building churches there as well as at Constantinople. She too had a province named after her, Helenopontus, as well as the cities of Helenopolis in Bithynia and in Palestina Secunda.

In 309, Constantine introduced a new gold currency, the *solidus* struck at 72 to the pound, which by 324 had become a standard that lasted unchanged until the eleventh century. The capture of the treasuries of his civil war rivals and the confiscation of temple treasures allowed large amounts of the new coinage to be introduced rapidly, thus removing from circulation the memorials of his predecessors. At the same time, there was an abandonment of the fixed relationship between gold coinage and coins in silver or bronze. The consequences of this uncoupling took time to become clear. First, since all imperial revenue collection in money was carried out only in gold, it changed the impact that inflation had on the state. The state was thus insulated from the impact of rising prices, themselves fueled by imperial minting of bronze used to pay salaries. This drove gold into becoming the de facto currency for all transactions, shown by the demands of officials to be paid in gold rather than in kind or in other metals. *Solidi* were continuously reminted, keeping the coinage at a very high level of weight (4.45 grams) and purity (usually around 97 percent). New *solidi* were required for accession donatives, though much of this cost was met by two accession taxes, the *aurum coronarium* and the *aurum oblaticum*. Constantine also introduced two new taxes payable to the *sacrae largitiones*, the *collatio glebalis*, a tax on senatorial lands, and the *collatio lustralis* (also known as the *chrysargyron*), a highly unpopular quinquennial tax on merchants and craftsmen.

THE FINAL STAGES OF CONSTANTINE'S REIGN

If Constantine had been hopeful that the Council of Nicaea had settled the problems of the church, he was disappointed. When Athanasius succeeded Alexander as bishop of Alexandria, he also inherited his hostility toward Arius and refused to accept the restoration of Arius as one of his priests. Athanasius also fell out with the local Melitians, and accusations were made against him to the emperor. Constantine

> wrote to his nephew Dalmatius the censor, who was then living in Antioch in Syria, directing him to order the accused to be brought before him, and after making a judgement, to punish those who were convicted (Socrates 1.27.20).

Before Dalmatius could assemble the accused and the witnesses, Constantine changed his mind. He decided to order the bishops whom he was sending to Jerusalem to dedicate the Church of the Holy Sepulcher to deal with these accusations and appointed the *comes* Dionysius to run the council.

When the bishops assembled at Tyre in May 335, Athanasius initially refused to attend, but the council sent a commission to Egypt to investigate. The accusations against Athanasius were sensational. One of his presbyters was accused of having overturned an altar, broken liturgical vessels, and burned sacred books, while Athanasius himself was supposed to have severed the hand of a certain Arsenius which was then used for magical purposes. When Athanasius appeared in front of the council, he was able to refute the charges, triumphantly producing Arsenius with both hands intact. This, of course, is Athanasius' account, which glosses lightly over the other charges. The assembled bishops, however, once reassured that Constantine believed that Arius was orthodox, deposed him. Following the verdict, Athanasius rushed to Constantinople and appealed to Constantine, who then wrote to the bishops at Tyre. Athanasius included this imperial letter in his *Defence against the Arians*:

> As I was entering on a late occasion to our eponymous and all-happy home of Constantinople, (I chanced at the time to be on horseback), suddenly Athanasius the bishop, with certain others whom he had with him, approached me in the middle of the road, so unexpectedly as to occasion me much amazement. God who knows all things is my witness that I should have been unable at first sight even to recognise him, if some of my people, on my naturally inquiring of them, had not informed me both who it was and under what injustice he was suffering. I did not, however, enter into any conversation with him at that time nor grant him an interview. But when he requested to be heard I refused and all but gave orders for his removal (86.6–8).

Athanasius' eagerness to make his point now overcame him to the extent that he omitted a paragraph from Constantine's letter while also softening its angry tone, which still comes through clearly enough in the edited version. We know this because the full text of the letter is preserved in the *Ecclesiastical History* of Gelasius, written in the late fifth century. Athanasius was successful in his appeal, since Constantine did not accept the verdict of Tyre immediately, but summoned the bishops to him. After they arrived, Athanasius was still deposed, albeit now because of a new accusation of interfering with the grain supply of Constantinople. When the emperor had finished his enquiries, Athanasius was exiled to Trier.

After the defeat of Licinius, Constantine spent most of his reign in Constantinople or on the Danube, though there were visits to Antioch (324), Rome (326), and Trier (328). The visit to Trier was part of a campaign against some Franks in 328/329, while Constantine fought against the Alamanni in 330. There were also campaigns in the Balkans, against Goths in 332, against

Sarmatians in 334 and 336. As a result of these Sarmatian victories, the *Origo Constantini* claims that Constantine settled "more than 300,000 Sarmatians of mixed age and sex throughout Thrace, Scythia, Macedonia, and Italy" (6.32). In contrast to the constant warfare on European frontiers, the Roman east had been mostly peaceful after the 290s, though Maximinus had been active in Persia and Armenia in 314 soon after the accession of Sapur II (309–379). After the defeat of Licinius, Constantine had given refuge to a Persian royal refugee, Sapur's brother Hormizd, though did not use his claim as a *casus belli*. But war flared eventually. In 335, Sapur occupied Armenia, removing the Christian king Tigran VII, grandson of Trdat, and placing his own nominee on the throne. When the Armenians appealed to Constantine, he named his nephew Hannibalianus as king of the Pontic region and sent Constantius to Antioch in 335 to manage the war. Constantine wrote to Sapur, unusually in his own hand, claiming to protect the Christians in Persia. This added a new dimension to the competition between Rome and Persia, leading to significant persecution of Christians under Sapur. Rivalry between the great powers and a desire to protect Christians are both adequate explanations, though there were others, like the tale of Metrodorus, who claimed that Sapur had stolen some jewels that he was carrying as a present from an Indian king to Constantine. When it was clear that Constantine would fight, Sapur sent envoys to Constantine. These were rejected, and Constantine died just outside Nicomedia on May 22, 337, in the first stages of the campaign, falling ill just after crossing to Anatolia from Constantinople.

Thus died the first Christian emperor. His reign was long and difficult, though unlike many periods of Roman history, most of Constantine's challenges were internal. The adoption of Christianity was to have great consequences for the emperor, the Empire, and the church. His great achievement was in creating unity. This was achieved by eliminating all imperial rivals and replacing the Tetrarchy with members of his own family, but also by bending all the bishops to his will. None of this was to last more than a few years after his death. Like the success of Diocletian in forging the Tetrarchy, this shows the central role played by the emperor in the success of the Roman state.

CONSTANTINE (337–340), CONSTANS (337–350), AND CONSTANTIUS II (337–361)

Following the death of Constantine, his body was taken to Constantinople, where he was buried by Constantius in the Church of the Holy Apostles. At Rome, he was deified by the Senate. According to Eusebius, who was following an official version of events that omitted mention of Dalmatius Caesar, the army then declared that only his sons could succeed. But a generation later, when justifying his seizure of power from Constantius II to the Athenians, Julian claimed that it was Constantius who was responsible for the soldiers' actions. Certainly Constantius' cousins, Dalmatius Caesar and Hannibalianus, were murdered at Constantinople, as was their father, Dalmatius the Censor, and Julius Constantius, another half-brother of Constantine. Numerous aristocrats also died in the purge, including Ablabius and Optatus. Dalmatius' territory was partitioned between Constantius, who received Thrace, and Constans, who received the dioceses of Dacia and Macedonia. The three brothers then met in Pannonia (probably in Sirmium) and took the title Augustus on September 9, although Constantine II was given precedence as the elder. This left field armies in Gaul (Constantine II), Illyricum (Constans), and the east (Constantius II). Constantine and Constans each had a *magister equitum* and *magister peditum*, while Constantius II divided his forces between the Balkans and the east, where he commanded personally, with a *magister militum* in each region. Similar arrangements took place with prefects, one for each emperor, though there was also one for Africa.

The coup took place while the Empire was still at war with Persia, and soon after Constantius left Antioch for Constantinople, the Persians laid siege to Nisibis for two months in summer 337. There was much else to do besides fighting in Persia. Constantine II restored the ecclesiastical exiles, so Athanasius returned to Alexandria and Marcellus to Ancyra. Constantius, busy with the Persians, appeared inclined to acquiesce to his brother's decision at this moment. After the death of the bishop of Constantinople in summer 337, a few bishops had consecrated the Nicene Paul as his replacement. Constantius expelled Paul and replaced him with Eusebius of Nicomedia. Then, at the Council of Antioch in 338, presided over by Constantius himself, Athanasius and Marcellus were again deposed. Athanasius left Alexandria in 339, but instead of appealing either to Constantine II, who had restored him in 337, or to Constantius II, who had deposed him, he went instead to Julius, the bishop of Rome (337–352). He arrived at the same time as Marcellus; Julius accepted both Athanasius and Marcellus as orthodox, presenting the issues to a western church council as a failure to follow the decision of Nicaea and suggesting that the eastern bishops were Arians. This set up the terms of western and eastern differences in church policy for the next half-century, western bishops mostly holding that the Nicene Creed was an adequate definition of faith, whereas eastern bishops generally saw it as an inadequate definition, even though they still used the creed as a touchstone of orthodoxy. At the same time, the bishop of Rome claimed the right to intervene in church affairs throughout the Empire, though this was rarely conceded to him. Misunderstandings might be inevitable given the complexity of the theological issues, but discussion is marked by the ambition and inflexibility of many of the participants.

In 340, two of the brothers fell out. Constantine II invaded Italy, allegedly because of a slight by Constans, but was killed in battle at Aquileia. The young Constans, still only seventeen years old, acquired all of his territory, now ruling the largest part of the Empire, all of Europe except Thrace. There were now field armies in Gaul under Constans; in Illyricum under the *magister militum* Vetranio, who reported to Constans; and in the east under Constantius. This structure was matched by three praetorian prefects, in the east, in Gaul, and a huge central prefecture of Italy, Illyricum, and Africa. Constans seems to have been under little military pressure, with only a Frankish attack in 342 and a visit to Britain in 343 being known. Constans repeated the ban on animal sacrifice in 341, while ordering temples to be closed. He also began the work of building a new church of St. Peter in Rome that now lies at the heart of the Vatican.

In January 341, a council of ninety eastern bishops met at Antioch in the presence of Constantius II to dedicate the Church of the Golden Octagon. They also considered again the case of Marcellus of Ancyra, then confirmed his deposition as a heretic in a conscious rejection of the ruling of bishop Julius of Rome. The consequences of this took time to show themselves, but in the meantime, other problems were emerging in the eastern church. After the death of Eusebius of Nicomedia late in 341, Macedonius was elected as bishop of Constantinople, but at the same time, the exiled Paul tried to reclaim his post. Following riots in the imperial city, in 342 Constantius sent the *magister equitum* Hermogenes to depose Paul. When Hermogenes was killed in further riots, Constantius marched immediately to the city with the intent of punishing it, but softened when met with a delegation that was submissive. Paul was exiled, and the bread distribution was halved. Athanasius, meanwhile, had moved on from Rome to Trier in Gaul, where he was joined by Paul. Following their appeals, Constans firmly asked Constantius to organize a church council to resolve their claims. The Council of Serdica took place in autumn 343 with significant representation from both eastern and western bishops. Constantius was unable to control the council, which split into western and eastern factions, neither of which was prepared to back down. Worse, when the western bishops restored Paul to Constantinople and Athanasius to Alexandria, Constans threatened to restore the two bishops himself if Constantius would not do so. Orthodoxy was not simply a theological matter, but an issue that could prompt civil war. Constans was only twenty at the time, and his youth may have led him to be aggressive over this issue. Constantius preferred to avoid conflict and restored both Paul and Athanasius in 345, though the western bishops did drop their support for Marcellus. Constans also faced a renewed Donatist problem. Two imperial officials, Paul and Macarius, distributing imperial largesse in Africa, were thought to be favoring Catholics. Confrontation was followed by violence, and a Donatist bishop was killed. The emperor was again cast as a persecutor, and more martyrdoms followed. Removing and installing bishops was easy for emperors, but resolving the differences between groups rarely prepared to compromise was another matter. For Constantius, it was a choice between civil war and upsetting his own bishops. He was also required to pay attention to the Persian war, fighting one (or two) battles at Singara (344 and/or 348) and resisting sieges of Nisibis in 346 and again in 350. The eastern bishops' unhappiness with Athanasius was clear, and he was deposed again at Antioch by another church council in 349, being replaced by George of Epiphaneia as bishop of Alexandria.

MAGNENTIUS SEIZES POWER, 350

Constantius' focus on Persia was then suddenly arrested by events in the west. On January 18, 350, the *comes* Magnentius seized imperial power in Gaul, exploiting the unpopularity of Constans. Constans fled, but was hunted down and killed at Helena in the Pyrenees. Magnentius' troops swiftly moved into Italy, while Britain, Africa, and Spain also supported him. Magnentius made his brother Decentius Caesar in Gaul. Magnentius then reached out clumsily to some eastern bishops. He wrote to Paul of Constantinople, who was soon arrested and executed, and sent two bishops to Athanasius in Alexandria. Although Athanasius later claimed that the letters he had sent to Magnentius were forgeries, another church council at Sirmium in 351 deposed him again and also reendorsed the Antiochene Creed of 342. The bishop of Rome Liberius then invited Athanasius to Rome. Although both Liberius and Athanasius tried to present the dispute as being over what they called Arian beliefs, it is unlikely that anyone else saw it as being that simple. Magnentius was, however, prevented from occupying Illyricum by the acclamation of the *magister militum* Vetranio on March 1, 350. Vetranio supposedly took the purple on the encouragement of Constantius' sister Constantia, and when she interceded with her brother, he sent Vetranio a diadem. There was also a brief revolt in Italy by Nepotianus, a nephew of Constantine, acclaimed on June 3, killed on June 30 by Magnentius' troops. It was not until the failure of the Persian siege of Nisibis that Constantius could move to the west, a clear statement that dealing with rivals for imperial power was less important than fighting external enemies. When Constantius reached Thrace, he was able to negotiate the surrender of Vetranio in December 350. Vetranio was exiled to Prusa in Bithynia, where he lived on a pension until his death of natural causes in 356. Although Constantius had left the east with a Persian war still raging, he appointed a Caesar to handle the east. This was his twenty-five-year-old cousin Gallus, acclaimed on March 15, 351, married to Constantius' sister, and sent to Antioch. Nepotianus' acclamation had shown that the House of Constantine was a real dynasty, but it also showed that emperor and army had to work together and that capricious behavior by an emperor could have fatal consequences.

The armies of Constantius and Magnentius prepared for a 351 campaign, with armies that might have included a few veterans of the war between Constantine and Licinius in 316. Constantius' preparations included encouraging various Franks and Alamanni to raid into Gaul, and they were able to win some victories against Decentius. Then Magnentius in spring 351 crossed the Julian Alps from Italy into Illyricum, moving into Pannonia down the Savus Valley. At the same time, Constantius' army advanced from Sirmium up the Savus Valley. After some maneuvering, Constantius II then attacked Magnentius at Mursa on September 28, 351, 30 kilometers north of Cibalae. Magnentius troops may have been wavering somewhat, as we hear of the defection of the *schola armaturarum* under Silvanus. Magnentius was defeated and his *magister officiorum* Marcellinus was killed, but he was able to retreat to Italy. The casualties were enormous, 54,000 according to the Byzantine historian Zonaras. Eutropius noted that "huge forces of the Roman Empire were consumed in that struggle, which were sufficient for any number of foreign wars and which might have brought many triumphs and security" (*Breviarium* 10.12). In 352, the war against Magnentius continued. His support remained strong, even as Constantius defeated him at Aquileia in 352 and then in 353 crossed the Alps into Gaul, defeating Magnentius for a third time at Mons Seleucus near Gap. Magnentius then committed suicide on August 10 when he heard of the loss of Africa and Spain to forces landed by Constantius from the sea, with Decentius hanging himself on August 18. Their heads were then severed by Constantius' men and sent around the Empire.

The victory over Magnentius left Constantius with a central imperial army with two *magistri militum* and regional field armies in Gaul, Illyricum, and the east. In the east, Gallus Caesar had his own prefect and *magister militum*. Reconciling the supporters of Magnentius with the victors was difficult, and some regiments of troops were sent to the east, in particular the regiments named Magnentiaci and Decentiaci. Ammianus is critical of the emperor and his investigations, noting that "no one easily recalls the acquittal of anyone under Constantius when matters were disturbed even by a whisper" (Ammianus 14.5.9); Constantius might have replied that his reign had seen plentiful disloyalty. The Alamanni and Franks whom Constantius had encouraged were still attacking Gaul, though the new *magister militum per Gallias* Silvanus, the defector during the Battle of Mursa, campaigned against them from Cologne and Trier, while Constantius operated against the Alamanni from Augst in 354 and 355. In Antioch, Gallus was beginning to behave in an unacceptable fashion. His consistory tried to help him, but the praetorian prefect Thalassius, "rather by opposing and scolding him at the wrong time, moved him to fury" (Ammianus 14.1.10), while the *comes Orientis* Honoratus chose to oppose an order to execute the city council of Antioch. Gallus ordered execution of the council because they had challenged his plan to deal with a famine. When Domitianus was sent as the new eastern praetorian prefect for Gallus, he also brought a command that he attend Constantius. Gallus arrested Domitianus, overruling his *quaestor* Montius, and then had both prefect and *quaestor* executed. Gallus would have known that Constantius could not accept this, but hesitated to seize power for himself. Eventually, he set out for Constantius' court, perhaps encouraged by messages suggesting that he would be advanced to the rank of Augustus. If Constantius had not already decided to remove him, then Gallus' holding chariot races in Constantinople as he passed may have been the final straw. Troops in cities on the way to Italy were moved out of the way, and once Gallus reached Poetovio he was arrested and moved to Pola, where he was hastily tried for the murder of Domitianus and Montius and executed.

Constantius moved into Italy in late summer 355, spending the next year at Milan. Athanasius wrote a *Defence before Constantius* (*Apologia ad Constantium*), but just as it was despatched, he was summoned to a church council at Milan that condemned him. The document we have with this title was rewritten by Athanasius after the events, yet the need to refute publicly charges against Athanasius is revealing. The document as we have it focuses on claims that Athanasius had prejudiced Constans against Constantius, had written to Magnentius, had used a new church in Alexandria before its formal consecration, and had disobeyed an imperial order to come to Milan. Liberius, bishop of Rome, did not attend the council, so he was arrested and brought to Milan. When he refused to accept Constantius' point of view on Athanasius, he was exiled and replaced by Felix (355–357). In Alexandria, Athanasius was deposed by the *dux Aegypti* Syrianus and his troops, and George of Epiphaneia was installed in his place; Athanasius, however, escaped into hiding in Egypt.

Then in 355, the *magister militum per Gallias* Silvanus was told of a forged letter showing him planning treason. His swift murder by his own troops, suborned by a negotiating mission led by the *magister militum* Ursicinus (in which the historian Ammianus Marcellinus was involved), probably forestalled another civil war. Constantius' own officials were thus as difficult to rule as were the bishops. With Gallus executed, Constantius had to find another colleague. At Milan on November 6, 355, he acclaimed his cousin (and Gallus' half-brother) Julian as Caesar. On the same day, Julian married another sister of Constantius, Helena. He was then sent to Gaul with Marcellus as *magister equitum*, Honoratus as praetorian prefect, and Saturninus Secundus Salutius as an adviser. Julian was born in 331 and was raised as a Christian, though he had been variously educated by Eusebius, bishop of Nicomedia; by the pagan eunuch Mardonius; and by George of Epiphaneia. From 348, he lived in Constantinople, where he met the Antiochene orator Libanius and was exposed to the pagan philosophical teaching of Maximus of Ephesus. In 351, he spent a few weeks in Athens at the same time as the Christians Basil of Caesarea (the correspondence between them continued when Julian was emperor) and Gregory of Nazianzus, but was also initiated into the Eleusinian Mysteries. Julian was soon to reject Christianity and when he later reflected on his apostasy defined this period in Athens as the moment of his conversion. At this point, his apostasy was secret and he continued to act as a reader in the church at Nicomedia.

One of the major administrative changes made by Constantius was the confiscation of the estates attached to cities, transferring them to the *res privata*. This deprived the cities of the Empire of one of their major sources of revenue. For the emperor, this would have helped compensate for the loss of revenue caused by imperial privileges for Christians. At the same time, with a continuing reluctance on the part of many to serve on city councils, it made sense to move control of city resources to the emperor, who was frequently now paying for things that had earlier been paid for by cities. Honoratus was appointed the first urban prefect for Constantinople in 359. The Constantinopolitan Senate was massively expanded by transferring senators living in the eastern Empire from the Roman Senate and directly appointing more senators as well as increasing their status to equal that of Rome by making all eastern senators *clarissimi* rather than *clari*. These measures, according to Themistius, increased the Senate from three hundred to two thousand by the reign of Theodosius I. The social mobility that had allowed Galerius and Diocletian to become emperors continued. Some soldiers, such as Arbitio, were famous for working their way up from private soldier to *magister equitum*, even becoming consul in 355. Other men, such as Datianus, consul in 358 and *patricius*, was the son of an attendant at the baths. After learning shorthand, he worked for Constantine and Constantius as a secretary and had been given the rank of *comes* by 345. To see such men succeed was distressing to men raised in an expensive educational system. Our source for Datianus is a speech of Libanius, an Antiochene orator, complaining of the failure of the emperor to grant one of his friends a post in the Senate. The speech complained of the injustice, running down many of the members of the Senate. Arbitio, Datianus, and the emperor would have had a very different perspective.

In 356, Julian continued Silvanus' operations against the Alamanni in northern Gaul while Constantius fought against the Alamanni in the south. During 357, Julian defeated the Alamanni under Chnodomarius in a battle at Strasbourg and then crossed the Rhine into Alamannia, though failing to cooperate in a combined operation with Barbatio in Raetia. Constantius visited in Rome in 357 to celebrate the victories in Gaul and Persia. While there, he removed the Altar of Victory from the Senate House in Rome and (following demonstrations in the Circus Maximus) allowed Liberius to return to Rome, now that he was prepared to condemn Athanasius and to accept the Creed of Sirmium. However, this was only a swift visit (the only visit to Rome of Constantius' career), and he was soon fighting against the Alamanni in Raetia before moving into Pannonia and wintering in Sirmium. From Sirmium, Constantius led preemptive strikes in 358 and 359 against the Sarmatians and Quadi, while Julian continued to fight on and across the Rhine. Much of what we hear of Julian at this period comes from Julian himself, or from Ammianus Marcellinus, an admirer. Ammianus tells the story of how Julian felt that Florentius' demands for additional tax assessments were unnecessary. To prove his case, he collected the taxes personally in Belgica Secunda, with the result that the annual demand for a *capitus* was reduced from 25 *solidi* to 7, an achievement that Ammianus then claimed applied to all of Gaul. The amount of the reduction is probably true, but Ammianus' account ignores the fact that this was possible only when the emperor himself was collecting the taxes of a single province. Why Julian thought the Empire needed less money is not quite so clear, though Ammianus did think that the burden of taxation was not evenly distributed, but fell more heavily on peasants than rich landowners. For Ammianus, the officials are the villains of the piece, with their corrupt ways, yet the refusal of the wealthy taxpayers to pay in full on time is glossed over.

At this time, too, eastern ecclesiastical politics changed, though in ways perhaps not immediately apparent to the emperor, local bishops, or local populations. Ecclesiastical politics after Nicaea can be broadly defined as being polarized over Arius, with western bishops being content with the Nicene Creed, though eastern bishops were less sure. The unity of the eastern bishops was now split by the ideas of Eunomius and Aetius. Their belief, usually described as Anomoian, was that the Father and the Son were not the same; this was not Arianism, but it did not fit well with the Nicene Creed, which defined Father and Son as the same (*homoousios*) or the more moderate and widely held eastern belief of similarity (*homoiousios*). In 357, Basil of Ancyra met Constantius II at Sirmium and proposed a council to unite the divided churches. He was hopeful that the term "like" (*homoios*) might be acceptable, though this would require revising the Nicene Creed. Constantius organized simultaneous eastern and western councils in September 359 at Seleucia in Isauria attended by about 150 bishops and Ariminum in Italy attended by more than four hundred bishops. Both councils were managed by imperial officials, the praetorian prefect of Italy Taurus in the west and the *quaestor* Leonas in the east. The two councils grudgingly accepted the Homoian Creed, though there was a significant group of *homoiousion* supporters at Seleucia. At Seleucia, other business included the cases of Cyril of Jerusalem, who had been deposed in 357, and of George of Alexandria, who had been accused of misconduct. Cyril was restored to his see at Seleucia, and George was deposed. For Constantius, it was a great triumph. As was to happen repeatedly over the next three centuries, however, a moderate consensus was overturned by a determined minority. In this case, some Nicene extremists, including Athanasius, were unable to accept a creed that was accepted by most Arians. With the eventual Nicene victory in the reign of Theodosius I (379–395), followers of the Homoian Creed, including Constantius and Valens (364–378), were caricatured as Arians in most theological writing. This is a partisan label that would not have been accepted by the Homoians themselves.

Following the reports from the councils of Ariminum and Seleucia, the Synod of Constantinople in 360 adopted the Homoian Creed. The Synod also deposed Macedonius, bishop of Constantinople, translating Eudoxius, bishop of Antioch, to replace him. Macedonius' name soon became attached to the belief that the Holy Spirit was not divine, and though it attracted much attention in the fourth century, Macedonianism was never a strongly organized movement. When Eudoxius was promoted to bishop of Constantinople (360–370), he was replaced in Antioch by Meletius. However, Meletius was deposed by Constantius II after only a month, when his views were discovered not to be as orthodox (i.e., Homoian) as expected, and replaced by Euzoius. Meletius retained many supporters, as did Paulinus (who had also been consecrated as bishop) who headed a Nicene community.

While the religious controversies were being worked through, Constantius marched east to return to the Persian war he had left a decade before. The war was not going well, with the key city of Amida being lost in 359. In February 360, Constantius ordered Julian to send Gallic troops to his army. Julian claimed that Constantius' orders provoked an insurrection by the army, who proclaimed him Augustus in Paris, but Julian was concealing the measures he had taken to make the insurrection happen, including assembling the troops, distributing copies of Constantius' letter, and entertaining the senior officers while making sure Florentius was absent. As soon as Constantius, at Caesarea in Cappadocia, heard of this unauthorized seizure of imperial power, he had a choice to make, whether to treat Julian as an imperial challenger (as he did with Magnentius), to accept the promotion (as Galerius did with Constantine) or to ignore it (as Gratian later did with Arcadius). Initially, he had no choice but to ignore the challenge because of events in Mesopotamia, where Singara and Bezabde also fell to the Persians, and he spent the campaigning seasons of 360 and 361 on the eastern frontier. Sabinianus, who had been *magister equitum* in the east, was relieved in 360, though an investigation by Arbitio and Florentius found that Ursicinus, the previous *magister equitum* in the east, was to blame. Ammianus Marcellinus, who had been part of Ursicinus' staff at Amida, quoted his general as refusing to be investigated except by the emperor. At the same time, Ammianus also claimed that Constantius was under the malign influence of Eusebius, the *praepositus sacri cubiculi*.

In April 361, Julian moved east. A swift advance on a broad front through north Italy and Noricum brought him into Pannonia, from where he occupied Illyricum as far as the pass at Succi. Spain and Italy went over to Julian, though Africa did not. Julian's position in Italy was also tenuous because the *agens in rebus* Gaudentius had been sent to Africa to divert the grain fleet to Constantinople. When some of the troops captured at Sirmium rebelled at Aquileia, Italy was lost to his control. It was only in response to Julian's offensive that Constantius abandoned the Persian war and marched east. He reached Cilicia but then fell ill and died at Mopsucrenae on November 3, 361, aged forty-four. He had no children. There was some discussion about acclaiming a new emperor, but practicality soon prevailed and Julian was accepted, averting the civil war. Constantius was buried in the Church of the Holy Apostles in Constantinople. He was a strong emperor, with a deep concern that officials be appointed only after they had gained relevant experience. At the same time, he was accused of excessive savagery toward men suspected of aspiring to the purple, though he had to deal with more civil wars than many Roman emperors.

JULIAN (361–363)

From Naissus, Julian marched rapidly to Constantinople, where he stayed until May 362. Almost immediately, he instituted a series of trials at Chalcedon where some of Constantius' civilian officials were tortured and killed under supervision of the retired *magister militum* Arbitio and several other military officers. Two praetorian prefects, Taurus and Florentius, were exiled, but after Ursulus, the *comes sacrarum largitionum*, had been executed, Julian was faced with such opposition that he claimed this occurred without his knowledge. As Ammianus noted, "from this [Julian] seemed timorous or did not sufficiently understand what was fitting" (22.3.9). The deaths of others, such as Paulus Catena, who had investigated the supporters of Magnentius with great enthusiasm, and Eusebius, the *praepositus sacri cubiculi*, attracted less dissent. The orator Claudius Mamertinus was also involved in these trials. On January 1, 362, Mamertinus delivered an extant panegyric of thanks for his consulate in Constantinople. He went on to become praetorian prefect of Italy, Africa, and Illyricum but was then removed from office in 365 following accusations of "peculation" by Avitianus, who was *vicarius Africae* under Julian. During this time, Julian deified Constantius. As a result of combining his *comitatus* with that of Constantius, Julian reduced the total number of officials, though his aspirations toward philosophy made his court a duller place. In the same way, his classical education led to measures that helped the cities. One was the restoration to cities of the estates confiscated under Constantius II, another making crown gold a voluntary contribution. Both measures displayed a denial of reality that must have involved overruling his advisers. Julian's behavior did not meet the expectations of all, even if they approved of some of his executions. Rather than dealing with a group of Egyptian petitioners, he sent them across the Bosporus to Chalcedon and promised to meet them there, then forbade ship captains to allow them to return. At the New Year celebrations for 362, he manumitted some slaves that he should not have. Mindful, perhaps, of Ulpian's ruling that the emperor was subject to the law, he then fined himself 10 pounds of gold. And famously, when Maximus of Ephesus entered the Senate House, Julian ran across the building to greet him. All this left Ammianus shaking his head, while the Christian historian Socrates noted that "a few men praised his actions, but the majority blamed him as tending to bring the imperial dignity into contempt" (3.1.53).

Another series of actions provoked far wider opposition, Julian's attempts to revive paganism. In the world in which he had been raised, there were numerous elements of paganism. Traditional religious practice continued among many of the aristocracy of Rome, and the Altar of Victory in the Senate House had only been removed by Constantius in 357. In the army, there were many vestiges of paganism, as shown by the greetings given by some veterans to Constantine I in the 320s: "Augustus Constantine, May the gods preserve you for us. Your security is our security" (*CT* 7.20.2). Most recruits were from the countryside, where in some areas traditional pagan practices remained strong into the sixth century, or barbarians. And the new regiments created by Diocletian, the Joviani and Herculiani, continued to head the precedence lists into the fifth century. At the same time, a growing number of imperial officials can be identified as Christians. Men such as Silvanus, *magister militum* in Gaul, on his way to church when he was assassinated in 355, or Helpidius, eastern praetorian prefect in 360–361, who had visited the hermits Antony and Hilarion in Gaza, were typical of Constantius' officials, not exceptional. Julian was out of step with an Empire in which Christians had received imperial support for half a century, while the paganism practiced by traditional aristocrats and in the countryside was very different from the intellectual Hellenism practiced by Julian.

On February 4, 362, Julian issued an edict that, like Constantine and Licinius' edict of 312, guaranteed freedom of religion. He also recalled bishops who had been exiled, permitted the reopening of pagan temples, allowed animal sacrifice to take place, and ordered the restitution of temple properties that had been alienated under Constantine. This was followed by a revival of Maximinus Daia's program of priests for each city and high priests for each province. This state-sponsored paganism was very different from traditional cults associated with particular gods, while the influence of Christianity is clear with Julian's requirements that these priests practice fairness, goodness, and benevolence, as well as being prohibited from the theater and ordered to establish hostels for the poor and to distribute alms.

He also rescinded the privileges granted to the church by Constantine and his sons. More alarmingly for many, in Ammianus Marcellinus' words, "this one thing was harsh and ought to be buried in eternal silence, that he prevented teachers of rhetoric and literature from teaching if they were followers of the Christian religion" (22.10.7). Julian's argument was that Christians had the choice either not to teach, or to teach pagan literature as truth: "I think it wrong that those men explaining the works of these writers [i.e., Homer and Hesiod] should dishonour the gods honoured by these writers" (Julian, *Ep.* 36). A traditional education was critical for political success, but aristocratic Christians did not want to have their children exposed to pagan beliefs without a corrective interpretation. Julian also attempted to rebuild the Second Temple in Jerusalem, which would have overthrown a prophecy of Jesus that "not one stone here will be left on another." According to Ammianus:

> Julian thought to rebuild the once proud Temple at Jerusalem at an excessive expense and gave this business to Alypius … When Alypius went vigorously to work, helped by the governor of the province, fearsome balls of fire erupting near the foundations continued their assaults until the workmen after repeated scorchings could no longer approach; he gave up the attempt (23.1.2–3).

It was remarkably different from Diocletian's persecution, which had attempted to use force to dismantle Christianity, and there were few martyrs. Julian was still the emperor for the Christians, even if he rejected their beliefs. Soon after Julian's accession, the patriarch of Alexandria, George of Epiphaneia, was murdered by the mob, along with several other imperial officials. He initially wished to take vengeance on the city but was persuaded to choose clemency over a massacre. Athanasius took up the bishopric of Alexandria again, only to be exiled again by Julian. The case of Artemius *dux Aegypti* in 360 is similarly ambiguous. A Christian whom Constantius II had ordered to bring the relics of the apostles Andrew, Luke, and Timothy to Constantinople, after his trial and execution, he was rapidly turned into a martyr. Artemius was tried by Julian following appeals by the Alexandrians, upset at his torture of a nun, Eudaemonis, while trying to track down Athanasius in 360 and at his stirring up riots by occupying the Serapeum. Unreasonable behavior seems as good an explanation of Artemius' trial and execution as an emperor seeking to destroy Christians. Similarly at Edessa, a violent clash between two Christian groups, whom Julian called Arians and Valentinians, resulted in an order to the provincial governor Hecebolius to confiscate the church's movable goods for the local soldiers and the lands to the *res privata*. Such direct anti-Christian action was exceptional, not typical.

JULIAN IN ANTIOCH AND PERSIA, 362–363

After a long summer in Constantinople, Julian left to continue the Persian war. With all imperial resources under his control, Julian was able to return to an offensive posture rather than continuing Constantius' strategy of a field army backing up fortified cities. He arrived at Antioch in June and spent the rest of the year there. Antioch was the biggest city of the Roman east, long accustomed to Roman imperial power. It was the headquarters of the *comes Orientis*, as well as of the *magister militum per Orientem*. It had a large imperial palace and a hippodrome. In the city, ecclesiastical politics had been turned upside down, probably as intended, by Julian's recent edict allowing the restoration of exiled bishops. Euzoius, approved by Constantius, was already in place and was soon joined by the returned Meletius. When Lucifer of Calaris arrived and appointed Paulinus as bishop, this created a situation where there were now three bishops for one city.

Between this and the arrival of the *comitatus*, the city was thus busier than usual. Julian's arrival was not auspicious. As part of his program of paganism, he had given orders for the restoration of the Temple of Apollo at Daphne. He soon arrived at the temple with his entourage in great excitement. John Chrysostom's *Homily to St. Babylas* claims that he was met by a single priest with a goose he had brought himself. If true, this was a humiliating moment. There were other challenges that were more deliberate. The abbess Publia organized a choir to chant when the emperor was passing:

> When he heard them [Julian] was very angry and told them to hold their peace while he was passing by. She did not, however, pay the least attention to his orders, but put still greater energy into their chant, and when the emperor passed by again told them to sing "Let God arise and let his enemies be scattered." On this Julian in anger ordered the choir mistress to be brought before him; and, though he saw that respect was due to her old age, he neither pitied her grey hair nor respected her high character, but ordered one of his bodyguard to box both her ears, and by their violence to make her cheeks red (Theodoret, *HE* 3.19.3–5).

Acts like this soon made Julian unpopular with the Antiochenes who were already suffering from food shortages when the emperor and the *comitatus* arrived. Pagan sacrifices in city led to problems with military discipline, especially with the brigade of the *Celtae* and *Petulantes*. Julian then fixed the price of food items in Antioch in an attempt to relieve the famine, but only in the city itself. Merchants thus bought up goods in the city to sell in its territory, exacerbating the shortages within Antioch. Julian was blamed for the shortages and even became the subject of popular songs. The New Year Festival of January 363 did not begin well, and the death of one of officiating priests at the Temple of Tyche was a bad omen. Julian celebrated taking the consulate together with Saturninus Secundus Salutius, the first time since the reign of Diocletian that a private citizen had held the consulate with the emperor. The army was given a donative. Some Christian soldiers apparently conducted the sacrifice to receive the payment, though others were executed. Julian's behavior was not what the Antiochene wanted, and at the New Year Festival, they made fun of, among other things, his philosopher's beard and the frequency of animal sacrifice, calling him a "bull-burner." All of this was well within social conventions; a few years earlier, the citizens of Edessa had publicly spanked a statue of Constantius II at a festival to make a point about the emperor's actions. Constantius did nothing.

Julian's response was different. He posted a satirical pamphlet outside the imperial palace at the Tetrapylon of the Elephants, the *Misopogon* (Beardhater), mocking himself, but also setting out a case for an inevitable clash between emperor and city. And then he left the city on March 5, 363, declaring he would never return and writing to the *praeses Ciliciae* Memorius, warning of his intention to winter at Tarsus. For Antioch to be so treated by the emperor was a significant worry. After posting the *Misopogon* and leaving, Julian was followed by a delegation of city senators. When he chose to receive them, he kept them waiting; it was not until the ninth hour that he received them, and even then promised that they would never see him again. Prophetic words.

Having left Antioch behind him, Julian led an army of 65,000 men against the Persians. He divided his troops into a larger force moving down the Euphrates and a smaller diversionary force commanded by his relative Procopius in Armenia. The presence of Sapur's refugee brother Hormizd in the army gave possibilities of fostering dissension among the Persians. Fearful of being caught between the two armies, Sapur kept his main army back, while the Suren led a delaying action against Julian. The Romans reached Ctesiphon, last attacked by the Romans in 298, on May 29, 363. The fleet was burned, as of no use for moving supplies upstream on either the Euphrates or the Tigris. After two weeks, the arrival of Sapur meant that the siege of Ctesiphon had to be abandoned. The Romans then left Ctesiphon and began withdrawing, this time following the course of the Tigris north, and shadowed by the Persians. There were numerous skirmishes and a battle at Maranga where the Persian elephants and armored cavalry were pushed back by the Roman infantry. But in one of these skirmishes at a place called Phrygia on June 26, 363, Julian was killed, rushing to engage some Persians harassing the rearguard and failing to put on his armor. The killer was unknown, though contemporary speculation was rife, suggesting the Saracens or a disgruntled Christian, as well as the more plausible Persian.

After Julian's death, the Roman Empire remained a Christian Empire. During the first half of the fourth century, both Constantine and Julian had tried to change the religion of the Roman Empire. Constantine succeeded, Julian failed. Before the early fourth century, there were not enough Christians for such an action to succeed; by Julian's time, there were too many. The adoption of Christianity brought new responsibilities for the emperor, but no corresponding advantages. And as Constantine's protection of the Armenian Christians in 335 and the threat of war by Constans after the Council of Sirmium showed, Christianity might involve the state in wars foreign and domestic. Julian's sole reign was short and spectacular. Like Constantine, his decisions show how much personal power the emperor had, moving authority back as far as possible to the cities. The same was true of his religious actions, moving back to a world of active paganism. But his actions were rapidly undone in the decade following his rule because, though the emperor might hope to impose change, his ability to do so was limited by reality. His idealism was not well suited to the world of the mid-fourth century, and had he lived, his falling out with Antioch would have been only the first of many such challenges to imperial power.

FURTHER READING

For much of this period, there is no connected primary narrative, in particular for the period 324–353. Zosimus provides a secular narrative based on Eunapius' *History* (of which some fragments survive), which is a heavily anti-Constantinian work. Zosimus can be supplemented by a number of short histories, in particular those of Festus, Eutropius, Aurelius Victor, and the anonymous *Epitome de Caesaribus*. From 354, the *History of Ammianus Marcellinus* provides a good guide since he was a soldier who took part in some of the events he described. These works tended to avoid mention of Christianity, but at the same time there arose a separate genre, that of ecclesiastical history, some of which have good coverage of secular events. Eusebius' *Ecclesiastical History* covered events down to 324, after which we have the continuations of Socrates, Sozomen, Theodoret, and parts of Philostorgius, though all preserve a fifth-century interpretation of events. From the fourth century, we have some documents written by the participants themselves, including Constantine's *Speech to the Assembly of the Saints* and numerous speeches and letters of Julian both before and after his accession, as well as some notices of proceedings of church councils. There are numerous panegyrics and the speeches of Libanius, Themistius, and Himerius. There are a large number of preserved works by Athanasius, though these are extremely partisan. There are several saints' lives that preserve many interesting anecdotes, in particular Athanasius' *Life of Antony*. Numerous laws from 313 onward are preserved in the *Codex Theodosianus*.

The best starting point for Constantine is the recent volume of papers edited by Lenski, N., *The Cambridge Companion to the Age of Constantine*[2] (Cambridge, 2011). See also the useful review article Barnes, T. D., "Constantine after Seventeen Hundred Years: The Cambridge Companion, the York Exhibition and a Recent Biography," *International Journal of the Classical Tradition* 14 (2007), 185–220. There are also an enormous number of monographs on Constantine including Bardill, J., *Constantine, Divine Emperor of the Christian Golden Age* (Cambridge, 2011). Very useful on the practicalities of politics is Drake, H., *Constantine and the Bishops* (Baltimore, 2000). There are also useful collections of documents in Lieu, S. N. C. and Montserrat, D., eds. *Constantine: History, Historiography and Legend* (London, 1998) and Lieu, S. N. C. and Montserrat, D., *From Constantine to Julian: Pagan and Byzantine Views* (London, 1996).

Licinius remains very obscure, though see Corcoran, S., "Hidden from History: The Legislation of Licinius," in Harries. J. and Wood, I., eds., *The Theodosian*

Code: Studies in the Imperial Law of Late Antiquity (London, 1993), 97–119 and Smith, R. R. R., "The Public Image of Licinius I: Portrait Sculpture and Imperial Ideology," *Journal of Roman Studies* 77 (1997), 170–202. On Julian, probably the best recent monograph is Tougher, S., *Julian the Apostate* (Edinburgh, 2007), though Bowersock, G., *Julian the Apostate* (Cambridge, MA, 1978) remains useful. There is a useful collection of documents and commentary in Lieu, S. N. C., *The Emperor Julian; Panegyric and Polemic* (Liverpool, 1989). For the visit to Antioch, see Gleason, M. W., "Festive Satire: Julian's Misopogon and the New Year at Antioch," *Journal of Roman Studies* 76 (1986), 106–119 and Van Hoof, L. and Van Nuffelen, P., "Monarchy and Mass Communication: Antioch A.D. 362/3 Revisited," *Journal of Roman Studies* 100 (2011), 166–184.

Other monographs include Barnes, T. D., *Constantine and Eusebius* (Cambridge MA, 1981) and *Athanasius and Constantius* (Cambridge, MA, 1993). Hanson, R. P. C., *The Search for the Christian Doctrine of God: The Arian Controversy, 318–381* (Edinburgh, 1988). On Rome and Constantinople, see Curran, J., *Pagan City and Christian Capital: Rome in the Fourth Century AD* (Oxford, 2000) and Grig, L. and Kelly, G., eds., *Two Romes: Rome and Constantinople in Late Antiquity* (Oxford, 2010).

The historiography of the latter part of this period is dominated by Ammianus Marcellinus. The best starting point remains Matthews, J. F., *The Roman Empire of Ammianus* (London, 1989), though Kelly, G., *Ammianus Marcellinus: The Allusive Historian* (Cambridge, 2008) builds on this. There are excellent volumes of collected papers, including Drijvers, J. W. and Hunt, D., *The Late Roman World and Its Historian: Interpreting Ammianus Marcellinus* (London, 1999) and den Boeft, J. et al., eds., *Ammianus after Julian: The Reign of Valentinian and Valens in Books 26–31 of the Res Gestae* (Leiden 2007).

3

THE MILITARY SITUATION, 260–395

The internal problems of the Roman Empire in the third and fourth centuries could all be managed, even if not in the way the emperor wished. Financial crises, arguments with bishops, or corrupt officials could not bring down the Empire rapidly, and solutions to these problems could sometimes be found in the imperial council. Defending the Empire against military threats was different. If not tackled effectively, external threats could destroy the Empire, whereas internal threats could only destroy a ruler or dynasty. This chapter begins by describing how the Romans made decisions. Then the resources of the Roman army are discussed before analyzing warfare in Europe (where the enemies were large numbers of barbarian tribes, occasionally uniting under competent leaders), with the Persians (where Rome faced a single organized state), and in Africa, Egypt, and the Levant (where the enemies were bandits operating on varying scales). The way in which the army fought civil wars is also described. Finally, the disastrous defeat at Adrianople in 378 is described, an event that eventually led to the collapse of the fifth-century western Empire.

The emperor's primary function was to defend the Empire. His subjects accepted demands for men and money in return for protection. The defensive system was built around the expectation that there would always be threats. Many of these threats were the result of factors that could not be controlled by the Romans, such as the leadership abilities of the barbarian kings, disruption following Roman civil wars, or famine causing food shortages in the *barbaricum*. Not surprisingly, then, the Romans saw their Empire as surrounded by enemies. The late fourth-century author of the *de rebus bellicis* reminded his audience "that the frenzies of the howling peoples are screaming round the Roman Empire everywhere, and barbaric cunning, concealed by natural positions, is attacking every part of the frontiers"

(Anon. *de rebus bellicis* 6). The destruction of one enemy thus led not to a lasting peace but simply the arrival of more barbarians. Unless dealing with Persia, terrorizing the enemy was thought to be good policy, the result of peace brought by a Roman army and the frequent outbreak of raids if the normal Roman presence on the frontier was reduced. Prisoners were often thrown to the beasts in the amphitheater as Constantine I did with the victims of his Frankish victories in 313 at Trier. And even when involved in negotiations, it was thought by some Romans to be acceptable to break their word. Ammianus Marcellinus' account of a Roman attack on a raiding band of Saxons in 370 concludes

> though a just arbiter of these things will condemn this act as perfidious and degrading, then after considering the affair, he will not think it shameful that a destructive band of bandits was destroyed once the opportunity was given (Ammianus 28.5.7).

Failure to defeat the enemies of Rome meant death and destruction within the Empire. Ammianus probably had in mind events such as the sacking of Antioch in 260, when he retells an anecdote of the betrayed city being surprised during a performance in the theater and an actor's wife rose to her feet, exclaiming, "Unless this is a dream, Look out! Persians!" (Ammianus 23.5.3). How to defend the Empire was a subject on which many contemporaries were prepared to give opinions. Not all were as well informed as Ammianus, who had seen the cruelties of war firsthand, notably in the siege of Amida in 359. Some of his contemporaries thought that it was possible to create a defensive system that could defeat all attacks on the borders of the Empire. Thus the author of the *de rebus bellicis* suggested that

> a proper care for the frontiers encircling the Empire on all sides is also helpful to the state: continuous forts will best provide for the protection of these ... so that the peace of the provinces, surrounded by this defensive belt, may rest unharmed in peace (Anon. *de rebus bellicis* 20).

This simplistic perspective was matched by others, such as Zosimus' description of Constantine's frontier policy:

> the frontiers of the Roman Empire were studded everywhere by the forethought of Diocletian, as I have already said [in a lost section] with cities, fortresses, and towers. And since the whole army made its home in these, it was impossible for the barbarians to cross, being confronted everywhere by forces able to resist their movements. But Constantine destroyed this security, by transferring a large number of soldiers from the frontiers and placing them in cities which did not need help (Zosimus 2.34.1–2).

And occasionally, members of the government might think that it was this simple. The *comes sacrarum largitionum* Ursulus was inspecting the ruins of Amida with Constantius II in 360 when he lamented, "See with what spirit the cities are defended by the soldiers, by whom, so that they may be so well-paid, the wealth of the Empire is already exhausted" (Ammianus 20.11.5). This remark earned Ursulus so much dislike among the soldiers that he was a fatal target in the bloodletting after Constantius' death in 361. And Zosimus' hostile description of Constantine's actions has to be read alongside the anonymous panegyrist who described Constantine's treatment of Maxentius' defeated troops after the Battle of the Milvian Bridge in 312:

> Now forgetful of the delights of the Circus Maximus, the theatre of Pompey and the familiar baths, they hold the Rhine and Danube, they stand guard, restrain banditry, and finally compete with the victors who defeated them in civil war to be pitted against the enemy (*Latin Panegyrics* 12.21.3).

Anecdotes such as these, subject both to the demands of the works in which they are contained and to the limits of the authors' knowledge, cannot be used to analyze Roman defensive systems.

IMPERIAL DECISION-MAKING

Rather than relying on this sort of material, analysis should start with the emperor's decision-making process. Decisions often had to be made swiftly on minimal information. Thus on the same day in 365, Valentinian I heard of an Alamannic attack and Procopius' revolt against his brother Valens in the east. The Alamanni were a known quantity,

> but as to dealing with the attempt of Procopius before it matured, [Valentinian] was distracted by doubting anxiety and disturbed by this most powerful reason, that he did not know whether Valens was alive or whether his death had led to the attempt on the throne. For Equitius [*comes per Illyricum*] had received a report of the tribune Antonius commanding troops in Dacia Mediterranea, which indicated nothing except a vague account which he himself had heard; and Equitius himself had not yet heard anything trustworthy, and reported the events to the emperor in simple words (Ammianus 26.5.9–10).

Gallienus faced the same problem in 260: should he avenge his father and stabilize the east or should he deal with the imperial challenger in Gaul? Such dilemmas would have been discussed in the imperial council (*consistorium*). As an assembly of senior officials, its membership varied, especially in emergencies. Constantius II called a meeting in Milan in 355 following news that might have pointed to a seizure of imperial power by the *magister militum per Gallias* Silvanus. Delay was dangerous, and the decision was soon made to send Ursicinus: "After a many-sided discussion, this was examined most closely, how Silvanus might be led to think that the emperor was still ignorant of his actions" (Ammianus 15.5.21). Ursicinus and a small staff soon set off for Cologne. Ammianus describes well the nervousness surrounding the mission, as Ursicinus' men, including Ammianus himself, had to improvise the removal of Silvanus without themselves falling victim to his suspicions. Similarly, in 360, news of the Caesar Julian's unauthorized assumption of the rank of Augustus reached Constantius in Cappadocia:

> Therefore, Constantius, wavering under the pressure of urgent matters, was unsure as to what to undertake, considering anxiously for a long time whether he should seek out Julian far away or drive back the Parthians [i.e., the Persians] who, as they threatened, were already about to cross the Euphrates; and being perplexed he often took counsel with his generals (Ammianus 21.7.1).

Having finally made the decision to march against Julian, fighting between the two emperors was averted by the death of Constantius II in Cilicia on November 3, 361. There was then further discussion in the eastern consistory, though now without the emperor:

> Those holding the first rank in the imperial court considered what to do or what they ought to attempt. And after checking with a few in secret as to the choice of an emperor, reportedly at the suggestion of Eusebius ... since the closeness of Julian made revolution inadvisable, Theolaifus and Aligildus, at that time *comites*, were sent to him to report the death of his relative and to beg him to put aside all delay and come to take over the East which was ready to obey him (Ammianus 21.15.4).

In all of these cases, the emperor was at a considerable distance from the area of concern. All of the participants were very aware of the time lag involved in information reaching them, the fact that the information they were discussing was incomplete and possibly wrong, and that the situation would have changed by the time any orders reached the area under question. The time lag varied. A day's travel for a mounted messenger was usually 20 to 40 kilometers, though the imperial post (*cursus publicus*) could easily manage around 80 kilometers per day. But when urgent news, such as the death of an emperor or the acclamation of an imperial rival, needed to be transmitted, much faster speeds could be achieved, though at a dreadful cost in horses. The *cursus publicus* relied on the availability of horses and when Constantine left the court of Galerius to join his father in 305; he was said to have killed the post horses en route to avoid being pursued. With such limits, even urgent information was sometimes several weeks old by the time it reached the emperor. Thus Valentinian in northern Gaul did not hear about Procopius' seizure of imperial power in Constantinople until at least a month after it took place. By this point, Procopius had control of all Thrace and was only kept out of Illyricum by the actions of Equitius, who had acted without orders from Valentinian. Events were thus moving faster than the emperor could react, and by early December, the earliest at which orders sent by Valentinian could have reached the area, Procopius had taken over Bithynia. Finally, the consistory was always advisory to the emperor. Valentinian I, for example, when he heard of the news about Procopius ignored the advice of some of his officials and observed that "Procopius was only the enemy of him and his brother, but the Alamanni were enemies of the whole Roman world" (Ammianus 26.5.13).

Although decision-making was centralized in the person of the emperor, most military force was dispersed along the frontiers. In the middle of the third century, some troops were located with a single emperor, but by the Tetrarchy the creation of multiple field armies allowed the Empire to deal simultaneously with problems in several different regions. Eumenius in a panegyric delivered in 298 praised Constantius for fighting Franks on the Rhine, Maximian fighting Moors in Africa, Diocletian putting down the revolt of Aurelius Achilleus in Egypt, and Galerius invading Persia. The need to fight on numerous frontiers required emperors to travel long distances repeatedly. In early February 313, Licinius left Carnuntum on the Danube for Milan to marry Constantine's sister Constantia. By April 30, he was back in the Balkans, where he fought Maximinus at Adrianople, crossed into Anatolia, and then forced the Cilician Gates. Licinius finally moved to Antioch in Syria at the end of the year, either on campaign against the Persians or preparing for it. This single year involved two campaigns and marching over 2,700 kilometers. In their travels, emperors were always accompanied by an imperial field army. The early fourth-century tombstone of Aurelius Gaius shows that he served on both the Rhine and Danube, crossing them frequently into the territory of the Carpi, the Sarmatians (four times), and the Goths (twice), as well as serving in Anatolia, Syria, Gaul, Spain, Mauritania, and Egypt. The same pattern was found in the middle of the fourth century, when the brigade of the *Celtae* and *Petulantes* served in Gaul under Julian, campaigned in Illyricum in 361 and in Persia in 363, and then returned to Gaul with Valentinian in 364. For emperors to lead their armies was expected, despite the risks. Valerian was captured in the course of campaigning against the Persians in 260, Constantius I had to be pulled over the walls of Langres on a rope to avoid a pursuing force of Alamanni, Constantius II was attacked by some Sarmatians while negating a peace treaty in 358, and Valentinian I was ambushed while scouting before the Battle of Solicinium in 368. On the battlefield, there were much greater risks, and Gallienus was wounded by an arrow in Gaul, Aurelian was wounded by an arrow at Palmyra, Constantine I was wounded in the thigh at Adrianople in 324, Julian was killed attempting to blunt a Persian attack on his rearguard in 363, and Valens died on the battlefield at Adrianople in 378. Roman emperors led from the front.

DIPLOMACY

Although armies were the most common tool used to create peace, there were other means of managing the frontiers. For most of the third and fourth centuries, relations with Rome's neighbors were governed by some form of treaty, whether imposed by diplomacy or through warfare. In Europe, this often involved a formal submission to the Romans, who took the opportunity to show their power. When Aurelian was negotiating with the Iuthungi in 270,

> he arrayed his soldiers as if for war so that he might alarm the enemy. When the arrangement satisfied him, he ascended a high stage, raised far above the ground … He requested that the Iuthungi should come forward. It so happened that when they saw this they were amazed and stayed silent for a long time (Dexippus, fr. 6).

Each treaty took account of local conditions, although the frequent conflict following the death of a Roman emperor suggests that they were seen as personal agreements between the emperor and barbarian leaders. Most treaties also required the return of Roman prisoners of war. Zosimus described Julian negotiating the return of prisoners from some Alamanni in 358:

> Caesar, seated on a high stage with the secretaries standing behind the stage, ordered the barbarians to produce the prisoners according to their agreement. As they came forward one by one and gave their names, the secretaries standing near Caesar checked the names in their lists. But on comparing those they had previously noted down and those now appearing before Caesar, and finding many more had been named by their fellow-citizens and villagers, they told this to Caesar. He then threatened the ambassadors with war for not giving back all the prisoners and at the

prompting of the secretaries named some from each town and village who were still missing (Zosimus 3.4.6–7).

Other terms imposed included the right to call on the barbarians as military allies, provision of recruits for the army, and the delivery of other resources, including grain and timber. A distrusted king could be replaced. In 360, Vadomarius, king of the Brisigavi, an Alamannic tribe, crossed the Rhine,

> fearing nothing during the deep peace … And when he saw the *praepositus* of the soldiers stationed there, talked to him briefly as usual, and what is more, so as not to leave behind any suspicion when he left, promised to come to dinner with him (Ammianus 21.4.3).

When Vadomarius arrived for dinner, he was arrested. This did not turn out badly for Vadomarius, who went on to a successful Roman military career in the east. He was succeeded by his son Vithicabius, who was assassinated in 368 after causing much trouble for the Romans. Replacing kings did not guarantee peace. When Valentinian I made Fraomarius king of the Bucinobantes in place of Macrianus, he was soon driven out by followers of the deposed king, and when the Quadic king Gabinius was killed in 373, his people attacked the Empire. The Romans also liked to break confederations and alliances. In 358, Constantius II made a separate peace with the Sarmatian king Usafer and with the Quadic king Araharius:

> Usafer was admitted to make an appeal, although Araharius protested obstinately, claiming that the peace which he had obtained should also extend to Usafer, as his partner, though of lower rank and accustomed to obey his orders. But after a discussion the Sarmatians were ordered to be freed from foreign control (Ammianus 17.12.14–15).

After negotiations, oaths were sworn and the Romans might take hostages, many of whom acquired Roman values. One Alamannic king, Mederichus, renamed his son after Serapis, an Egyptian mystery god, as a result of his time as an exile. Treaties might also result in Roman payments to barbarians. One such was Julian's accusation that his prefect Florentius had promised to pay 2,000 pounds of silver (= 111 pounds of gold) to some Germans to allow free passage for a Roman fleet down the Rhine. These payments were less than the costs of wars and may also have freed troops to operate elsewhere, but as Julian's accusation shows there could be a substantial political cost. For many, especially those a long way from the frontier, any payment by the Romans to barbarians was viewed as a shameful tribute. For others, any means used to avoid war might be counted a success. Finally, a favored ruler might be given an honorary Roman office. The focus on the leadership of barbarian tribes suggests that this was seen as the best use of Roman resources.

Roman treaties with the Persians were very different from treaties in Europe or Africa. Romans and Persians traditionally informed each of other of changes of ruler. There was either a formal state of war or peace between the two empires, with peace controlled by written documents. The few details we have for the third or fourth centuries are similar to the much more detailed examples from the sixth century. Negotiations were always carried out through envoys. Thus Sicorius Probus, leading an embassy to the Persian king Narse in 298–299, claimed that he did not have any independent power and that he had not received instructions from the emperors. On all of the Roman frontiers, negotiated peace was highly desirable, but military action continued to occur.

IMPERIAL RESOURCES

Maintaining the Roman army and thus the Roman state required the extraction of surpluses of money, supplies, and men and their transportation to areas of military need. This was an immense process whose constant demands attracted the hostility of many. Thus the fourth-century author of the *de rebus bellicis* referred to "the enormous expenditure on the army … from which the whole working of the tax system is suffering" (Anon. *de rebus rellicis* 5.1). Keeping the army up to strength required constant attention. John Lydus, writing under Justinian and working in the office of the eastern praetorian prefect in Constantinople, had access to official records and provides a figure for the entire Roman armed establishment. He claimed that Diocletian had an army of 389,704 and a navy of 45,562, a figure that is plausible. An army of four hundred thousand men serving twenty-year terms would have required a minimum annual intake of twenty thousand men simply to maintain its strength if all men served full terms, an assumption that ignores attrition from desertion, accidents, disease, and death or injury in battle.

There were several ways in which the Empire obtained the required men. The majority of soldiers were conscripts of different types. In theory, military service was hereditary. Although St. Martin, son of a soldier, tried to avoid service, he was conscripted at fifteen years old and served as a *scholarius* in Gaul for five years under Constantius II. Sons of veterans were supplemented by annual levies. A panegyrical description of Constantius I's settlements of defeated Chamavi and Frisii in Gaul claimed that "if he is called to the levy, he hurries up, is improved by service, straightens his back, and is proud to serve with the name of soldier" (*Latin Panegyrics* 8.9.4). Even if true, not all were as ready to serve. The *praefectus* Abinnaeus in Egypt received a letter begging for an exemption for the writer's nephew: "He is the son of a soldier and his name has been given so that he should serve. If you can release him again, it is a fine thing to do … But if he must serve, please safeguard him from going abroad with the levy for the field army" (*P.Abinn.* 19). Others were so desperate to avoid service that they mutilated themselves, as recorded in a law of Constantine I that was then reissued in the reign of Valentinian I. Other troops were conscripted from prisoners or served as a result of peace treaties made with a defeated enemy. There were also volunteers from within and beyond the empire; their motivations may have included adventure, plunder, pay, or food. Some of these volunteers had contracts that limited their area of service; in a fourth-century case, men from across the Rhine had negotiated a restriction of service to north of the Alps (Ammianus 20.4.4). Although there was a constant need for men, not all were taken; imperial tenants, slaves, heretics, *curiales*, and men less than 5' 7" (1.65 meters) were excluded at various times. And like all armies, the Romans had difficulties in recruiting enough troops. We thus often hear of extensive recruiting campaigns before a war. Before Constantine invaded Italy in 312, he began "levying troops from the barbarians he had conquered, both Germans and other Gauls, and those collected from Britain" (Zosimus 2.15.1). Similarly, Constantius II went to great lengths to recruit troops before his war with Julian in 361, when "levies were ordered throughout the provinces, every order and profession was troubled, delivering clothing and weapons and siege-engines, even gold and silver and a manifold provisions of all kinds as well as various sorts of baggage animals" (Ammianus 21.6.6).

Although recruits came from all over the Empire, in the third century the Balkans had a good reputation, providing many emperors and officers, as well as the names of two new types of cavalry regiment, *Dalmatae* and *Illyriciani*. In the fourth century, there were still many Balkan soldiers, while Gauls and Germans were also prominent. Many Franks, for example, served in the *scholae* in the fourth-century west, though they had numerous Pannonian colleagues such as St. Martin and Valentinian, the future emperor. So many recruits came from outside the Empire that the army is sometimes described as "barbarized." Thus Constantine made extensive use of Germans for the 312 campaign, while Julian offered recruits from across the Rhine to Constantius II in 360. Despite the extensive use of men recruited from outside the Empire, third- and fourth-century Roman regiments were mostly composed of men born inside the Empire.

At the start of the third century, most army officers were aristocrats of senatorial or equestrian rank, not professional soldiers, and military posts were only part of a political career controlled by the emperor. But during the third century, many senatorial aristocrats stopped holding military positions, reflected by the claim that Gallienus banned senators from holding military commands. This separation of civil and military hierarchies created a professional officer class based on ability rather than inherited wealth and thus led to an imperial aristocracy. Men of all social groups could advance within the army and even become emperor. Examples of this social mobility included the emperors Diocletian, son of a freedman, and Galerius, who had been a herdsman. By the middle of the fourth century, Magnentius, whose mother was a Frank, was acceptable as an emperor.

However, regardless of their origins, most Roman officers had long military careers before being placed in charge of armies. Volusianus, consul in 261, had commanded a pair of legions as well as three units of guards (one cavalry, two infantry), and before this had been the first centurion (*primus pilus*) of another legion, all on his way to becoming praetorian prefect under Gallienus (*ILS* 1332). There were occasions when men might be felt to have been promoted too quickly, as Ammianus reported of Agilo in the reign of Constantius II, though he also claimed that under the same emperor, "no one who had not endured the dust of war was put in command of soldiers" (21.16.3). Many of those promoted to unit commands held the office of *protector Augusti;* during the third century, they were attached to the comitatus, but by the early fourth century were often attached to a *magister militum.* Some became *protectores* after long service, such as Abinnaeus, who served for thirty-three years in the *Parthosagittarii*, though sons of senior officers and barbarian royalty could be fast-tracked, such as Hariulfus, son of the Burgundian king Hanhaualdus. Promotion was a competitive process. Both Gallienus and Aurelian were murdered because they were thought to have planned to execute subordinates, Aper was killed by Diocletian in a struggle to succeed Numerianus, and Theodosius the Elder's execution in 373 was the result of such rivalries. At lower levels, the stakes were less significant but competition was still present. When Abinnaeus arrived at Alexandria ca. 340 to be appointed as *praefectus* of the *Ala Quinta Praelectorum*, he found other officers claiming the same position, and it was only after a petition to Constantius II that he took up his post. Men such as Abinnaeus were professionals. Another was Traianus Mucianus, whose career, recorded in a Greek inscription from Augusta Traiana in Thracia, involved at least nineteen different positions in the late third century.

As a professional army, along with a command structure there were processes of discipline and reward. In Persia in 363, when three cavalry regiments broke in the face of Persian attacks, Julian dismissed the two surviving tribunes and executed ten of the men, while after the capture of

Maiozamalcha, he awarded siege-crowns to several men in the presence of the army. The army also fed its men. The basic ration system was simple, with each soldier receiving a food allowance (*annona*) and cavalrymen receiving a fodder allowance (*capitus*) as well. Ranks above private soldier received multiple allowances, with a *biarchus* (a sort of corporal) receiving two *annonae* and one *capitus*, and a *dux* receiving fifty *annonae* and fifty *capitus*. These rations were provided by the state either in kind (according to a fixed tariff) or commuted to money payment at a rate of four *solidi* per allowance. Arms and equipment, including cavalry horses, were also provided by the state. When soldiers retired after twenty years, they received small cash payments or larger values of land, oxen, and seed-corn. They also received tax privileges that were more significant than the discharge bounties, though not a direct cost to the state.

There was far more to the process of collecting these allowances than just the state paying for the goods. During the early third century, collecting the supplies for Roman expeditionary forces was the responsibility of a local procurator. He issued demands to provincial governors, who in turn dealt with individual cities. A register of letters from Panopolis in the Thebaid regarding the impending visit of Diocletian and the *comitatus* in 298 mentioned at least forty-seven local two-man teams assigned to collect, receive, and redistribute supplies. Similar efforts would have been needed wherever the emperor or his armies went. From the reign of Constantine, these duties were usually carried out by the praetorian prefect. The quantities of supplies needed meant planning for large military movements usually took place months ahead, making it difficult for the Romans to achieve strategic surprise. Such stockpiles could be enormous; Ammianus Marcellinus described the collapse of a stack of dried fodder at Batnae in Osrhoene in 363 that apparently killed fifty men.

The total cost of the army was much greater than the sum of the costs related to individual soldiers. There was a large amount of equipment, including boats, ships, tents, artillery, and wagons, to be maintained. There were also consumables, such as spears and arrows, firewood, rope, and paper or papyrus for recordkeeping. This material, like the food and fodder, had to be transported to the armies from wherever it was produced, the responsibility of the *cursus publicus*. There was also constant process of building and maintaining fortifications carried out by all emperors, as suggested by a law of Valentinian I in 364, which instructed the *dux Daciae Ripensis* to construct towers (*turres*) annually at "opportune places" along the frontier (*CT* 15.1.13). Maintenance of city defenses was theoretically the duty of the individual cities, though in practice the state often paid for this too. All of these costs occurred in peace, but when armies took to the field there was a sudden demand for all sorts of material, especially recruits and pack animals. Deferred maintenance sometimes needed to be done in a hurry, as when Probus, praetorian prefect of Italy, Illyricum, and Africa, cleaned up the defenses of Sirmium in 374 in preparation for an attack by the Quadi and Sarmatians.

He cleaned out the ditches, which were choked with rubble, and put in order the greatest part of the walls, which had been neglected and ruined completely by the length of peace as far as the battlements of the high towers (Ammianus 29.6.11).

THE DEPLOYMENT OF ROMAN ARMIES

In 260, most Roman troops were assigned to frontier provinces under the command of provincial governors. Some of these commands were very large; in Syria, there were three or four legions and about twenty *auxilia* regiments, totaling perhaps thirty thousand men, almost 10 percent of the Empire's military forces. In crises or for planned offensive campaigns, these commands were reinforced by troops and guards accompanying the emperor. In the third century, the *excubitores* provided close security for the emperor while the ten cohorts of praetorians supported by a cavalry regiment of *equites singulares* provided an elite battlefield force. From the creation of the Tetrarchy, if not before, the praetorians were split between the emperors. By the reign of Diocletian, several cavalry regiments of *scholae palatinae* had been added, while Constantine (and perhaps Licinius) dissolved the praetorians. By the end of the fourth century, the *Notitia Dignitatum* records seven eastern and five western *scholae*. In addition to these guards, there were troops attached to the emperor, both whole legions such as *Legio II Parthica*, but also detachments of others. By the mid-third century, this collection of troops had become a permanent field army, known informally as the *comitatus*, usually led by the emperor with the assistance of a praetorian prefect. On some occasions, prefects were put in charge of troops, as when Volusianus led an army of Maxentius against Domitius Alexander in Africa in 309. From the 260s, a cavalry commander (whose exact title is uncertain) led the cavalry regiments of the *comitatus*, a post held by Ballista, Aureolus, Claudius, and Aurelian. From the 280s, most field armies were commanded by emperors, although in some situations praetorian prefects still acted alone. When Diocletian formed the Tetrarchy, each emperor had his own *comitatus*, so there were first two, then four field armies.

It was in the reign of Constantine that a distinction between the field army troops (*comitatenses*) and the troops left in the border provinces (now usually known as *limitanei*) first became visible. Constantine also created a new rank of *magister militum* to lead the *comitatenses*, eliminating the command role of praetorian prefects. The terminology used by contemporaries to describe these generals is often imprecise; on May 27, 349, Silvanus was described as *magister militum* and *magister equitum et peditum* in two laws issued in Sirmium (*CT* 7.1.2, 8.7.3). After Constantine's death in 337, his sons divided his imperial field army into three separate armies in Gaul (Constantine II), Illyricum (Constans), and the east (Constantius II), which they led with the assistance of *magistri militum*. By 350, the army on the Persian frontier was commanded by the *magister equitum* Ursicinus (though the emperor Constantius II was also present), and in the west there were armies in Illyricum (under the *magister militum* Vetranio) and in Gaul (under the emperor Constans). After Constantius II became sole emperor in 353, the imperial field army was recreated, supplemented by three regional field armies under *magistri militum* in Gaul, Illyricum, and the east. When Valentinian and Valens divided the Empire in 364, they also divided the imperial field army between them. This structure of eastern and western imperial armies, with regional field armies in Gaul, Illyricum, and the east, supplemented by a fourth regional army created in Thrace during the 370s, continued little changed into the fifth century.

These armies did not have permanent bases, but in Gaul and Illyricum often wintered at Trier and Sirmium, while the Thracian army was usually based at Marcianopolis, the eastern at Antioch. The western imperial army was based in Italy, usually at Milan, the eastern imperial army at Constantinople. Sometimes small expeditionary forces were detached from these armies under a *comes rei militaris*. By the end of the fourth century, some of these expeditionary forces had become permanent detachments, recorded in by the *Notitia Dignitatum* in Africa, Spain, Britain, Illyricum (attached to the western Empire), and Isauria. These armies were supported by fleets of warships (for fighting) and merchantmen (for supply and transport of troops). In the west, the main Roman fleet was at Ravenna, although there were smaller fleets elsewhere in Italy, in Gaul, Africa, and Britain. In the east, the main fleet was based first at Nicomedia and then at Constantinople. There was no separate naval hierarchy, so naval expeditions were commanded by generals.

It is not until the fourth century that we have any reliable figures for the size of Roman field armies. At Cibalae in 316, Licinius led thirty-five thousand men and Constantine twenty thousand. These figures are similar to Ammianus' claim that in 357 the Gallic field army under Julian had approximately ten thousand infantry and three thousand cavalry while Barbatio led twenty-five thousand to thirty thousand men from the imperial army in Raetia. His figures are similar to the estimates based on the number of regiments recorded by the *Notitia Dignitatum* at the end of the fourth century (Gaul 34,000; western Illyricum 13,500; Thrace 24,500; Illyricum 17,500; and the East 20,000). Larger armies were occasionally created by reinforcing regional field armies with the central imperial armies. Julian in 363 combined the eastern and western imperial armies with the eastern field army to create a force of at least sixty-five thousand for his Persian war; Zosimus' text at this point is unclear as to whether a force of eighteen thousand was part of this force or in addition to it (3.12.5–13.1). In any case, this was an exceptional situation when a single emperor could draw on the resources of the entire Empire at a time when there were no other commitments; smaller armies of ten thousand to twenty thousand were more typical. These sorts of figures are much smaller than Zosimus' report of Constantine leading 98,000 men against Maxentius' army of 188,000 in 312, though such figures might represent troops under arms rather than field army strengths.

By the mid-fourth century, multiple regional field armies gave greater flexibility than depending on intervention by an emperor, as was typical of the Tetrarchic system. In 357, the Caesar Julian and the *magister peditum* Barbatio were able to campaign against Alamanni on the Rhine, Constantius II fought on the Danube against Sarmatians, and the *magister equitum* Ursicinus watched the eastern frontier. At the same time, frontier commanders (perhaps less so on the Persian frontier) had considerable freedom to conduct their own operations, only calling for assistance if they were unable to deal with a situation. When Charietto, *comes per utramque Germaniam*, was defeated by raiding Alamanni in 366, a larger force drawn from the imperial and regional Gallic armies was sent under the leadership of Jovinus, *magister equitum*.

The regiments that made up these armies had long histories. In the middle of the third century, many units such as *Legio III Augusta* could trace their ancestry back to the first century AD. At the end of the fourth century, there were still many regiments named after emperors of the First Tetrarchy, such as *Legio III Diocletiana* and *I Maximiana*. Many other regiments, however, were destroyed or renamed, so we hear of no units named after Maxentius or Licinius. Although there was continuity of some units, their structures changed. In the early third century, legions were composed of five thousand infantry optimized for hand-to-hand combat, but by the end of the third century, many eastern legions had created subunits of *lanciarii*, missile-armed infantry, and *promoti*, light cavalry, which strengthened their combined arms capacity. Thus *Legio II Traiana* in the Thebaid in Egypt in 299 had a main body based at Apollon, some *lanciarii* at Ptolemais, and some *promoti* at Tentyra. By the early fourth century, many of these subunits became independent regiments. These changes increased field army legions, which were smaller (ca. 1,200 strong) and more tactically flexible than the larger legions of the early Empire. In the west, field army legion strength was also reduced, with tactical flexibility added by a new type of infantry unit, the *auxilia palatina*. Some of these were existing units of border troops transferred into the field armies, but many were newly created, particularly by Constantius I and Constantine I. During the late third century, numerous new cavalry regiments were also formed, generically known as Illyriciani.

Allied barbarians were sometimes attached to the central imperial armies for particular campaigns, especially during civil wars. Constantine used Rhine barbarians against Maxentius in 312, while Licinius used Goths against Constantine in 324. Other contingents of Goths fought with the Roman army against the Persians in the east in 359 and 363, while Burgundians helped Valentinian against the Alamanni in 370. Occasionally, these groups could act in Roman interests but without the support of Roman troops, as when the Taifali fought against the Sarmatians in 358.

The growth of the *comitatus* in the third century led to a separation of function between these troops and the troops on the borders, though it was not until the reign of Constantine that two distinct hierarchies were created. Diocletian began to reassign the border troops from provincial governors to a new class of military officials, the *duces*. However, in Isauria and Tripolitania, both areas of low population and difficult military problems, the provincial governor continued to command troops well into the fourth century. *Duces* were often responsible for more than one province, such as the *dux Pannoniae Primae et Norici Ripensis* or the *dux Eufratensis et Syriae*. They at first reported to a provincial governor, although by the reign of Valentinian I had become responsible to their regional *magister militum*. At the end of the fourth century, there were three commands in Britain and the English Channel area, eleven along the Rhine and Danube, five in northern Africa, and nine on the eastern frontier (including Egypt). There were few differences between border and field army troops, and so regiments were sometimes transferred from the *limitanei* into the field armies, where they were given the status of *pseudocomitatenses*. However, some specialized training is suggested by the lack of preparation for siege warfare of some Gallic *comitatenses* transferred in 359 from Gaul to Amida on the eastern frontier. This serves also as a reminder of the fact that Roman armies carried out regular exercises at both the unit and army level.

OPPOSITION AND OPERATIONS IN EUROPE

The overall effectiveness of the defensive system can be judged by its lack of major change between 260 and 395, although there were many minor changes, especially in regional command structures, and local adaptations of practice. But except on the Persian frontier, there were no great changes in the way that operations were conducted. The defensive system placed Roman strengths in intelligence and logistics against barbarian weaknesses in these areas. As far as possible it avoided battle as a risky endeavor. The system's major weakness was that it often responded slowly to attacks, which combined with the inability to keep all enemies out meant that civilians suffered. However, such considerations only had military importance if the Empire had to fight in two areas at the same time, a situation that rarely arose during the fourth century.

In Europe, the Roman Empire extended as far as a Roman general was able to march, but for most purposes ended at the Rhine or Danube. In the third century, there were two areas where administrative zones crossed these rivers, the Agri Decumates across the upper Rhine and Dacia, a province across the Danube, though both were abandoned during the reign of Aurelian. In Britain, Hadrian's Wall provided a similar function to river borders, but Britain and Gaul also had coastlines exposed to raids from the sea. The lands outside the Roman Empire, sometimes described as the *barbaricum*, were inhabited by numerous peoples. Across the southern Rhine were the Alamannic tribes, including the Iuthungi, Bucinobantes, Semnones, Lentienses, and Brisigavi. Writers of short histories such as Aurelius Victor or Eutropius referred to them simply as Alamanni or Germans, but contemporary sources closer to the frontier tended to refer to the smaller units. Thus the Augsburg altar recorded a victory over the Semnones and the Iuthungi in 260 and Ammianus mentions an attack by Constantius II against the Lentienses in 354. In the northern Rhineland, tribes living along the Rhine included the Bructeri, Salii, Chamavi, and Cherusci, though both Roman and modern historians often described such groups as Franks. On the Upper Danube were the Sarmatians (Limigantes, Argaragantes, Rhoxolani), and on the lower Danube the Goths (Visi, Tervingi, Greuthungi). There were also numerous other smaller tribes all along the frontier such as the Scotti and Picti who threatened Britain or the Burgundians, Vandals, and Taifali in central Europe. These groupings were cultural, not political, and there were frequent clashes between different Frankish or Gothic tribes.

These communities were village-based and for the most part, agricultural, though along the Danube there was some pastoralism. They were dominated by aristocracies who valued military success. No Germanic society was literate, even if there were occasional instances of writing. The consequence of a decentralized society and minimal literacy was a limited logistical organization. The financial resources available were limited with the result that only a few troops had body armor or helmets and swords were rare. There were few cavalry. Individual skills at riding or with weaponry were often strong, as suggested by Aurelius Victor's description of the Alamanni as "a people who fight wonderfully from horses" (21.2), but there was little to no training as units in complex maneuvers. Most Germanic armies were composed of large numbers of spear and shield armed infantrymen, thickened up by aristocrats and their retinues, often with armor and swords, sometimes mounted. On occasion, they might fight behind circles of wagons. Despite their weak military skills, these tribes were able to cause significant problems for the Romans. They were at their most dangerous under capable leaders such as Cniva, who brought together several Gothic groups to defeat Decius at Abrittus in 251 or Chnodomarius, who united seven Alamannic tribes at Strasbourg in 357.

The Roman defensive system worked well at stopping raids carried out by a few hundred men. Ammianus Marcellinus noted that his history omits many battles, "because their results were not worthwhile and because it is not fitting to stretch out a history with insignificant details" (Ammianus 27.2.11). One small raid that Ammianus did describe involved six hundred Franks who in winter 357 occupied two deserted forts on the river Meuse. After they were starved into surrendering, they were sent to Constantius II for use as soldiers in the east. Most *limitanei* units were stationed in forts or towns on the Roman side of the border with detachments in a dense network of smaller forts and watchtowers. In a few cases, there were bases across the Rhine or the Danube used as listening posts and jumping-off points. The defenses of Roman cities and forts were characterized by walled circuits with projecting towers and ditches defended by garrisons with large numbers of missile weapons and bolt-shooters. Given the small size of most raids and the limited barbarian capacity for siege warfare, these defenses were usually effective at resisting assaults. They were more vulnerable to surprise attacks, such as the raid led by the Alamannic leader Rando against Mainz in 368, which coincided with a Christian festival. They were also vulnerable to blockade, and Cologne eventually fell to the Franks in late 355 because it was not relieved by a Roman army. When attacks penetrated the border, it was common for the population and their livestock to take shelter in hilltop refuges or other defended sites. Because of their logistical weakness, problems in assaulting defensive structures, and lack of a strong command structure, barbarians tended to scatter into small groups within the Empire, often hiding in forests or marshes. The Romans could do well against such dispersed enemies. In 366, some Alamanni suffered when the *magister equitum* Jovinus

> learnt from a trustworthy scout that a band of plunderers, having laid waste the nearby villas, was resting by a river. Coming closer and hidden in a valley made obscure by the thick growth of trees, he saw some washing themselves, others dyeing their hair red as was their custom, and yet others drinking. And taking advantage of an opportune moment, he immediately gave a signal with the horns and broke into the bandits' camp (Ammianus 27.2.2–3).

Although this Roman strategy was effective militarily, there was a significant cost to the local population. Nor was it always successful. Sebastianus, *magister peditum* in Thrace in 378, hoped to delay any Gothic activity until they retreated or starved. In response, the Gothic leader Fritigern began to concentrate his men, fearful of Sebastianus' nibbling attacks, and taking the risk of being attacked by the Romans in a field battle. And since pinning the enemy down was difficult, it could lead to hurried attacks by the Romans. In 357, despite their tiredness following a long approach march and being heavily outnumbered, Julian's men wished to attack the Alamanni at Strasbourg because they could see the enemy. Field battles such as Strasbourg were infrequent, in part because the Romans preferred to avoid them as far as possible because of the inherent risk; this would be exacerbated by rushing into battle. Although the Romans won most field battles, they were occasionally defeated. Thus in 251, the Goths defeated Decius at the Abrittus; in 352/353 the Alamanni defeated Decentius and in 357 Barbatio; and, most spectacularly, Valens was defeated by Fritigern's Goths at Adrianople in 378, a battle that started prematurely.

When battles occurred, both sides usually deployed with infantry in the center, cavalry and light troops on the wings. The most dangerous moment for the Romans was the initial barbarian charge, but if this could be resisted, then Roman training and armor usually carried the day. Julian's victory over the Alamanni at Strasbourg in 357 shows many of these characteristics. We have three accounts, by Ammianus, Zosimus, and Libanius. Of these, Ammianus' is the most detailed; his naming of three of the four dead tribunes and giving a precise number of Roman deaths suggest use of an official source. Julian led thirteen thousand men, including some cataphract cavalry and the infantry regiments of the *Cornuti, Bracchiati, Batavi, Reges,* and *Primani*. Julian deployed his infantry in the center, with cavalry on both flanks, the left refused, the best troops on the right. He was opposed by an Alamannic force of thirty thousand to thirty-five thousand made up of seven tribes in a confederation under Chnodomarius. The Alamanni deployed with their right wing resting on a canal, their center was composed of multiple lines of infantry stiffened with a group of *optimates* (aristocrats) and their followers, and the left wing was held by most of their cavalry supported by light infantry. Chnodomarius was stationed on the left, while his nephew Serapio led the right flank. After an exchange of missiles, the Alamanni charged "with more rage than reflection." The shock of the Alamannic attack pushed back the Roman cavalry on the right flank after a cataphract officer was wounded, but they rallied behind their infantry. In the center, although the impetus of the Alamannic charge failed to break the first Roman line, a second wave of *optimates* broke through before being repulsed by a second line of Roman troops. The Roman follow-up then routed the Alamanni, pursuing them into the Rhine and capturing Chnodomarius. There were 247 Roman casualties to 6,000–8,000 Alamanni, a disparity typical of ancient battles (Ammianus 16.12; Libanius, *Or.* 18.53–68; Zosimus 3. 3.3–5).

The defensive system was usually reactive, but on some occasions the Romans were able to take the initiative, for example Maximian crossing the Rhine against some Franks in 287, Constantine's crossing of the Danube against Sarmatians in 336, or the Alamannic wars of Valentinian I, which involved numerous strikes across the Rhine at the same time as Valens was campaigning across the Danube against the Goths. These strikes into the *barbaricum* required crossing the Rhine or Danube. In 294, Diocletian built forts across the Danube at Aquincum (Budapest) and Bononia (Vidin), in 309–310 Constantine built a new bridge over the Rhine at Cologne to serve a new fort on the opposite bank at Divitia (Deutz), and in 328 he built another bridge across the Danube at Oescus. It was also possible to ferry troops over rivers by boat or to build pontoon bridges, as used by Valens to cross the Danube against the Goths in 367 and 369. Valens' attack on the Greuthungi in 369 is typical:

> Having broken into the *barbaricum*, after continuous marches, he attacked the warlike people of the Greuthungi who lived far away. And after some minor struggles, he forced into flight Athanaric, at that time the most powerful ruler (*iudex*) who dared to resist with a force he believed to be adequate, in fear for his life (Ammianus 27.5.6).

Once in enemy territory, the Romans tried to destroy settlements and take as many prisoners as possible while the barbarians attempted to avoid contact or to ambush the Romans. In 357, Julian sent troops across the Rhine into Alamannia after his victory at Strasbourg:

> ... great spirals of smoke were seen at a distance, showing that our men had broken in and were devastating enemy territory. This broke the spirit

of the Germans and they fled ... When they had left the soldiers marched on freely and plundered rich villas of their cattle and crops, sparing none; and having taken prisoners, they set fire to and burned down all the houses which had been carefully built in Roman style (Ammianus 17.1.5–7).

On a few occasions, there was more sophisticated planning with two converging armies marching through the *barbaricum* to a common objective. This maneuver was successfully carried out by Valentinian I in 375 against the Quadi, but a similar operation in 357 was ruined by the Alamanni, who defeated the southern arm of the pincer under Barbatio.

Despite all the Roman victories, there were no permanent solutions to the problems of barbarian raids. Although the continuous violence was frustrating for local inhabitants on either side of the border and Roman soldiers, barbarian societies valued military success above all else, which tended to prompt continuous attacks. The lack of significant change in the location of the Roman borders in the third and fourth centuries suggests that the Roman defenses worked reasonably well. As a result of the constant cycle of violence, there was a slow improvement of both military systems so that the battlefield performance of the fourth-century Roman army, with its heavy infantry well supported by cavalry and missile troops, was far in advance of that of the first century AD. But the barbarians had learned much too and were more dangerous opponents in the fourth century than they had been earlier.

THE PERSIAN FRONTIER

In Europe, the Romans were clearly very different from their enemies in terms of resources, military capacity, political organization, and culture. The Persians, on the other hand, were seen by the Romans as rivals in many ways. Both empires could inflict severe damage on the other, but ultimate military defeat was much harder to achieve given the size of the two states, even after the Romans had sacked Ctesiphon or the Persians had sacked Antioch. In the sixth century, the *magister officiorum* Peter the Patrician wrote:

> It is obvious for all mankind that the Roman and the Persian Empires are just like two lamps; and it is necessary that, like the eyes, the one is brightened by the light of the other and that they do not angrily strive for each other's destruction (Diocletian fr. 13).

The frontier between Rome and Persia was very porous. Having heard rumors about Sapur II's plan to attack Mesopotamia in 359, Ammianus

Marcellinus, serving as a *protector* on the staff of the *magister militum* Ursicinus, was sent to Jovinianus in an attempt to learn about the Persian preparations. Jovinianus was a Persian noble who had been a Roman hostage in Syria as a young man and, although he had become the Persian governor of Corduene, still hoped to return to live in the Roman Empire. Jovinianus entertained Ammianus and assisted him in observing Persian activity. However, at the same time as Ammianus was spying in Persia, another Roman, Antoninus, was deserting to the Persians. As a merchant trying to escape debtors, he had little hope of being welcomed in Persia in his own right, so earned his acceptance by gathering information about Roman military dispositions, then becoming an adviser to Sapur and guiding the Persian attack.

The Sasanid dynasty ruled the Persian kingdom, which stretched from the Roman border as far as India, from a capital at Ctesiphon (close to modern Baghdad). The Sasanid king was known as the king of kings (*shahanshah*), ruling a combination of provinces and dependent kingdoms. This role as king of kings could mean carefully managing subordinates. When the son of Grumbates, king of the Chionitae, was killed at Amida in 359, Sapur's plan to bypass the city had to be abandoned and a siege instead took place to avenge the loss and placate Grumbates. Unlike the Roman Empire, the Persians had a small number of powerful and long-lived aristocratic families, often referred to only by their family names, like Suren or Karen. Although the majority of Persians were Zoroastrians, there was a significant Christian minority. Roman emperors from Constantine onward sometimes claimed to act as protectors of Christians, though this could prompt persecution in Persia. This Empire had numerous cities, minted large quantities of silver coins, and made great use of writing for administration. When Sapur I (240–272) erected a boastful inscription at Naqsh-i Rustam, he used Greek, Pahlavi, and Parthian. This inscription named officials, including Mard, the head of scribes, and Papak, the master of ceremonies. The presence of Valash son of Seleucus in this inscription and the use of Greek in some of the palace floor mosaics at Bishapur are suggestive of continuing Hellenic culture. Persian forts and cities were well defended. Zosimus describes defenses of the city at Pirisabora: "On the east side it was enclosed by a deep ditch and palisade of strong timber. Large towers stood along the ditch, from the ground up to the middle built of baked bricks bonded with asphalt, then above of baked bricks bonded with gypsum" (Zosimus 3.17.5).

Roman–Persian hostilities were dominated by sieges and field battles. Persian kings led many of campaigning armies, though they tended to watch battles rather than lead troops in combat. The core of the Persian army was regiments of mailed heavy cavalry levied from the aristocracy to supplement the royal cavalry regiment of the Immortals. These did much of the fighting, supported by levies of poor-quality infantry and more effective contingents of mercenary infantry (Daylami) and light cavalry (Huns). Some armies included elephants obtained from India, fielded at sieges at Nisibis in 350 and Amida in 359 and on the battlefield in 363 at Maranga and Sumere. Ammianus describes a Persian force near Ctesiphon in 363:

> Against the Romans, the Persians opposed ordered regiments of cataphracts in such close order that the gleam of moving bodies covered with closely fitting plates of iron dazzled the eyes of those who looked at them while the whole multitude of horses was protected by coverings of leather. The cavalry was backed up by units of infantry who, protected by oblong curved shields covered with wickerwork and raw hides, advanced in very close order. Behind these were elephants, with the appearance of walking hills (Ammianus 24.6.8).

These armies inflicted significant several battlefield defeats on the Romans, including Barbalissus in 253, and Narse's two defeats of Galerius in the same region in 296/297. But Roman forces also won many victories over the Persians. The Roman forces based in the east were well suited for these confrontations, with many regiments of heavily armored cavalry (*cataphracti* and *clibanarii*) focusing on hand-to-hand combat supported by regiments of horse archers. Roman infantry, trained, armored, and festooned with short-range missiles, provided an excellent base for the cavalry. There was a strong emphasis on rapid moves to contact to minimize the time of exposure to Persian archery, notorious for its speed of shot.

Unlike the European enemies of Rome, the Persians were very capable at siege warfare. Their logistical network was strongly developed, being able to supply the army besieging Nisibis in 337 for nine or ten weeks. This gave plenty of time to apply their sophisticated offensive siege techniques, including the use of siege towers and battering rams, tunneling, and siege ramps. The siege of Dura on the Euphrates in 256 shows these techniques. There were at least three elements to the Persian assault. One was an attack on the main gate of the city, shown by surviving burning and a large number of projectile points, many embedded in mud-brick walls in the gate area. This suggests an attempt to burn the gates supported by archers whose arrows were intended to keep the defenders' heads down. A second element was a siege mound opposite the southwest corner of the city, constructed of an earth fill between mud-brick walls. The remains of this mound are still over eight meters tall, higher than the stone walls of the city, though the Romans added height to the city wall with mud-bricks to counter the ramp as it was built. The main assault was planned to take place using a wheeled siege tower that would have approached the wall up the paved surface of the assault ramp. This paving was made of fired bricks produced in the Persian camp, clear evidence of a professional approach to siege warfare. To ease the assault, the tower to the right of the ramp was undermined to stop it enfilading the attackers on their unshielded side. There was also an assault mine, running under the ramp, dug with the intent of allowing the attackers to enter the city at the same time as the main assault started. The Romans, however, detected this and dug their own countermine. When this was fired, it destroyed the assault mine, and the surface of the ramp collapsed. A third element was a Persian mine under the city wall. The Romans also detected this and dug their own countermine. Despite the countermine, the Persians were able to fire their mine, weakening the city wall but failing to collapse this section because of a recently built thickening rampart. Although we know much about the siege, we do not know whether the city fell to attack from one of these three areas or to a separate assault, or if it surrendered.

The Persian objectives for waging war appear very different from those of the Romans. In general, Persian offensives were large-scale raids rather than attempts to conquer territory. Frequent features of these campaigns were thus the deporting of prisoners to Persia and the negotiation of ransoms from individual Roman cities in return for not sacking them. Sapur I, for example, in his inscription from Naqsh-i Rustam boasted that "we captured the emperor Valerian with our own hands and the others, the praetorian prefect and senators and officials, all those who were the leaders of that force, and we made all of them prisoners and deported them to Persis" (*Sapur Inscription* 18).

Although the Roman frontier was the biggest military commitment for the Persians, they were also forced to spend significant efforts on defending their northern frontiers in the Caucasus and on the steppe against nomad threats. Here they had similar problems to the Romans in Europe, i.e., an inability to create long-term peace. But between Rome and Persia there were usually clearly defined states of war and peace. The Roman frontier with Persia can be divided into three zones: the Caucasus, Armenia, and Mesopotamia. In the Caucasus, there were three kingdoms: Lazica in the west on the Black Sea, Iberia in the south-central Caucasus, and Albania in the east on the Caspian Sea. Both Lazica and Iberia were allied to Rome, and there was little interaction with the Persians at this point. Several members of the Iberian royal family were Roman hostages at Constantinople. Others were soldiers, such as Bacurius, who commanded a regiment of archers at Adrianople in 378, then was *dux Palestinae*, before becoming *comes domesticorum* and dying at the Battle of the Frigidus in 394. There was more interaction with the Persians in Armenia. Most Armenian territory lay in the mountain valleys of the Anti-Taurus Mountains. The difficult terrain made it difficult for the Armenian royal family, from the dynasty of the Arsacids, to dominate the various Armenian aristocratic families, of whom the most prominent were the Maimakonians, the Akruni, and the Bagratuni. Armenian society supported numerous cities, was (after the conversion of Trdat III in 314) mostly Christian, and had its own language, culture, and literature. In general, western Armenia was more influenced by Rome, eastern Armenia more by Persia. Armenian armies had good light infantry and some excellent aristocratic cavalry. Though they were not a great threat to either Rome or Persia, they were a useful ally. The result was a region that was hard for either empire to subdue, but in too important a location to ignore. Numerous campaigns followed until the region was partitioned in 387.

The main area of Roman confrontation with Persia lay in the Tigris and Euphrates valleys of Mesopotamia. The Roman defensive system here was very different from Europe because of the limited options for military movement. The problems of feeding and watering large forces in the hot climates of the Near East meant that large armies were usually confined to river valleys, particularly the Euphrates, although small groups of raiders could operate in the desert. The river valleys were blocked by fortresses or cities, with the result that sieges played a major role in most wars. With the limited routes, the need to collect supplies before campaigning, and a permeable frontier, it was almost impossible for either state to achieve strategic surprise. Although the frontier remained in the same general area, unlike in Europe there were significant changes in the manner in which the east was defended.

In the third century, Roman strategy was based on offensive campaigns in the Euphrates Valley, sometimes accompanied by supporting forces from Armenia, as in the campaigns of Galerius in 298 and Julian in 363. At the same time, there were several Persian offensives marching up the Euphrates in 252, 256, and 260. In these campaigns, the cities at Barbalissus, Callinicum, and Dura Europus were important defended points. Galerius, after an initial defeat, was successful in Mesopotamia in 296–297 and in Armenia in 298. After the capture of Nisibis in 298, Diocletian and Galerius met and negotiated a treaty with Narse (293–302). This peace extended Roman control across the Tigris, which marked the edge of Roman territory. Three cities in this new territory, Nisibis, Amida, and Singara, were heavily fortified. There then followed peace until the end of Constantine's reign, although there were campaigns in Armenia. For the next four decades, there was almost continuous warfare, in part because of the long reigns of the two rulers, Sapur II (309–379) and Constantius II (337–361). Because of Diocletian's annexation of territory, the main area of operations was now in the Tigris Valley. Amida had been briefly captured by the Persians in 336, but was soon reoccupied by the Romans and refortified. There followed one (or two) major battles at Singara (344 and/or 348) and three Persian sieges of Nisibis (337/338, 346, and 350), none of which was successful. After 350, hostilities ceased until the Persian capture of Amida in 359. Constantius' planned counterattack was abandoned because he had to deal with Julian's seizure of power, but in 363 Julian used the resources of a unified Empire to resume a strategy of offensive campaigning, leading 65,000 men down the Euphrates Valley as far as Ctesiphon.

When Julian was killed retreating from Ctesiphon, his successor Jovian was forced to give up the territory gained by Diocletian to extricate the army from Persia. He surrendered Nisibis, and the border now moved back to the Chabur River. The 363 treaty was vague about Armenia and the Caucasus, and Persian aggression continued. In Iberia, there was a division of the kingdom into pro-Roman and pro-Persian parts, but in Armenia, the Romans won a victory over the Persians at Vagabanta in 371. However, subsequent Armenian kings were unable to build consensus among their aristocracy, and in 379 the Persians appointed their own king, so dividing the kingdom. By 387, Rome and Persia had demarcated spheres of influence.

AFRICAN AND LEVANTINE FRONTIERS

In Africa, Egypt, and the Levant, the Romans were faced with a military situation similar to Europe in many ways. These frontiers were long, about 4,000 kilometers in Africa, while the Levantine frontier added a further 1,000 kilometers. The size of the region required a large allocation of imperial resources. A few cities had been imposed on the Roman-controlled edges of these regions, but within and beyond the Empire, there was still an underlying network of villages and tribes, many of them nomads subsisting on flocks of sheep and goats, though still providing Roman soldiers and paying taxes. Without clearly defined borders, a Roman urban landscape thus shaded gradually into a land without Romans. Since the steppes and deserts were unable to support large populations, defense was mostly concerned with low-intensity warfare. A late fourth-century situation shows the artificiality of describing these peoples simply as Roman or barbarian. Ammianus Marcellinus described Nubel as a king of the tribe of the Iubaleni, but he also erected an inscription at Rusguniae in Mauritania Caesariensis that describes his dedication of a church to house a part of the True Cross. This inscription also mentions Nubel's service as *praepositus* of the *equites armigeri iuniores*, a cavalry regiment in the African field army (*CIL* 8.9255). And one of his sons, Firmus, had also joined the Roman army, but had rebelled against the Romans in 373. To deal with this revolt, Valentinian I sent an army from Europe under the command of Theodosius the Elder. During the war, Nubel's family was divided, with three of his sons, Mazuca, Mascezel, and Dius, fighting with Firmus, but another, Gildo, fighting under Roman command. When Firmus revolted, he was supported by the city of Caesarea, many local churches, and at least two regiments of Roman troops. It is thus not surprising that there was no political unity in any of these frontier regions, though as in Europe occasionally strong alliances arose under talented leaders. For most of these areas, we can do little more than name some of the tribes. In the eastern area of Mauritania there were the Quinquegentiani (Five Peoples). Ammianus' account of Theodosius' campaign in this region includes the names of fourteen tribes, the Iubaleni, Tyndenses, Massinissenses, Mazices, Musones, Baiures, Cantauriani, Avastomates, Cafaves, Bavares, Caprarienses, Abanni, Isaflenses, and Iesalenses (29.5). In Numidia, near Carthage, tribes included the Bavares and the Fraxinenses, in Tripolitania and Libya the Austuriani, and in Cyrenaica the Marmaridae.

Farther east, to the south of Egypt, raids of various tribes of Blemmyes and Nubians provided an occasional threat. These societies had kings, with some spectacular royal tombs discovered at Ballana in Nubia, and made occasional use of writing. In the Levant, the Romans had alliances with many Saracen groups, so numerous that Theodoret in the fifth century mentioned "numerous tribes of Ishmael" (*Curatio* 9.14). Few of the names that we hear of in the fourth century, such as the Assanitae, can be traced into the fifth century. Although their leaders are often described as phylarchs, the term means only tribal leader and has no technical value. These alliances were most useful in terms of scouting and intelligence, though the Saracens could provide troops for the Romans, as in the 378 campaign when Queen Mavia sent some men to Thrace.

In all of these frontier regions, there were no central places or written systems of administration (despite the occasional erection of inscriptions), so the military capacities of the various peoples were limited. Logistical weaknesses meant that assembling large forces was difficult. The majority of their raiders were unarmored cavalry, though many would have ridden to battle on camels and then fought on foot. Weapons were mostly spears and knives, with swords and bows being less common. They were most dangerous when raiding, when their mobility and small numbers were assets, but in battles their lack of armor and training put them at a severe disadvantage when facing Roman troops. Finally, their abilities to undertake sieges were very limited. The Roman forces deployed along these frontiers were thus concerned mostly with intelligence and policing. An inscription from Syria erected in 334 records that,

> when Vincentius, acting as *protector* at Basia, observed that many of the farmers had been ambushed and killed by the Saracens while fetching water for themselves, he constructed a new reservoir for the water (*AE* 1948.136).

There were numerous fortifications along these borders, ranging from large fortresses holding several regiments to small towers guarded by a handful of men. These chains of defensive works were improved by all emperors and local commanders. With the size of the region to be monitored and the number of Roman troops available, it was impossible to stop all raids, but it was rare that major intervention from outside the region was needed. However, Maximian fought in Mauritania and Numidia in 297–298, and Theodosius the Elder fought in Mauritania in 373. Egypt saw operations by Galerius in 295 and by Diocletian in 297–298 and 301/302, and some troops led by the *magister militum per Orientem* Julius fought against the Saracens in the 370s.

ROMAN CIVIL WARS

Roman relations with external enemies were very different from relationships with internal enemies. When a claimant to imperial power arose, the incumbent could only accept the new emperor or fight. The motivations for men to seek imperial power for themselves varied, though a lack of confidence in the current emperor was a major factor. Embassies seeking recognition were often sent by the challenger. These attempts were rarely successful, and even when recognition was granted, they rarely lasted long. Galerius recognized Constantine I in 305, Constantius II recognized Vetranio in 350, and Theodosius I recognized Magnus Maximus in 384. In the case of Constantine and Theodosius, hostilities quickly followed, while Vetranio was soon exiled to Bithynia without fighting taking place, leading Philostorgius to suggest that Vetranio was put up as emperor by Constantius' sister to stop Magnentius capturing Illyricum. Since accepting a new emperor would encourage others, most challenges resulted in war. Another way of resolving an imperial challenge was assassination. During the late third century, several emperors were murdered by rivals, including Gallienus in 268 and Aurelian in 275, while Julian's troops feared his murder in 360. In some cases, as with the Gallic Empire in 260 or Vaballathus' acclamation in 267, it took some time for the central Empire to respond. While attempting to eliminate their rival, both rival emperors needed to maintain political support. Ignoring a rival was tantamount to accepting their legitimacy, and this was particularly true of the Gallic Empire in the 260s. The longer Maxentius controlled Rome in 307–308, the more difficult it was for Galerius to portray him as illegitimate. The dependence of the city of Rome on imported African grain meant that it was vital for the emperor controlling Rome also to control Africa. Where this was not the case, as in Julian's seizure of power in 360, the holder of Africa was able to put economic pressure on the Italian faction. Thus an expedition was launched against Africa by Constantius II from the east in 352/353, and Julian had a force ready to cross from Sicily in 360.

Campaigns usually continued until one faction's leader died. Thus the first attempt to remove Maxentius failed when Severus was abandoned by his men outside Rome in 307 and captured. After successive defeats by Licinius in 313, Maximinus Daia committed suicide at Tarsus, as did Magnentius after defeats by Constantius II. The civil war between Julian and Constantius II was stopped in its initial stages by the natural death of Constantius. Once a rival emperor was captured, he was usually executed. Constantine did not execute Licinius immediately in 324, but by 325 he had executed his rival (who was his brother-in-law) together with Licinius' son (who was also Constantine's nephew). But there were a few exceptions. Aurelian spared both Tetricus and Vaballathus, while Vetranio was exiled by Constantius II in 350. The head of a defeated emperor was usually removed and placed on a stake and either paraded around the Empire or placed over city gates. After his defeat at Nacoleia, Procopius' head was sent to Gaul, while the heads of both Magnus Maximus and Eugenius were displayed at Ravenna.

Roman strategy for fighting civil wars was very different from that for fighting barbarians. The resources available to both sides were similar, while they both had the same objective, to remove the opposing emperor. Most civil wars thus resulted in field battles. Since the effectiveness of the Roman army was roughly uniform, the larger army was more likely to win and we hear of massive recruitment programs that included large contingents of barbarians. Thus Magnentius and Magnus Maximus hired Franks and Saxons, while Licinius, Constantius II, Procopius, and Theodosius I all hired Goths. The uncertain but usually fatal prospects for the supporters of the defeated faction could make for long wars; Constantius II had to defeat Magnentius in three battles over three years, starting at Mursa in 351. These civil war battles could be very bloody, especially among the officers; Magnentius' *magister militum* Romulus fell at Mursa. Other defeated generals committed suicide, such as Andragathius in 388 and Arbogast in 394. However, persecution of a defeated faction was rarely carried out beyond its upper ranks. When Theodosius the Elder executed or mutilated troops supporting Firmus in 373, Ammianus reports that he was criticized by some contemporaries and the soldiers "deserved to have been punished more leniently." Ammianus disagreed, but he was writing in the reign of Theodosius' son (29.5.23). When the civil war was over, whoever was victorious continued to rule. In some cases, it was the challenger, as with Aurelian, Diocletian, Constantine I, and Julian.

In the initial stages of a civil war, imperial officials had to decide quickly whether to support the new emperor or to remain loyal to the old one. A wrong choice could prove fatal. In 361, Julian tried to restrict information going to Britain since he did not trust Lupicinus, who had recently led an expeditionary force to the island. Misunderstandings also occurred, and also in 361 Julian's troops were let into Sirmium when the city thought that their shouts of "Augustus" referred to the arrival of Constantius II. Naval and siege warfare were often influential. The wars between Diocletian and Carinus, Constantine and Licinius, Magnentius and Constantius II, Julian and Constantius, and Theodosius I and Magnus Maximus and then Eugenius were all between one emperor holding Italy (and sometimes Illyricum) and another holding territory in the east. The Mediterranean Sea was thus important as a means of outflanking the enemy. Constantius II built a fleet in Egypt to support his campaign in Italy against Magnentius in 351–352, then sent it against Carthage and then to Spain, while Theodosius I supported his land expedition against Magnus Maximus in Italy with a fleet in the Adriatic. Even when the conflict did not develop into an east–west confrontation, sea power was of great importance. It was not until Constantius I had built a substantial fleet that he could cross to Britain to defeat Allectus. Campaigning within the Empire often meant that cities had to be captured. Aureolus was besieged in Milan by Gallienus and then by Claudius II in 268, and Constantine I had to storm Milan and Verona before marching on Rome in 312. The Battle of Mursa in 351 was preceded by Magnentius' siege of the city, and Constantius' pursuit afterward was halted by the need to besiege Aquileia.

Since civil wars usually ended only with the death of one of the emperors involved, struggles tended to be long and bloody. The Battle of Mursa was fought between Magnentius and Constantius II on September 28, 351. Constantius was hopeful of using his cavalry superiority on the plains, while Magnentius pinned his hopes on an ambush laid in the stadium outside the city. Neither plan worked, leading to the two infantry bodies becoming locked in a bitter combat that lasted until nightfall. Zonaras, writing in the twelfth century but with access to some good source material, claimed that Constantius was reduced to tears by the losses. These were huge: 30,000 of the 80,000 men led by Constantius and 24,000 of the 36,000 men led by Magnentius (13.8). Because of the likely death toll, there were frequently last-minute negotiations and attempts to suborn troops of the other faction when two armies came face to face. We thus hear of the desertion of Carus by his troops at Margus in 284, of the collapse of Severus' army outside Rome in 306, and fears of desertion by Galerius when he approached the city soon afterward. Other defections were smaller. Silvanus and his regiment of the *schola armaturarum* abandoned Magnentius at Mursa in 351 and three of Constantius' regiments that Julian found at Sirmium in 361 initially joined him before turning back to Constantius.

The numerous civil wars of the third and fourth centuries cost the Empire much manpower. Despite their destructiveness, they were seen as an occasional internal problem. Fighting foreign enemies, on the other hand, was a duty for every Roman emperor. Emperors were sometimes lost in battle, such as when Decius was defeated by Goths at Abrittus in 251 and Valerian was captured by the Persians in 260. These defeats, like many other Roman defeats, did not have disastrous consequences. However, in one of these routine campaigns against barbarians, Valens was killed and his army mangled at Adrianople on August 9, 378.

THE BATTLE OF ADRIANOPLE, 378

In 376, the eastern emperor Valens consulted with the consistory about appeals from several groups of Goths who wished to enter the Empire. After long debate, these Goths were admitted, but two years later they defeated the Romans at Adrianople in what the contemporary historian Ammianus Marcellinus described as the worst Roman defeat since Hannibal's victory at Cannae in 216 BC. With hindsight, it is easy to suggest that allowing the Goths to settle was not a good idea, but in 376, Valens was following precedent, and the case was made that this settlement would bring both present taxpayers and future recruits. Barbarians had been settling in the Roman Empire since the first century BC, and many of these settlements had disappeared without trace. But in this settlement, when problems with supplying the settlers with food were poorly handled, armed intervention by the Romans in 376 and 377 was necessary. By 378, it was clear that this had become a war, not a settlement operation, and Valens himself arrived at the head of the imperial army to handle events in person. Additional troops were also requested from the west, and Gratian himself was reported as leading them.

By June, Valens had reached Thrace and then advanced against the Goths. In the first few days of August, the scouts who were keeping track of the Goths reported that there were only ten thousand near Adrianople. Valens set up a fortified camp outside the city. Ammianus reports a debate over whether the army should wait for the Gallic troops under Gratian, who were close, though it was unclear how long it would take them to reach the battlefield. Valens wanted to fight, hoping to destroy what he thought was an isolated part of the Gothic army. He was opposed by Victor, *magister equitum*, and others. Elsewhere, Victor is described by Ammianus as being "foresighted and careful." Valens overruled his generals.

Valens left the court behind, but marched toward the Goths in full battle kit (armor, weapons, a water bottle and rations, woolen or cotton clothing, boots). It was August, so the weather was hot, probably in the low 30°s C. As the army marched, it was preceded by scouts who now reported that the Goths had camped in a circle of wagons. When the Romans began to deploy for battle, the Goths attempted negotiations, and Richomeres, Gratian's *comes domesticorum*, volunteered to go to their camp as a hostage. It is thus possible, even at this point, that battle might have been avoided. What followed illustrates the wisdom of Roman military manuals, with their repeated recommendation to avoid battle as far as possible because of its unpredictability.

The negotiations broke down as a result of an impulsive attack by two Roman regiments, the *Scutarii* (led by the tribune Bacurius) and the *Sagittarii* (Cassio), possibly drawn into combat through their eager skirmishing. As these two regiments engaged, other Roman units were drawn into contact along the main battle line, with infantry on the Roman left flank soon advancing as far as the Gothic wagons. Even at this point, though the battle had started prematurely, there was no particular cause for concern.

However, it suddenly became apparent that the Roman scouting had missed some of the Goth cavalry who now arrived behind the Roman left flank, striking the Roman battle line, which was already engaged to its front. There was a confused period of heavy fighting, followed by a Roman withdrawal in serious disorder. Even at this stage, however, we hear of the brigade of *Lanciarii* and *Mattiarii*, both *legiones palatinae*, fighting well. When the troops around Valens needed reinforcing, Victor went to bring the reserves up to assist the emperor. In the confusion, they had already been committed elsewhere. Valens took refuge in a farmhouse, still fighting hard. The Goths were aware only of the fierce resistance here, so fired the building. Although some of the emperor's bodyguards escaped, the emperor died and his body was never recovered. Fighting continued, and the battle was only brought to a conclusion by nightfall.

It was a disaster. The Roman casualties were high, but unknown with Ammianus claiming that "barely a third of the army escaped" (31.13.18). He also recorded the fallen officer, probably using an official casualty report, counting thirty-five tribunes as well as Trajan, *magister militum*; Sebastianus, *magister peditum*; Valerian, *tribunus stabuli*; and Equitius, *cura palatii*. What went wrong? There was nothing about the Gothic army that the Romans had not seen before. There may have been some complacency, but this was not a revolution in military science. There is no simple answer, only a series of errors and mishaps. These included Valens' decision not to wait for Gratian, the misreporting of the numbers of Goths, the premature opening of the battle, the arrival of the Gothic cavalry at the wrong place and time, the premature use of the reserves, and the death of Valens. None of these was catastrophic in itself, but it took all of these events together to make the disaster. Thus the battle itself does not suggest a structural deficiency in the army, a conclusion supported by the lack of subsequent changes. But the consequences of Adrianople were far greater than the battlefield defeat. Valens' death left the nineteen-year-old Gratian as emperor over the whole Empire. Following debate in the consistory, he withdrew to the west rather than continuing to advance against the Goths. Although Theodosius was soon appointed emperor for the east, he chose to settle the Goths quickly on generous terms rather than prolong campaigning in an attempt to destroy them. Both decisions would have been difficult to make. Even if settling the Goths was not the best course of action, it was what Valens had planned to do in 376. The subsequent war with Magnus Maximus in Italy, only five years after the settlement of the Goths, could not have been predicted. This helped build a sense of Gothic unity, strengthened by the war against Eugenius in 394. And then Theodosius died in 395, leaving two young emperors, a divided empire, and a Gothic settlement that had been given a sense of identity. It was only then that the true impact of Adrianople started to become clear.

FURTHER READING

The history of Ammianus Marcellinus, an officer who had fought in Gaul and on the eastern frontier in the middle of the fourth century, is invaluable, particularly for its detailed accounts of Julian's expedition against Persia, as well as the Battles of Strasbourg and Adrianople. Much of our knowledge of the organization of the army is based on the *Notitia Dignitatum*, compiled at some point after 395. This lists the army's regiments and for border troops their bases, together with the commands to which they are assigned. The *Notitia* is a challenging document to understand, though good introductions are Brennan, P., "The User's Guide to the *Notitia Dignitatum*: The Case of the *Dux Armeniae* (ND Or. 38)," *Antichthon* 32 (1998), 34–49, and Kulikowski, M., "The *Notitia Dignitatum* as a Historical Source," *Historia* 49 (2000), 358–377.

Most modern scholarship on the Late Roman army suggests that it was an efficient organization, a change from half a century ago. Few works cover the whole of this period, though for the late fourth century, see Elton, H., *Warfare in Roman Europe: AD 350–425* (Oxford, 1996), Nicasie, M., *Twilight of Empire* (Amsterdam,

1998), and the essays on the Late Empire in Sabin, P., van Wees, H., and Whitby, Michael, eds., *Cambridge History of Greek and Roman Warfare* (Cambridge, 2007) are also valuable. For discussions of Roman foreign policy (though these are often heavily concerned with individual campaigns rather than theory), Blockley, R. C., *East Roman Foreign Policy* (Leeds, 1992) and Errington, R. M., *Roman Imperial Policy from Julian to Theodosius* (Chapel Hill, 2006). On diplomacy, see Nechaeva, E., *Embassies – Negotiations – Gifts: Systems of East Roman Diplomacy in Late Antiquity* (Stuttgart, 2014). On civil war, there is not much in English, though see Wardman, A. E., "Usurpations and Internal Conflicts in the Fourth Century AD," *Historia* 33 (1984), 220–237.

Numbers are discussed in Coello, T., *Unit Sizes in the Late Roman Army*, BAR S645 (Oxford, 1996). For recruiting, see Speidel, M. P., "Raising New Units for the Late Roman Army: *Auxilia Palatina*," *Dumbarton Oaks Papers* 50 (1996), 163–170, Tomlin, R. S. O., "*Seniores-Iuniores* in the Late Roman Field Army," *American Journal of Philology* 93 (1972), 253–278, and Zuckerman, C., "Two Reforms of the 370s: Recruiting Soldiers and Senators in the Divided Empire," *Revue des Etudes Byzantines* 56 (1998), 79–140.

On barbarians, for the Rhine, see Drinkwater, J. F., *The Alamanni and Rome* (Oxford, 2007); and for the Danube, see Batty, R., *Rome and the Nomads* (Oxford, 2007). For Persia, see Dodgson, M. and Lieu, S. *The Roman Eastern Frontier and the Persian Wars, 226–363* (London, 1991), Greatrex, G. and Lieu, S. N. C., *The Roman Eastern Frontier and the Persian Wars, AD 363–630* (London, 2002), Frye, R., *A History of Ancient Iran* (Munich, 1984), and Dignas, B. and Winter, E., *Rome and Persia in Late Antiquity* (Cambridge, 2007). On eastern frontier warfare, Coulston, J. C., "Roman, Parthian and Sassanid Tactical Developments," in Freeman, P. and Kennedy, D., eds., *The Defence of the Roman and Byzantine East, BAR S297* (Oxford, 1986), 59–75 and Charles, M. B., "The Rise of the Sassanian Elephant Corps: Elephants and the Later Roman Empire," *Iranica Antiqua* 42 (2007), 301–346. For Dura, see James, S., *Excavations at Dura-Europos Final Report VII: The Arms and Armour and Other Military Equipment* (London, 2004) and James, S., "Stratagems, Combat and 'Chemical Warfare' in the Siege Mines of Dura-Europos," *American Journal of Archaeology* 115 (2011), 69–101.

4

THE LATE FOURTH CENTURY, 363–395

Julian's death on campaign in Persia marked the end of the House of Constantine. The following half-century was dominated by the arrival of the Huns, the entrance of numerous Goths into the Roman Empire, and the inability of the Romans to defeat or assimilate the Goths. At the same time, the failure of imperial attempts to create ecclesiastical unity continued and eventually resulted in the establishment of the Nicene Creed as orthodoxy. This period is dominated by the rule of Valentinian, Valens, and Theodosius, three capable warriors with strong personalities. Despite their marked abilities, they constantly clashed with their subordinates, a similarly capable group. Julian died from his wounds during the night of June 26, leaving the Roman army leaderless as it was withdrawing from Persia.

JOVIAN (363–364)

There was little time for musing or debate, though there was enough of this that Ammianus (who was part of the expedition) identified two factions, one of the Gallic army, i.e., Julian's people, and one of the court of Constantius II. The eastern praetorian prefect Saturninus Secundus Salutius, famous for his incorruptibility, found favor, but he refused the position. Suddenly, again according to Ammianus, following some confusion and to the surprise of the council, Jovian was acclaimed as Augustus on June 27, 363. Flavius Jovianus was born in 331, of a military family, and had served as a *protector domesticus* under Constantius II and Julian. Jovian was Christian and Salutius was a pagan, but there is no mention of these facts being raised, suggesting that continuing Julian's pagan practices was not considered a priority.

As emperor, Jovian's first task was to extract the army from Persia as rapidly as possible. He therefore agreed to a thirty-year peace with the Persians, giving up three of the five satrapies acquired by Diocletian, i.e., Arzanene, Zabdicene, and Corduene, as well as Moxoene, Rehimene, and fifteen border fortresses. Singara and Nisibis were evacuated and given to the Persians. The blood shed for Nisibis during three sieges made this a decision that sparked outrage among contemporaries, including the historian Ammianus, who described it as "ignoble." Jovian also promised not to assist the Armenian king Arsak III against the Persians. Once he had made this unpopular peace with the Persians, Jovian led the army out of Mesopotamia. Despite the Roman expressions of outrage, the peace was remarkably successful. It was not until the early years of the sixth century that there was again sustained warfare between Romans and Persians in Mesopotamia, a marked contrast to the third and early to mid-fourth centuries.

By the end of September, Jovian had reached Edessa. The first edict preserved from his reign concerned the distance to which soldiers could be sent to transport straw, modifying a law of Julian, but also suggesting a cessation of the immediate military crisis. Favor to Christians and imperial finances coincided in another edict, which reclaimed the estates to the *res privata* that Julian had given to pagan temples. It was also at Edessa that Jovian received various bishops who had rushed to meet him, though he hoped to avoid getting entangled in disputes between Christian factions. According to the historian Socrates, after receiving a petition from the Macedonians, Jovian said that "I hate contentiousness, but love and honour those rushing to unanimity" (Socrates 3.25.4). Nonetheless, he was faced with immediate problems on arriving at Antioch, where he found three bishops claiming the see, the Homoian Euzoius, and two Nicenes Meletius and Paulinus, divided over Apollinarianism (the idea that Christ had a human body and a divine mind). Jovian backed Meletius, who had the largest number of supporters. After spending the autumn at Antioch, he buried Julian at Tarsus and was on the way to Constantinople when he died of natural causes at Dadastana in central Anatolia on February 17, 364; he was buried in Constantinople.

VALENTINIAN AND VALENS: THE BEGINNING

After Jovian's death, the army continued to march for a few more days until it reached Nicaea, where the officers again debated, though in a calmer situation than the council in Persia eight months earlier. Ammianus mentioned the involvement of both civil and military officials in the discussions over whom to appoint. Salutius' name was not discussed, but first Equitius and Januarius were suggested, then rejected, before finally Valentinian's name met with approval. Valentinian was a forty-two-year-old Pannonian from a military family (his father had served as *comes Africae* and *comes Britanniarum*), who had fought in Gaul under Julian and was currently tribune of the *Schola Secunda Scutariorum*. He was absent from the army, and it was not until February 26 that he was acclaimed in Nicaea. Although Julian had ruled the empire alone, it was clear that Valentinian needed a colleague. When Valentinian consulted the consistory, "when they were all silent, Dagalaifus who was at that time *magister equitum*, answered boldly, 'if you love your relatives', he said, 'best of emperors, you have a brother; if you love the state, seek another to wear the purple'" (Ammianus 26.4.1). A few weeks later, Valentinian acclaimed his younger brother, the thirty-six-year-old *protector* Valens, as Augustus on March 28, 364, at the Hebdomon in Constantinople.

The two brothers then marched into the Balkans as far as Sirmium, where they split the empire between them, with Valentinian taking the western part of the Empire, i.e., the prefecture of the Gauls and the prefecture of Italy, Illyricum, and Africa, while Valens took the prefecture of the Orient. This division was based on seniority and did not match the brothers' linguistic skills. Valens' Greek at this point was limited, whereas Valentinian was fluent. The brothers also redivided the army into two parts, allowing many of the troops that Julian had brought from Gaul to be returned. The brothers turned to men that they knew to replace some of Julian's appointments. This resulted in the promotion of many Pannonians to high ranks, such as Equitius, also a tribune of the *scholae* but soon promoted to *comes*, and Leo, who had become *magister officiorum* by 371. However, there were too many posts to be filled for the whole government to be composed of Pannonians, leaving plentiful opportunities for others. One of these was Petronius Probus, from Verona in northern Italy. He was appointed in 364 as praetorian prefect of Illyricum, now separated from Italy and Africa. Probus was the most successful of the senatorial aristocracy of Rome in the late fourth century, holding the consulate in 371 and being praetorian prefect four times. There were still ways in which the old families could contribute to the Empire, but they did involve adapting to the Empire's patterns, not the other way around. Another major organizational change was the carving of a new diocese of Aegyptus out of Oriens, administered by a *praefectus Augustalis*.

The two brothers now moved to their respective parts of the Empire. They never met in person again, but they worked closely together on many matters, especially financial affairs. Julian's order to make crown gold voluntary was revoked at once. Whereas Julian had been an advocate of local

Figure 10. Latin letter of Valens to Eutropius ca. 371 regarding civic estates, Curetes Street in Ephesus (Photo: author).

autonomy, the emphasis changed to a greater use of imperial officials to replace local tax collectors. An Italian inscription shows provincial governors being ordered to compare tax rolls (*breviaria*) with archive records, while a new census in Asiana and Pontica in 371 resulted in a series of detailed inscribed tax records from these dioceses. At the same time, in response to a delegation from Ephesus, Valens wrote to Eutropius, proconsul of Asia, noting that the imperial estates in the province of Asia alone contained 6,736.5 *iuga* of arable land and 703 *iuga* of *agri deserti* (tax exempt land), which between them produced an income of 11,000 *solidi*. This Latin inscription was given a prominent place in Ephesus on Curetes Street. (Figure 10). Julian had restored the recently confiscated city estates to their cities; his edict was now reversed, though in 371 a third of the revenue of these estates was reassigned to the cities specifically for use on urban defenses. From the perspective of the emperors, this reduced the ability of local taxpayers to influence local officials and thus increased imperial income, while also removing responsibilities from city councils that were often understrength and functioning poorly. Cities probably described it in terms of imperial interference, like the new appointment structure of the Defender of the Community (*defensor civitatis*), an office already in existence in the early fourth century. They were now selected for each city by the praetorian prefect from retired imperial officials, with the duty of providing swift justice for the city's poor as well as assisting in forwarding cases to be heard by the provincial governor. The office may not have always worked well, but is a striking example of the imperial willingness to listen to their subjects.

At an imperial level, the mints of the Empire were reorganized so that most gold coins were produced by the mint accompanying the emperor, though gold coins continued to be minted at praetorian capitals. There was a growing emphasis by the state and by those who could enforce their demands on payment in gold, and from the 370s the *collatio lustralis* appears to have been collected in gold only, as opposed to the gold and silver levied before. The increasing demand for state payments to be made in gold (as inflation resistant) had already been eased by Constantine's seizure of the treasuries of pagan temples. Then, during the mid-fourth century, the Empire began to mine vast quantities of gold from a new source, probably in the Caucasus, with dramatically higher platinum levels than the existing gold in circulation. The combination of slightly more effective tax collection combined with an increase in imperial gold production resulted in an Empire which from the mid-fourth century was far richer than the Empire of the mid-third century. In this Empire, gold was far more widely available than in previous centuries and used for more transactions.

There were significant changes in the dignitaries granted to officers, especially military officers. Ammianus contrasted this period with Constantius II's reign, when "no one was promoted to *dux* with the clarissimate. They were, as I myself remember, *perfectissimi*" (21.16.2). The rank of *illustris* was widened to include prefects and *magistri militum*, as well as the *magister officiorum*, the *comites rei privatae, sacrarum largitionum, domesticorum*, and the *quaestor*. There was also a continued expansion of the senatorial order, to the discomfort of the Senate in Rome. This expansion was also of significance to city councils, since every man promoted to the Senate of Rome or Constantinople was one fewer *curialis* for his hometown. Libanius in Antioch complained of Constantinople running to fat on the sweat of provincial cities, though at the same time he was prepared to support his pupils and friends in their attempts to gain such promotions for themselves. These complaints of too rapid promotions of unsuitable men seem more likely to reflect Ammianus' and Libanius' prejudice than reality. For other commentators, they could be seen as signs of social mobility and a world of opportunity. And for every senator bemoaning the dilution of his order, there was an imperial official pleased at being promoted because of his hard work. The rewards of promotion could be huge, and help explain why competition between aristocrats was often so intense

VALENTINIAN I (364–375)

After leaving Sirmium in 364, Valentinian moved to Italy, where he stayed for a year before moving to Gaul. He had a son, Gratian, from an earlier marriage, but soon after his arrival in Italy married Justina, wife of the former emperor Magnentius and a relative of Constantine. Here he found a church that was almost entirely Nicene, though there were occasional problems such as the continuing presence of Donatists in Africa. Valentinian tried to avoid involvement in ecclesiastical matters and when approached at the very start of his reign about a Church Council by Hypatian, bishop of Heraclea, he replied, "Since I am one of the laity, it is not right for me to meddle in these things" (Sozomen 6.7.2). Such a detached position was rapidly challenged by riots in Rome between supporters of Ursinus and Damasus, both candidates for the bishop of Rome following the death of Liberius in 366. After numerous deaths, Valentinian banned Ursinus and his supporters from the city. Imperial tolerance made many Christians happy, at least until it appeared that tolerance really did mean tolerance for all, including Auxentius, the Homoian bishop of Milan. While prepared to investigate and then reject Nicene accusations that Auxentius was an Arian, Valentinian ignored a Church Council that Damasus had summoned to condemn Auxentius. When Auxentius died in 374, a new bishop of Milan was elected, Ambrose, who was at that point not a priest, but the *consularis* of Aemilia et Liguria. In ability, persistence, and belief in the Nicene Creed, he matched Athanasius, but he was also an imperial aristocrat, son of one of Constans' praetorian prefects in Gaul. Not every bishop was from this sort of family, but an increasing number were, while those of lesser status were a loss to their cities' councils. Ambrose was to be a major figure in both church and imperial politics for a quarter of a century, though his acclamation, in which he was rushed through the clerical grades, was a clear violation of Canon 9 of Nicaea. Nonetheless, his appointment was an important stage in moving imperial theology from a Homoian to a Nicene stance.

Secular affairs were similarly complex. In 363, Leptis Magna in Tripolitania had appealed to the *comes Africae* Romanus for help against the raids of the Austuriani. When Romanus arrived from Carthage with his troops, he demanded supplies and four thousand camels from the city. Since four thousand camels would be able to carry the rations for ten thousand infantry for four months, Romanus' demands were the right size to carry the supplies for a small force for a summer's campaigning. However, this was too much for Leptis, particularly after the city's territory had been devastated by the Austuriani. When the camels were not forthcoming, Romanus refused to intervene. After Valentinian's accession in 364, a provincial delegation bearing golden statues from Tripolitania was sent to the emperor in Italy. The delegates also complained about Romanus, who in their telling had failed to defend their territory. As soon as Romanus heard of this, he immediately sent a message to Remigius, the *magister officiorum*, but more importantly, a relative, who then wrote a report for Valentinian. Faced with two contradictory versions, Valentinian promised an investigation. The emperor's problem was in knowing what really happened, and for this his own man was needed. This investigation had not yet begun when a second attack followed by the Austuriani on Leptis Magna and Oea, and further reports were sent to Valentinian, by now in Gaul. Valentinian deputed the *tribunus et notarius* Palladius, already on his way to Africa to pay soldiers, to investigate. Palladius investigated and reported that there were no grounds for the complaint. But when Palladius returned to Trier, he found a second Tripolitanian delegation had arrived with further complaints and was sent back to investigate further, this time in the company of Dracontius, the *vicarius Africae*. Since the complaints still appeared unfounded, once Palladius returned to court, several members of a second provincial delegation were executed together with the provincial governor Ruricius, who had submitted a false report.

Romanus was later dismissed and arrested by Theodosius the Elder in 373. At this point, an investigation into Romanus' estate produced documents showing that he had colluded with Palladius. When Palladius was summoned to court, he committed suicide. Once Romanus was dismissed and Palladius dead, new details began to leak out. Gratian, by now emperor, ordered further investigation by the *vicarius Africae* and the *proconsul Africae* that revealed that Romanus had persuaded several citizens to make false statements. At a subsequent enquiry at the imperial court in Milan in 377, Romanus produced witnesses whose evidence led to him being acquitted. Almost all of our evidence for the affair comes from Ammianus, who was no friend of Romanus, though Zosimus also notes the rapacity of Romanus. How guilty Romanus really was is by now unknowable. The complexity of relationships with subordinates is similar to that of finance; terms such as severity or efficiency often depend as much on the writer as the actions being described.

By late 365, Valentinian had moved to Gaul. He fell seriously ill at Paris in 367 and there were fears that he would die. Ammianus' account shows a court divided, with Rusticus Julianus, *magister memoriae*, and Severus, *magister peditum*, both being canvassed as possible successors. Following his recovery, Valentinian had his son Gratian (b. 359) from his first marriage acclaimed as Augustus on August 24, 367. There was continued fighting on the Rhine, and Britain came under attack from Picts, Scotti, and Attacotti. Here, Valentinian sent the *comes* Theodosius the Elder, who restored order as well as creating a new province of Valentia in western Britain. When Theodosius returned to Gaul, he was promoted to *magister equitum*. During 368, Valentinian transferred troops from Illyricum and Italy to Gaul and began a series of campaigns against the Alamanni. He crossed the Rhine himself, accompanied by Gratian, and defeated some Alamanni at Solicinium. Here, he was ambushed while scouting before the battle, and though he escaped, the *cubicularius* carrying his helmet was lost, along with the imperial helmet. In 369, there was some fighting against Saxon raiders in northern Gaul, and preparations were made for a major campaign in 370, involving an attack by Valentinian across the upper Rhine, a second Roman expedition launched from Raetia, and an allied force of Burgundians entering Alamannia from the east. Although these elaborate preparations were upset by another Saxon attack from the north, requiring the diversion of Roman troops and the cancelation of the northern part of the operation, the southern arm of the attack led by Theodosius the Elder was successful. Prisoners taken were settled in northern Italy. In 372, Valentinian returned to the offensive, crossing the Rhine again and unsuccessfully trying to capture the stubborn Alamannic king, Macrianus. Finally, in 374 he made peace with Macrianus.

Valentinian was a dedicated emperor who took much of the ruling of the Empire on himself. He was a very intense individual and Ammianus reported that the emperor had a pair of bears named Goldflake and Innocence kept in cages near his bedroom. Despite his fierceness, Valentinian could be challenged. When in the late 360s a senatorial delegation requested that senators should not be tortured, the delegates' request was heard in the consistory. Valentinian denied that he permitted torture, but was contradicted by the *quaestor* Eupraxius. By 374, Eupraxius had been appointed urban prefect of Rome, so his career did not suffer from his frankness. This request emerged from an investigation at Rome when an ex-*vicarius* named Chilo claimed that an attempt had been made to poison him and his wife; as the investigation proceeded, claims of magic were made, and several senators were executed and exiled. Valens was similarly harsh when it came to accusations of magic. In other cases, Valentinian could be very mild, as shown by the scolding delivered to Festus, proconsul of Africa in 367, whose office had been imitating the letters used by the imperial chancery. Valentinian simply ordered this practice to stop. But not all problems were resolved as simply. In 373, the African aristocrat Firmus was accused by the *comes Africae* Romanus of murdering Zammac, Firmus' brother. Romanus sent reports to this effect to the court, while Firmus tried to present his point of view, but it was blocked by Remigius, the *magister officiorum*. With no hope of being able to present to Valentinian, Firmus revolted; the *magister equitum* Theodosius was sent to Africa. Although Firmus attempted to negotiate, Theodosius pursued him aggressively, and Firmus committed suicide in 374. Our main source for this is Ammianus, writing during the reign of Theodosius' son, the emperor Theodosius I (379–395). He treated Theodosius generously, perhaps using a panegyric as a source, but whether Firmus had really killed his own brother remains unclear. What is easier to understand is the difficulty for the emperor of finding out what was happening, particularly if his own officials were keeping information from him.

There was a second consequence of these accusations against Firmus. The withdrawal of troops for Theodosius' expedition encouraged the Quadi and Sarmatians to begin raiding across the Danube in 374. Troops were now moved from Gaul to Pannonia, while Valentinian himself arrived in spring 375. He made peace with the Sarmatians before crossing the Danube by pontoon bridge to attack the Quadi. When the Quadi sued for peace, their envoys were admitted to a meeting of the consistory at Brigetio. In the course of their justifying their actions, Valentinian, in Ammianus' words "overwhelmed by a violent anger" (30.6.3), was struck by an attack of apoplexy. He was hurriedly rushed from the room but soon died, aged only fifty-four, on November 17, 375. Valentinian's reign was relatively free from external and internal challenges, certainly different from that of his brother, though like his brother Valens he was said to be greedy and cruel. He was an active emperor, but a remote figure, respected rather than loved.

VALENS (364–378)

After leaving his brother at Sirmium, Valens returned to Constantinople by December 364. Here, he was warned of Gothic hostility and began preparations for a campaign on the Lower Danube, sending troops back from the eastern frontier to Thrace. However, he himself left Constantinople in the late summer of 365 and had reached Caesarea in Cappadocia by October. As some of Valens' troops passed through Constantinople on their way to the Danube, Julian's distant relative Procopius persuaded them to acclaim him emperor on September 28, 365. Procopius had fought in the Persian campaign of 363 and was well known to the army; born at Corycus in Cilicia, he spoke excellent Greek, but, more importantly, represented the House of Constantine. Thrace soon fell under his control and with it the rest of the troops that Valens had been assembling for the Gothic campaign; he also summoned allies from the Goths and other barbarians beyond the Danube. The recently promoted *comes per Illyricum* Equitius blocked the passes leading westward, confirming his loyalty to Valentinian, who promptly promoted him further to *magister militum per Illyricum*. Procopius then crossed into Anatolia and persuaded other troops of Valens to fight for him. Valens, moving back from Cappadocia, was able to confine Procopius to western Anatolia until the rest of his army arrived from the eastern border, but could not prevent the fall of Nicaea and Cyzicus to Procopius. Procopius could not sustain his early success and was now faced with enemies on two fronts, Equitius in Thrace and Valens in Anatolia. Once the main body of Valens' troops arrived, he swiftly defeated Procopius at Nacoleia, after which the challenger was captured and executed on May 27, then his severed head sent to Valentinian. Following Procopius' death, his relative Marcellus seized the purple in Thrace, hoping for Gothic support, but he too was soon captured and executed. The walls of Chalcedon were partially demolished because the population had jeered at Valens and called him a *"sabaiarius"* (beer drinker). The stones were taken across the straits to Constantinople and used to build the baths called Constantinianae. Valens also built the major aqueduct for the city which still bears his name, another sign of the spectacular growth of the city.

Unlike in the west, Valens faced a complex religious situation immediately. The decades after Nicaea had resulted in several different Christian factions emerging. The dominant group was the Homoians, who had been supported by Constantius II, and were strongest in Constantinople and Antioch. They were usually described as Arians by their opponents in fourth-century and later writings, though they would not have used this term for themselves. The two other major eastern groups, the Nicenes, with strength in Cappadocia and Alexandria, and the Homoiousians, mostly located in Constantinople and western Anatolia, were less strong. Valens, like Constantius II, was a Homoian. He is harshly treated by most Christian writers because of the eventual victory of Nicene Christianity in the east. These writers sometimes saw Valens' death at Adrianople as God's punishment, but during his reign this was all unforeseeable. At first, Valens restored a number of bishops who had been exiled, but in an attempt to bring some order to the church he reexiled those bishops who had been exiled by Constantius and restored by Julian, including Meletius of Antioch. An exception was made for the Nicene Athanasius, allowing him to remain in post, probably for fear of provoking rioting in Alexandria. However, after the death of Athanasius in 373, Valens imposed a Homoian bishop Lucius on Alexandria, though force had to be used.

From 372, Valens was resident in Antioch in Syria, living in the huge palace complex on an island in the River Orontes on the northern side of the city. Malalas claimed that Valens was so enchanted by Antioch that he embarked on a series of major construction projects, including a rebuilding of the Forum, which was decorated with a large column topped with a statue of Valentinian. Within this vast complex, the business of government continued as usual. We thus have an imperial response to Leontius, the *consularis* of Phoenice, confirming that the *collatio lustralis* was to be paid by all merchants, apparently canceling an earlier ruling that collectors of murex (the Latin, delightfully, is *conchylioleguli*) were to be exempt. Other aspects of government were less formal:

> Between the palace and the river lies a road leading to the fields in the suburbs which was used by those coming out of the city's gates. Proceeding along this, the godly Aphraates was going to the military parade ground, to carry out the care of serving his divine flock. The emperor looking down from a gallery in the palace saw him going by, a goat hair cloak thrown over his shoulder and though aged, walking vigorously. When someone said that this was Aphraates on whom much of the city was hanging, [Valens] said to him "Where are you going? Tell us" (Theodoret, *HE* 4.26.2–3).

Even if the candor with which Aphraates answered Valens was exaggerated by Theodoret, Romans wanted to believe in the accessibility of the emperor to their holy men. More often, however, it was sordid events that took up the emperor's time. In the course of a financial investigation, a certain Palladius claimed that three men, Fidusius, Pergamius, and Irenaeus, had used divination to find out who was to succeed Valens. Fidusius was arrested and admitted the crime, as well as implicating some others, including Euserius *vicarius Asiae*. Valens was outraged and the investigations continued, with some of the victims being tortured. Even Ammianus (who was in Antioch at this point) is forced to admit that there may have been something to Valens' concern, citing an attack by one of the *Scutarii* when Valens was napping after lunch in the hills near Antioch. Living in Antioch also forced Valens to address the problem of the multiple competing bishops, all of whom claimed legitimacy. He confirmed Euzoius, left alone the Nicene Paulinus (recognized in Alexandria and the west, though not accepted elsewhere in the east), and expelled Meletius, whose Nicene theology was closer in alignment with the more recent Cappadocian readings of Nicaea than that of Paulinus. The decision was one based on a desire for peace, not the creation of a single orthodoxy.

Before he reached Antioch, however, Valens continued the campaign against the Goths, which had been aborted by Procopius' seizure of imperial power. In 367, he crossed the Danube via a pontoon bridge, then forced the Goths into the hills. In 368, campaigning was impossible because of floods but in 369 Valens crossed the Danube again. The Goths under Athanaric again avoided battle and sued for peace. Valens and Athanaric finally met on boats in the middle of the Danube, then Valens headed east. He arrived in

Antioch in spring 370 and spent most of the next seven years there. Conflict with the Persians now took place entirely in Armenia and the Caucasus, unlike earlier in the fourth century when it was mostly in Mesopotamia. Persian aggression since the death of Julian had resulted in the Persian replacement of the Roman-appointed king of Iberia, Sauromaces, by his cousin Aspacures. At the same time, the Armenian king Arsak had surrendered to Sapur in 368 and his son Pap fled to the Romans. In 369, Valens sent troops to restore Pap to Armenia and Sauromaces to Iberia. At first, events turned out well for the Romans as Aspacures and Sauromaces agreed to divide Iberia between themselves and deep in Armenia a Roman force won a battle against the Persians at Vagabanta in 371. After this, an armistice was agreed and Pap placed on the Armenian throne. But when Pap was suspected of giving his allegiance to Sapur, he was summoned to the emperor at Antioch. After a period of detention at Tarsus, he escaped captivity and fled to his kingdom, pursued by Roman troops. Although it seemed that good relations could be restored, at a Roman banquet in 374 Pap was assassinated and replaced by Varazdat (374–377). With the removal of Pap, trusted by neither Rome nor Persia, an intense series of negotiations followed. These were abandoned when Varazdat was deposed by Manuel Mamikonian in 377; he appealed to Valens, while Manuel appealed to Sapur. Valens began preparations for war, but was soon distracted by events in Thrace.

THE ARRIVAL OF THE GOTHS

When Valentinian died, there were already two *Augusti*, his son Gratian, aged sixteen, in Trier, and his brother Valens in Antioch. Nonetheless, the generals with the army at Brigetio, led by Equitius, *magister militum per Illyricum*, and Merobaudes, *magister peditum*, acclaimed Flavius Valentinian II (375–392), Gratian's four-year-old half-brother, as Augustus on November 22. This supposedly protected the young Valentinian by stopping other soldiers from acclaiming a different candidate, but it may also suggest some discomfort by the generals with the idea of Gratian as emperor. At the same time, there was a settling of scores among Valentinian's generals, and orders were sent to Carthage to execute Theodosius. Since Theodosius' son was soon to become emperor, our primary sources are understandably reticent about his death. However, Merobaudes was later instrumental in the final acquittal of Romanus, who had earlier been arrested by Theodosius. Theodosius thus happened to be away from court at a critical moment and was eliminated by a rival. Valentinian's body was sent to Constantinople to be buried in the Church of the Holy Apostles, though it did not reach the city until December 28, 376. The fifth-century historian Zosimus claimed that the western Empire was then divided between the two emperors, with Valentinian II ruling the prefecture of Italy, Africa, and Illyricum, while Gratian was in charge of Gaul. Since Valentinian was aged only four, any such division was nominal at this point, and his Empire was ruled by Gratian. Despite Valentinian's youth, however, Gratian included him in the imperial college immediately and coins were issued in his name. With Gratian now appointing imperial officials, the extra opportunities for Pannonians provided by Valentinian now went elsewhere, to Gauls and to the Roman senatorial aristocracy. Thus Gratian rewarded his childhood tutor Ausonius. He had already had a successful career, becoming *quaestor* under Valentinian, but by 377 was Gallic prefect and by 378 held a joint prefecture over Gaul, Italy, and Africa and then held the consulate in 379. Ausonius' son Hesperius held both offices with his father, then continued to hold the Italian prefecture after his father retired in 379. The aristocracy of Rome benefited too, in particular from better communication with imperial officials that came from a greater engagement with the imperial court. Nonetheless, Gratian remained in Gaul until 378, usually at Trier, concerned like all fourth-century emperors with the Franks and Alamanni

Unlike the Rhine, the strategic situation on the Danube, which had remained relatively constant since the late third century, now began to change rapidly. For some years now, the Romans on the Danube had been hearing reports of the arrival of a new barbarian people, the Huns. As the Huns entered the Danube basin, they came into contact with the Goths. Some Goths such as Athanaric and his followers fled, some resisted, others submitted to the Huns. Then in 376 several groups of Goths led by Fritigern requested permission to cross the Danube:

> The Romans stationed on the river bank said that they could do nothing without the decision of the Emperor. When this report was brought to the Emperor, there was much discussion, and after many opinions had been aired on both sides in the imperial council, the proposal seemed good to the Emperor (Eunapius fr.42).

Valens hoped to settle the new immigrants peacefully and use them as recruits for the army, following the practice of numerous earlier emperors. At the same time, other Goths were refused permission to enter the Empire. The new arrivals were disarmed and supplied by the Romans, but plans to settle them were disrupted by the incompetence and greed of some Roman officials. They may have been overwhelmed by the numbers, estimated by Eunapius at two hundred thousand. These difficulties led to outbreaks of violence and, as the Romans began to lose control, more Goths crossed the Danube. Following a bungled attempt to murder Fritigern, the *comes rei militaris* Lupicinus was defeated outside Marcianopolis. As the violence spread in late 376, Valens sent additional troops while Gratian also sent western soldiers to Thrace under the *comes domesticorum* Richomeres. Fighting continued in 377 when the combined Roman armies under Richomeres fought an inconclusive battle at Ad Salices. Although at the start of winter of 377 the Romans had forced the Goths into Scythia, they were unable to maintain the blockade and had to withdraw south behind the Haemus Mountains.

The two emperors then planned a joint campaign in 378 against the Goths, leaving Trier and Antioch with the intent of fighting in Thrace. As Gratian began to march eastwards, the withdrawal of troops from the Rhine led to an attack by an Alamannic confederation led by King Priarius. Gratian turned back, defeated the barbarians at the Battle of Argentaria before crossing the Rhine and forcing the Alamanni to submit. Delayed by this victory, Gratian then continued his march east, reaching Sirmium in August, then pressing on to Castra Martis. By now, Valens had left the eastern frontier and had arrived in Thrace in June with reinforcements, reaching Adrianople. Then Richomeres arrived with a letter from Gratian, advising Valens to wait for his arrival. Castra Martis to Adrianople is some 400 kilometers or just over three weeks of hard marching. Valens summoned the consistory, and though some advised fighting, others advised waiting. Motivated by a desire to win his own victory before the recently victorious Gratian arrived, and perhaps misled by poor intelligence, Valens engaged the united Goths at Adrianople on August 9, 378. A disastrous defeat followed, with the destruction of much of the eastern field army and the death of Valens (see Chapter 3).

Like his father before him, Gratian clearly needed an imperial colleague and could not rely on his half-brother since Valentinian II was still only eight. And as in the crises following the deaths of Julian and Jovian, rather than picking a general from his or Valens' court, Gratian appointed a lower-ranking military figure, Theodosius, as *magister militum* but with the intent of further promotion. In making this decision, Gratian was influenced by Eucherius, *comes sacrarum largitionum*, but also Theodosius' uncle. Theodosius, the son of the *magister militum* executed at Carthage in 375, was born in Spain ca. 346, and had already reached the rank of *dux*. While at Sirmium Gratian also issued a general edict of toleration, though this was rescinded in 379 in Milan, probably following a remonstration by Ambrose. As soon as Theodosius had won some victories over the Sarmatians and Goths, Gratian acclaimed Flavius Theodosius I (379–395) as Augustus at Sirmium on January 19, 379. Soon after this, Gratian returned first to Italy and then Gaul.

On his accession, the immediate problem for Theodosius was the various Gothic groups in the Balkans. Many of the other Goths who had recently entered the Empire and were serving as troops in the east had already been massacred by Julius, *magister militum per Orientem*. There were two main groups of Goths, one led by Alatheus and Saphrax, who attacked Pannonia; the other under Fritigern was in Thrace. Gratian therefore transferred control of the dioceses of Macedonia and Dacia to Theodosius, though retaining control of the diocese of Illyricum. Theodosius used Thessalonica as his capital for the campaigning seasons of 379 and 380, leading combined eastern and western forces, and it was not until November 24, 380, that he entered Constantinople. The Romans slowly recovered control of Thrace from the Goths. A final Gothic settlement was celebrated on October 3, 382, which, although its terms are unclear in detail, involved settlement in exchange for military service. These Goths were settled along the Danube in Thrace. Gratian was in Pannonia in the summer of 380 and again in 382, finally coming to some agreement with the other Goths under Alatheus and Saphrax.

By late 380, Theodosius was secure enough to begin paying attention to ecclesiastical affairs. Although Valens had favored the Homoians, Theodosius chose to back the Nicene faction, a viewpoint generally accepted in the Latin-speaking parts of the Empire. The direction desired by both emperors was soon evident, with an edict of February 27, 380, to the entire population of the Empire, making it clear that the Nicene doctrine followed by Damasus in Rome and Peter in Alexandria was to be defined as orthodoxy. With the publication of this edict, it was clear that Demophilus, Valens' patriarch of Constantinople, would probably soon be forced to leave office. In a pre-emptive move, a priest named Maximus from Alexandria was consecrated as patriarch in Constantinople in the autumn. An ambitious priest in the imperial city, Gregory Nazianzus, who was a friend of Maximus, felt betrayed and saw the hand of Peter of Alexandria in this, but there is no certainty. With his credentials in hand, Maximus then went to Theodosius in Thessalonica. Like Constantius II when confronted with Paul in 337, Theodosius refused to accept this coup attempt, and the Council of Constantinople later underlined this rejection. Our descriptions of the audience are not flattering to Maximus, but he was able to be heard by the emperor himself before, as Gregory of Nazianzus joyously wrote, he was rejected "like a dog" (*de vita sua* 1001–1012). A few weeks later, Theodosius entered Constantinople on November 24, and at a meeting with Demophilus ordered him to accept the Nicene Creed. Demophilus refused to do, and on November 26 he left the city, continuing to run a church outside the walls. Theodosius still had to enter the Great Church as emperor to take control in what was clearly a tense moment. However, with no imperial sympathy, without a leader with the tenacity of Athanasius, and without an ally like the Pope, the Homoians began to lose ground.

With control of the city and having rejected Maximus, Theodosius now needed a patriarch. He promised the post to Gregory, and in January 381 summoned a church council to Constantinople. The council in May was attended by 150 bishops, almost entirely easterners. When combined with the recent public confrontation and expulsion of Demophilus, Gregory of Nyssa's description of the city's excitement is unsurprising:

> The whole city is full of it, the squares, the marketplaces, the crossroads, the alleyways; old-clothes men, money changers, food sellers: they are all busy arguing. If you ask someone to give you change, he philosophizes about the Begotten and the Unbegotten; if you inquire about the price of a loaf, you are told by way of reply that the Father is greater and the Son inferior; if you ask "Is my bath ready?" the attendant answers that the Son was made out of nothing (*de Deitate Filii et Spiritus Sancti*).

The assembled bishops proclaimed Gregory of Nazianzus patriarch at the start of the council, but he had resigned by the end, victim of the fact that he had to be transferred from Sasima in Cappadocia in violation of the fifteenth canon of the Council of Nicaea; his writings on the matter are bitter, but suggest he did not have the stomach for the job. Theodosius then chose a Cilician senator, Nectarius, from a list of candidates provided by the bishops at the council; despite his secular background, he was acceptable to both the emperor and the assembled bishops and was consecrated before the end of the council. Although the proceedings of the council itself do not survive, we have several of the canons, including a condemnation of Homoian thought and a declaration that Constantinople should be second in precedence to Rome alone, a canon whose significance only became apparent once an emperor was permanently resident in Constantinople. The fourth canon rejected the claim that Maximus had ever been a bishop. The council also took steps to sort out the problem of multiple bishops in Antioch. Euzoius had died in 378, while Meletius died during the council itself. However, rather than accepting Paulinus, Flavianus was named as patriarch of Antioch (381–404). Soon after the council, on July 30, Theodosius issued a law to eastern provincial governors naming those bishops from whom it was necessary to take communion to be considered orthodox. These included Nectarius, Timothy of Alexandria (the successor of Peter), and Diodorus of Tarsus, but no bishop of Antioch was named.

The council was successful for Theodosius, but the inevitable unhappy bishops now moved to the west. Maximus went to Italy where he was able to persuade a council at Aquileia in September 381, presided over by Ambrose, to accept him as Patriarch of Constantinople. This was an easy claim to make given the unconventional appointment of the secular Nectarius though ironic given Ambrose's own appointment to the episcopate. Maximus reached Gratian's court too, even presenting a book to the emperor. Two letters from Ambrose to Theodosius survive regarding this issue, the first demanding the restitution of Maximus, the second an apology explaining that "we will not say by whose mistake or by whose fault, in case we give the impression of spreading rumours and empty gossip" (Ambrose, *Ep.* 14.2), suggestive of a stinging rebuke from Theodosius. The first letter, however, indicates a wider context, with the intimation by Ambrose that he was writing in response to a suggestion from Theodosius' imperial colleague Gratian. Although Ambrose may have thought he was dealing with religious issues, Gratian and Theodosius were negotiating to control the Empire. Gratian was still only twenty-two and perhaps was startled by the assurance with which his junior colleague was behaving.

After his arrival in Constantinople in 380, Theodosius remained in or close to the city until 387, and then again between 391 and 394. It was during this period that Constantinople first settled into the role of being a second imperial capital; Constantine, Constantius II, and Valens had spent little time in the city, even though they had helped it grow to rival the other major eastern cities of Antioch, Ephesus, and Alexandria. During Theodosius' reign, this growth continued. The Gothic wars brought many Goths to Constantinople as hostages, slaves, soldiers, or supplicants; Athanaric finally reached Constantinople in January 381, dying two weeks later and being buried with great ceremony. Others included westerners, particularly Spaniards such as Maternus Cynegius, who was eastern praetorian prefect and held the consulate with Theodosius in 388. Theodosius' ability to offer positions to his Spanish acquaintances was similar to Valens' ability to help Pannonians, i.e., there were more opportunities for those who spoke Greek. But there were plenty of talented men from other regions, such as Rufinus the Gaul and the Italian Postumianus, prefect in either the east or Illyricum. At the same time, easterners were not neglected, and the family of the Lycian (and pagan) Tatianus did very well under Theodosius, Tatianus holding the office of eastern praetorian prefect and his son Proculus being *comes sacrarum largitionum* and then urban prefect of Constantinople. The senatorial order continued to grow, though there was always a careful balance between increasing the number of senators at the expense of local decurions. Libanius was sadly disappointed at the failure of his friend Thalassius to be admitted to the senate, with a dozen letters being preserved of attempts to overturn the decision. The city's architecture also continued to grow. The Obelisk of

Theodosius, which now stands in the center of the Hippodrome, arrived in 390. It had originally stood in the Temple of Amun in Egyptian Thebes under Tuthmosis III (1479–1425 BC) before being moved to Alexandria by Constantius II. Then Theodosius' urban prefect Proculus had it moved to Constantinople, boasting about erecting the obelisk in thirty days (see Figure 11). Theodosius also built a palace for his wife Flacilla in the Eleventh District of the city. The Theodosian Forum opened in 393, on the Mese, the main street of the city to the west of the Forum of Constantine. And a church for the head of John the Baptist was built at the Hebdomon, part of a flood of relics now entering the city, and accompanied by a growth in the number of monks and monasteries. In a moment of great irony, the body of Julian was later transferred from Tarsus to the Church of the Holy Apostles. Most spectacularly, a new victory arch, known as the Golden Gate, was built outside the city on the road to the Hebdomon. This became the imperial entrance to the city, the starting point of imperial *adventus*.

Well aware of the uncertainties of the imperial succession over the past two decades, Theodosius had his six-year-old son Arcadius proclaimed Augustus at the Hebdomon on January 19, 383. This was not accepted by Gratian, who was still the senior Augustus, and Theodosius seemed content not to push the issue; no eastern laws mention Arcadius until mid-384, and no western coins were issued in Arcadius' name at this point. This was a very different response to that of Constantius II when Julian promoted himself to Augustus in 361. From 381, Gratian was living in northern Italy, which brought him into closer contact with the Roman Senate. In 382, at the urging of Ambrose, he removed the Altar of Victory from the Senate House in Rome. A gold statue of the goddess and an Altar of Victory had stood here since the Battle of Actium in 31 BC, and sacrifices at the altar opened every session of the Senate. The altar had been removed once before, by Constantius II in 357, but was then restored by Julian. Even after the imperial adoption of Christianity, emperors had continued to hold the title *Pontifex Maximus*. According to Zosimus, Gratian refused to accept this, though some modern historians reject his account. After Gratian's removal of the altar, the prominent pagan Symmachus led a delegation of senators asking for its restoration. Gratian also received a delegation of Christian senators, led by Bishop Damasus, arguing that they would not come to the Senate if the altar was restored. Gratian refused to change his mind.

Like the affair of the Altar of Victory, the purely Christian events surrounding Priscillian were also brought to the imperial court. Priscillian was a well-educated Spanish aristocrat who had acquired a local following for his beliefs in southern Gaul and northern Spain, including two bishops

Figure 11. Base of the Obelisk of Theodosius, Constantinople 390, showing the emperor in the *kathisma* at the Hippodrome, accompanied by senators in front and guards behind. (blackboard1964/Shutterstock.com)

from unknown sees, Instantius and Salvianus. When they were condemned for heresy by a church council at Caesaraugusta (Saragossa) in Tarraconensis in 380, Instantius and Salvianus consecrated Priscillian as bishop of Avila in Lusitania. Faced with bishops who would not accept their authority, the council, led by Ithacius of Sossuba, appealed to Gratian and were rewarded with a rescript exiling all heretics "beyond the face of the earth." But Priscillian, Instantius, and Salvianus could also appeal. They traveled to Italy, but Damasus in Rome and Ambrose in Milan both refused to meet them. Salvianus died at Rome, but Macedonius, Gratian's *magister officiorum*, was now persuaded to restore Priscillian and Instantius. With the backing of the governor of Lusitania Volventius, Ithacius was now deposed. He fled to Trier, where he gained the support of the praetorian prefect Gregorius. Gratian was now trying to find out what was really going on, as Macedonius had sent men to Trier, where Ithacius had gone into hiding. Macedonius was thought to have taken bribes to ensure that an investigation into Ithacius takes place in Lusitania under Volventius rather than in Trier. Now the political situation was changed with Magnus Maximus' seizure of imperial power in Gaul 383. Ithacius was still in Trier and now took advantage of the proximity of an emperor to appeal directly to Maximus. This resulted in the emperor ordering a church council to be held at Bordeaux in 384. Instantius was deposed, but Priscillian refused to accept the authority of this council and appealed directly to Maximus. There followed two hearings at Maximus' court in Trier, first with Ithacius making accusations of witchcraft in front of the praetorian prefect. Having determined Priscillian's guilt, the prefect then consulted with the emperor, who confirmed the sentence. Ithacius now tried to recant, aware that his accusation would cost a man's life, but it was too late. Like Valentinian and Valens, Maximus could not let an accusation of practicing magic go uninvestigated. A retrial took place without Ithacius, with Patricius, *patronus fisci*, as accuser, in front of Maximus himself. Following this trial, Priscillian and several followers were executed ca. 386 and their property confiscated. The affair provoked protests from some bishops, including Siricius of Rome, Martin of Tours, and Ambrose, that a bishop should not be condemned to death.

Magnus Maximus, *comes Britanniarum*, seized the purple in Britain in June 383 and crossed to Gaul. Maximus was, like Theodosius, from Spain; he had served with the emperor's father in Britain and in Africa against Firmus. Gratian immediately aborted his campaign against the Alamanni and marched from Raetia across the Alps to Paris, where he met Maximus. As Gratian had become an adult, he seems not to have had the same affinity with the army that his father had, while his enthusiasm for a new regiment of Alans had turned other soldiers away from him. Only twenty-four, he might have grown into the role of emperor, but after five days of skirmishing and negotiations Gratian's army went over to Maximus. Gratian fled toward Italy but was caught and killed at Lyons on August 25, 383. He was cremated and his ashes eventually reached Milan, where he was buried. Maximus now controlled Britain and Gaul, while Spain and Africa soon went over to him. Italy, however, continued to be held by the twelve-year-old Valentinian II. From Theodosius' perspective, having only just made peace with the Goths, going to war was a risky choice. By 384, he had agreed to recognize Maximus. Valentinian was allowed to continue to rule in Italy, being represented in a mission to Trier by the bishop Ambrose, but as compensation Theodosius returned the dioceses of Dacia and Macedonia that had been handed over by Gratian in 379. At the same time, Theodosius began appointing the senior officials for Valentinian. For Maximus, the negotiated peace meant his seizure of power had been accepted. By late 386, the eastern praetorian prefect Cynegius was ordering imperial portraits of Maximus to be set up in cities, including Alexandria, and a few coins minted in Constantinople recognized him as Augustus; the reverse legend of CONCORDIA AUGGGG on *solidi* refers to four emperors, i.e., Theodosius, Arcadius, Valentinian, and Maximus. Soon after Maximus' accession, his infant son Victor was also acclaimed Augustus, though no coins were minted for him in Theodosius' territory nor was he accepted by Theodosius.

For Theodosius, even with the Goths settled, Nicene orthodoxy imposed, and a peace made with Maximus, there were still plenty of other crises that required attention. In the east, the Persian king Sapur had expelled Sauromaces from Iberia in 379, and in Armenia he had appointed his own king, Xusro. Sapur's death in 379 after a long reign filled with hostility toward Rome gave a new opportunity for peace, especially as his successor Ardasir II (379–383) was focused on domestic affairs. Then in 384, another Persian embassy arrived in Constantinople, to announce the accession of a new king, Sapur III (383–388). This built on the division of Armenia between two kings in 379, accepting the inability of any Armenian monarch to impose unity. The result was a partitioning of the kingdom in 387 into Armenia ruled by the pro-Roman Arsak IV and Persarmenia under the pro-Persian Xusro. After the death of Arsak in 389, the Arsacid monarchy was dissolved and these provinces were incorporated into the Roman Empire, though ruled by hereditary satraps. These functioned just like Roman governors, so Gaddana, satrap of Sophene, was sent instructions about crown gold in 387. Iberia remained partitioned. In the Balkans, a group of Greuthungi, Goths who had remained across the Danube in 378, requested permission to enter the Empire. Zosimus records two stories. In one, the request was refused but the Goths attempted to cross anyway; in the other, they were attacked after negotiating a crossing. But in both versions, the *magister peditum* Promotus destroyed the Gothic force before it could enter the Empire.

Despite the acceptance of Maximus, relations between Trier and Milan were tense. Campaigns by Valentinian II's generals against the Alamanni in 384 and Sarmatians in 386 were a reminder not just of the incessant barbarian pressure, but also of the army still in Italy. And though Valentinian was young, he was rapidly growing up. Symmachus was urban prefect in 384. When he complained to Valentinian about the quality of the imperial personnel assigned to his office (*Relatio* 17), he received a tart reminder from the emperor, "there must be no questioning of the imperial judgement: it is close to sacrilege to doubt whether he whom the emperor has chosen is worthy" (*CT* 1.6.9). Symmachus' ideas of management clearly did not include the concept that it was up to him to get the best out of his people. Nonetheless, he and his staff worked hard, submitting forty-nine reports (*relationes*) to Valentinian over a period of six months, i.e., an average of two reports per week. Symmachus also led another attempt to restore the Altar of Victory, though this too was rejected. Then in early 386, Valentinian issued an edict in the names of Theodosius and Arcadius as well as in his own name that granted freedom of worship to the Homoians. It was a clear sign that Valentinian was beginning to think for himself, but it was also part of what is usually described as a struggle with Ambrose, bishop of Milan. We know about this only from Ambrose's account and material influenced by it. Ambrose's version is preserved in a series of letters that is clearly incomplete and written to justify his actions. When the emperor demanded from Ambrose the use of the Basilica Portiana, outside the walls of the city, possibly only for occasional ceremonies rather than permanently, the bishop refused and justified himself in the consistory. When faced with a renewed request for use of a different church, the New Basilica, Ambrose shut himself up in the church, which he claimed was then besieged by troops. He refused to attend another summons to the consistory. But the claim that he was also walking around Milan at the same time and yet was not arrested suggests that Valentinian may have had a different conception of what was happening. Valentinian's tentative handling of Ambrose reflects the looming presence of Maximus as well as his lack of experience. At about the same time, the same tensions appeared in the east after a riot in Antioch in 387. Riots were common enough in large Roman cities, and some, such as Alexandria, were notorious for their population's volatility. But in Antioch, statues of the emperor were pulled down; this was unacceptable.

The immediate cause of this riot was, according to the eyewitness Libanius, an imperial demand for an increase of taxation. This demand came at a bad time for all cities in the Empire, since they had just paid crown gold for the fifth anniversary of Arcadius as Augustus in January 387 and were preparing for the tenth anniversary of Theodosius in January 388. At Antioch, moreover, the city had also suffered from several years of poor harvests. When the city council was informed of the increased taxes, they sent a delegation to the provincial governor, Celsus. At the same time, the Antiochene mob looked for the bishop Flavianus, but they were unable to find him. This mob then went to Celsus' palace but was unable to break in; the governor's house had perhaps had its gates reinforced since 353, when an Antiochene mob had burned an aristocrat's house and killed the governor Theophilus. They then attacked the bronze imperial statues, dragging them through the city on ropes, and the imperial portraits painted on wood. The lawlessness was over quickly, as the *Comes Orientis* deployed troops before noon. Many of the rioters were executed, some being burned alive, others thrown to the beasts. An official report was sent the same day to Constantinople, about nine days' travel, less if the messenger hurried.

Now that the excitement was over, the city was fearful. Urban rioting was common, but overthrowing imperial images was a direct challenge to imperial authority. The emperor had the right to massacre the population, lower the city's status, execute *curiales*, or confiscate property. The city immediately sent a delegation of the bishop Flavianus and Hilarius, a local senator, to Constantinople, catching up with the messengers on the way. When they arrived in Constantinople, they were seen by the emperor and made a good impression on him. Meanwhile, as John Chrysostom said in a sermon preached while waiting, the city was in suspense, "when the wrath of the Emperor is expected to come as a fire from above" (*Homilies on the Statues* 2.4).

Theodosius enacted some initial punishments, making Antioch subordinate to Laodicea; closing the hippodrome, theaters, and baths; and suspending the free distribution of bread. He also sent two officials to investigate, the *magister officiorum* Caesarius and the *magister militum per Orientem* Ellebichus, who was usually based at Antioch. Once the commissioners had arrived in Antioch, they were approached by many monks, including the hermit Macedonius, who, speaking in Syriac, told them bluntly that it was easy to remake statues when they had been pulled down, but impossible, even for the emperor, to bring the dead back to life. His words had to be translated for Caesarius and Ellebichus. Though his intervention is described by Theodoret as being influential on Theodosius, any impact it had was delayed and didn't stop Caesarius and Ellebichus from arresting the city council. Then the investigations started, graphically described by John Chrysostom:

… when I entered the court, other sights I saw which were still more awful; soldiers armed with swords and clubs, and strictly keeping the peace for the judges within. For since all the relatives of those under trial, wives and mothers and daughters and fathers, stood before the doors of the lawcourt; in order that if any one happened to be led away to execution, yet no one inflamed at the sight of the calamity might raise any tumult or disturbance; the soldiers drove them all far off; thus preoccupying their mind with fear (*Homilies on the Statues* 13.1).

Once the investigation was over, a recommendation for clemency was taken to the emperor by Caesarius while Ellebichus remained in the city. About two weeks later, Flavian returned, the city was relieved of its punishment, and Easter was celebrated.

Much revolved around imperial readiness to listen. Theodosius may have been reluctant to punish Antioch, but he would also have been reluctant to allow such behavior to go unpunished. All of a sudden, mercy can become seen as weakness, and Theodosius did not want to suggest to Magnus Maximus that he was weak. The city knew that the *Comes Orientis* had sent a report to the emperor, but they wanted to tell the story their way. Their ambassadors confessed the city's guilt, but did well enough that Caesarius and Ellebichus were sent to investigate with a positive mandate and Hilarius was thought to owe his promotion to governor of Palestina because of his great virtue in this matter (Zosimus 4.41.3). But as the emperor and his servants listened, they also knew that the reports they received need not be telling the truth. As with the Romanus affair, the emperor needed to investigate himself, so he sent his own men. Once the investigation determined it was a riot, not a conspiracy, they recommended clemency to the emperor.

Any fear of Maximus was well placed. In summer 387, he broke the peace and stormed across the Alps. Valentinian fled first to Aquileia, then to Thessalonica as Italy fell into Maximus' hands. Following the arrival of the refugee Valentinian II and his mother in late 387, Theodosius was left with a choice: he could accept the situation as it was and avoid further civil war, or he could restore Valentinian to power. There were good reasons for following each course, but eventually Theodosius chose to support Valentinian. In September 387, he married Valentinian II's sister Galla in Thessalonica, this marriage soon producing a daughter, Galla Placidia. The likely outcome of the civil war was unclear enough to contemporaries that when Theophilus, bishop of Alexandria, sent the presbyter Isidore to Rome with gifts, he also wrote two letters of congratulations, one for Maximus, one for Theodosius. This war was similar to the 351–353 war between Magnentius and Constantius II, setting the eastern part of the Roman Empire against the western part.

But it was crucially different because of the presence of large numbers of recently settled Goths in the Balkans. Maximus encouraged some of these Goths to fight against Theodosius, while Theodosius chose to recruit large numbers into his army, as well as raising allied contingents from the Alans, Iberians, and Armenians.

In spring 388, Maximus crossed the Julian Alps and occupied Pannonia. Theodosius launched a three-pronged attack. He led his main force into Pannonia in June, while other generals led a marine assault on Sicily and Italy and marched from Egypt to Africa. In the Adriatic, Theodosius' troops avoided Maximus' fleet, landed in Sicily, and defeated Maximus' troops there. And in Pannonia, Theodosius marched up the Savus, captured Siscia, and then defeated Maximus' main army in battles at Siscia and Poetovio. He then crossed the Alps to Italy, successfully laying siege to Aquileia and capturing Maximus. Timasius and Arbogast played a significant role in this campaign. Maximus was executed by Theodosius near Aquileia on August 28, 388, his son Victor soon afterward by Arbogast at Trier. His wife and two daughters were spared.

As well as restoring Valentinian and punishing the supporters of Maximus, Theodosius was also aware that his rule required the support of the Italian senatorial aristocracy. One of the most prominent, Quintus Aurelius Symmachus, was accused of being a strong supporter of Maximus. His career to this point was typical of the Italian senatorial aristocracy, *corrector* of Lucania et Bruttium, proconsul of Africa, and urban prefect. It was highly successful, but also very safe, involving few interactions with the imperial court where the politically ambitious went. In 388, after Maximus' occupation of Italy, Symmachus had delivered a (now lost) panegyric to him at Milan on behalf of the Senate. When Maximus was defeated, Symmachus, after perhaps burning his panegyric, took refuge in a church at Rome, and it was only after the intervention of Pope Leontius that he was given the opportunity to make a speech of apology and panegyric to Theodosius at Milan. This allowed Theodosius to show mercy, and Symmachus was awarded the consulate for 391. The stability of the imperial house was stressed with the *decennalia* of Theodosius, and then in the summer of 389 further reinforced when Theodosius visited Rome in the company of Valentinian and the four-year-old Honorius (see Figure 12).

Theodosius' understandable concern with the west may have led to less attention being paid to more local affairs. Christians were becoming more confident in acting against non-Christians. While Cynegius was eastern praetorian prefect (384–388), he encouraged the dismantling by monks of several pagan shrines and temples, including Apamea. Others were less controlled, such as the bishop of Callinicum in Osrhoene, who encouraged his

Figure 12. Silver plate (*missorium*) of Theodosius I issued as part of the celebrations for his *decennalia* in 388, showing the emperor with both of his sons. (Printed with permission of Real Academia de la Historia)

congregation to burn a synagogue and a temple of the Valentiniani, a gnostic sect. Theodosius ordered the bishop to repay the costs out of his own pocket, though this was soon overturned. Then an edict of 391 repeated Constantine's banning of pagan sacrifice throughout the Empire. This was soon followed by the destruction of the Serapeum, the temple of Serapis, in Alexandria, led by Theophilus, patriarch of Alexandria. This was the largest temple in the city; its destruction marks the beginning of the end of civic paganism, which was still hanging on despite over half a century of bans on animal sacrifice, image worship, and keeping temples open. Though there were still numerous pagan temples still operating in the 390s, it was clear not only that Christianity was here to stay, but that the Empire itself was becoming a Christian Empire. Theophilus was not content with destroying the buildings, but paraded the cult images in an insulting fashion in the city. Here, his zeal only proved that paganism was not yet dead. Violence followed, and the *comes Aegypti* Romanus and the *praefectus Augustalis* Evagrius were required to intervene with soldiers to restore order. Theophilus soon built churches on the site of the Serapeum complex, one of which housed the bones of John the Baptist (though his head was now in Constantinople).

The events at Callinicum had an impact in the west, where Theodosius soon clashed with Ambrose of Milan. Theodosius ordered the bishop of Callinicum to rebuild the burned synagogue at his own expense. When Ambrose asked for a lesser penalty, Theodosius was prepared to give ground. At this point, he had many things on his mind, not least the need to smooth relations with the Italian aristocracy in the immediate aftermath of his victory over Magnus Maximus. As part of this program, he visited Rome in 389, accompanied by the five-year-old Honorius, who was presented to the Senate. His willingness to compromise with Ambrose was part of this program, though he did not go as far as Ambrose wished. It was only when he pressed the case while the emperor was taking communion that Theodosius acceded to Ambrose's wishes. This, at least, is the story told by Ambrose in a letter published after the death of Theodosius (Ambrose, *Ep.* 40, 41), but we have no sense of how the emperor told the story.

In 390, Ambrose again chose to challenge Theodosius. In Thessalonica, the *magister militum per Illyricum* Butheric had arrested a popular charioteer. When the urban mob pressed for his release, Butheric refused. A riot followed in which Butheric was killed. Subsequently, in a confused situation, a massacre took place, with supposedly seven thousand being killed. It is not clear who was responsible for events on the ground, but the ultimate responsibility belonged to the emperor. Theodosius agreed to do penance for the massacre in front of Ambrose, but only on his terms. Again, in terms of contemporary sources, these events are known only through Ambrose's writings in which he, not surprisingly, claimed the leading role.

These relationships between Theodosius and Ambrose rapidly became a major part of the standard Christian histories of the fourth century. Thus Theodoret, one of the ecclesiastical historians of the fifth century, focused on the confrontation in Ambrose's church, claiming that Theodosius,

> after making his offering, as he was accustomed, remained within at the rail, but once more the great Ambrose was not silent and taught him the distinction of place. First, he asked him if he wanted anything; and when the emperor said that he was waiting for participation in the divine mysteries, Ambrose sent word to him by the chief deacon, saying that "the inner place, O Emperors, is open only to priests; to all others it is inaccessible; go out

and stand where the others stand; for purple makes emperors, but not priests" (*HE* 5.18.20–1).

Theodosius' relations with Ambrose need to be considered not only as confrontations between the two men, but also as a problem of imperial rule. Ambrose was able to exploit Theodosius' need to restore political unity in Italy, but the emperor's other actions at Thessalonica and Antioch illustrate what Theodosius could do. There were also limits to episcopal intransigence, as bishops such as Athanasius, Chrysostom, and Nestorius knew well, and few other bishops had anything like the success of Ambrose if they challenged the emperor. And when history was told in this way, Theodosius, unlike Constantius II or Gallus, managed to avoid being seen as a cruel tyrant

Now that Theodosius had restored Valentinian II as western emperor, he was faced with the problem of restoring order on the frontiers, similar to that faced by Constantius II after his victory over Magnentius in 353. The Rhine frontier had been battered by Frankish raids that started when Maximus marched to Italy. Quintinus, one of the generals left in command of Maximus' forces in Trier, pursued a group of Franks across the Rhine, but his men suffered badly in confused fighting in swamps and forests. Theodosius left Arbogast as the regent of Valentinian II, who by summer 389 had moved his court to Trier. Arbogast led another expedition, which crossed the Rhine in the winter of 391, ravaging the territory of the Bructeri and Chamavi. Theodosius remained in Italy, though by the summer of 391 he had returned to Constantinople, leaving Valentinian, now aged twenty, to rule the western Empire from Trier. Valentinian's relationship with his *magister peditum praesentalis* Arbogast did not develop well, as he rejected Arbogast's claims that Theodosius had asked him to look after him. In an attempt to smooth over relations, Ambrose, trusted by both, had been invited to visit Trier. In 392, when Valentinian ordered Arbogast to march into Italy, Arbogast refused. Valentinian soon afterward tried to dismiss Arbogast, but the general tore up the letter, saying that as Valentinian had not appointed him, he could not dismiss him. According to Zosimus, Valentinian wrote to Theodosius for his assistance, without success. The twenty-one-year-old emperor soon afterward committed suicide at Vienne on May 15, 392. Arbogast sent his body to Milan, where he was buried with Gratian.

Following Valentinian's death, there was time for Arbogast to negotiate with Theodosius, who probably demanded that Honorius be accepted as emperor in the west. Arbogast was not ambitious for himself, but could foresee that Theodosius was married to Valentinian's sister and that surrender would probably result in his own death. He had little choice but to revolt, and on August 22, 392, Arbogast raised Eugenius to the purple at Lyons in Gaul. Eugenius was an obscure *magister scrinii*, but still was soon supported in Gaul, Spain, and Britain. Further embassies were sent to Theodosius, though to no effect, while Theodosius' refusal to accept Eugenius' nominees for the consulship of 393 and his acclamation of Honorius as Augustus at the Hebdomon on January 23, 393, made it clear that war would soon follow. In April 393, Eugenius advanced to Italy, which now had little choice but to accept him as emperor. It was not until the spring of 394 that Theodosius marched west. In the interim, Eugenius received several embassies from senators in Rome requesting the restoration of the Altar of Victory. In need of support with a war against Theodosius looming, yet as a Christian unwilling to restore the altar, he compromised by giving some private funding to prominent individuals for pagan sacrifices. After the defeat of Eugenius, writers of Christian history invented a pagan revival that was then used to glorify both Ambrose and Theodosius. But before Theodosius' invasion, Eugenius' coins and inscriptions were simultaneously naming as *Augusti* Theodosius, Arcadius, and Eugenius, though their legends were no different from those of Valentinian II.

The animated debate concerning the Altar of Victory was described by pagan aristocrats in terms of Roman tradition. This description masked the reality that by the end of the fourth century, membership of the Senate and the holding of imperial office were the same. There were a few senators who followed the path of entry from their parents or via the office of *quaestor*, but the majority of their colleagues had entered as a result of imperial service. Provincial governors, most of whom only served for a year, were now members of the Senate, as were regimental commanders, *notarii*, senior *agentes in rebus*, and many other senior officials in the *comitatus*. The orders no longer ran the Empire, but they did represent a convenient body, especially in Constantinople, to reflect aristocratic opinion throughout the Empire. However, when the Senate met in Rome, it was dominated by the traditional Italian aristocracy, which was not such a good reflection of western aristocratic feelings. Senatorial status also brought immunity from local municipal responsibilities, hence Libanius' simultaneous desire to see his friend Thalassius acquire it, while complaining that Constantinople was sucking men out of local councils.

Theodosius left Constantinople in May 394 with a Roman army supported by contingents of allied Goths, Alans, and Iberians. His army was commanded by Timasius, a veteran of the 388 campaign against Maximus, and Stilicho. Stilicho is first heard of on a diplomatic mission to Persia ca. 383, after which he married Serena, the niece of Theodosius, and was promoted to *magister utriusque militiae* for this campaign. By September, Theodosius had reached the western foothills of the Julian Alps, where he defeated Eugenius in the two-day bloody battle of the Frigidus on September 5–6, 394:

> In that part where the Romans were engaged with the Romans, the battle was well-matched: but where the barbarians were fighting for the Emperor Theodosius, the men of Eugenius were doing much better. But the emperor, seeing the barbarians dying, being in the greatest danger, throwing himself on the ground, he called God for help, and his request did not fail ... A violent wind arising turned back the missiles shot by Eugenius' men on themselves, and carried those from his men with a greater force against their enemies; so strong was the emperor's prayer (Socrates 5.25).

This was the Bora, a local wind that often blows strongly from the east. Theodosius was also helped by the defection of part of Maximus' army under the *comes* Arbitio. Other writers mention heavy casualties among the Goths who led Theodosius' assault. Eugenius was executed on September 6, 394, and his head carried around Italy; Arbogast committed suicide a few days later. The allied troops were now dismissed. The Goths had now fought two campaigns in just over a decade after being settled in the Roman Empire. These wars interrupted their process of assimilation, giving the Goths a sense of community within the Roman state that had not occurred with earlier settlements.

After his victory, Theodosius visited Rome and then moved to Milan. Restoration of order was even more difficult than six years earlier, though now it was clear that his successor would be his youngest son, Honorius. Stilicho, who had married Theodosius' niece, was now appointed *magister utriusque militiae* in the west. Other prominent figures also had to reestablish their relationships with Theodosius. Ambrose had left Milan, keeping out of the way of the court; perhaps mindful of the clashes he had had with Theodosius, Eugenius left him unmolested, making reconciliation easy. Symmachus had a more difficult situation, having celebrated his son's quaestorship with spectacular games in 393. There was little time for these tensions to settle before Theodosius fell ill late in 394.

When Theodosius fell ill, he appointed Stilicho as the guardian of both Honorius and Arcadius. This, at least, was what Stilicho claimed, and it seems quite likely that the dying Theodosius was worried about both his sons. The emperor died at Milan on the evening of January 17, 395, having appeared in the Hippodrome in the morning. Following a period of mourning of forty days, Ambrose gave a speech that praised his humility and his martial skills, but was explicit that Stilicho had been appointed regent for both sons. As Ambrose claimed, Theodosius had left the Roman Empire in good condition for his sons. Every enemy he faced had been defeated, religious unity had been created, and a few disturbing remnants of paganism had been overturned. Both parts of the Empire appeared equally strong. However, the appointment of Stilicho as guardian to both boys conflicted with Theodosius' earlier appointment of Rufinus, the eastern praetorian prefect as guardian of Arcadius and the mandates that the two powerful and ambitious men claimed were in conflict. Whether it was their ambition that was at fault, or whether a dying father forgot what he had done or changed his mind, Theodosius had set in motion renewed discord between the two parts of the Empire at a time when the need for concord was greater than ever.

FURTHER READING

The primary sources continue to be dominated by Ammianus Marcellinus, whose history covered events to 378, supplemented by Zosimus' history, which covers the entire period in reasonable detail, drawing on Eunapius of Sardis for the period 270–404. Two short histories were written under Valens by Eutropius and Festus. There are good *Ecclesiastical Histories* by Socrates, Sozomen, and Theodoret, though these were all written in the middle of the fifth century, as well as substantial fragments of the Eunomian historian Philostorgius, whose work covered events from the reign of Constantine to 425. There is much anecdotal information contained in saints' lives, e.g., the *Life of St. Martin* by Sulpicius Severus, as well as collections of lives of monks, such as the *Historia Religiosa* of Theodoret. There are increasing amounts of episcopal writings, including collections from Ambrose, Augustine, Athanasius, Basil of Caesarea, and John Chrysostom, though frequently partisan. Secular letter collections such as those of Libanius and Symmachus, and a reasonable amount of court and private rhetoric, including speeches by Themistius, Libanius, Himerius, and others exist, though these are often as partisan, similar to the Latin poems of Ausonius and Claudian.

The best history of the whole period remains Matthews, J. F., *Western Aristocracies and Imperial Court* (Oxford, 1975). Despite the abundant primary source material, good studies of emperors and their reigns are rare, notably Lenski, N., *Failure of Empire* (California, 2002) on Valens. For Theodosius I, there is a series of outstanding articles by Errington, R. M., "The Accession of Theodosius I," *Klio* 78 (1996), 438–453, "Theodosius and the Goths," *Chiron* 26 (1996), 1–27, "Christian Accounts of the Religious Legislation of Theodosius I," *Klio* 79 (1997), 389–443, and "Church and State in the First Years of Theodosius I," *Chiron* 27 (1997), 21–72. On young emperors, see McEvoy, M., *Child Emperor Rule in the Late Roman West, AD 367–455* (Oxford, 2013). Many of the discussions of Ammianus Marcellinus also cover the history of this period.

For western religious politics, McLynn, N., *Ambrose of Milan* (Berkeley, 1994) is excellent, while Barnes, T. D., *Athanasius and Constantius* (Cambridge, MA, 1993) is more useful for this period than the title implies. On Priscillian, see Burrus, V., *The Making of a Heretic. Gender, Authority, and the Priscillianist Controversy* (Berkeley, 1995). For a study of the intersection of elite culture and power, see Brown, P., *Power and Persuasion in Late Antiquity* (Madison, 1992). On economics and the gold supply, Banaji, J., *Agrarian Change in Late Antiquity* (Oxford, 2001) is first rate but demanding.

On the Goths and their entrance into the Empire, differing perspectives are provided by Heather, P., *Goths and Romans 332–489* (Oxford, 1991) and Kulikowski, M., *Rome's Gothic Wars* (Cambridge, 2006). For the early source material, Heather, P., "Cassiodorus and the Rise of the Amals: Genealogy and the Goths under Hun Domination," *Journal of Roman Studies* 79 (1989), 103–128 is essential reading.

5

THE EARLY FIFTH CENTURY, 395–455

With the succession of Theodosius I by his sons and grandsons Honorius and Valentinian III in the west, Arcadius and Theodosius II in the east, the two parts of the Empire began to take different directions. These emperors did not lead their armies in the field, and imperial campaigning came to an end. Imperial government became more fixed, in Rome or Ravenna in the west, in Constantinople in the east, and disputes over the correct form of Christianity continued to divide the Empire. Most importantly, the West was weakened by the loss of territory, in Britain, Gaul, Spain, and in particular Africa, losses that were to bring it to collapse before the end of the century. This was also a very confusing period, and many contemporaries were often as ignorant about events as we are. Particularly in the west, there were often too many crises for the state to cope with, and the imperial regime understandably concentrated on its own survival. This more limited focus helped feed the sense of aristocratic disconnection from the Empire and the gradual loss of territory. Territory was lost to outside enemies, but also to barbarians settled on Roman territory who then ceased to be Roman allies and instead ran independent kingdoms.

Like Julian's death in 363, Theodosius' death at Milan on January 17, 395, brought the problem of the imperial succession to the fore. In theory, it was dealt with by the appointment of regents, the *magister militum* Stilicho in the west for the ten-year-old Honorius, the eastern praetorian prefect Rufinus in the east for the seventeen-year-old Arcadius. But Stilicho claimed to have been appointed as regent over both sons, setting the two parts of the Empire into an uneasy coexistence. The death of Theodosius is often seen both as the end of an effective Roman Empire and as the beginning of the permanent division of the Empire into eastern and western parts. Although this had happened by the middle of the fifth century, this was a gradual development, and both emperors were highly concerned for imperial unity in both secular and religious matters.

THE EASTERN EMPIRE: ARCADIUS (395–408)

Arcadius was seventeen when his father died. Although he had held the rank of Augustus since 383, the dominant figure in Constantinople was the eastern praetorian prefect Rufinus, who in 394 had been left as Arcadius' guardian by Theodosius. Nonetheless, it was clear that Arcadius would soon be ruling in his own right, and it was not long before he took steps to secure his succession by marrying Eudoxia, daughter of the general Bauto, on April 27, 395. Then in the summer, Stilicho led the combined eastern and western field armies east from Italy, escorting the body of Theodosius. Tensions ran high between the two armies, as might be expected given the two recent civil wars. Although Stilicho conducted some operations against Alaric, in revolt in Thessaly at the head of a group of Goths, he soon released the eastern troops to Constantinopolitan command and returned to the west, leaving Alaric unsubdued. The cortège bearing Theodosius arrived first, and the emperor was buried at the Church of the Holy Apostles in Constantinople on November 8. The eastern field army, led by Gainas, arrived a few weeks later. As they returned to Constantinople, they were met by the emperor and Rufinus on November 27 outside the city at Theodosius' triumphal arch (later turned into the Golden Gate). What should have been a spectacular reaffirmation of imperial power turned into a disaster as Rufinus was assassinated in front of the troops and the emperor. For Arcadius, this was probably the event that caused him to avoid any military activity for the rest of his reign. Unlike his father and the majority of previous emperors, but just like his brother Honorius in the west, Arcadius ran the Empire from the palace. His age had little to do with this, since Gratian had been leading armies when he was seventeen. Nor did a failure to lead troops affect his popularity when he left the palace, since on a visit to the church at Carya in Constantinople,

> all who lived around this holy building assembled to see the Emperor; and some, being outside the building, hurried to occupy the streets in order to get a better view of the emperor and they went to see the escort around him. But others followed him, until everyone, including the women and children, were outside the building (Socrates 6.23).

As with the sons of Constantine, dividing the Empire caused significant tensions between the two brothers, in this case exacerbated by the presence of the Goths in the Balkans. The poet Claudian claimed that Stilicho had abandoned his campaign against Alaric because of a demand from Arcadius to return the eastern armies. How far Claudian should be believed is a difficult question as he was trying to justify Stilicho's failure to defeat Alaric. The dioceses of Dacia and Macedonia had been administered from Constantinople during the later years of Theodosius' reign, and though Honorius requested their return, Arcadius refused, and this was a continuing source of tension between the brothers. The ecclesiastical administration had not changed, however, so the bishop of Thessalonica administered these two dioceses and reported to the Pope.

The murder of Rufinus had been organized by Gainas, the *comes rei militaris* assigned to lead the eastern troops back to Constantinople. Subsequently, Rufinus was accused by some of aiming at the throne and of inviting Huns and Goths into the Empire. In the period of opportunity that followed, the eastern generals fell out among themselves. The *magister militum* Timasius, who had fought alongside Stilicho at the Frigidus, and the ex-*magister militum* Abundantius were condemned by a court presided over by another ex-*magister militum*, Saturninus. Other competition can be seen in the transfer of several offices that Rufinus had aggregated to his position, including the *cursus publicus*, command of the *scholae palatinae* and the *fabricae*, to the *magister officiorum* Marcellus. Victims of Rufinus, such as Tatianus, were reinstated, but this brought with it further disruption. Although there were many winners and losers, the most spectacular case was the *praepositus sacri cubiculi* Eutropius. As a eunuch, he attracted much hostility, well seen in Claudian's vituperative masterpiece, the two volumes of *in Eutropium* (against Eutropius), reflecting the tensions between east and west. Eutropius was both unpopular and successful, exploiting the competition between the other powerful men at Arcadius' court to advance himself. However, the accusation that he could dominate government is based on an unquestioning acceptance of the emperor as supreme authority. Thus during the struggles between the generals, Eutropius was able to get himself sent with some troops against some Huns who had crossed the Caucasus in 395 and raided south, reaching Syria, Cappadocia, and Cilicia. Winning some successes, Eutropius was appointed consul in 399, though this was not acknowledged in the west, and *patricius*. Both military command and the consulate were unprecedented for a *praepositus sacri cubiculi* in the fourth century and suggest Arcadius leaning on a man he trusted as dependent on himself, rather than the hard men created by his father.

As well as fighting among themselves, many of the military men were also focusing elsewhere. Alaric led his Goths into Greece, plundering widely. He was turned away from Thebes and Athens, according to some because

Alaric saw Athena patrolling the walls and Achilles at the head of their troops. Although Stilicho returned from the west and landed in the Peloponnese in 397, he was undercut when Arcadius declared him a public enemy and appointed Alaric as *magister militum per Illyricum*. Alaric may have seen this as gaining a Roman command similar to that of other Goths, such as Gainas, Tribigild, and Fravitta. Arcadius is more likely to have seen Stilicho's landing as a second western intervention in his part of the Empire, an extremely presumptuous move by his younger brother. When the *comes Africae* Gildo declared that he would henceforth report to the eastern emperor, Arcadius was thus happy to accept, though with the awareness that this would involve him in more tensions with Honorius.

One of the Roman commanders in the Hunnic campaign, Tribigild, revolted in early 399 in Phrygia, ambitious for the sorts of honors that other Goths had received. Gainas (now promoted to *magister militum praesentalis*) and Leo (*magister militum*) were sent against him, but Leo was defeated. Gainas was able to exploit the crisis not only to advance himself but also to get revenge for his exiled military colleagues Timasius and Abundantius. Eutropius was dismissed and fled to the Hagia Sophia, where he took refuge under the altar. John Chrysostom, the new Patriarch appointed in 398 with a reputation as a highly effective preacher at Antioch, preached a sermon while the eunuch cowered. John's opening quotation from the Bible's *Ecclesiastes*, "vanity of vanities, all is vanity," rang through the church as he demanded to know "where is the applause which greeted you in the city, where is the acclamation in the hippodrome and the flatteries of the spectators?" (*Homilium in Eutropium*). Eutropius was soon hauled from the church, first exiled to Cyprus, and then executed in Chalcedon. Then Gainas tried to obtain the consulate and a Homoian church at Constantinople from Arcadius for the use of his Gothic troops; this was similar to Valentinian II's request opposed by Ambrose in Milan. Arcadius was prepared to accede to the request for a church, though Chrysostom was opposed to it, speaking out boldly in front of the emperor. The emperor also appointed the new eastern praetorian prefect Aurelianus as consul for 400, not Gainas.

From this point onward, there was a shift in imperial policy toward the Goths, changing from accommodation to opposition, resulting in Alaric leaving the Balkans and moving to Italy in 401. With the campaign against Tribigild over, Gainas returned to Constantinople in April 400 with new demands. Following a meeting between Arcadius and Gainas at Chalcedon, the emperor exiled Saturninus, Aurelianus, and a certain John, one of Arcadius' counselors, and then installed Caesarius as eastern praetorian prefect. Although Gainas was now the dominant figure, his naked use of military power made many uncomfortable. In July, a panicky population burned a church containing a number of Goths and attacked some of Gainas' troops. Arcadius then summoned the *magister militum per Orientem*, Fravitta (himself a Goth), to remove Gainas from office. Gainas resisted and was defeated and his army destroyed. Fravitta was rewarded with the consulate for 401 and appointed to Gainas' position; his ethnicity was of no importance to Arcadius. Arcadius erected a column in 402 in Constantinople to commemorate the victory; a statue of the emperor was later placed on top in 421. The iconography of the base shows clearly the pairing of Rome and Constantinople and of Honorius and Arcadius (see Figure 13).

Although the early years of Arcadius' reign were dominated by political crises, the business of government continued as usual. The Egyptian Anthemius had served as *comes sacrarum largitionum* and then as *magister officiorum* before being appointed as eastern praetorian prefect in 405. He was also responsible for starting the construction of a new walled circuit for Constantinople in 404, not to be finished until 413. These new walls were six kilometers long, enclosing an additional area of ca. 600 hectares, doubling the defended area of the city. There were other moments of great imperial ceremony, with the acclamation of his wife Eudoxia as Augusta on January 9, 400, and his son Theodosius as Augustus at the Hebdomon on January 10, 402. There were celebrations too for the birth of their four daughters, Flacilla, Arcadia, Pulcheria, and Marina. Many visitors came to the city, like Synesius from the city of Cyrene in Pentapolis on an embassy requesting a reduction in the city's taxes. Another was bishop Porphyrius of Gaza in Palestina Prima, trying to get a temple of Zeus closed in his city. In Constantinople, he met the patriarch John Chrysostom for advice. The *Life of Porphyry*, written by Mark the Deacon, claimed that John could not present the petition himself because Eudoxia, angered by a property dispute, had blocked his access. Therefore, he suggested that Porphyry approach one of Eudoxia's eunuchs, Amantius, for help. Amantius brought Porphyrius to Eudoxia, who listened to his appeal, but when she put the request to Arcadius, he turned it down. Apparently, he feared that granting the request might disturb the flow of taxes from the city. However, soon after Eudoxia gave birth to Theodosius in April 401, she was able to finesse a petition to be granted by the infant emperor; miraculously, the petition received by the infant was that of Porphyrius regarding the closure of the temple. Although Mark the Deacon makes this a story of Christian success, it shows not only Arcadius' concern for tax collection and public order but also the minimal influence of Eudoxia.

Figure 13. Base of the Column of Arcadius, Constantinople, 402, showing both emperors as a sign of imperial unity.

ARCADIUS AND CHRYSOSTOM

Other new arrivals in Constantinople initially seemed less controversial. Concern regarding their supposedly Origenist teachings had led Theophilus, patriarch of Alexandria (385–412), to excommunicate three Egyptian monks, Ammonius, Eusebius, and Euthymius, and deposed a fourth, Dioscurus, from the bishopric of Nitria. These monks, collectively known as the Tall Brothers, fled to Constantinople in late 401, where John cautiously received them. When the monks delivered petitions to Arcadius and Eudoxia in June 402, Arcadius then summoned Theophilus to Constantinople and appointed John, probably to his horror, to investigate his actions.

Theophilus chose to move slowly, traveling overland so as to give time to bring his supporters together. He was also helped by John himself, who was discovering that the freedom he had had in Antioch was not present in the imperial city. In particular, a recent sermon against extravagant feminine dress had been assumed by some to be an attack on Arcadius' wife Eudoxia; the sermon itself is lost, but from similar sermons by John written in Antioch, it probably focused on lavish dresses, jewelry, and makeup. Moreover, John's personality was less pleasing than his rhetoric, and he had already upset a number of local clergy. In particular, his overhauling of church finances caused hostility and trimming of the patriarch's household, while his devotion to the rich widows of Constantinople, especially Olympias, had set tongues wagging.

When Theophilus finally arrived in Constantinople in August 403, he was received as the guest of the empress. Instead of being the subject of an enquiry himself, he was able to coordinate a synod that investigated John's behavior; Theophilus' realism in coming to terms with the Tall Brothers is matched only by John's political naiveté. With the emperor failing to back his patriarch, the Synod of the Oak held in Chalcedon in autumn 403 rapidly resulted in John's deposition by the assembled bishops and then banishment by the emperor. Unpopular though he may have been with Theophilus, many priests, monks, bishops, and the emperor, John was still a superb preacher who had a strong popular following in Constantinople. Rioting in his favor was such that in a dramatic about-face by the emperor, he was recalled only a day later. When the emperor gave orders for another ecclesiastical court to assemble, Theophilus left Constantinople for Alexandria and John resumed office.

Despite his narrow escape, John seems to have learned little. A few weeks later on a Sunday in November 403, the urban prefect Simplicius erected a silver statue of Eudoxia on a column with a dedicatory inscription (still extant) near Hagia Sophia, accompanying the installation with speeches and mimes. With his service disturbed, John denounced the dedication ceremonies. Then a few days later, he began an angry (and now lost) sermon with the words, "Again Herodias raves; again she is troubled; she dances again; and again desires to receive John's head on a platter," a remarkably unwise allusion to the events surrounding the death of John the Baptist. Arcadius was slow to act, but had little choice; he could not allow his dignity to be undermined by his own bishop. Despite the inevitability of John's fall, Arcadius proceeded slowly. The bishops summoned for the second synod met with the emperor in person and condemned John. Arcadius banned John from his church at Easter and after keeping him under arrest for two months exiled him to Cucusus in Armenia Secunda. Arcadius showed great patience, John refused to show contrition. As the patriarch left the city to go into exile, there were riots among his supporters and the Hagia Sophia (soon rebuilt) and the Senate House were both burned down.

Arcadius died in the palace on May 1, 408, aged about thirty. Despite the copious evidence for Arcadius' reign, we know little about the emperor himself. He is traditionally seen as being weak. Synesius' description of Arcadius as a "jellyfish" is often quoted (Synesius, *de Regno* 14D), although no modern historian believes that the speech was given in front of the emperor. Politics was always a dangerous business, but the early part of Arcadius' reign appears particularly troubled. In particular, at this point he seems to have been unable to impose himself on his officials, though this is perhaps unsurprising given his youth. Nor was seeing Rufinus murdered in his presence only ten months after his father's death likely to inspire him to challenge his officials early in the reign. In later years, the Empire was more stable as Arcadius began to assert himself. And unlike the clashes between Theodosius and Ambrose, Arcadius was clearly master over his bishop

THEODOSIUS II (408–450)

Arcadius was succeeded as eastern emperor by his six-year-old son Theodosius II on May 1, 408. Theodosius reigned as sole emperor for forty-two years, the longest reign of any Roman emperor though close in length to Augustus' rule in the first century and the thirty-eight years of Justinian's principate. As Theodosius was even younger than Honorius when he became emperor in 395, his early years were necessarily guided by others. At first, this role was played by Anthemius, who had already been praetorian prefect of the east for four years, although Antiochus the eunuch acted as his tutor and was also said to be influential. The Persian king Yazdgard I (399–421) was supposedly his guardian according to Arcadius' will, though any such role, if it existed, was only nominal. Anthemius was only one of several powerful men in the consistory. Two crises early in the reign would have made it clear that he needed cooperation to guide the state. One crisis was military, in which Uldin, a Hunnic king, crossed the Danube. After his defeat, a number of his followers, including some Sciri, were settled in Bithynia. This settlement disappeared within a century, suggestive of the considerable ability of Roman culture to absorb immigrants. The other crisis was secular, a riot in Constantinople after the grain fleet from Egypt had not arrived as expected. The house of one of Anthemius' colleagues, Monaxius the city prefect, was burned down in the chaos. The various responses to these crises would have required discussion in the consistory in front of the emperor. Expressing strong views was acceptable, but the violence of the competition early in Arcadius' reign had shown the wisdom of moderation; the politics in the early part of Theodosius' reign were noticeably less intense. Tensions with the west caused by Stilicho also disappeared with his death in 408, and some eastern troops were sent to Italy in 410 to help Honorius against the Goths.

Anthemius died in 414 and in the same year, the emperor's sister Pulcheria was acclaimed as Augusta on July 4. The ecclesiastical historian Sozomen, writing in 439, claimed that Pulcheria "governed the Roman empire excellently and with great orderliness" (9.1.5). This claim involves ignoring Theodosius himself, by now aged twelve, and reflects the difficulty of knowing what was actually happening in the palace. Other contemporaries explained government in different ways. Socrates and Theodoret, contemporaries who wrote ecclesiastical histories similar to that of Sozomen, say nothing about Pulcheria's role in government, though they do mention her piety. Sozomen also wrote that Plinta, *magister militum in praesenti* between 419 and 438, was "the most powerful of those then in the palace" (7.17.14). And others saw different figures as being influential. The Egyptian Isidore of Pelusium wrote to Antiochus, *praepositus sacri cubiculi* in 421, claiming that Antiochus controlled the Empire, though this may be flattery (*Ep.* 1.36). A very different view of what was happening in the palace comes from a law of 418 that rejected a request for a group of merchants on Pulcheria's estates to be exempted from paying the *collatio lustralis* (*CT* 13.1.21). Like Eudoxia, Pulcheria was a prominent public figure, but she was not involved in the day-to-day government of the Empire.

There were other tensions outside the imperial palace. In Alexandria, Hypatia, a classically educated and thus pagan mathematician, had been appointed as a professor of philosophy. She was well connected here, being a friend of Orestes, the *praefectus Augustalis*, and was a well-known figure famous for her bluntness. Following an attack by some Jews in the city on some Christians, the Patriarch Cyril expelled Jews from the city. Orestes complained about this to the Emperor, but disorder continued, and Orestes himself was stoned. It was in this highly charged environment that Hypatia was murdered by a group of *parabalani*, a body of Christians appointed by the patriarch to tend the sick, though often mobilized as enforcers. Such treatment of Roman officials often elicited a harsh response from the emperor. The emperor was faced with contradictory reports from Cyril and Orestes,

Figure 14. Trier Ivory, usually thought to show the arrival of the relics of St. Stephen at the imperial palace in Constantinople in 421 (Treasury of Trier Cathedral).

so sent a certain Aedesius to investigate and report back. The *parabalani* were soon limited in number in a law of 416 because of the terror they had caused, and their membership was controlled by the *praefectus Augustalis* (*CT* 16.2.42).

In Constantinople on June 7, 421, Theodosius married a girl much like Hypatia, daughter of a philosopher in Athens. Born Athenais, she had converted to Christianity before the marriage and took the name Eudocia. Several children followed: a son Arcadius, who died young; and two daughters, Eudoxia (acclaimed as Augusta on January 2, 423) and Flacilla, who also died young. Eudocia also wrote poetry, some of which survives. Theodosius' sisters and wife intensified the Christian feelings of the Constantinople, taking advantage of the permanent imperial residence in the city in a way that had not been possible before. Pulcheria, for example, built several churches, including a church for relics of Stephen the Protomartyr in the Great Palace, to which was later added the arm of Stephen, brought to Constantinople from the Holy Land by Eudocia (see Figure 14). In 438, the remains of John Chrysostom were returned to the city and placed in the Church of the Holy Apostles alongside the emperors. The palace and its associated buildings thus had a highly Christian feel, very different from the military camp that had characterized the court of Theodosius I and earlier emperors. This atmosphere was very influential on Peter the Iberian, a twelve-year-old hostage from the Iberian royal family, who arrived ca. 429. He remained in the city until 437, when he escaped from the palace and traveled to Palestina to become a monk.

During the first decade of Theodosius' reign, a period when his uncle Honorius in the west was under intense military pressure, the eastern Emperor faced no major foreign challenges. With the death of the Persian King Yazdgard I in 421, the previously good relations with the Sasanids deteriorated rapidly, and when the new king, Vararanes V (421–438), began to persecute Christians, a short war erupted in 421. A Roman army led by the *magister militum* Ardabur marched through Armenia to Mesopotamia and laid siege to Nisibis. This force withdrew on the approach of Vararanes himself, but was victorious in a battle in 422, after which peace was made. At the same time, western events began to affect Theodosius. First, in 421 Honorius declared Constantius Augustus without consulting Theodosius. Theodosius' refusal to accept Constantius as emperor was followed by rumors that Constantius was planning a war against the east before his death in September 421. Then Honorius and his stepsister Placidia managed to fall out. In early 423, Placidia was expelled from Ravenna and arrived in Constantinople, bringing along her children Valentinian and Honoria. By August, Honorius was dead and John had claimed the western Empire. Theodosius now had a choice to make: whether to recognize John, or go to war to press the claim of his cousin Valentinian. He chose family, so Constantius was now retrospectively recognized as Augustus, and on October 23, 424, Valentinian was acclaimed as Caesar in Thessalonica. Military action followed in 425, when Ardabur led a Roman army into Italy that captured and executed John. Theodosius had planned to visit Rome himself for the acclamation of Valentinian as Augustus, but when he fell ill he sent the *magister officiorum* Helion in his place. With the restoration of the Theodosian dynasty in the west and a successful conclusion to the Persian war, the twenty-three-year-old Theodosius probably felt confident in his Empire. But over the next decade, life for the young emperor suddenly became far more complicated with serious division between his bishops and the growth of the Hunnic confederation.

In December 427, Sisinnius, the patriarch of Constantinople, died. After much discussion, Nestorius was appointed to replace him. Nestorius was a man with ambition, and in his inaugural sermon he made a promise to Theodosius: "Give me, emperor, the earth cleansed of heretics, and I will give back heaven to you. Put down the heretics with me, and I will put down the Persians with you" (Socrates 7.29). He also managed to create a debate in the city by claiming that it was inappropriate for Mary to be called Mother of God (*Theotokos*). Nestorius thus started a chain of events that were to take up vast amounts of imperial energy for the next two centuries. There is plentiful source material, much of it written by the participants, but little of it is impartial. News of Nestorius' views on Mary was rapidly disseminated. Some bishops were not concerned or supportive, but others, in particular Cyril of Alexandria, found his views objectionable. Cyril proceeded in two ways. He engaged the support of Pope Celestine, though his description of Nestorius' actions was rather misleading. Celestine incautiously condemned Nestorius without investigation. Celestine's views of the accusation and of his powers to depose an eastern bishop were not universally shared by eastern bishops, never mind Theodosius. Cyril also wrote a document himself condemning Nestorius, the so-called Twelve Anathemas. With this, he was overreaching and provoked a prolonged refutation by Theodoret of Cyrrhus. Faced with conflict over the views of his patriarch and with an unhappy Pope, Theodosius summoned a universal church council to meet at Ephesus in June 431, appointing the *comes domesticorum* Candidianus to preside.

The previous universal councils at Nicaea and Constantinople, though often spirited, had been able to come to clear decisions. Nothing like this was to happen at the First Council of Ephesus, where, despite the imperial instructions, there was no debate between the dissenting groups of bishops. Nestorius arrived on time, soon followed by Cyril with many of his supporters. The Antiochene contingent, led by John of Antioch and including Theodoret, was delayed. After several days when the Antiochenes had still not arrived, Cyril overrode Candidianus and held a council in which 197 bishops deposed Nestorius. When the easterners finally arrived, they also held a separate council in which forty-three bishops deposed Cyril and condemned the Twelve Chapters. Both factions then reported to the emperor.

The civic turmoil in Constantinople caused by the council in 381 and by the deposition of John Chrysostom in 403 was now repeated. The archimandrite Dalmatius, who had not left his cell in forty-eight years, came to the imperial palace in Constantinople at the end of June 431 accompanied by a large crowd. Having entered the palace, Dalmatius showed the emperor the letter he had received from Cyril at Ephesus recording the deposition of Nestorius. It was a moment of great drama. There was also a public demonstration at the Hagia Sophia in early July 431. By now it was clear to Theodosius that Nestorius was unpopular, but there was no certainty about what would happen next. At the end of July, Theodosius summoned a small group of bishops to meet him at Chalcedon in September. Cyril knew that Theodosius had still not yet made up his mind and so hoped to create a favorable climate of opinion at court. He therefore encouraged Dalmatius to see the emperor again and sent out a slew of presents. The majority of these were not sent to imperial officials but to those Cyril hoped could influence them, such as Heleniana, the wife of Florentius, the assessor of the eastern praetorian prefect. The main effort was directed toward the *cubicularii*. The dispatch of one hundred pounds of gold to both the *quaestor* and the *magister officiorum* reflects Cyril's desperation as imperial officials were not allowed to accept gifts while in office. Since the preserved gift list totals more than one thousand pounds of gold as well as numerous luxury goods, it is not surprising that three contemporaries, Theodoret, Nestorius, and Acacius of Beroea, accused Cyril of bribery. Theodosius finally accepted the exile of Nestorius and the reinstatement of Cyril in September 431. This resolved the dispute over Nestorius, but it was still necessary to reconcile the Antiochene and Alexandrian churches. More negotiations followed, and Theodosius by April 433 had been able to produce the Formula of Reunion acceptable to both Cyril and John. However, some of John's bishops did not accept the formula and withdrew from communion with him. Theodosius now ordered the *quaestor* Domitianus to tell the Cilician bishops to recognize John or be exiled. This order was opposed by the eastern praetorian prefect Taurus (son of the prefect Aurelianus exiled in 400), who warned the emperor that it would cause such disturbances that Cilicia would be the same as Thrace, referring to recent Hunnic raids, and claimed that tax income would be reduced. Despite his bluntness, Taurus went on to serve a second term as prefect in the mid-440s. The Formula of Reunion was clumsy, but it could be made to work as long as the participants were prepared to compromise.

At the same time as trying to bring order to the church, Theodosius was also grappling with the rising power of the Vandals and the Huns. The Vandals had crossed from Spain to Africa in 429. To reinforce the western defenses, the *magister militum* Aspar was sent with troops to Carthage in 431, remaining there until 434. In Europe, early Hunnic activity was concentrated around the Great Hungarian Plain on either bank of the River Theiss, opposite the western diocese of Illyricum and the eastern diocese of Dacia. Until the 430s, these Hunnic tribes had both raided the Empire and fought as mercenaries for eastern and western empires. But from the 430s, one Hunnic leader Rua was able to build a powerful confederation. Like other barbarian confederations, not all the members of Rua's alliance wished to be ruled by him. Priscus noted that the Amilzuri, Itimari, Tounsoures, Bosici, and other tribes had attempted to escape Rua's power. Rua was succeeded ca. 434 by the brothers Bleda and Attila. In their first negotiations with the Romans, they were concerned to receive back royal fugitives who had fled to the Romans and to stop the Romans from receiving further fugitives. When the Romans did return two Hunnic royalty, the children Mama and Atakam, they were promptly impaled. The Romans also doubled the annual payments to the Huns from 350 to 700 pounds of gold. Along with these great wars, there

Figure 15. Petition of Appion, bishop of Syene, to Theodosius II (SB 20,14606). (Licensed under CC BY 3.0)

were continuing minor problems on all frontiers. Near Syene in the Upper Thebaid, the bishop Appion wrote in Greek to Theodosius requesting to be assigned some troops to defend his churches. A copy of the petition was forwarded to the Dux of the Thebaid, with an annotation by Theodosius himself in Latin (see Figure 15).

While this military and religious activity was taking place, the internal affairs of the Empire continued. On October 29, 437, Valentinian III and

Theodosius' daughter Licinia Eudoxia were married in Constantinople. This was a spectacular moment in Roman history, the first time since 395 that emperors from both parts of the Empire had been together in the same city and the last occasion in Roman history that this was to occur. Sadly, we have no descriptions of the ceremony and celebrations, even though the talented western poet Merobaudes was probably present. At this time, Valentinian III transferred the Pannonian provinces and the city of Sirmium to Theodosius II, though he kept the other parts of the diocese of Illyricum, i.e., Noricum and Dalmatia, under western control. The same year saw the completion of one of Theodosius' great projects, the compilation of the Theodosian Code. This work, which had started in 429, attempted to assemble all laws with universal validity issued by emperors since the reign of Constantine. Over 2,500 edicts were excerpted and sorted into sixteen books. Like the marriage of Valentinian and Eudoxia, it was a reaffirmation of the Roman Empire, showing that it was a single organism even though it had two heads. Huge efforts were required of the compilers to assemble the raw material, often using provincial archives from both east and west, showing that there were no central archives available. This compilation, as well as the length of Theodosius' reign, means much legislation is preserved. The issuing of edicts banning pagans, Jews, Samaritans, and heretics from imperial service and forbidding pagan sacrifices suggests that these were still continued practices. Other actions included laws restricting the building of new synagogues, though permitting repairs to existing buildings, ordering the removal of lime kilns near the palace, and ordering shops in the porticoes by the Baths of Zeuxippus to devote some of their income to repairing the baths. The process of legislation is well illustrated by three laws, which postdate the code, concerning the rights of some accused to select which court would have jurisdiction (*praescriptio fori*). The first, from September 440, was directed to Cyrus, the eastern praetorian prefect. Two months later, a second law clarified that it was meant to cover non-military *comites* and tribunes but not soldiers. Then in March 441, a third law clarified the status of civilian support staff in the offices of *magistri militum*. Together, they suggest a committee process in which laws were read aloud and the full implications were not always immediately clear, but also continued readiness to change and correct government processes. Another law of 444 responded to a report of the eastern praetorian prefect Zoilus that a certain decurion of Emesa, Valerianus, had claimed the rank of *illustris* to which he was not entitled. Theodosius stripped Valerianus of his rank and restored him to the city council, but exacted no further punishment (*Novellae of Theodosius II* 15.2). Valerianus' attempt to evade local responsibilities is strikingly similar to Thalassius' attempt half a century earlier.

Following the Vandal occupation of Carthage in 439, Theodosius planned another African expedition. The organization for this took place at the same time as a brief Roman war against the Persians in 440. In 441, the expedition against Africa reached as far as Sicily before it was recalled when the Huns crossed the Danube. They occupied Sirmium, Ratiaria, Viminacium, Singidunum, and Margus (delivered to the Huns by the treachery of its bishop) before advancing to capture Naissus, then Philippopolis and Arcadiopolis. The ability of the Huns to capture so many cities so quickly had much to do with the withdrawal of Roman troops for wars in Persia and Africa, though they were more skilled at siege warfare than many contemporary barbarians. Nonetheless, they were not invincible and the town of Asemus in Moesia Prima was able to resist them. When peace was negotiated, Attila and Bleda demanded the return of fugitives; some Hunnic royalty in Roman territory killed themselves rather than be handed over him. After this campaign, the praetorian prefect of Illyricum Apraemius moved his headquarters from Sirmium to Thessalonica.

In 445, Attila murdered Bleda and became sole ruler over the Huns. By this point, he had a fearsome reputation, but was still only one of the many problems that Theodosius had to face. The Hun confederation had now grown to reach the Black Sea, incorporating numerous Gothic groups as well as the Gepids and the Akatziri. It was still fragile, and Theodosius had already unsuccessfully attempted to detach the Akatziri. Then in 447, the Huns again crossed the Danube following the Roman refusal to hand over more fugitives to Attila. Attila captured Marcianopolis and reached Thermopylae in Greece, though he was turned back by the defenses; he then defeated Arnegisclus in a hard-fought battle at the River Utus before winning another victory in the Chersonesus and threatening Constantinople. The city's walls had been damaged by an earthquake earlier in the year, with fifty-seven towers collapsing, and so had to be hurriedly repaired. Rather than test the defenses, Theodosius negotiated peace with the Huns again, trebling the previous payments to 2,100 pounds of gold per year. The demand for 6,000 pounds of back tribute produced an effect visible in Constantinople, according to the contemporary, Priscus:

> To these payments of tribute and other monies which had to be sent to the Huns they forced all taxpayers to contribute, even those who for a period of time had been relieved of the heaviest category of land tax through a judicial decision or through imperial liberality. Even members of the Senate contributed a fixed amount of gold according to their rank. To many their

high station brought a change of lifestyle, for they paid only with difficulty what each had been assigned by those whom the Emperor appointed to the task, so that formerly wealthy men were selling on the market their wives' jewellery and their furniture. This was the calamity that befell the Romans after the war and the outcome was that many killed themselves either by starvation or by the noose (Priscus fr. 9.3).

As a piece of rhetoric, this is wonderful. Priscus' outrage that even senators had to pay taxes does not fit well with modern theories of progressive taxation, while others might wonder why he (or any other source) did not name any of the many who had committed suicide. The senators could probably afford this. A generation earlier, Olympiodorus claimed that in the 420s senators at Rome often had an annual income of one thousand pounds of gold or more; although many individuals might be richer than eastern senators, westerners were probably no richer as a group. Further fugitives were also demanded, some of whom were executed by the Romans when they refused to return to the Huns.

In addition to facing problems with the Vandals and the Huns, Theodosius by the late 440s was also troubled again by religious disputes. A certain Eutyches was the archimandrite of the monastery of Job near the Hebdomon in Constantinople, as well as being the godfather of Chrysaphius. Eutyches was accused by Flavianus, patriarch of Constantinople (446–449), of believing that Christ had only one nature, the divine, which subsumed the human, a very Cyrillian point of view. Others also disagreed with Eutyches' views, including Theodoret, who wrote a dialogue attacking Eutyches, the *Eranistes*; and Domnus, patriarch of Antioch (441–449), who wrote to the emperor complaining. In November 448, Flavianus convened a meeting of the bishops who happened to be in Constantinople on business, a standing assembly usually known as the Home Synod. Here, thirty bishops from provinces including Isauria, Thrace, Helenopontus, Africa Proconsularis, and Pisidia condemned Eutyches. Nonetheless, Eutyches' belief, which we know about only from the perspective of Flavianus, was accepted as orthodox by both the patriarch of Alexandria Dioscurus (444–451) and by Theodosius II. The tensions between Antioch and Alexandria over the nature of Christ, which were unresolved since the First Council of Ephesus in 431, thus resurfaced. As the extent of the dispute became clear, Theodosius remarked that it would be "intolerable to overlook such a gross impropriety, lest this might appear to involve outrage against the Almighty" (*Acts of the Council of Chalcedon*, First Session #24). He therefore summoned the bishops to meet at the Second Council of Ephesus in August 449, which deposed Flavianus and accepted Eutyches as orthodox.

THE SECOND COUNCIL OF EPHESUS, 449

By the time Theodosius summoned his bishops to meet at Ephesus, the fragile peace he had built in 433 between the Antiochene and Alexandrian bishops had been destroyed. Theodosius took a different approach to managing this council, appointing Dioscurus, patriarch of Alexandria, to run it rather than a secular official. The main business of the council was the emperor's desire to reverse the condemnation of Eutyches that had taken place at the Home Synod in 448. Furthermore, Theodosius confined Theodoret of Cyrrhus, the leading Antiochene theologian, to his see and specifically banned him from attending. This was a severe blow to those who disagreed with Cyrillian theology. Theodoret was outraged at this and wrote letters to several senior officials, including Anatolius. Despite having been shown a letter "written by the hand of the emperor" and confirming that he had abided by its terms, he asked Anatolius to find out if such an order had really been sent and

> if no order of the kind has really been issued, to let me know; but if the letter really comes from the victorious emperor, tell his pious majesty not readily to believe lies nor give a hearing only to the accusers, but to demand an account from the accused (*Ep.* 79).

There were several sessions of the council. In the first session, Dioscurus managed the 135 assembled bishops to approve the rehabilitation of Eutyches, following the line desired by the emperor. Flavianus was also deposed. He was then imprisoned in mysterious circumstances and died soon afterward. However, two years later at Chalcedon many bishops claimed that they had acted only under duress. Basil of Seleucia, for example, asserted that he was forced to accede when "armed soldiers burst into the church and there stood the monks around Barsauma and the *parabalani* [lay brethren controlled by Dioscurus] and another great crowd" (*Acts of Chalcedon*, First Session # 851); these were the same *parabalani* who had murdered Hypatia only a generation earlier. These claims of duress need to be considered in light of the need of those bishops who had followed Dioscurus at Ephesus in 449 to justify their now turning against him.

Another controversy involved Pope Leo. After the Home Synod, Flavianus had sent an account of the proceedings to Leo. Leo in reply wrote a document that has become known as the Tome of Leo. In addition to a condemnation of Eutyches, it included a statement of faith stressing the human and divine natures (dyophysite) within Christ. Leo's envoys, the bilingual bishop Julian of Cos and the Deacon Hilary (later Pope Hilary), went to the council, but though received, the tome was never read. This prompted Leo to describe the meeting as a robber council (*latrocinium*). For all Leo's bluster, the tensions between his document and the more nuanced miaphysite (i.e., focusing on the unity of the two natures in Christ) statement that most easterners preferred were not yet exposed. These issues were bypassed in 449, and the council made no statements regarding faith, though it reaffirmed the principle that the Nicene Creed was sufficient and that there should be no innovation regarding this or the First Council of Ephesus.

Other issues were discussed at another session, whose records have survived only in a Syriac translation. As a result of his hostility toward Cyril in the 430s, Bishop Ibas of Edessa had been accused of being a Nestorian, a term that by now had little to do with views actually expressed by Nestorius himself. Ibas' enemies had first approached Domnus, patriarch of Antioch, but were not received. They then appealed to Flavian in Constantinople and to the emperor. This appeal prompted Theodosius to request that Chaereas, *praeses* of Osrhoene, investigate; these materials were read out as part of the proceedings at Ephesus against Ibas. They include, as required by Constantine in his law of 331 (*CT* 1.16.6), a record of all the acclamations made in front of Chaereas. Chaereas not only forwarded their petitions to the emperor, but also sent them to the *magister officiorum* and to the praetorian prefects of the East, Italy, and Illyricum. At one point in the local petitions, the *comes* Theodosius from Edessa requested that Chaereas

> convey these instruments to his excellency, the Master of divine Offices, so that through the means of his Excellency the Victorious and divine Crown may be informed of them, and to the Glorious and Illustrious Prefects, and to the powerful *magister utriusque militiae*, the ex-consul. Will your Highness also instruct, by your Letters, the Holy Archbishops of Constantinople the Opulent, and of Alexandria (the Great), as well as the Venerable Domnus, the Archbishop of Antioch, and the Holy Bishop of Jerusalem, Juvenal, and Eustathius and Photius, the Holy Bishops of Tyre and Berytus, who have had to be judges in this affair? (108–109).

As a result of his proven hostility to Cyril, Ibas was deposed. After the council, Theodosius wrote to Dioscurus again regarding the affirmation of faith:

> Your Piety, having then taken copies of it, will despatch it to the Venerable Bishops of the Royal City of Constantinople and Jerusalem, and to the other Metropolitans in order that all those bishops suffragan to them may sign it also and forward it to us with those letters, notifying the same to us, and (in order that) every one of the bishops who has a copy may read it in Church before all the people. But before anything else, your Piety with all your suffragan bishops will append your signatures and forward the same to the auditory of our Serene Highness (369).

As the council showed, events within the Empire often related to each other in complex ways. Following the marriage of their daughter, Theodosius' wife Eudocia set out to visit the Holy Land in 438, returning with many relics. Eudocia was friends with the Egyptian Cyrus, consul for 441, urban prefect twice, the second time holding this office at the same time as he was eastern praetorian prefect (439–441). Like many other aristocrats, Cyrus wrote poetry and sponsored construction; a suburb of Constantinople where he built a Church of the Theotokos came to bear his name. More unusually, he had the reputation of being incorruptible. Cyrus was not the only aristocrat building in Constantinople during Theodosius' reign. The urban prefect Aetius built a large cistern in 421, and the eunuch *praepositi sacri cubiculi* Antiochus and Lausus both built extravagant houses near the Hippodrome. Cyrus, however, was exceptional, and his popularity became such that the Hippodrome crowd (where Theodosius favored the Greens) praised him in front of Theodosius, leasing to his dismissal from office and appointment as bishop in Cotiaeum. Another important contemporary was Chrysaphius, a eunuch who held the rank of *spatharius* (sword-bearer) in the imperial household. Chrysaphius' influence has been seen in the withdrawal of Pulcheria from the Great Palace to the Hebdomon and of the withdrawal of Eudocia to the Holy Land. By the sixth century, Eudocia's self-imposed exile was being explained in romantic terms, as the result of a suspected affair between Eudocia and the ex-*magister officiorum* Paulinus, himself executed in 444. Like other eunuchs, Chrysaphius was able to make himself important by his closeness to the emperor. Aristocratic competition was intensified by Theodosius' holding eighteen consulates himself, reducing the opportunities available. At the same time, long tenures of office also reduced the opportunities available for promotion to the highest ranks. Helion was *magister officiorum* for at least fifteen years, while Aspar appears to have been *magister militum* from 424 to 471 and Plinta was *magister militum praesentalis* between 419 and 438. The long tenures, however, did mean that many *magistri militum* and praetorian prefects did become consuls. It is also remarkable how many sons of prefects and general were successful in reaching *illustris* rank, also suggestive of a limited group.

As with the difficult choices to make about religious groups, Theodosius also had choices to make concerning the Huns. These choices included military approaches, whether attacking the Huns or simply bolstering the defenses, finding allies, murdering Attila, or buying him off. For a brief period after the 447 war, Attila had been able to impose a demilitarized zone on the Roman bank of the Danube between Singidunum and Novae. At this point, the policy of appeasement was in disarray, while the military approach was clearly also not feasible. Then in 449, the Romans changed strategies and attempted the assassination of Attila. Chrysaphius organized a plot, described in detail by Priscus, which had the backing of Theodosius and the *magister officiorum* Martialis. The plot failed, and Attila demanded the surrender of Chrysaphius. Chrysaphius had maneuvered himself into an influential position, but only at the cost of making numerous enemies. He was also unpopular with a certain Zeno (an Isaurian, but not to be confused with the later emperor) first recorded as *magister militum per Orientem* in 447 and appointed consul for 448. Zeno had taken the daughter of Saturninus, who had been betrothed to one of Attila's secretaries, and married her instead to the *comes rei militaris* Rufus. Rufus' brother was Apollonius, *magister militum praesentalis* from 443 to 451. When Attila complained to Theodosius about the broken engagement, the emperor confiscated the girl's property, an act which Zeno blamed on Chrysaphius. Immediately afterward, the *magister militum* Anatolius and Nomus, *patricius* and ex-*magister officiorum*, were able to negotiate a new wife for Attila's secretary and the Hunnic withdrawal from the demilitarized zone. This was the high-water mark of the Huns, but Attila was still north of the Danube and the emperors in Ravenna and Constantinople. Although his plot to murder Attila had failed, Chrysaphius retained the support of Theodosius. Soon afterward, Theodosius suspected that Zeno might declare himself emperor, probably as a result of rumors started by Chrysaphius. Theodosius' planned actions against Zeno were not followed through aggressively, either because the suspicions were unfounded or because of his death.

Theodosius II died in a riding accident on July 28, 450, aged only forty-eight. The first few years of his reign depended very much on his advisers, but once past these opening years, he faced few serious threats to his Empire despite the length of the reign. Although there was no danger of the Empire collapsing, Theodosius was unable to resolve the problems caused by the Vandals, the Huns, and his bishops. Reversing the Vandal occupation of Africa was probably within the capacities of the eastern Empire, but defeating the Huns on the Danube would only lead to some other barbarian group taking their place. As for the problems caused by religion, no fifth-century emperor was able to resolve them. Despite all the other challenges faced by the emperor, the creation of the Theodosian Code may have been his greatest triumph.

MARCIAN (450–457)

The childless Theodosius was succeeded by Marcian, acclaimed emperor at the Hebdomon on August 25, 450. The new emperor had been born in

392 in Thrace and had a military career, campaigning in Africa in 431 and reaching the rank of tribune. He had a daughter Euphemia from an earlier marriage, but no son, nor would any come from his marriage to Theodosius' sister Pulcheria. The month-long interregnum after the death of Theodosius was significant. The acclamation of Marcian was taken without the approval of the senior Augustus, Valentinian III, though there certainly was time to consult. Marcian was not accepted as legitimate by the west until 452. Deciding how to handle this would have involved much discussion in the consistory. The major figures of Aspar and Zeno continued to serve the new regime, but Chrysaphius was soon executed. Zeno was made *patricius*, but after his death, Aspar's son, Ardabur, was promoted to his position of *magister militum per Orientem*.

Marcian's first concern was the Huns, who as recently as 447 had been plundering outside the imperial city. Unlike Theodosius II, however, he refused to pay subsidies to Attila. Marcian may have been persuaded by Zeno, but he probably made the decision knowing that Attila was planning to go to war against the west. Marcian's judgment that the Huns could be challenged proved correct. Following Hun campaigns in Gaul in 451 and Italy in 452, Attila died of natural causes in 453. Since the Hun Empire had been built on his personality, his sons were unable to compel the subject peoples to accept their authority. This collapse is also suggestive of what might have happened if Chrysaphius' plan to murder Attila had succeeded. The Gepids led a revolt that defeated the Huns at the Battle of the Nedao in 454, after which the confederation collapsed. Some of the Huns and their subjects entered the Empire and took up service as Roman troops. Others settled on Roman terms in 454–455 when Marcian placed several groups of Goths in Pannonia Prima and Valeria, though Sirmium remained Roman controlled.

Like many new emperors, Marcian was surprised at what he found at the court. Less than two months after his proclamation, a law regarding appeals to the emperor declared that "you see columns, you see infinite throngs of people arriving, flowing in not only from neighbouring provinces, but also from the farthest borders of the Roman world, and bringing complaints against their enemies" (*Novellae of Marcian* 1). In the same year, he banned *clarissimi* and *spectabiles* from the provinces from holding the praetorship. Financially, Marcian was confident, writing off arrears of taxes, and between 452 and 455 he abolished the *collatio glebalis*, a senatorial land tax. These measures would have been well received by the urban senators of Constantinople, though perhaps not so happily by the praetorian prefects, the *comes rei privatae*, or the *comes sacrarum largitionum*. Nonetheless, by the end of his reign there was a surplus of over one hundred thousand pounds of gold.

With a new emperor, those who objected to the results of the Second Council of Ephesus could try to reopen the issues. Pope Leo was unhappy with the treatment of his Tome, and Theodoret had many supporters who agreed with his rejection of Cyril's Twelve Anathemas. By acceding to Leo's request for further action, Marcian may have been hopeful of conciliating Valentinian III, who at this point had not accepted him as an imperial colleague. The Council of Chalcedon was held in October 451. Marcian took a far more forceful approach than Theodosius, appointing the *magister militum* Anatolius to preside and sending a huge number of secular officials, including the eastern praetorian prefect Palladius, the urban prefect Tatianus, and the *magister officiorum* Vincomalus. These proceedings are preserved in their entirety, including transcripts of parts of the Home Synod of 448 and the Second Council of Ephesus in 449. The council was well attended by eastern bishops, and even Nestorius was invited. But like the Second Council of Ephesus, the emperor's desired outcome was clear from the start of the council. The first session began with a condemnation of the views of Christ's nature approved at Ephesus only two years earlier. Though often described as "monophysite," the nature of Christ was not a significant topic at Ephesus for the eastern attendees. Nonetheless, condemning the council required some deft maneuvering, though Dioscurus' aggression in 449 made it possible for many bishops to claim that they were acting under duress. More difficult was forcing the acceptance of the Tome of Leo. Although this satisfied western bishops, its strict dyophysite approach, stressing the separate divine and human elements of Christ, failed to deal with the theological issues raised at the First Council of Ephesus. Particularly problematic was the tome's treatment of Eutyches, accepting uncritically Flavianus' distortion of his position. Nonetheless, the emperor's men forced the issue. By creating a false choice between Leo and Dioscurus, they were, like Constantine at Nicaea, able to impose unity. A new definition of faith was agreed in the fifth session on October 22, and then Marcian himself, together with Pulcheria, attended the sixth session of the Council of Chalcedon on October 25, 451, to approve the new definition.

The dyophysite declaration of Chalcedon set the stage for the next half-century of ecclesiastical politics, with many bishops struggling to understand and, worse, to explain how the orthodoxy of 449 had been overturned. Theodoret and Ibas were restored, while Dioscurus was deposed and exiled to Gangra in Paphlagonia, being replaced as bishop of Alexandria by Proterius (451–457). Civic disorder in Alexandria followed rapidly, and many of the population, led by Peter Mongus and Timothy Aelurus, refused to accept Proterius. Florus, holding the combined offices of *comes Aegypti* and *praefectus Augustalis*, had to bring in additional troops, close baths, and stop all public entertainments before order could be restored. In subsequent sessions, the council conducted other business, carving a patriarchate at Jerusalem out of the patriarchate of Antioch, though limited in jurisdiction to the three provinces of Palestina. The monks in these provinces refused to accept Juvenal's authority and created their own bishop, Theodosius. Here too, troops had to be deployed to reassert order since Juvenal was unable to return to his see without them. Flavianus was restored as patriarch of Constantinople. The council also granted control of the dioceses of Pontica, Asiana, and Thrace to the bishop of Constantinople and, making a reality of the patriarchate that had grown up over the past half-century, assigned the city the same privileges as Rome though second to that city. As might be expected, this decision was strongly opposed by Leo's delegates, whose grounds for objection were noted but ignored.

Although the Huns were the most important part of Marcian's dealings outside the Empire, there were other issues. In the west, the murder of Valentinian III in 455 was soon followed by the Vandal sack of Rome. During this, Geiseric captured Valentinian's wife Eudoxia and her two daughters Placidia and Eudocia. Placidia's husband, Anicius Olybrius, went to Constantinople and persuaded Marcian to send envoys to Geiseric, unsuccessfully requesting the release of the imperial women. After the death of Valentinian, Marcian refused to accept the legitimacy of the recently acclaimed western emperor Avitus and designated consuls himself for both parts of the Empire in 456 and 457. In the Caucasus, there was a short Roman campaign in Lazica, where the northern parts, known as Suania, were attempting to secede. The Romans were able to impose unity by forcing King Gobazes to abdicate in favor of his son. And in Constantinople, Pulcheria died in July 453 and was buried in the Church of the Holy Apostles. Notable imperial construction included the Column of Marcian, which was built on the main road to the city center south of the Church of the Holy Apostles.

Marcian was sixty-five when he died in Constantinople on January 27, 457, and was buried with his wife in the Church of the Holy Apostles. Financially and militarily, it was a successful reign. At his death, the situation in the east was very similar to that at Arcadius' accession in 395. The imperial borders were in roughly the same place, though there were now a new set of problems exposed by the Vandal occupation of Africa. The Huns had suggested the military weakness of the Empire, though their threat appears to be similar to the problems posed by the Goths in the 370s and 380s. The Persian frontier continued to be peaceful. In religious terms, however, the reign was disastrous. The councils of Ephesus and Chalcedon had created significant ecclesiastical disunity within the east as well as forcing conflict with the west. Despite the religious problems, the early fifth century was little different from the late fourth century for the eastern Empire. But over the same period, the outlook for the western Empire had worsened dramatically.

THE WESTERN EMPIRE: HONORIUS (395–423)

When Theodosius died, Honorius succeeded him in the west. He faced significant problems during his reign and has been left with a poor reputation. According to Bury, "His name would be forgotten among the obscurest occupants of the Imperial throne were it not that his reign coincided with the fatal period in which it was decided that western Europe was to pass from the Roman to the Teuton" (*History of the Later Roman Empire*, volume 1, 210–211). As Honorius was only ten years old at his accession, the Empire was initially dominated by the regent Stilicho. Stilicho had earlier married Theodosius' niece; then in 398, he became the emperor's father-in-law when Honorius married his daughter Maria. Stilicho's dominance, like Rufinus' in the east, is seen in the reorganization of offices. In the *Notitia Dignitatum*, the *magister militum per Gallias* lost his own entry and was incorporated into a chapter showing the distribution of all military forces in the west under the command of Stilicho, holding the office of *magister peditum*.

Honorius' court was initially based at Milan, but after the Goths had been expelled from Italy in 402, it moved to Ravenna, though he occasionally visited Rome. Located in the marshes at the mouth of the Po Valley, Ravenna was easy to defend, as well as being a port. It was also better suited than Rome to be the capital of an Empire that needed to focus on the Balkans and on communications with Constantinople. However, an imperial presence in Italy in a city other than Rome continued the disjunction that had grown up from the mid-fourth century between the Emperor and the aristocracy of the city of Rome.

The question of policy toward Alaric's Goths was to dominate western Roman politics for the next two decades. Honorius did not have the resources or good enough generals to defeat them in the field, while at the same time the plans he put into place were constantly being upset by other events, in particular the failure of his brother Arcadius to cooperate in the early years of the reign. This began as early as 395, when Stilicho led the combined eastern and western field armies back from Italy through the Balkans, escorting the body of Theodosius to Constantinople. Arcadius then requested that Honorius abort Stilicho's operations against Alaric.

Worse, a western landing in the Peloponnese in 397 intended to help Arcadius against the Goths resulted in the recognition of Alaric as *magister militum per Illyricum* and the declaration of Stilicho as a public enemy. Furthermore, Arcadius encouraged the request by the *comes Africae* Gildo to report to him rather than to Honorius, resulting in the threat of cutting off the grain supplies to Rome. Honorius sent Gildo's brother Mascezel against him, resulting in a swift victory and the return of Africa to western control. In 401, Alaric and his Goths, no longer welcome in the east, moved into Italy. There were inconclusive battles with Stilicho at Pollentia and Verona in 402, following which Alaric retreated to Pannonia and Dalmatia. Most of our evidence for these events comes from Stilicho's poet Claudian, reflecting criticism of his continued failure to defeat Alaric. Alaric's ability to stave off defeat was considerable, but he was also unable to defeat the Roman army. When Stilicho was faced by a less capable leader, the result was very different. Another Gothic king, Radagaisus, led his people over the Alps in 405. Stilicho met them near Florence with thirty regiments and destroyed them in a victory that matched contemporary expectations of what the Roman army should be able to do against the barbarians. A triumphal arch was then erected in Rome in honor of the victory, dedicated to Arcadius, Honorius, and Theodosius. The Latin-speaking dioceses of Dacia and Macedonia had been under eastern control since 378. Now that Alaric was in Pannonia, it made sense to Honorius to use the Goths to pressure Arcadius to return the dioceses of Dacia and Macedonia. He was also being pushed by Pope Innocent, who was concerned about the exile of John Chrysostom. Honorius' pressure can be seen in a letter from 405 to his brother, in which he complains about the honors given to images of Eudoxia, but also mentioned the lack of information about events in the Balkans (*Collectio Avellana* 38).

Honorius' hopes of regaining Dacia and Macedonia, however unlikely, were upset by events on the Rhine. Around 402, the capital of the Gallic prefecture was moved from Trier on the Rhine to Arles on the Mediterranean. Soon after this, at the end of 406, large numbers of Suevi, Alans, and Vandals arrived on the Rhine, fighting their way west through the Franks before crossing the river. With Honorius focusing on the Goths, two emperors appeared in Britain, Marcus and Gratian, who both ruled very briefly before being succeeded by Constantine III. He crossed to Gaul in early 407 and was rapidly accepted as emperor. The speed of Constantine's advance gave Honorius little time to react. Order was soon restored on the Rhine, in part by recruiting many of the invaders to fight for Constantine. By late 407, Constantine's troops had garrisoned the passes through the Alps. Some of Honorius' Spanish relatives raised troops, prompting Constantine in spring

408 to send his son and Caesar, Constans, and a general, Gerontius, across the Pyrenees.

Honorius was now faced with two simultaneous problems: commitments to Alaric and a need for action against Constantine. In early 408, he went to Rome to extract money from the Senate to pay off Alaric in Noricum. The sum proposed, four thousand pounds of gold, was clearly beyond Honorius' available resources at this point, as he was fighting wars against Alaric and Constantine and deprived of half the western Empire. The senators were, understandably, reluctant, with the ex-urban prefect Lampadius making a memorable speech claiming that this was not a peace (*pax*) but a pact (*pactio*) of slavery. However, rhetoric is cheap, war is not, and the Goths were at the door. Then news arrived of the death of Arcadius in Constantinople on May 1, 408. Honorius wished to go to bury his brother, but Stilicho argued that he should not abandon Italy when it was threatened by both Constantine and Alaric. He was probably right, but there was a cost to this. Both emperor and general then left Rome for northern Italy, but news of their disagreement left Stilicho vulnerable. Stilicho also hoped to send Alaric against Constantine, setting one threat against another; whoever won, Honorius would benefit. Stilicho was now faced with a rumor, apparently started by the *magister scrinii*, Olympius, that he planned to make his son Eucherius emperor in Constantinople in place of Theodosius. On August 13, 408, while the army was being assembled at Ticinum to march against Constantine, Olympius' whispers boiled over into mutiny, suggesting the intensity of the army's feeling of loyalty toward the emperor, not to its commanders. The hostility to paying off Alaric led to the death of the praetorian prefects of Gaul, Limenius, and Italy; Longinianus, the prefect of Rome; as well as the Gallic *magister militum* Chariobaudes, the *magister equitum* Vincentius, the *magister officiorum*, and the *comes sacrarum largitionum*. Also killed was the *quaestor* Salvius, cut down while clasping Honorius' feet. It was like the murder of Rufinus in front of Arcadius, but so much worse. Stilicho was at Bononia, the only high official to escape. It was not until later in the day that Honorius, without chlamys or diadem, managed to calm the troops. With the massacre of Stilicho's supporters, Honorius was persuaded or decided that Stilicho had to go and declared him a public enemy; he surrendered and was executed at Ravenna on August 23. A witch hunt of Stilicho's friends and supporters followed, though this produced no evidence for any wrongdoing. Honorius repudiated his wife Thermantia, Stilicho's daughter. Eucherius had taken refuge in a church at Rome, but on imperial orders was taken from the church and executed. Afterward, Stilicho's wife Serena, the emperor's mother-in-law, was strangled; Zosimus later claimed this was on account of her pagan sympathies. A monument in the Forum at Rome, inscribed to commemorate Stilicho's defeat of Radagaisus in 406, soon had his name chiseled out (*ILS* 799).

Following the murders, a host of new imperial officials were appointed, Olympius as *magister officiorum*, Turpilio as *magister equitum*, and Varanes as *magister peditum*. The estates of the executed officials were confiscated by the emperor, though the income from these seems unlikely to have covered the taxes lost by remissions to Italy of both regular taxation and the senatorial *collatio glebalis* detailed in a law of September 13, 408 (*CT* 11.28.4). At the same time, the new voices in the consistory led to a new policy against Alaric, moving from conciliation and negotiation to hostility. An embassy sent by Alaric with a request to be allowed to settle in Noricum was rejected. One can imagine the debate in the consistory, a probably subdued Honorius, a ranting Olympius, a new praetorian prefect who had just learned that the accounts would not add up, and some quiet and doubtful *magistri militum* making promises they knew that they could not deliver. There was, however, an end to the hostility between the two parts of the Empire. Soon, western ports were reopened to eastern shipping, and Theodosius sent some troops to help his uncle. Although Alaric wished to continue the peace established by Stilicho, Olympius' faction was committed to war. So in October 408, Alaric entered Italy and, with the Roman army unable to offer opposition, marched straight to Rome, which he besieged. The senators chose to negotiate with Alaric themselves. One would like to know where Lampadius was at the moment that Alaric demanded everything from the city but their lives. A second embassy produced a more reasonable, yet still chilling, five thousand pounds of gold and thirty thousand pounds of silver. The money was raised by a levy from the senators and given to Alaric, who withdrew from the city. The elite of Rome probably felt abandoned by their emperor at this point, with the Roman army nowhere to be seen. Soon afterward, the wealthy aristocrats Melania the Younger and Pinianius left for the Holy Land after selling their estates, another sign of the growing marginality of the city of Rome to some of the aristocracy. While dealing with the Goths, there was still the regular business of government to attend to. Following riots at Calama and Utica in Africa in June 408 that left a bishop dead and a church burned, Possidius of Calama and two other bishops traveled to the imperial court at Ravenna in the autumn, perhaps meeting Pinianius and Melania as they traveled south. At issue was the severity of the imperial response to the riots, a topic that had already split the African church. At the end of the year, we find Augustine writing to Olympius, asking him to confirm that laws against heretics issued earlier were genuine, since some "claim that these were issued without the knowledge and consent of the emperor" (Augustine,

Ep. 97.2). Pressure from Augustine was successful and a law of January 15, 409, confirms that previous laws were still in force.

Honorius was so short of resources that when Constantine in Gaul asked for recognition, he received an imperial robe. A funerary inscription from Trier attests Constantine and Honorius holding a first consulate together, though Honorius and Theodosius were the official consuls (*IG* XIV Supp. 2559), perhaps an example of Constantine's aspirations rather than Honorius' acceptance. Constantine's position was shown to be weak, however, as the Vandals, Alans, and Suevi crossed from Gaul into Spain in September 409. Constantine now promoted Constans to Augustus and sent him back to Spain. Before he arrived, however, news arrived that his *magister militum* Gerontius had promoted a certain Maximus to Augustus at Tarraco.

In 409, Athaulfus, Alaric's brother-in-law, entered Italy with further troops to reinforce the Goths. The war faction now lost the support of Honorius. The emperor exiled Olympius to Dalmatia and reopened negotiations with the Goths, sending Pope Innocent (401–417) to Alaric. Finally, his new Italian praetorian prefect, Jovius, managed to negotiate a truce with Alaric. Alaric's request was for land in Italy, Dalmatia, and Noricum; some gold and grain; and the honor of *magister utriusque militiae*, a rank that he had been granted before by Arcadius. Honorius wrote back that the other terms might be acceptable, but not the generalship. In late 409, Alaric again besieged Rome; with no sign that Honorius would rescue them, the Senate came to terms. Alaric now tried a new strategy, trying to work within Roman power structures rather than against them, by acclaiming Priscus Attalus, the urban prefect, as emperor on November 3, 409. Attalus' power was even more circumscribed than that of Honorius, being confined to central and southern Italy. Nonetheless, he promised in a speech to the Senate that he would take control of the eastern Empire. The grain supply for the city was of more immediate concern, and a small force was sent to Africa. Alaric meanwhile marched on Ravenna, where Honorius wavered and offered to share imperial power with Attalus too. But with the arrival of eastern reinforcements, and news of the defeat of Attalus' troops in Africa, Honorius' nerve returned, and his plans to flee to the east were abandoned. Alaric was still, despite the Roman inability to defeat him, unable to defeat the Romans. Attalus was unpopular too, with Rome suffering from Heraclius' interruption of the grain supply. Alaric thus deposed Attalus in July 410, and Honorius pardoned his officials. Renewed negotiations between Honorius and Alaric soon broke down again, however, and a frustrated Alaric returned to Rome and laid siege to the city again. On August 24, 410, Rome fell to the barbarians.

ALARIC IN ROME, 410

News of Alaric's sack of Rome rippled like a shockwave through the Roman Empire. The city was well used to violence, and only a century earlier had seen Constantine defeat Maxentius outside its gates, then build a monument commemorating his triumph in a civil war within the city itself. But Alaric was a barbarian and thus an enemy of all Romans. The last time any barbarian had occupied Rome was in 387 BC, when Brennus led his Gauls against the city. Jerome had difficulty in writing, "My voice comes to a halt and sobs interrupt my words as I dictate. The City was captured which had captured the whole world" (*Ep.* 127.12). However, his grief did not stop him from reworking a line from one of Horace's letters. He was just as emotional in the prologue to his *Commentary on the Book of Ezekiel*, describing the sack as "when the brightest light of all lands was extinguished or, rather, when the Roman Empire was decapitated."

The city was sacked over three days. The sack was not like that of a city falling to siege, but more of an organized plundering. Galla Placidia, Honorius' half-sister, was captured during the attack and held as a Gothic hostage. Orosius writing a few years later noted that, "although the memory is recent, whoever saw the multitude of the Roman people themselves and heard their talk would think that 'nothing happened', as they themselves say, unless perhaps he were to notice some burnt ruins still visible" (*Historia adversus paganos* 7.40.1). Other forms of damage also persisted. According to Procopius, the Goths were let into the city by Anicia Faltonia Proba, the widow of the praetorian prefect Sextus Petronius Probus, because she felt pity for the starving population. Writing in the middle of the sixth century, Procopius' vision of the distant past was often very different from that of contemporaries. In particular, his tale regarding the emperor's response is, though often quoted, part of the canon of fantasy woven around all emperors:

> They say that in Ravenna the Emperor Honorius was informed by one of the eunuchs, obviously the keeper of the poultry, that Rome had been lost. And crying out, he said, "And yet it just ate from my hands!" For he had a very large rooster called Rome; and when the eunuch putting together his words explained that it was the city of Rome that was lost to Alaric, the emperor with a deep breath answered "But I, my friend, thought that my bird Rome had died." So great was the ignorance of this emperor, as they say (Procopius, *Wars* 3.2.25–26).

However, it was easier to tell these sorts of stories than it was to explain the complexities of imperial politics, aristocratic disconnection, tax collection, and military failure. As the city fell, many fled, such as Anicia Faltonia

Proba, who, together with her daughter and granddaughter, went to Africa. Augustine commented on the flow of refugees in several of his sermons. Moreover, in response to those who had asked whether God had failed Rome by allowing the city to be sacked, Augustine wrote one of his most important works, *The City of God*. It ranges widely over its subject matter, but returns always to the focus on the irrelevance of earthly matters when compared to the spiritual.

Despite the sack of Rome, Alaric could not impose his will on Honorius. He marched south through Italy, planning to cross over to Africa from Sicily, though his fleet was wrecked in a storm. He then died and was succeeded by Athaulfus. Honorius now had new opportunities regarding the Goths, and his new *magister utriusque militiae* Constantius advocated a policy of cooperation with the Goths in place of the unsuccessful policy of confrontation, i.e., a return to Stilicho's ideas. The fact the emperor's half-sister Galla Placidia had been taken prisoner when Rome was sacked may have helped this change of imperial policy. More decisive, however, would have been Constantine's crossing into Italy from Gaul. Constantine was hopeful that the *magister equitum* Allobichus would betray Honorius, but the emperor found out about the negotiations and had the general murdered. Constantine then withdrew from Italy.

This was the point at which Britain drifted away from the Roman Empire. Although in 406 the island had been sufficiently committed to the Empire to produce three emperors, once Constantine had removed large numbers of troops the problems in Gaul and in particular on the Rhine were greater priorities. A letter from Honorius in 410 requesting the cities to look to their own defenses shows a continuing imperial commitment to the island, though there remained too many distractions in Gaul for anything to be done in the next decade. With no mint in London, coins had to be imported from Gaul to pay officials and soldiers. From the first decade of the fifth century, there are significant coin hoards, such as the Hoxne treasure, and eastern coins minted ca. 406 were still reaching Hadrian's Wall before 410. After this, collapse was rapid and there are only a handful of Roman coins from the period after 410. By the time bishop Germanus of Auxerre visited in 429, Britain was Roman no more.

In 411, Constantine's regime in Gaul suddenly collapsed. The troops of the emperor Maximus, who entered Gaul from Spain, besieged Vienne, captured and executed Constans, and then besieged Constantine in Arles. Nor could he rely on Honorius being distracted by the Goths. When an army of Honorius led by Constantius arrived outside Arles, many of Maximus' troops returned their loyalty to Honorius, Maximus withdrew to Spain where he went into hiding, and Constantine surrendered and was executed.

Despite his death, Constantine's Empire continued when the Gallic aristocrat Jovinus was declared Augustus at Mainz on the Rhine. He had support from the Alans and Burgundians and was soon joined by Athaulfus, who had fallen again into opposition to Honorius, acting on the advice of Attalus. Jovinus took control all of Gaul and was quickly able to mint coins at Trier, Arles, and Lyons.

The year 413 saw further improvement in Honorius' fortunes, although the year started badly, when Heraclianus, *comes Africae* and consul for 413, rebelled and crossed over to Italy. Here he was defeated by the *comes rei militaris* Marinus, who pursued Heraclianus back to Africa, then defeated and executed him. The usual investigations followed, though Marinus' treatment of the rebels was soon deemed too harsh, and he was recalled and dismissed. When Heraclianus' son-in-law Sabinus fled to Constantinople, he was arrested and sent to Honorius. At the same time, Athaulfus, no longer able to cooperate with Jovinus, began to work with Honorius again, offering peace and the heads of Jovinus and his brothers Sebastianus and Sallustius in return for grain supplies. When his offer was accepted, he defeated the rebels and sent their heads to Italy for display (see Figure 16). But then the Romans failed to supply the promised grain, Athaulfus refused to return Galla Placidia, and then he married her in January 414. By his marriage to the emperor's stepsister, Athaulfus may have seen himself as marrying into the imperial household; it is unlikely that Honorius saw the relationship in the same light. Athaulfus' ambition is shown by the Spanish historian Orosius, who quotes an eyewitness on his views

> that he eagerly desired to obliterate the Roman name and to make all Roman territory a Gothic empire, in both deed and word, so that, to speak colloquially, Gothia should be what Romania was and Athaulfus should be what Caesar Augustus once was (Orosius 7.43.5).

Roman relationships with the Goths changed again in 415 when Athaulfus was murdered. Only after some confusion did a new king emerge, Vallia, who soon came to terms with the Romans. In return for food supplies, he promised to fight against other barbarians in Spain and to return Galla Placidia and Attalus to Honorius. Vallia kept his promises. In summer 416, Honorius was in Rome, repairing some of the physical and emotional damage from the Gothic sack. He displayed Attalus in triumph to the Senate before exiling him, while on January 1, 417, Galla Placidia married Constantius. In Spain, the Goths fought so effectively against the Siling Vandals and the Alans that these peoples were absorbed into the kingdom of the Asding Vandals.

After these campaigns, the Goths were settled in Aquitania Secunda in 418; while this was occurring, Vallia died and was succeeded by Theoderic I

Figure 16. Page from the *Ravenna Annals* for 412 showing the severed heads of the emperor Jovinus and his brothers Sebastianus and Sallustius on display in Ravenna (Merseburg Cathedral Library, Germany, MS 202, eleventh-century copy of sixth-century original).

(418–451). As with most settlements of barbarians within the Empire, we have no details of the mechanics of this settlement, though there is no reason to expect them all to have been handled in the same way. Settling the Goths of 418 and almost all other subsequent settlers on imperial estates and *agri deserti* would have been the simplest process. This would have had little impact on the majority of Roman aristocrats, thus accounting for the minimal impact of these settlements in the primary evidence. From 418, an independent Gothic state in southern Gaul slowly evolved that can now be described as Visigothic. During the early years of the kingdom, the Visigoths fought for Rome as allies under the terms of their treaty, participating in a Roman expedition led by Castinus against the Asding Vandals in Baetica in 422. Although the Romans were initially successful, capturing Maximus, who had again claimed imperial power when they were defeated by the Vandals, the Visigoths deserted, which aborted the campaign.

After the death of Ambrose in 397, no western churchman other than the Pope had the same impact on the emperor. However, his ability to influence Honorius was limited since Honorius, like other late fourth-century emperors, spent most of his time in northern Italy. Nonetheless, Honorius was still involved in church matters. In Africa, there were still lingering problems with Donatism, which were addressed by the Council of Carthage in 411. In Rome, the British monk Pelagius had argued that man could achieve salvation through himself alone, i.e., without the assistance of God, But when he arrived in Africa in 411, his views were strenuously opposed by Augustine. Pelagius then went to the east, where he was found orthodox in two synods held in Palestina in 415, though he was still condemned by Pope Innocent of Rome. However, he still had numerous supporters in Rome itself, especially among the senatorial aristocracy, and was able to present his version of events before Innocent's successor Zosimus (417–418), who was prepared to accept his arguments. Augustine then used his connections at the imperial court so that Honorius issued an edict to Palladius, praetorian prefect of Italy, on April 30, 418, condemning Pelagius and his followers as heretics and expelling them from Rome. Zosimus then also condemned him, though Pelagius' supporters rioted in Rome. Faced with opposition from both the emperor and the Pope, Pelagianism soon disappeared from Italy, though there were still adherents in Britain. In 418, after the death of Zosimus, two successors, Eulalius and Boniface, were elected in Rome. The urban prefect, Aurelius Anicius Symmachus, wrote a report about the disputed election to Honorius; five days later, Honorius wrote back from Ravenna, prompting a reply from Symmachus after a further five days. Honorius at first backed Eulalius, but after an appeal from Boniface's supporters he removed both Eulalius and Boniface from Rome and summoned a synod at Ravenna. When this was inconclusive, he planned a larger council at Spoletum, inviting bishops from Africa and Gaul as well as from Italy. This would have taken place after Easter, so Honorius took measures to make sure that services would be conducted in Rome. On the same day, March 15, we have preserved an imperial letter to Bishop Achilleus of Spoletum delegating this responsibility to him, as well as announcements made to Symmachus, to the Senate, and to the people of Rome. The planned council was then canceled when Eulalius returned to Rome without imperial permission, leading Honorius to appoint Boniface. Rome and Ravenna lay some 300 kilometers apart over the Apennines; even this routine correspondence was thus moving at a speed of over 60 kilometers per day, suggestive of the continued efficiency of the *cursus publicus*. This is very different from the perspective of the Gallic aristocrat Rutilius Namatianus, who describes a journey to Gaul through a devastated Italy in late 417. His short poem, *De reditu suo*, describes floods and collapsed bridges making land travel so difficult that despite the lateness of the season, he traveled by ship. One of the reasons for Rutilius' return was probably the re-creation of the Gallic provincial council. This had fallen into abeyance after the invasions of 406 and the subsequent civil wars, but was now reestablished, though, like the transfer of the prefecture capital to Arles, focusing Gauls on the Mediterranean and away from the Rhine.

Constantius III was acclaimed Augustus at Ravenna on February 8, 421, and at the same time his wife Galla Placidia was made Augusta. By now, they had two children, Justa Grata Honoria and Placidus Valentinianus, who, since Honorius was still childless, continued the Theodosian line. Although Honorius was the senior Augustus, the accession of Constantius was not accepted by Theodosius II in the east. The last few months of Constantius' life were wretched. He started preparations for a campaign against Theodosius to force his acceptance. And he

> regretted his elevation, that he no longer had the freedom to leave and go off wherever and in whatever manner he wished and could not, because he was Emperor, enjoy the pastimes which he had been accustomed to enjoy (Olympiodorus fr. 33).

Six months later, Constantius died of pleurisy on September 2, 421. Honorius soon managed to fall out with his stepsister. This falling out soon spread to Honorius' generals, with Bonifatius fleeing to Africa rather than campaigning with Castinus. Placidia's disruptive effect was so bad that early in 423 she was exiled; she took her children and went to her uncle in Constantinople.

A few months later, Honorius died of oedema (like his father) on August 15, 423. He was buried in Rome with his wives. Honorius has often received negative assessments by historians, but despite the significant challenges posed by both internal and external enemies, he died of illness after a reign of twenty-eight years. There were some successes. The Visigoths were neutralized, various imperial challengers were seen off, and hordes of barbarians across the Rhine, in Spain, and in Italy had been eliminated. As long as the western emperor controlled the resources of the west, as in the reigns of the late fourth century, there was no reason to expect the western part of the Empire to have collapsed within half a century. However, with the diminution of these resources, change was inevitable, with the Italian aristocracy in particular suffering as they lost control of their estates in areas occupied by the barbarians.

JOHN (423–425)

Following the death of Honorius, there was an interregnum of three months. It was not until November 20, 423, that John, previously *primicerius notariorum*, was acclaimed Augustus at Rome, sufficient time for several exchanges of messages between west and east. These messages would have discussed various permutations of government, including sole rule by Theodosius, the acclamation of Honorius' nephew and Theodosius' cousin Valentinian, and the acceptance of John. No agreement could be reached, and some of John's envoys were imprisoned. Although John's supporters included the *magister militum* Castinus, other western generals such as Bonifatius in Africa refused to accept him. Bonifatius was rewarded by Theodosius with the title of *comes Africae* and even fought off a military expedition sent by John in 424. With the breakdown in negotiations and Theodosius' acclamation of Valentinian as Caesar, John prepared for war. He sent Aetius, one of his palace officials, to the Danube, where he recruited a number of Huns to reinforce his army against Theodosius' expedition. In early 425, the invading eastern army force captured Aquileia, then defeated John's forces in northern Italy. John was executed and Castinus exiled. It was only after this battle that Aetius arrived with supposedly sixty thousand Huns and fought an inconclusive battle against the eastern Romans. Following the battle, Aetius dismissed the Huns in return for the position of *magister militum* in Gaul.

VALENTINIAN III (425–455)

Following the defeat of John in the early summer, Placidus Valentinianus, the son of Constantius and Galla Placidia, was acclaimed as Augustus in Rome on October 23, 425, exactly a year after his proclamation as Caesar. The young Valentinian III was betrothed to Theodosius' daughter Eudoxia, though he was still only six years old. As with Honorius, Arcadius, and Theodosius at their accessions, some sort of guardianship arrangement was therefore necessary. Yet even before he had been acclaimed as Augustus, the government of Valentinian was exerting his authority. An edict of July 425 threatened Pelagian bishops with expulsion if they did not convert to Catholicism. Laws issued in 426 concerned the rights of freedmen and the testatory rights of apostates. Soon after his accession at Rome, Valentinian moved to Ravenna, where he remained until 437. His mother Galla Placidia is often said to have been influential in his government, though Felix, holding the same combination of offices as Stilicho and Constantius, i.e., *patricius* and *magister militum*, was initially the most important figure. Felix was faced with two rivals for influence, Aetius and Bonifatius, who had been on different sides in John's reign. Aetius held the position of *magister militum per Gallias*, where in 427 he relieved a siege of Arles by the Visigoths and in 428 fought in northern Gaul against the Franks. In 429, he was promoted to the second *magister utriusque militiae*. Bonifatius remained in Africa, but in 427, when he refused a summons to the palace, Felix sent two unsuccessful expeditions against him. Then in 430, Felix died at Ravenna in a mutiny, with one source claiming that he was murdered by Aetius for plotting against him.

Although Honorius' reign had been a difficult one, by 425 the western Empire appeared to have weathered the crisis. Imperial unity had been restored, and though Britain and parts of Spain had been lost, there were good reasons for the Romans to be optimistic. Yet thirty years later, at the end of Valentinian's reign, there was no cause for optimism and the western Empire was teetering on the brink of dissolution. One problem was the frequent focusing of energies of the Roman state on internal rather than external problems, for example in the east during the reign of Arcadius and in the west just after the murder of Stilicho. But the main cause of this sudden collapse of western power was the Vandal occupation of Africa. In 429, the Vandals, led by their king Geiseric (428–477), crossed over from Spain to Africa. In the sixth century, Procopius claimed that eighty thousand people crossed, perhaps twenty thousand to thirty thousand warriors. Procopius and another sixth-century writer, Jordanes, claimed that Bonifatius had invited the Vandals in, but there is no fifth-century evidence of this, and it is tempting to explain this rumor as the propaganda of Aetius. Indeed, Bonifatius fought against the Vandals, though in 430 he was defeated in battle and then was besieged for a while in Hippo, where the bishop Augustine died in the siege. Roman hopes rose with the arrival of an eastern army led by Aspar in 431, although this force was also defeated by Geiseric. Bonifatius then returned to Italy in 432 to be appointed as *magister militum* and *patricius*, while Aspar remained in Carthage until 434. Western Roman efforts against the Vandals were now derailed by the outbreak of civil war, which broke out between Bonifatius and Aetius in 432. This conflict between Roman generals was a new development within the west, though similar to the revolt of Gainas in the east under Arcadius. Bonifatius won the battle of Ariminum in January, but he was mortally wounded. Aetius went first to his rural estates in Italy, but after an attempt on his life, he fled to the Huns. Bonifatius' son-in-law Sebastianus now became *magister utriusque militiae*. Aetius must still have had friends in the palace since in 433 he was restored to the position of *magister utriusque militiae* and Sebastianus took refuge in the east. In 435, Aetius was then appointed patrician.

Although quickly resolved, the civil war forced Valentinian to abandon the attempt to hold Africa and instead to negotiate with the Vandals. He sent Trygetius to Geiseric in 435, making a peace that granted Geiseric control of Numidia, the two provinces of Mauritania, and Tingitania. The Romans were still holding Carthage and the prosperous provinces of Africa and Byzacium, but their failure to defeat the Vandals, particularly with the ability and initiative already displayed by Geiseric, was ominous. At the same time, Valentinian was forced to make concessions to the Huns, granting them control of Savia and Valeria in 435, though at this point much of the diocese of Illyricum (excluding Sirmium) had already been effectively lost to Roman control and Sirmium itself was captured by the Huns in 441.

The ecclesiastical issues faced by Valentinian were very different from those faced by Theodosius. The youth of Honorius and Valentinian, combined with their understandable concentration on secular matters, often allowed the Pope to act as an independent figure representing all western bishops. This was very different from the relationship that the eastern emperor had with his patriarchs. With few dissident opinions among the bishops and only one patriarch, the western emperor was rarely asked to resolve ecclesiastical affairs, though he was often asked to support the decisions of the Pope. Eastern bishops would appeal to the Pope when it suited them, though the eastern emperor was more reluctant to accept his authority. When Pope Celestine (422–432) received a misleading letter from Cyril in Alexandria regarding Nestorius, he swiftly condemned him. Like most bishops in the West, Celestine believed that Nicaea was a sufficient definition of orthodoxy. Most bishops in the east were aware of its shortcomings. This inevitably led to differing responses to theological disputes, not helped by the weakness of many western bishops in understanding the subtleties of theological argument in Greek. Having discussed Cyril's accusations at a Synod at Rome in 430, Celestine then sent delegates to the First Council of Ephesus in 431, where they watched the imposition of the sentence of exile on Nestorius.

Once he was eighteen, Valentinian returned to Constantinople in 437 for his wedding to Eudoxia on October 29. This was soon followed by the promulgation of the *Codex Theodosianus* in 438. Both of these events were major propaganda occasions for the Empire. Like the creation of the illustrated version of the *Notitia Dignitatum* a generation earlier, these events showed significant imperial concern for imperial unity, though like Tetrarchic propaganda they also betray the fact that this unity was under great stress. Following Valentinian's return to Italy, he spent the next few winters in Rome and summers in Ravenna. With the death or exile of Castinus, Felix, and Bonifatius, Aetius had emerged as the dominant general in the administration of Valentinian. He had much to do, as the western Empire was now faced with military demands in four areas, within the Empire in Africa, Spain, and Gaul, and at its edges in Gaul and Pannonia. This was a major change from the beginning of the reign of Honorius, when most Roman energies were concentrated on the Rhine frontier and the Balkans. At the same time as the military demands had increased, the loss of territory had reduced the military resources available. Aetius, following his restoration to power, concentrated most of his energies in Gaul, attacking the Burgundian kingdom on the Rhine in 436. In 437, he sent some Hun mercenaries against them, a campaign that destroyed their state and formed the basis of the medieval German epic poem the *Niebelungenlied*. These victories were followed by settlements of Alans in the Rhone Valley (440) and Armorica (442) and of Burgundians in Savoy (443). Aetius' defeat of the rebels in Armorica brought the Gallic holy man Germanus to Ravenna in 448 appealing to the emperor for their pardon. When not trying to intercede in the palace, Germanus, whose *Life* was written by another Gaul Constantius of Lyons, resurrected the son of Volusianus, *cancellarius* (an office staff member) of Sigisvultus, *patricius* and *magister militum*; and exorcised a demon from the foster son of Acholius, the *praepositus sacri cubiculi*. Germanus then fell ill, during which time he was visited by the Augusta Eudoxia. When he died, there was a competition for his relics, with Galla Placidia getting the reliquary with his bones, but Peter Chrysologus, bishop of Ravenna (ca. 433–450), was able to get his hands on Germanus' cloak with a hairshirt inside it. At the same time as securing the Rhine frontier, Aetius fought several battles against the Visigoths, including a siege of Narbo in 436 and a victory at the unknown Mons Colubarius in 438. Similarly in Spain, the general Merobaudes (who has left some good poetry) tried to stem an expansion of the Suevi, who had taken advantage of the departure of the Vandals. All of these efforts kept much of Gaul and Spain under Roman control, but were insufficient to allow any restoration of Roman power. Valentinian would have hoped that, over time, the various barbarian settlements would be absorbed within the Empire.

Before much progress could be made in absorbing the new immigrants, events in Africa took a significant turn. Although peace had been made with the Vandals in 435, in 439 Geiseric broke the peace, occupied Carthage, and then in 440 attacked Sicily. Valentinian even issued an edict encouraging the population of Italy to take up arms to defend themselves. As the Vandals took control of Carthage, they imposed Arian bishops and began persecuting, resulting in a flood of refugees to the imperial courts at Ravenna and Constantinople. Valentinian listened to their appeals, for example exempting them from lawsuits for debts (unless they held land elsewhere) until Africa was recaptured. Others scattered more widely, and a series of eight letters from Theodoret in Eufratensis survive, asking for help for the Carthaginian city councilor Celestiacus. Losing control of Africa was not just a western problem, and though a major eastern expedition was launched in 441, Theodosius was forced to abandon this because of Hun attacks on the Balkans. Following this, a new treaty was made in 442 in which the Romans regained control of the provinces of Tripolitania, the two Mauritanias (Sitifensis and Caesariensis), and some of Numidia, while the Vandals kept the rest of Numidia, Byzacium, and Africa Proconsularis (Zeugitana), which included Carthage. Geiseric's son Huneric was sent to Rome as a hostage but also betrothed to Valentinian's young daughter, Eudocia (born ca. 438–439). This planned marriage of a member of the imperial house to a barbarian king was reminiscent of the marriage of Placidia to Athaulfus a generation earlier. In 445, a delegation from the remaining African provinces came to Rome, appealing successfully for tax reductions; although they had been Vandal occupied for over a decade, they were still, at least in Valentinian's eyes, to be treated like all Roman possessions. Peace between the Romans and the Vandals lasted until 455.

The loss of Africa was a critical event for the west. The loss of Britain and parts of Spain would have had a small impact on tax revenue, while the Visigothic settlement in Gaul was occasionally producing allies. Africa was completely different. This was not only a wealthy region, but one that had exported large quantities of grain to Rome. This prosperity allowed the Vandals to build a fleet, allowing them to challenge the Roman dominance over the Mediterranean. The western inability to pay troops soon became clear with a new sales tax levied only in the western Empire in 444, the *siliquaticum*, levied at a rate of one *siliqua* per *solidus*, at all markets and on all written contracts.

Valentinian soon found himself in close contact with the new Pope, Leo (440–461). Leo is especially well known because of the preservation of 150 of his letters. Some of the refugees from Africa who arrived in Rome were accused of Manicheism, of concern to Leo but also to Valentinian, who issued an edict condemning them, while Leo also had to deal with resurgent Priscillianism in Spain. Other problems were more over power than theology. In 445, Valentinian issued an edict to Aetius, making it clear that the Pope had authority over Arles, where bishop Hilary had been appointing and deposing bishops. Leo had objected to this as being an ecclesiastical issue. Valentinian agreed, but his enforcement mechanisms were secular and expressed in orders to Aetius, *magister utriusque militiae*. Furthermore, if any bishop was summoned to an ecclesiastical court at Rome, the provincial governor could compel him to attend (*Novellae of Valentinian* 17). Leo also took a firm direction in his relations with the eastern bishops. His forceful condemnation of Eutyches and Nestorius was strongly expressed in June 449 by the so-called Tome of Leo, a letter sent to Patriarch Flavian of Constantinople (Leo, *Ep.* 28). Leo was not at all happy with Dioscurus of Alexandria's ignoring of the Tome at the Second Council of Ephesus, which he soon claimed was a "robber council" (*latrocinium*). He was far happier with the results of the Council of Chalcedon, though he continued to be baffled at ongoing eastern dissent with the council.

After 450, Valentinian spent the rest of his reign in Rome. There were negotiations with the east after his cousin's death in 450, and it was not until 452 that he accepted the acclamation of Marcian as eastern emperor. Then in 450, following rumors that his elder sister, Justa Grata Honoria, was having an affair with her estate manager, Valentinian planned to marry her to a senator, Bassus Herculanus, who held the consulate in 452. Honoria was then supposed to have sent a ring to Attila, who treated this as a proposal of marriage. When Valentinian discovered his sister's actions, he was so angry that his mother Placidia had to intervene to have Honoria exiled rather than executed. Attila claimed that the failure to deliver Honoria was justification to invade the western Empire. He invaded Gaul in 451 in a spectacular but poorly conceived expedition with no clear objective. After Attila's unsuccessful siege of Orleans, Aetius met the Huns at the Battle of the Catalaunian Fields, his Roman army supplemented by Visigothic allies led by King Theoderic. After an inconclusive battle, the Huns retreated to the Danube. In 452, Attila invaded Italy. He was able to terrorize the Po Valley, capturing Aquileia and Milan. Soon afterward, he received a Roman embassy that persuaded him to withdraw from Italy. Pope Leo was one of the members of the embassy, but supply problems and an outbreak of disease were more influential in persuading Attila to abandon the campaign. When Attila died in 453, the threat posed by the Huns disappeared almost overnight.

During a meeting in September 454 in which Valentinian and Aetius were involved in financial planning, Valentinian, with the help of the eunuch *primicerius sacri cubiculi* Heraclius, murdered Aetius in the palace at Rome. Boethius, praetorian prefect of Italy, was also killed, though Aetius' son Gaudentius was spared. In revenge, on March 16, 455, Valentinian was murdered on the Campus Martius at Rome by two of Aetius' followers. Writing in the sixth century, John of Antioch suggested that "Valentinian was doomed to come to ruin by destroying the bulwark of his own sovereignty" (fr. 201.2). Yet emperors had forcefully removed senior generals, as Honorius did with Stilicho in 408 and Leo was later to do with Aspar in 471, with lesser consequences. It was the murder of the 36-year old Valentinian that was more significant. He left no heir or clear successor, and so all the problems that he and Aetius had been grappling with now were able to grow. At the beginning of his reign in 425, there were already independent kingdoms of Vandals, Suevi, Visigoths, and Burgundians on Roman territory, while Britain had been completely lost to the Western Empire. And then control of Africa was lost. For the western Roman Empire, although the collapse that followed was not inevitable, it was no longer unforeseeable. Without a strong Empire, there was little incentive for aristocrats to support the Empire. In the east, on the other hand, the Roman emperor continued to have enough resources to grapple with the same intractable problems that were starting to tear the western Empire apart.

FURTHER READING

There is no reliable narrative for the whole period, though the *Ecclesiastical Histories* of Socrates, Sozomen, and Theodoret, all written in the middle of the fifth century, provide a useful start for the early part of the century. We also have substantial fragments of the *Ecclesiastical History* of Philostorgius, drawing on Olympiodorus of Thebes, whose history covered 407–425. For the early period, these can be supplemented by Zosimus' secular history, which covers the entire period in reasonable detail, drawing on Eunapius of Sardis for the period to 404 and then Olympiodorus to 410. For the middle of the fifth century, the *Ecclesiastical History* of Evagrius is particularly useful, drawing on the *History of Priscus of Panium* covering ca. 434–474, which is otherwise only available in fragments. Various chronicles in east and west also provide chronological signposts. There is much imperial legislation contained in the *Codex Theodosianus* to 438, with various *Novellae* after that. We also have the *Notitia Dignitatum*, a list of imperial offices dating to the early fifth century. There is also much anecdotal information contained in saints' lives, e.g., of Porphyry of Gaza or Germanus of Auxerre, as well as a collection of lives of Syrian monks, the *Historia Religiosa* of Theodoret. There are increasing amounts of episcopal writings, including collections from John Chrysostom, the fascinating *Bazaar of Heraclides* by Nestorius, various Papal letter collections, as well as letters of Theodoret, Synesius, and Firmus of Caesarea; all these materials are highly partisan. There are versions of the proceedings of the councils of Ephesus in 431 and 449 and of Chalcedon in 451. There is a reasonable amount of court and private rhetoric, including speeches by Synesius, Merobaudes, and others. The Latin poems of Claudian and Rutilius Namatianus are informative, and some information can be gleaned from the many epigrams preserved in the *Anthologia Palatina*.

The complexity of this period and lack of good source material have deterred many authors from writing books about emperors, though there is no shortage of detailed studies. An excellent overview is provided by Maas, M., ed., *The Cambridge Companion to the Age of Attila* (Cambridge, 2015). For the eastern Empire, there are good works on parts of Arcadius' reign by Cameron, A., and Long, J., *Barbarians and Politics at the Court of Arcadius* (Berkeley, 1993) and Liebeschuetz, J. H. W. G., *Barbarians and Bishops* (Oxford, 1991). On Chrysostom, see Kelly, J. N. D., *Golden Mouth* (London, 1995) and Liebeschuetz, J. H. W. G., *Ambrose and John Chrysostom: Clerics between Desert and Empire* (Oxford, 2011). For Theodosius II, Millar, F., *A Greek Roman Empire* (Berkeley, 2006) provides an excellent introduction, as do the various essays in Kelly, C., ed., *Theodosius II: Rethinking the Roman Empire in Late Antiquity* (Cambridge, 2013) and Elton, H. W., "Imperial Politics at the Court of Theodosius II," in Cain, A., and Lenski, N., eds., *The Power of Religion in Late Antiquity* (Aldershot, 2009), 133–142. A challenging perspective, though one rejected here, is provided by Holum, K., *Theodosian Empresses* (Berkeley, 1982). Most work on Marcian's reign has to be viewed through the perspective of the Council of Chalcedon, though a useful alternative perspective is provided by Burgess, R. W., "The Accession of Marcian in the Light of Chalcedonian Apologetic and Monophysite Polemic," *Byzantinische Zeitschrift* 86/87 (1993/1994), 47–68. For the climate of politics in the eastern Empire in the fifth century, Brown, P., *Power and Persuasion in Late Antiquity* (Madison, 1992) is an excellent introduction.

For the west, one means of approaching the reign of Honorius is provided by Cameron, A. D. E., *Claudian* (Oxford, 1970), another by Matthews, J. F., *Western Aristocracies and Imperial Court AD 364–425* (Oxford, 1975). See also Kulikowski, M., "Barbarians in Gaul, Usurpers in Britain," *Britannia* 31 (2000), 325–345, Drinkwater, J. F., "The Usurpers Constantine III (407–411) and Jovinus (411–413)," *Britannia* 29 (1998), 269–298, Hermanowicz, E. T., "Catholic Bishops and Appeals to the Imperial Court: A Legal Study of the Calama Riots in 408," *Journal of Early Christian Studies* 12 (2004), 481–521, and Lipps, J., Machado, C., and von Rummel, P., eds., *The Sack of Rome in 410 AD: The Event, Its Context and Its Impact* (Wiesbaden, 2013). For Valentinian's reign, there is surprisingly little, though see Mathisen, R. W., "Sigisvult the Patrician, Maximinus the Arian, and Political Stratagems in the Western Roman Empire c. 425–40," *Early Medieval Europe* 8 (1999), 173–196, Sivan, H., *Galla Placidia* (Oxford, 2011), and Traina, G., *428 AD: An Ordinary Year at the End of the Roman Empire* (Princeton, 2009).

Religious affairs are covered in different ways by McGuckin, J. A., "Nestorius and the Political Factions of Fifth-Century Byzantium: Factors in His Personal Downfall," *Bulletin of the John Rylands Library* 78 (1996), 7–22 and Wessel, S., *Cyril of Alexandria and the Nestorian Controversy* (Oxford, 2004). For the Council of Chalcedon, see de Ste. Croix, G. E. M., and Michael Whitby, "The Council of Chalcedon," in de Ste. Croix, G. E. M., ed., *Christian Persecution, Martyrdom and Orthodoxy* (Oxford, 2006), 259–319, Price, R. and Whitby, M., eds., *Chalcedon in Context: Church Councils 400–700* (Liverpool, 2009), and the introduction to Gaddis, M. and Price, R., tr., *The Acts of the Council of Chalcedon* (Liverpool, 2007). On the Pope, see Cooper, K. and Hillner, J., eds., *Religion, Dynasty, and Patronage in Early Christian Rome, 300–900* (Cambridge, 2010), Sessa, K., *The Formation of Papal Authority in Late Antique Italy* (Cambridge, 2011), and Dunn, G. D., ed., *The Bishop of Rome in Late Antiquity* (Farnham, 2015).

On barbarians, Heather P. J., *Goths and Romans, 332–489* (Oxford, 1991), and very differently, Kulikowski, M., *Rome's Gothic Wars* (Cambridge, 2007), and Kelly, C., *The*

End of Empire: Attila the Hun and the Fall of Rome (New York, 2008). For a perspective on the Huns as causing the collapse of the Empire, see Heather, P. J., "The Huns and the End of the Roman Empire in Western Europe," *English Historical Review* 110 (1995), 4–41, with further developments in Heather, P., "Why Did the Barbarian Cross the Rhine?" *Journal of Late Antiquity* 2 (2009), 3–29. There has been much debate about barbarian settlements, ultimately in response to Goffart, W., *Barbarians and Romans, A.D. 418–584* (Princeton, 1980). Critics include Barnish, S. J. B., "Taxation, Land and Barbarian Settlement in the Western Empire," *Papers of the British School at Rome* 54 (1986), 170–195. See also Goffart, W., "The Technique of Barbarian Settlement in the Fifth Century: A Personal, Streamlined Account with Ten Additional Comments," *Journal of Late Antiquity* 3 (2010), 65–98, and Halsall, G., "The Technique of Barbarian Settlement in the Fifth Century: A Reply to Walter Goffart," *Journal of Late Antiquity* 3 (2010), 99–112.

Regional studies include Drinkwater, J. F. and Elton, H. W., eds., *Fifth-Century Gaul: A Crisis of Identity?* (Cambridge, 1992); Poulter, A., ed., *The Transition to Late Antiquity, on the Danube and Beyond: Proceedings of the British Academy* 141 (Oxford, 2008); and Conant, J., *Staying Roman: Conquest and Identity in Africa and the Mediterranean, 439–700* (Cambridge, 2012).

6

THE LATE FIFTH CENTURY, 455–493

With the loss of Africa to the Vandals and the failure of Majorian and Leo's attempts to reoccupy it, the Roman Empire in the west rapidly collapsed. Only fifteen years after the death of Majorian in 461, the last Roman emperor in the west had been replaced in 476 by a barbarian king in Italy. In the east, however, the Empire continued almost unchanged. The political collapse was so sudden that contemporaries had little time to react before the Empire in the west disappeared. The failure was not one of defeat on the battlefield, but the result of financial weaknesses which led to a failure of the western Empire to retain the allegiance of enough of its aristocracy. After the middle of the third century, there had been a separation between the imperial and the senatorial aristocracy, but both would unhesitatingly have described themselves as Romans. However, by the late fifth century, several very different visions of Roman identity had begun to emerge. Zeno, Aspar, Ricimer, Pope Leo, Pope Simplicius, Theoderic Strabo, Aegidius, and Odovacer would all have described themselves as Romans, yet all had very different definitions of what this meant. These differing visions occurred at the same time as, and partly stemmed from, the collapse of Roman secular power in the west. However, the simultaneous occurrence of diverging visions in the east suggests that what it meant to be Roman was continuing to change.

The ability of the Roman state to dominate Europe militarily was now greatly diminished. It was still the most powerful state in the Mediterranean, but it was no longer powerful enough to destroy its enemies, merely to defeat them. The Empire should not be written off, however, and looking ahead to the sixth century and the Justinianic reconquests, the Empire in the east still retained great military power. But in the late fifth century, Roman control of the western Mediterranean

collapsed. There were a number of reasons for this, but the most important of these was financial incapacity. With the loss of so much western
territory in the first half of the century, especially the wealthy provinces
in Africa, western imperial revenues were massively reduced. At the same
time, there was little diminution of the need for resources. Indeed, with
the rise of the Vandals as a naval power, the need for resources was even
greater, since the Empire in both east and west now also required a major
fleet in the Mediterranean. Thus the Empire collapsed in the west but survived in the east; its failure was not inevitable.

Despite the continued ideal of imperial unity, both parts of the Empire
continued to have separate but interrelated histories. With the growing
weakness of imperial power comes an increase in the number of political actors
and thus the complexity of the narrative presented here. Contemporaries
probably also found this confusing. Many of them took advantage of the
opportunities this presented, but others retreated from the chaos by isolating
themselves or clinging to a lost past. Like the previous chapter, this is divided
into two parts. The story of the east is told first, as this provides a backdrop
against which to view the collapse of the western Empire. Eastern continuity
is important to consider since it suggests that the Roman Empire was not
bound to fail. This allows us then to examine the events in the west in an
attempt to isolate causes of collapse, as opposed to changes in the nature of
the Roman Empire at this period.

In most of the east, life was little different from the previous century,
but in the west, in Africa, and in the Balkans, urbanized life in the Roman
fashion was changing rapidly for the worse. Few provincial governors are
attested in the late fifth century, though this phenomenon is partly an
artifact of the evidence, as there are few provincial governors recorded in
eastern provinces too. The concept of imperial unity, worked for so hard
by Theodosius II and Valentinian III, was now much harder to achieve.
Although the latest eastern law preserved in the west is from the reign of
Marcian, the *Codex Justinianus* appears not to contain any western laws
issued after the creation of the *Codex Theodosianus*. However, as late as the
reign of Glycerius, western legislation continued to name all four praetorian prefects. This failure to exchange laws does not mean the empires
were separate states, though the failure of the western Empire does high-
light the differences. Continued cooperation is attested by the joint campaign by eastern and western emperors against the Vandals in 468; the
sending of the easterners Anthemius, Olybrius, and Nepos as emperors
to the west; and a unified system of law and coinage. At the same time,
travel between east and west is clearly shown by eighty-nine gold coins
found in the grave of the Frankish king Childeric, buried at Tournai in

northern Gaul in 481, including three of Basiliscus minted in 475/476 and fifteen of Zeno.

LEO I (457–474)

There was no heir apparent in the eastern Empire when Marcian, without a son, died in 457. His son-in-law Anthemius was *patricius* and in 455 held the consulate with Valentinian III; he was a strong candidate to succeed, but he was passed over. It was not until two weeks after the death of Marcian that Leo was acclaimed at the Hebdomon in Constantinople on February 7, 457. There was no emperor in the west, so Leo automatically became the senior Augustus. He was a Balkan soldier who had reached the rank of tribune in the infantry regiment of the Mattiarii. Leo's wife was Verina; they had two daughters, the elder Ariadne and the younger Leontia (born 457).

Leo's coronation is the first known to involve the patriarch of Constantinople, an addition to the traditional roles played by the army and Senate. The detailed account in the *de caeremoniis* makes clear the significant role played by the *magister militum* Aspar, still prominent thirty years after he had helped depose the western emperor John in 425. Following a vote of the Senate, there was a meeting at the Hebdomon Palace that included the *archontes*; various soldiers; Anatolius, patriarch of Constantinople; and Martialis, *magister officiorum*. After the proclamation in the Hebdomon, Leo traveled with Aspar to the Senate House in the city. Although Aspar held both positions of first *patricius* and *princeps Senatus*, he was not the only influential figure in the palace in the first few years of the reign. Marcian's son-in-law Anthemius continued to serve as *magister militum* under Leo and fought in the Balkans in the 460s. Other prominent figures included Olybrius, who had married Placidia, daughter of Valentinian III; he was in Constantinople, and his prestige would have increased after she was released by the Vandals in 461.

Among the first items of business for Leo was the west, where there was no emperor after Avitus had been deposed in October 456 by Majorian and Ricimer. When Majorian was finally acclaimed, it was without approval from the east. Although Majorian's elevation could have been a cause for military intervention, neither the sick Marcian nor the new emperor Leo had any appetite for confrontation, and Majorian was accepted by the east as a legitimate emperor during 457. A second critical issue also involved both east and west. Leo was faced with the fact that the Council of Chalcedon had not resolved the issues originally brought up at the First Council of Ephesus in 431, while the Second Council of Ephesus had also provoked the opposition of Pope Leo. Leo was probably still finding his feet as emperor when, a few weeks after his accession, an anti-Chalcedonian group in Alexandria consecrated Timothy Aelurus as patriarch, even though there already was an incumbent patriarch Proterius (who had replaced Dioscurus). When Aelurus was arrested, riots followed in which Proterius was murdered on March 28, 457, and Dionysius, *comes Aegypti*, had to deploy troops to restore order. Supporters of both factions sent petitions to the emperor Leo.

Faced with this crisis, the emperor at first suggested another church council, though he was advised against this by Anatolius, bishop of Constantinople. Anatolius may have been somewhat skeptical of their efficacy, and may also have been concerned to avoid further provoking Rome over Canon 28, which had made Constantinople equal in dignity to Rome and also gave the patriarch the reasonability of appointing the metropolitan bishops in the dioceses of Asiana, Pontica, and Thracia. Leo therefore tried a different approach, writing to all the metropolitan bishops in the eastern Empire, enquiring whether they thought there should be another council, what they thought about Timothy Aelurus (attaching copies of the petitions from Alexandria in favor and against Timothy), and what they thought about the Council of Chalcedon. The responses suggested that Chalcedon was universally supported and Aelurus universally condemned, with the singular exception of Amphilochius of Side. The uniformity, however, of the responses provoked comment even in the sixth century, while there are numerous problems in matching the lists of addressees and signatories. Leo decided that Aelurus' consecration was illegal, removed Aelurus by force in 460, and appointed a new pro-Chalcedonian bishop, Timothy Salofaciolus (460–475). Aelurus was first exiled to Gangra in Paphlagonia, and then to Chersonesus, from where he continued to press his claim. Leo's firm stance in favor of Chalcedon eased relations with Pope Leo somewhat, and these continued with Hilary (461–468), then Simplicius (468–483). In the east, the majority of bishops were prepared to accept Chalcedon, but there remained many who would not. In Antioch, after Martyrius was deposed following accusations of Nestorianism in 469, the anti-Chalcedonian Peter the Fuller was acclaimed bishop. After Martyrius was reinstated, Peter was exiled to the Oasis in Egypt, though he soon escaped to Constantinople to the monastery of the Akoimetoi.

On the eastern frontier, peace with the Persians generally continued, though the Persians by midcentury had been able to take control of Lazica. Now that the whole of the Caucasus was under Persian control, they were faced with the problem of controlling barbarians such as the Saraguri moving south. The Persians demanded a contribution from the Romans for the defense of the passes, though the Romans refused. The Balkans posed much more trouble for the Romans. After the collapse of the Hunnic confederation in Marcian's reign, new barbarian groups such as the Slavs and Bulgars began entering the transdanubian *barbaricum* while other groups crossed the Danube and entered the Empire. These included two major Gothic groups: the Thracian Goths, later led by Theoderic Strabo; and a group of Goths led by Valamir, who had been living under Hun domination in Pannonia. Sirmium remained lost to the Romans. Valamir began raiding the western Balkans in 459. This eventually led to a negotiated peace in 461, with the Romans giving an annual subsidy of three hundred pounds of gold in exchange for peace and a hostage, Theoderic the Amal, who was taken to Constantinople. As in the late fourth century, the presence of any barbarian group in the Balkans was a difficult problem for the Romans. Neither group of Goths was interested at this point in creating their own state but were instead attempting to find a place within the Roman world. Once the disruption caused by the collapse of Attila's Empire had settled, the Romans were able to restore order, particularly after Leo's brother-in-law Basiliscus was promoted to *magister militum per Thracias* in 464 and began winning battles. Dengizech, one of Attila's sons, was soon reduced to asking for land and money from the emperor; he was killed by the Romans in 469 and his head used to decorate the walls of Constantinople.

At the same time as high politics and foreign wars, the business of government continued. A recently discovered inscription posted in a public area outside the office of the governor of Palestina Prima at Caesarea lists the fees for services, charging, for example, eight *siliquae* for a record of a trial (*SEG* 53.1481). Administrative changes included a minor revision of the office of the *magister militum per Orientem* by 472, adding *comites* to Pamphylia, Lycaonia, and Pisidia, probably because of banditry in the Taurus. The same law also shows that the *comitiva* in Pontus had been renamed the *dux utriusque Ponti*, while the single ducate of Eufratensis and Syria had been divided into two commands (*CJ* 12.59.10). In Constantinople, there was a great fire in September 464, which Evagrius described as burning for four days: "all that was built with an eye to unsurpassable magnificence, all that was put to public or private use was at one stroke reduced to hills and mounds of all kinds of rubble, impassable obstacles, the jumbled remains of former beauty" (Evagrius 2.13). Leo constructed no major new buildings in Constantinople, though the cistern of Aspar built in 459 reflects the continuing growth of the city, as does the new official residence for the eastern praetorian prefect. Leo's energies were focused more on relics, bringing the relics of St. Anastasia of Sirmium, among others, into the city, and though he tried to obtain the body of Symeon Stylites from Syria after his death in 459, he had to make do with the saint's tunic. Leo also met with local holy men, including Daniel the Stylite, a Mesopotamian saint who had come to the city after visiting Symeon the Elder in Syria. Christianity was by now so dominant that accusations of being a Hellene (i.e., a pagan) led to the trial of Isocasius, who had been *quaestor* in 465. He was removed from office and sent to Bithynia for trial. Following intervention by his friends, his trial was moved to Constantinople, where he was acquitted of paganism and converted to Christianity. Other men and women were also adorning the city, such as John Studius, consul for 454, who built a monastery perhaps in 462 in Psamathia near the Golden Gate of Theodosius, and Mark the *silentiarius*, who erected a column for the recently arrived ascetic Daniel. From the beginning of his reign, Leo had benefited from the support and experience of Aspar and his family. Aspar had been instrumental in the acclamation of Leo, and his family benefited, with his younger sons Patricius holding the consulate in 459 and Herminericus in 465. In 466, a certain Isaurian named Zeno brought letters to Leo. These letters showed that Aspar's eldest son, Ardabur, *magister militum per Orientem* and consul, in 447 had written to the Persians, inciting them to attack the Empire and agreeing to cooperate with them:

> The Emperor received the man and understating the importance of the letters he ordered a *conventus* to be held; when the Senate had met, the Emperor produced the letters and commanded that they should be read aloud by Patricius who was *magister officiorum* at that time in the hearing of all the senators. After they had been read the Emperor said, "What do you think?" And when everyone was silent, the Emperor said to the father of Ardabur, "These are fine things that your son is practising against the Emperor and the Roman State" (*Life of Daniel the Stylite* 55).

The life of Daniel was written in the 490s and records a well-known event, so we can be fairly comfortable with the veracity despite its dramatic nature. By distinguishing between the actions of Ardabur on the one hand and of Aspar and Patricius on the other, Leo was able to make Aspar's best choice the disowning of Ardabur. The calling of the *conventus et silentium* suggests Leo's need to justify his actions in such a way that Aspar would be left with no choice but to concur. Ardabur was dismissed from his office and Jordanes was appointed as *magister militum per Orientem*. Another beneficiary of these events was the Isaurian soldier Zeno, who was appointed *comes domesticorum* and married Leo's eldest daughter, Ariadne.

The increasing weakness of the western Empire meant that Leo was repeatedly dragged into its affairs. The wife and daughter of Valentinian III, captured after the sack of Rome in 455, were sent by the Vandals to Constantinople in 461. Initial good relations soon soured after the death of

Libius Severus in 465, when there was an interregnum that lasted until Leo designated Anthemius, Marcian's son-in-law, as western Augustus in early 467. Both consuls were easterners in all years between 464 and 467. Even though a new emperor could be sent to Italy, this did not solve the problem of the Vandal attacks on or the lack of resources in the west. Leo therefore sent an envoy to the Vandal king Geiseric in Africa, threatening war if he did not leave Italy and Sicily. When Geiseric rejected the envoy, a joint expeditionary force from both parts of the Empire was assembled. The great expedition was a failure. According to Candidus, the expedition cost 64,000 pounds of gold and 700,000 pounds of silver, a dramatic reminder of the cost of active campaigning. The expense also shows the continued wealth of the Empire, putting into perspective the supposedly ruinous subsidies paid to the Huns two decades earlier. Various explanations were advanced for the disaster. Amphibious operations are perhaps the most complex of military operations, and it is best to accept military failure. Contemporaries, however, focused on treachery by either Basiliscus, though he had become a convenient scapegoat after his execution in 476 by Zeno, or Aspar, murdered by Leo in 471. There is no reason to believe either of these men betrayed the Empire. Moreover, after the expedition, Aspar was again the leading military figure at the court. In 470, he even persuaded Leo to acclaim his son Patricius as Caesar, although Patricius was forced to forswear his "Arianism." There were enough "Arians" in Constantinople, like the *magister militum* Jordanes, who converted to orthodoxy following an intervention by Daniel the Stylite, that there was a church outside the city walls reserved for their use. But Arianism was not acceptable in an emperor, and so there were public demonstrations in the Hippodrome by the patriarch Gennadius and another prominent monk, Marcellus, archimandrite of the Akoimetoi, about the faith of Patricius. Following his public endorsement of Chalcedon, Patricius was acclaimed as Caesar and married Leo's younger daughter, Leontia. The return to favor of Aspar's family was soon overturned when the *magister militum per Thracias* Anagastes revolted in 470. During Anagastes' negotiations with Leo, it was revealed that his rebellion had been encouraged by Aspar's son Ardabur. With this evidence of renewed treachery by Ardabur, Leo decided that he was too dangerous to let live. Aspar, Ardabur, and probably Patricius were thus murdered in the palace in 471. Leo subsequently tried to justify the bloodbath by presenting Aspar as a barbarian and as an Arian. This was harsh treatment for a family that had given three generations of service to the Empire and Leo's subsequent nickname "the Butcher" was well deserved. The immediate beneficiary of the murders was Zeno. He was soon appointed *magister militum praesentalis* and his son Leo, born in 467, was acclaimed as Caesar in 472.

The actors in domestic politics and military leadership changed dramatically in the second part of Leo's reign. Apart from Leo's massacre, there was the departure of first Anthemius and then Olybrius to the west in 467 and 472 respectively, and the marginalization of Basiliscus after the African disaster. But there were plenty of domestic rivals who might challenge the presumption that Zeno's son might inherit, including Jordanes and Anagastes. These internal distractions meant that when the leader of the Thracian Goths, Theoderic Strabo, revolted in 473, he was able to negotiate the position of *magister militum praesentalis*. At the same time, the Pannonian Goths, led by Theodemir, moved into Macedonia in 473 and settled. Leo was confident enough at this point to send a third emperor to the west, Julius Nepos, with further troops. He did not see the results, having already fallen so ill in late 473 that the young Leo II was promoted to Augustus on November 17, 473. A few months later, Leo died of dysentery, aged seventy-three, on January 18, 474.

Leo's reign saw the last sustained attempt by the east to prop up the western Empire. Although these efforts were unsuccessful, his ability to project force and the subsequent Justinianic reconquest of Africa showed that the attempt was well within Roman capabilities. What Leo could not do was change the way in which the Italian and other western aristocracies viewed the Empire. Less than a century earlier, Theodosius I had imposed his son Honorius on the west, but none of the three emperors sent by Leo was successful in gaining real support from the Italian aristocrats. Otherwise, Leo's reign saw little progress in resolving the problems posed by the presence of Gothic groups in the Balkans or the Council of Chalcedon, both problems that were left to his successor.

ZENO (474–491)

Leo II ruled alone for a few days before his father Zeno was appointed Augustus on January 29, 474. Aged only seven, Leo II's rule could only be nominal, and after his death from illness in November 474, Zeno reigned alone. Zeno had had a military career under Leo, first being heard of serving in the east in 466. He then came to Constantinople and, following the removal of Ardabur, became *comes domesticorum* and married Ariadne, Leo's eldest daughter, in 467. Zeno was unpopular during his reign and seems always to have been short of money, although his financial difficulties were at least partly the consequences of the cost of Leo's Vandal expedition. There were also accusations of favoring Isaurians too much. The problems faced by Zeno were similar to those faced by Leo, in particular the Goths in the

Balkans and what to do about Chalcedon. As in Leo's reign, rivalry between generals could be intense, and Theoderic Strabo, one of the *magistri militum praesentales*, murdered Heraclius, *magister militum per Thracias*, in revenge for Heraclius' involvement in Aspar's murder in the palace. Theoderic was dismissed, but before he could cause trouble, Zeno was faced with a challenge in the imperial city.

BASILISCUS (475–476)

In early January 475, only two months after the death of Leo II, Zeno was faced by a conspiracy led by Basiliscus, the brother of Leo's wife Verina and thus Zeno's mother-in-law. Basiliscus had a military career under Leo before holding the consulate in 465, commanded the failed expedition against the Vandals in 468, and was involved in the coup against Aspar in 471. He was acclaimed as Augustus on January 9, 475, supported by Verina; his nephew Armatus, who was *magister militum per Thracias*; the Isaurian Illus; and the recently dismissed Goth Theoderic Strabo. After some fighting in the capital, Zeno withdrew to Ourba (probably Olba) in the lowlands of Isauria with his wife, mother, and, most importantly, much of the treasury. For a while, he retained control of Syria, but this was lost when an army under Illus arrived. Zeno then abandoned Ourba and retired to mountainous Sbide deeper in Isauria, where he was besieged by Illus.

Basiliscus was accepted in both east and west and secured the accession by appointing his son Marcus as Caesar, then Augustus. Gaining power was easier than keeping it, and he was still faced with the same problems as Zeno at his accession as well as a civil war. With the Empire still reeling under the costs of the 468 expedition, with much of the treasury still in Zeno's hands, and with the required accession donatives coming only a few months after accession donatives for both Leo II and Zeno, Basiliscus was in financial difficulty. His measures taken to raise income caused great unpopularity with one historian claiming that "he was so greedy for money that he did not leave alone even those who pursued mean and mechanical occupations" (Suda B.164). Even so, he just could not collect enough gold and the purity of Basiliscus' *solidi* was the lowest of all fifth-century eastern emperors. One of Basiliscus' earliest decisions involved a delegation of anti-Chalcedonian monks from Alexandria who had originally intended to petition Zeno. This resulted in Basiliscus issuing his *Encyclical* on April 6, 475, which attempted to resolve the problems caused by Chalcedon. It did so by renouncing all the innovations at Chalcedon that were contrary to Nicaea, but also making it clear that Nestorius and Eutyches were heretics and denying the Tome of

Leo. Like Leo's *Encyclical*, this represented the new direct imperial approach to resolving ecclesiastical issues. At first, it appeared to be a great success. According to Evagrius, a council of five hundred bishops assembled at Ephesus in summer 475 to sign the *Encyclical*. Basiliscus also restored Peter the Fuller to Antioch and Timothy Aelurus to Alexandria (with Timothy Salofaciolus retiring to a monastery at Canopus in Egypt). However, the *Encyclical* was not well received everywhere. In Constantinople, the patriarch Acacius enlisted the support of Daniel the Stylite (who even descended from his column) and other Constantinopolitan monks to oppose it, although Daniel's initial approach to Basiliscus in the Hebdomon Palace was rebuffed. Equally predictably, the denial of the Tome of Leo meant the encyclical was rejected by the Pope.

Other problems were beginning to arise for Basiliscus. There was another major fire in Constantinople that burned the Palace of Lausus and many of its famous statues. Basiliscus failed to keep promises made to Illus and to Armatus, who returned their allegiance to Zeno, as did Theoderic Strabo. Theoderic the Amal also joined Zeno. At this point, Basiliscus was so desperate for support from the city as to issue a *Counter-Encyclical* which rescinded the encyclical and expressly reaffirmed the rights of the patriarch of Constantinople to control the provinces in Asia. It was not enough, and in August 476 Zeno returned to Constantinople. When Basiliscus fled to the Great Church, Zeno promised not to execute him but exiled the whole family to Cappadocia, where they were starved to death.

Now restored, Zeno first rewarded his supporters. He fulfilled his promise to Armatus to make his son Basiliscus Caesar in 476; soon after he had Armatus murdered and forced his son to become a priest. Theoderic the Amal was appointed as *magister militum praesentalis*, and great favor was shown to various Isaurians, in particular Illus, who was appointed as consul for 478, and Illus' brother Trocundes, consul for 482 (though Illus also took Zeno's brother hostage at this point). At the same time, all of Basiliscus' acts were annulled, Peter the Fuller was exiled from Antioch, and plans were made to depose the anti-Chalcedonian Timothy Aelurus in Alexandria, though he died first in 477. Zeno restored the pro-Chalcedonian Timothy Salofaciolus (477–482), but another anti-Chalcedonian, Peter Mongus, was also consecrated locally and claimed the see.

Other problems were equally intractable. In 476, the eastern praetorian prefect Erythrius resigned rather than increase taxes. His successor, Sebastianus, sold offices, an action that probably brought in more complaints than the money raised justified. Finances also affected policy toward the two groups of Goths in the Balkans under Theoderic Strabo and Theoderic the Amal: "The emperor therefore, summoned his council and asked its advice as to what he should do. They said that the treasury did not have the resources to offer payments and wages to both parties, since 'we cannot supply our own soldiers without difficulties'. They left it to the emperor to decide which of them should be chosen as a friend" (Malchus fr. 15). Zeno decided to support Theoderic the Amal, but when a Roman army did not arrive as promised, Theoderic came to an agreement with Strabo. Zeno first tried to turn Theoderic the Amal against Strabo again by promising a marriage to Anicia Juliana, the daughter of Olybrius. These negotiations are preserved in some detail in Malchus, who records Zeno offering Theoderic not just Anicia Juliana, but also one thousand pounds of gold, forty thousand pounds of silver, and an annual income of ten thousand *solidi*. When this failed, he acceded to the promotion of Strabo, but dismissed Theoderic the Amal, sending Sabinianus, *magister militum per Illyricum*, against him in 479. Such policies did not inspire trust and encouraged rumors. During this campaign, Zeno was said to be planning to hand Thessalonica over to Theoderic the Amal. The populace rioted, threatening to burn down the palace of the praetorian prefect and turning over the statues of Zeno. Then the crowd was calmed by the bishop, and no violent imperial retribution took place.

Zeno, however, had good reasons to be suspicious of many of those around him. In 478, his mother-in-law Verina promoted an attempt on Illus' life. When she was caught, Zeno turned her over to Illus, who imprisoned her in Isauria. Even in prison, Verina continued to act against Zeno, now encouraging her other son-in-law Marcian (who had married Leontia) and Theoderic Strabo to revolt in 479, a revolt swiftly and decisively quashed by Illus, though it involved fighting in the corridors of the Great Palace. When the coup failed, Marcian was exiled to Cappadocia, and Theoderic Strabo was again deprived of his position. Now that Zeno had upset both Gothic groups, they allied, plundering Thrace and in 481 making an unsuccessful attempt on Constantinople. Soon afterward, Theoderic Strabo died after being thrown from his horse and was succeeded by his son Recitach. Zeno again showed favor to Theoderic the Amal, reappointing him as *magister militum praesentalis* in 483, making him consul for 484, and settling his people in Dacia Ripensis and Moesia Secunda. He also murdered Recitach in Constantinople, with the result that the Thracian Goths now disappeared, some becoming Romans, others joining Theoderic.

If the Gothic problems had become simpler, Zeno's life did not become that much easier. In 482, he made an attempt to resolve the continuing tensions caused by the Council of Chalcedon. The statement of faith at Chalcedon, heavily influenced by western theology, stressed the existence of both the human and divine natures of Christ. The opponents of this view, often described as monophysites (though they preferred the term "orthodox"), focused on the unity of the two natures in Christ. In an attempt to bring adherents of both two views together, Zeno issued a religious statement that became known as the *Henotikon*. Basiliscus' *Encyclical* had already suggested that a moderate approach initiated by the emperor might be successful in gaining widespread support. The *Henotikon* was skillfully written, probably by Acacius, patriarch of Constantinople. Like the *Encyclical*, it accepted the Nicene Creed, the Twelve Anathemas of Cyril, and condemned both Nestorius and Eutyches. However, it passed over Chalcedon in near silence, specifically taking the approach of moderation rather than the more inflammatory tone of the *Encyclical*. Nonetheless, the *Henotikon* provoked widespread opposition among some eastern bishops, particularly the patriarchs of Antioch and Alexandria, and some monks in Constantinople, especially the Akoimetoi. Zeno soon expelled John Talaia, patriarch of Alexandria. Most significantly, like the *Encyclical*, ignoring the Tome of Leo made the *Henotikon* unacceptable in the west. When Pope Felix III (483–492) excommunicated Acacius in 484, he caused a schism that lasted until the reign of Justin. The problems posed by Chalcedon were close to insoluble, given the differing concerns of eastern emperor and Pope. Nonetheless, there were real efforts made to resolve the division. One index of the intensity of the diplomacy surrounding the *Henotikon* is the career of Uranius, an *agens in rebus* based in Constantinople. He is first heard of carrying imperial letters to Bishop Calandion in Antioch (479–485) before carrying letters from Zeno to Simplicius in Rome in 482, then bringing Simplicius' reply back. Later in 482, Uranius carried other letters of Zeno to Alexandria. Acacius was succeeded as patriarch by Fravitta (488–489) and then Euphemius (489–496), who tried to heal the schism by denouncing Peter Mongus. Euphemius' refusal to remove Acacius and Fravitta from the diptychs of the Constantinopolitan church meant that Felix rejected the attempt.

LEONTIUS (484–488)

Zeno's relations with Illus had never been good and continued to deteriorate. In 481, Ariadne tried to have Illus killed, so Zeno sent him to Antioch, promoting him from *magister officiorum* to *magister militum per Orientem*. Then in 483, Zeno asked Illus to release Longinus, his brother, whom Illus had taken hostage in 476 when restoring Zeno to power. When Illus refused to do this, he was dismissed from office. He then rebelled in 484, releasing Marcian from prison in Isauria. After Zeno sent out an army led by Leontius, another

Isaurian, Illus, with the assistance of Verina, declared Leontius Augustus at Tarsus on July 19, 484. The rebels then moved to Antioch in Syria, where they were supported by the patriarch Calandion (479–484), who had refused to acknowledge the *Henotikon*. Here, Verina issued her own Chalcedonian edict. Leontius occupied Antioch for twelve days (July 27–August 8), during which time a few coins were hurriedly minted and he formed a full administration, including men such as Aelianus, who had been Zeno's eastern praetorian prefect in 480. Any confidence that Leontius felt was soon dashed. A second imperial expedition arrived, under the command of Ioannes the Scythian. This army, which included a contingent of Goths under Theoderic, rapidly defeated Leontius at Antioch and pursued him to Isauria, where the remaining rebels were then besieged for four years at the fortress of Papirius. At first, Illus made appeals for help to Odovacer, the Persians, and the Armenian satraps. When these appeals brought little support, Illus lost interest in the fighting and instead turned to reading. Verina died during the siege, though her body was later sent to Constantinople for burial alongside her husband. Finally, the fortress was betrayed in 488. Leontius was executed at Seleucia and his head taken to Constantinople, where it was impaled on the walls. Illus was also executed, and Calandion was deposed as patriarch, being replaced by Peter the Fuller.

Despite the distractions of the war against Leontius, there was much military activity in the east during this period. Illus' appeal to the Armenian satraps produced little support for Leontius, but did prompt a change in the government in Armenia, where four of the five hereditary satraps were replaced with governors appointed by the emperor. In addition, a *comes Armeniae* was created to oversee the region's defense. There was a campaign by Zeno's brother Longinus against the Tzanni in 485. And in the same year, Zeno demanded control of Nisibis through an envoy, Eusebius, sent to King Peroz I (459–484); Eusebius even accompanied the king on an expedition in 483 against the Hephthalite Huns. Nonetheless, the request was unsuccessful. There was a Samaritan revolt in ca. 484. When this was quelled, the defeated leader Justasas was executed and his head sent to Constantinople, while the synagogue at Mount Gerizim was converted into a church to St. Mary.

While Zeno was attempting to put down Leontius' revolt in Anatolia, in Europe Theoderic revolted again in 486. This was calmed by one of his sisters, who was living in Constantinople as a companion of Zeno's wife Ariadne and stopped Theoderic from attacking Constantinople. With negotiations restarted, Zeno was able to persuade Theoderic to leave the Balkans and to attack Odovacer in Italy. Zeno's relationship with Odovacer had been peaceful to this point, but he now seized an opportunity to get rid of Theoderic. Theoderic left Novae at the head of his Goths in 488 and entered Italy in August 489. At the same time, Zeno was also encouraging the Rugi in Noricum to attack Odovacer.

As with other emperors, the tone of Zeno's surviving laws varied widely. An early edict in October 474 displays surprise at the number of petitioners, requesting that "no one hereafter dare to annoy the favourable ears of our piety by pouring out petitions concerning treasure either looked for in his own land or another place or concerning treasure found by another or by himself'" (*CJ* 10.15.1). Another law required imperial officials to remain in their area of administration for fifty days after their assignment was over in case there were accusations against them, and a third restricted the patriciate to consuls, urban and praetorian prefects, the *magister officiorum*, and *magistri militum*. Despite being the gateway to such honors, the consulate was proving harder to fill, and no eastern consuls were appointed in 480, 481, 483, 484, 485, or 488. Among building work in the capital, the Royal Stoa was restored by Illus. The interest shown by Leo in relics continued when St. Barnabas' copy of the Gospel of Matthew was brought to Constantinople from Cyprus and placed in the Church of St. Stephen in the imperial palace.

Zeno's court was an interesting place. Isaurians had a poor reputation: the bishop Theodoret in the middle of the century noted that "when many people speak against the Isaurians, they say that they carry off money and love gold and look for too much" (Theodoret, *Ep.* 40). But many Isaurians were more cultured. The *magister officiorum* Illus was looking for a speaker on the nature of the soul, and so asked Marsus, another Isaurian soldier, for a recommendation. Marsus suggested Pamprepius, a pagan Egyptian philosopher who had been educated in Athens and went on to become *quaestor* in 479. Ioannes, praetorian prefect of Illyricum in 479, was also known for his interest in culture. Men such as Ioannes and Illus served as literary patrons for professional poets like Christodorus and Panolbius. These writers flowed around the various groups in the palace, of whom the Isaurians were the most prominent. Some of the Isaurians were attracted to the company of another Zeno, the illegitimate son of the emperor, while later on they clustered around his brother Longinus; both men had reputations for dissolute behavior. The emperor's wife, Ariadne, and mother-in-law, Verina, were the focus for the numerous soldiers from the Balkans, many of whom were Goths. They included Marcian and Anthemius, sons of the Anthemius who had been emperor in the west. Marcian had married Verina's other daughter, while Anthemius was married to Herais, patron of Daniel the Stylite. There were other groups too, including the previous generation of Balkan soldiers, represented by Areobindus, son of Dagalaiphus (consul in 461), who married

Anicia Juliana, the granddaughter of Valentinian III and daughter of the western emperor Olybrius.

All of this imperial blood could bring tension to the court. In addition to the attempts to seize the throne, by Basiliscus, Leontius, and Marcian, other plots were discovered before they reached fruition. Dionysius, eastern praetorian prefect, was executed in 480, together with Epinicus and Thraustila, for plotting against the emperor. And the pagan Severianus, who had been offered a senior administrative position by Zeno on condition that he convert to Christianity (he rejected the offer), was later accused of being involved in a plot with the intent of reviving paganism. Some of these plots were discovered because of informers, but Zeno was also prepared to use astrologers. In 490, the patrician Pelagius was put to death. In the sixth century, it was reported that the *comes* Maurianus, "who knew about mystical things," predicted that Zeno would be succeeded by a *silentiarius*. Since Pelagius had been a *silentiarius* before becoming a patrician, he was executed.

Zeno died on April 9, 491. Even in death, his reputation was so poor that according to the medieval populist historian Cedrenus he was buried alive and for two days was heard screaming from the tomb, "have pity on me" (Cedrenus, p622). Despite his unpopularity, Zeno was able to survive a number of serious challenges and remain emperor. However, he died without an heir; his son Leo had died in 474, while an illegitimate son also predeceased him. There was thus a moment of uncertainty before the acclamation of the next emperor, Anastasius.

THE WEST

The brief interregna after the deaths of several eastern emperors were far less significant than the transitions of imperial power in the west. Here, the twenty-one years and nine emperors between the murder of Valentinian III and the deposition of Romulus in 476 made the period complex and confusing for modern historians and for contemporaries. In addition to the political complexity, the primary evidence becomes very scarce. Between 455 and 476, for example, we can identify only two provincial governors in Italy: an anonymous *consularis* of Flaminia et Picenum in 458, and Rogatianus *consularis* of Tuscia Suburbicaria in 459. Both are known from laws of Majorian concerned with routine administration. Rogatianus had written to the emperor requesting advice on an adulterer who had evaded exile. Majorian was in Arles, but had a *quaestor* with him and provided a response. The lack of inscriptions was not confined to the west, and in the same period no provincial governor can be identified in either of the Syrian provinces or in Lycaonia, Isauria, Mesopotamia, and Osrhoene. The Empire was changing, but so too was the evidence we use to describe it.

During the first half of the fifth century, the Roman Empire was under threat in the west and had lost territory in Britain, Gaul, Spain, and Africa. Yet at the death of Valentinian III, few Romans would have thought that the Empire would have disappeared in the west within the next generation. The invasion of the Huns in 452 and the sack of Rome in 455 made it clear to the Italian aristocracy that their leadership was failing to protect them; earlier in the century, Honorius still had armies at his disposal, but with the successive losses of territory, the military resources available to Valentinian III and his successors were too limited.

PETRONIUS MAXIMUS (455)

In the west, the period after the assassination of Valentinian III was one of political confusion. On the day after the murder, March 17, 455, officials at Rome acclaimed Petronius Maximus as emperor. The swiftness of the decision meant that there was no consulting Marcian, the senior Augustus. Maximus had been twice urban prefect, twice Italian praetorian prefect, and twice consul as well as being patrician. Before the acclamation, there was a brief discussion in Rome as to whether the general Majorian was a better candidate, but though he was supported by Eudoxia, Valentinian's widow, Maximus had more support in Rome. After his proclamation, Maximus married Eudoxia and made his son Palladius Caesar; Palladius married one of Eudoxia's daughters. These marriages made clear a claim to continue the dynasty of Valentinian.

Maximus' reign was so brief that little can be said about it. Coins were struck and one of Maximus' *magistri militum*, Avitus, was sent as an envoy to the Visigoths in Toulouse. But with Valentinian's death, the treaty that he had made with the Vandal king Geiseric in 442 lapsed. Geiseric immediately occupied the rest of Roman Africa, taking control of the provinces of the Mauritanias, Tingitania, and Numidia, while a fleet sailed to Italy and landed near Rome. Maximus panicked, fled, was deserted by his bodyguard, and then was mobbed and died on May 31. Palladius died with him. The Vandals entered Rome three days later and sacked the city for two long weeks, taking many prisoners, including Maximus' wife Eudoxia, her daughters Eudocia and Placidia, and Aetius' son Gaudentius, as well as the treasures of Jerusalem from Titus' capture of the city in 70. This was traumatic for the city, but far less significant than the sack by Alaric in 410.

EPARCHIUS AVITUS (455–456)

With the Vandals still in Italy, the imperial officials in Rome were not sure what to do. While they talked, others acted; the *magister militum* Eparchius Avitus was declared Augustus at Arles in Gaul on July 9, 455. Avitus, originally from Clermont in Gaul, had served as a soldier under Aetius as well as being Gallic praetorian prefect in 439. With no obvious candidate of their own, the Italians accepted the well-qualified Avitus as emperor. The eastern emperor Marcian never accepted him.

At his accession, Avitus had all sorts of military problems with few resources to deal with them. In northern Gaul, Roman control of the English Channel had been lost, allowing Germanic raiders to reach Armorica, the Atlantic coast of Gaul, and even Spain. In western Gaul, there was now a substantial Burgundian kingdom, while in southern Gaul there was a Visigothic kingdom. Both of these kingdoms had developed into independent states from their original status as settlements within the Roman Empire. Nonetheless, Avitus was able to persuade the Visigoths and Burgundians to attack the Suevi in Spain. They defeated, captured, and executed the Suevic king Rechiarius at the River Urbicus in Galicia in October 455, after which the Suevi split into several factions fighting for the kingship. This expedition was a diplomatic triumph, achieving Roman aims at no cost to the Romans themselves.

Avitus himself left Gaul for Rome in September 455. After his arrival, he soon became unpopular in the city which was suffering from famine as well as trying to recover from the Vandal sack. Although it is likely that any emperor would have been poorly received in this situation, the appointment of Gauls to almost all of Avitus' senior positions would not have made him popular with the Italian aristocracy. In 456, Avitus had some military success against the Vandals, whom the *comes* Ricimer defeated off Sicily and then off Corsica, for which he was promoted to *magister militum*. This did not help Avitus in Rome, where the problems in food supply focused attention on the Goths and Gauls he had brought with him. Then Avitus stripped the ornamental bronze from some public buildings to pay off the Gothic soldiers, which caused further resentment among the Romans. He returned to Gaul in early 456 before moving to Ravenna, where he executed the *patricius* Remistus, his other *magister militum*, on September 17. This led some of the Italian army, led by Ricimer and the *comes domesticorum* Majorian, to revolt. Ricimer, with a Suevic father and Visigothic mother, had served as a soldier under Aetius and had married into the Burgundian royal family. As Avitus attempted to withdraw from Italy, he was defeated in battle and captured at Placentia on October 17, 456. He was forced to become a bishop at Placentia, but he died soon afterward, starved to death by Majorian. His son and daughter were allowed to live.

MAJORIAN (457–461)

In the months after Avitus' deposition, Majorian and Ricimer were unable to come to an agreement with the eastern emperor Marcian before he died on January 26, 457. The situation changed a little with Leo's acclamation as eastern Augustus on February 7, 457; on February 28, he granted Ricimer and Majorian the honors *patricius* and *magister militum*, respectively. Then Julius Valerius Majorianus was acclaimed Caesar on April 1, 457. Like his colleague Ricimer, Majorian had served as a soldier in Gaul under Aetius. He had retired, but after the murder of Aetius he was recalled by Valentinian. Majorian's elevation to Augustus did not occur until December 28 at Ravenna.

Like Avitus, Majorian was faced with a combination of military challenges in Gaul and Africa and a lack of money and manpower to deal with them. One of the results of the financial problems was that the quality of his *solidi* was markedly low; in 455, there had been accession donatives offered by both Petronius Maximus and Avitus as well as the quinquennial *vota* for Valentinian's thirtieth year. Like Avitus, Majorian went on the offensive, suggesting that some Romans believed that they could improve the situation. He began a program of shipbuilding and recruiting additional troops from the Danube. Reestablishing imperial authority in Gaul was a delicate matter following the removal of Avitus. To accomplish this, Majorian appointed Aegidius, another of Aetius' followers, as *magister militum per Gallias*. At the same time, he sent Petrus, *magister epistularum*, with an army in early 458 that recaptured Lyons from the Burgundians after a long siege. After this, the Burgundians remained at peace with the Romans during the lifetime of their king Gundioc (455–473/4). Majorian then arrived in Gaul himself in November 458 and wintered in Lyons, the first emperor to lead troops in the west since Theodosius. The good relationship that Avitus had had with the Visigoths died with him, and Aegidius and Majorian were forced to campaign against Theoderic II.

A long letter by Sidonius Apollinaris to his friend Montius (*Ep.* 1.11) tells us about a banquet hosted by the emperor Majorian at Arles in 461. Sidonius was from a family of prominent Gallic aristocrats in the area around Lyons. His father and grandfather had been Gallic praetorian prefects, while Sidonius himself went on to become urban prefect of Rome in 468. During the year, an anonymous pamphlet was circulating among the *comitatus* containing satire pointed at named individuals. It was clearly the work of an accomplished poet, but who? The victims wanted to know. One of them, Paeonius, had claimed it was Sidonius. The result was that as Sidonius walked in the Forum, he was the object of popular attention, some positive, some negative. The next day he was invited to dinner by the emperor. Sidonius describes a traditional and intimate dinner, with only six other guests, including Severinus, consul for the year; Magnus, consul for the previous year; and Paeonius. This Paeonius had earlier played a prominent role in the interregnum between Majorian and Severus, acting as praetorian prefect in Gaul. He was also involved in the *coniuratio Marcellana*, a poorly understood event that seems to have involved a plan to make someone emperor, probably hatched in the interregnum after Avitus' deposition. Majorian had heard of the accusation that Sidonius had written the anonymous satire, though Paeonius declined to make the accusation in front of the emperor. Sidonius' account is the only one we have, so we may doubt that the dinner was quite as witty as Sidonius painted it. Nonetheless, his spontaneous generation of a short poem in response to Majorian's request was clearly talked about, hence Montius' request for an account that Sidonius was only too pleased to publish.

Once southern Gaul was secure, Majorian sent Aegidius north, where he fought against Frankish tribes around Trier and Cologne, not entirely successfully. The emperor entered Spain in 460, and in a swift offensive against the Suevi recaptured the province of Carthaginensis. Once he had secured the region, Majorian started to assemble a large fleet (Priscus mentions three hundred ships) for operations against the Vandals. A naval battle followed at Elece just north of Carthago Nova in Carthaginensis, which was won by the Vandals. Majorian now made peace with them and, leaving Spain under the control of the *magister militum* Nepotianus, went back to Arles. When he finally returned to Italy, he was deposed by Ricimer at Dertona in Liguria and then executed five days later on August 7, 461.

Majorian's reign was the last time that there was a Roman imperial presence in Spain, and after this the Romans paid no attention to the peninsula until the mid-sixth century. Africa and Gaul were closer, paid more taxes, and produced more recruits than Spain, so they were higher strategic priorities. And now that the Visigoths were also involved in Spain, both they and the Vandals would need to be dealt with in any Roman attempt to reclaim control of the peninsula. With the murder of Majorian, Ricimer was now the dominant political figure in the west. His authority was tenuous, based more on a dominant personality and military position than a firm control of the mechanisms of government.

LIBIUS SEVERUS (461–465)

After Majorian's death in August, there was again a delay before Libius Severus was acclaimed emperor in November 461 at Ravenna. Severus is a very obscure figure and nothing is known of him before becoming emperor except that he was from Lucania in Italy. The murder of Majorian by Ricimer would have made Leo suspicious of any emperor put forward in the west, and Leo never accepted Severus. In addition to the foreign and financial problems facing the emperor, by murdering Majorian, Ricimer had also attracted the hostility of the *magister militum per Gallias* Aegidius and another military friend of Majorian's, Marcellinus, who moved to Dalmatia. Aegidius refused to accept Severus and began making preparations to invade Italy. Severus therefore appointed Agrippinus as *magister militum per Gallias*, though most of the Gallic army remained loyal to Aegidius. At this point, the Roman forces in Italy, Dalmatia, and Gaul were now facing each other, not the external enemies of the Empire. Short of troops, Agrippinus turned to the Visigoths for help, but when he gave them control of Narbo he exceeded his orders; by October 463, he had been replaced as *magister militum per Gallias* by the Burgundian king Gundioc, who was probably a relative of Ricimer. Despite the removal of Agrippinus, his policy was successful. The Visigoths marched to Orleans in 463, and though they were defeated, this did stop Aegidius from invading Italy. When Aegidius was murdered in 464/465, his son Syagrius took over control of his army. Syagrius played no further role in imperial politics, suggesting that Gallic belief in the Empire was starting to fade. Half a century earlier, such ambitious men had seized imperial power or tried to control it, but in the late fifth century it was also possible to ignore it. Northern Gaul now passed outside the Roman Empire.

Most of our evidence for Severus' reign concerns Gaul, but he also faced renewed Vandal problems in Italy since their treaty with Majorian ended with his death. Geiseric began sending raiding parties to Sicily and Italy in autumn 461 and annually in spring thereafter, as well as occupying Corsica, Sardinia, and the Balearic Islands. At this point, the eastern emperor Leo was able to persuade Marcellinus in Dalmatia to cooperate with Severus, though at some point after this reign, Sicily was occupied by the Vandals. Then Severus died in Rome on November 14, 465. There were contemporary accusations that Ricimer had him poisoned, though other contemporaries suggested that the general was innocent. With Severus' death, the task of finding another emperor fell to Ricimer again; this time, he requested assistance from the east.

ANTHEMIUS (467–472)

The negotiations between Leo and Ricimer took sixteen months. During this time, Ricimer appears to have acted as head of state, though without making himself emperor. This reluctance of generals to claim imperial power for themselves is a characteristic of the fifth and sixth centuries in both east and west, a significant difference from the third and fourth centuries. Finally, Leo sent Anthemius, son-in-law of the emperor Marcian, to the west with a large army in 467. Anthemius had had a successful military career in the Balkans under Marcian and Leo. He was also accompanied by Marcellinus, whom he appointed patrician, an act that Ricimer interpreted as challenging him. Soon after his arrival, Anthemius was acclaimed Augustus near Rome on April 12, 467.

Once Anthemius arrived, his relationship with Ricimer was critical. Ricimer had paid a high price in return for the promised eastern expedition against the Vandals. The relationship started well, with Ricimer's marriage to Anthemius' daughter Alypia late in the year. In Rome, we hear of the urban prefect, Sidonius Apollinaris, who had used the *cursus publicus* to travel to the city, celebrating the arrival of ships bringing grain and honey, which he hoped would settle a populace anxious about the food supply to the city. And though few laws are preserved from Anthemius' reign, those that survive show the continuing functioning of the imperial system. The emperor was still receiving petitions from his subjects. In one case, a dispute between two *illustres* over property granted by a previous emperor, Anthemius took advice from Leo. Anthemius spent his entire reign in Rome.

Anthemius marshaled what resources he could against the Vandals and the Visigoths. In 468, Leo's Vandal expedition was launched, with the western forces under the command of Marcellinus. He was able to reoccupy Sardinia, but after the defeat of the main expedition was murdered in Sicily, probably at the order of Ricimer. In southern Gaul, the Visigothic king Theoderic II was succeeded in 466 by Euric (466–484), who was ambitious, capable, and aggressive. In 471, he besieged Arles. In an attempt to relieve the city, Anthemius sent one of his sons, Anthemiolus, to Gaul, but he was defeated and killed by the Visigoths and the city fell. This was the last case of Roman imperial intervention in Gaul, and though there was continued resistance to the Goths by individual cities, such as Clermont, chronicled by Sidonius Apollinaris, Roman control of southern Gaul was now almost entirely lost.

Arvandus had served two terms as praetorian prefect in Gaul in the 460s, but his second prefecture was interrupted by series of accusations leading to his arrest and transport to Rome. Our main source for these events is a letter from Sidonius Apollinaris, who had just finished a term as urban prefect in Rome (*Ep.* 1.7). Though Sidonius is a well-informed contemporary, his letter is a part of a highly polished selection of correspondence designed to show him in a good light. In Rome, charges were laid on behalf of the provinces by a trio of Gallic aristocrats, Tonantius Ferreolus (who had been Gallic praetorian prefect when Attila invaded Gaul), Thaumastus (Sidonius' uncle), and Petronius (who later suggested that Sidonius publish some of his letters and then helped him in the project). Following this, Arvandus was arrested in 469 in Gaul and sent to Rome for trial. While awaiting trial, he was kept in custody by another Gallic aristocrat, Flavius Asellus, currently serving as *comes sacrarum largitionum* and a known friend. There were several charges against Arvandus, including bribery. The most serious was based on an intercepted letter that his secretary, also under arrest, claimed had been written to the Gothic king Euric, dissuading him from making peace with the "Greek emperor" and encouraging him to take over control of Gaul and share it with the Burgundians. The trial took place in the Senate, where Arvandus admitted to writing the letter, apparently in the belief that he could only be convicted of treason (*maiestas*) if he was aiming at making himself emperor. Found guilty, he was condemned to death. Successful appeals by his friends, including Sidonius, reduced the sentence to exile.

The initial hopes for Anthemius' reign thus crumpled. Without the financial resources offered by Africa, there was little hope now for the western Empire to recover, and the remaining years are a sad tale. When in 470 Anthemius executed Ricimer's friend Romanus, *patricius* and ex-*magister officiorum*, for treason, Ricimer left Rome and assembled an army of six thousand men at Milan. Insults began to fly, with the emperor describing Ricimer as a "skin-clad Goth," while the general called him "an excitable Galatian" (Ennodius, *Life of Epiphanius* 67, 53). Although Ennodius, bishop of Ticinum, was able to organize a reconciliation between the two for a while, this collapsed early in 472. Ricimer then summoned his Burgundian nephew Gundobaudes, *magister militum per Gallias*, and laid siege to Rome in March.

ANICIUS OLYBRIUS (472)

According to Malalas, Leo sent Olybrius (a westerner who had married Valentinian III's younger daughter Placidia) to mediate in the dispute between emperor and general. This was a very different response to an overmighty general compared to Leo's own murder of Aspar in the palace at Constantinople the year before. If Olybrius had been sent to mediate, Leo may have been surprised when Ricimer acclaimed Anicius Olybrius as Augustus in April 472, especially as Olybrius is not known to have held any political or military offices. Anthemius fought on for five months, but in July 472 Ricimer's troops finally broke into the city, capturing and killing Anthemius. Within weeks of his victory, Ricimer died on August 19, 472. Olybrius then promoted Gundobaudes to *patricius* to replace him. A few months later, Olybrius died of dropsy at Rome on November 2, 472.

GLYCERIUS (473–474)

Another interregnum followed, with Gundobaudes replacing Ricimer as the dominant figure in Italy, while appointing his brother Chilperic as *magister militum* and *patricius* in Gaul. After five months, Gundobaudes acclaimed the *comes domesticorum* Glycerius as emperor at Ravenna on March 3, 473. Like Olybrius, Glycerius is not known to have held any other offices before this point, but he still had an imperial administration. On April 29, 473, an edict was issued at Rome concerning the ordination of priests in the names of the four praetorian prefects, Aurelianus, Dioscurus, Himelco, and Protadius. This is the last known imperial edict to be issued in the western Empire. Although Glycerius recognized Leo's administration, Leo did not reciprocate.

Anthemius had been able to send expeditions against Africa and Gaul, even though these had failed. Now Glycerius was faced with barbarian invasions of Italy. In 473, the Visigoth Euric sent an army under Vincentius into Italy, but it was defeated and killed by the *comites* Alla and Sindila. Nothing is known of Vincentius' background, but his Roman name is suggestive of the sorts of choices open to Romans in the late fifth century. For many, working for barbarians was a good choice, while the Germanic names of Alla and Sindila suggest the opposite, i.e., the attractions of Roman service to those of non-Roman origin. Around the same time, some Goths led by Vidimir entered Italy from Pannonia, though they were bribed by Glycerius to leave Italy and join the Visigoths. But what was attractive for some was not enough for others, and Gundobaudes left

Italy after his father's death late in 473 or early in 474 to become one of the kings of the Burgundians.

JULIUS NEPOS (474–480)

Glycerius' elevation was not accepted by the eastern emperor Leo, who wanted to appoint Julius Nepos to succeed Anthemius. Nepos was *magister militum Dalmatiae* in 473, having succeeded his uncle Marcellinus in this previously unattested post; he was also husband of a niece of Leo. Leo died before the expedition was launched, but it took place in the joint reign of Leo II and Zeno. After landing at Portus near Rome, Julius Nepos entered Rome in June 474 and was acclaimed Augustus. Glycerius surrendered and was exiled to Salona, where he served as the city's bishop.

Nepos and Zeno together made a treaty with the Vandals. On Glycerius' exile, there was a division between those Gauls who wished to remain in the Empire and those who preferred to give up on the Empire and remain under Burgundian rule. Nepos appointed a prominent Gaul, Ecdicius, son of Avitus, as *patricius* and *magister militum per Gallias*, and some *solidi* were minted in Arles. However, any hope of exerting power in Gaul was soon quashed by Ecdicius' transfer to Italy. Soon afterward, Ecdicius was replaced as *magister militum* by Orestes. Nepos negotiated a peace with the Visigothic king Euric, making him *patricius* and giving up the provinces of Aquitania in return for Arles and Marseilles.

ROMULUS (475–476)

When Nepos ordered Orestes into Gaul in late August 475, Orestes revolted. Nepos retired to Dalmatia, where he continued to rule as Augustus until 480. Orestes declared himself *patricius* and a month later, on October 31, 475, acclaimed his son Romulus as Augustus at Ravenna. Probably fed up with irregular pay, the army demanded land to secure their livelihood, and when Orestes refused this, one of his officers, Odovacer, took up the cause. His troops marched from Ticinum to Placentia where they captured Orestes on August 28, 476. Ravenna was then stormed and Orestes' brother captured on September 4:

> Entering Ravenna, Odovacer deposed Augustulus from ruling, and taking pity on his youth he granted him his life, and because he was beautiful he even gave him an income of six thousand *solidi* and sent him to Campania to live freely with his relatives (*Anonymus Valesianus* 8.38).

The deposition of Romulus is frequently seen as the end of the western Roman Empire. Such a judgment is very much a later view. Contemporaries would have seen his deposition as part of the ongoing practice of western politics, with imperial power still being represented by both Julius Nepos and Zeno. The first statement that we have that the western Empire was no more came in an entry in the *Chronicle* of Marcellinus Comes, writing in Constantinople around 518: "with this Augustulus the Western Empire of the Roman people perished" (sa 476). But after this, Marcellinus moved rapidly on; for him, it was not a significant moment.

ODOVACER (476–493)

The eastern emperor Zeno, who in summer 476 had just regained control of Constantinople from Basiliscus, then received embassies from both Odovacer (sent by the Senate of Rome) and Nepos. Having considered his choices, Zeno appointed Odovacer as *patricius*. He did not try to restore Nepos to power, but instructed Odovacer to recognize him as emperor. Odovacer accepted this, issuing coins in the names of Zeno and of Nepos. At the same time, Zeno recognized Odovacer. Thus a prefectural edict from Mylasa in Caria issued at some point between 480 and 486 names Boethius, prefect of Italy, along with the prefect of the east and Illyricum. In Italy, Odovacer held the position of emperor, but not the title, referring to himself as king; in a Sicilian land grant to Pierius, he was referred to simply as "king Odovacar" (*P.Ital.* 10–11). Nonetheless, he had a full set of officials, including the Italian praetorian prefect Basilius (consul in 480), who during the election of Pope Felix III in 483 was described as acting on behalf of "the most distinguished king Odovacer," an annual consul recognized in the east, a *comes domesticorum*, and a *magister militum*. He also restored some sections of the Flavian Amphitheater (Colosseum), where beast hunts continued to be held. Odovacer was now relatively secure in Italy, though unable to do much outside the peninsula.

Nonetheless, the lack of an imperial title mattered to contemporaries. In 476, the Visigothic king Euric occupied Marseilles and Arles. He then wrote to Zeno, who granted the Goths control of the captured cities. Odovacer's authority at this point was weak, and with the recent western disorder his reign might have been expected to be short-lived. The battles necessary to unseat Orestes and rebellions led by the *comes* Brachila in 477 and by Adaric in 478 suggest that Odovacer did not have the unanimous support of the Italian army. But after the death of the Vandal king Geiseric in 477, Odovacer was able to negotiate peace with the Vandals and the return of

Sicily. A second threat was removed in 480 when Julius Nepos was murdered at a villa in Salona in Dalmatia. Photius' epitome of Malchus suggests that Glycerius, who had been deposed by Nepos, was involved. In 481 Odovacer occupied Dalmatia.

Though secular relations were generally good, religious relations between east and west soon collapsed after the publication of the *Henotikon* in 482. When Simplicius became Pope in 468, there was a Roman emperor in the west, but at his death in 483 only a king of Italy. This removed any immediate check on Simplicius' independence. The situation was further complicated by the difficulties of the theology, particularly because Simplicius was working with a limited knowledge of events in the east; the fact that the Tome of Leo was ignored in the east meant resolution of the schism was even more difficult. Soon after his election as Pope in 483, Felix III (483–492) was faced with responding to Zeno's *Henotikon*, horrifying to him in that it was an imperial edict, not the result of a church council. And he also chose to support the refugee patriarch from Alexandria, John Talaia. Felix acted boldly, summoning Acacius, the patriarch of Constantinople, to Rome to explain his conduct. Perhaps not surprisingly, the legates carrying these letters were imprisoned as soon as they landed in Constantinople. Felix then held a synod in Rome on July 28, 484, in which he deposed and excommunicated Acacius in Constantinople, Peter the Fuller in Antioch, and Peter Mongus in Alexandria. He also wrote directly to Zeno, ordering him, under threat of excommunication, to abandon Acacius. Felix's view of his powers differed greatly from both that of Zeno and the bishops of the east. Threatening Zeno's bishops may have been acceptable, but threatening the emperor himself was not. Schism followed between eastern and western churches, though after the death of Acacius in 489 Felix made an unsuccessful attempt to restore communion between the churches.

At the same time as religious tensions between the two parts of the Empire escalated, there were growing secular problems. In 486, Zeno had encouraged the Rugi to attack Noricum so that Odovacer might be distracted from intervening in the Balkans in favor of Leontius, currently in revolt in Isauria. In response to the attack, Odovacer crossed the Danube, wintered in enemy territory, and defeated the Rugic king Feletheus in late December. Onoulphus, Odovacer's brother, had recently left the eastern army and in 487 led a second campaign against the Rugi.

With the failure of the Rugi to depose Odovacer, in 488 Zeno sent Theoderic the Amal against him in Italy, with orders to rule in his place until Zeno arrived there. Zeno may not have been concerned about who the victor was, while for Italy the consequences were similar whether Odovacer or Theoderic was victorious. In early 489, Odovacer was defeated by Theoderic at the river Isonzo, at the foot of the main pass across the Julian Alps. He retreated to Verona, where he lost a second battle and then retreated to Ravenna. By this point, what was left of his kingdom was beginning to disintegrate as some men under the *magister militum* Tufa retreated to Milan, pursued by Theoderic. Tufa surrendered on April 1, was given a command in the Gothic army, and sent against Odovacer. But then he returned his allegiance to Odovacer, who now advanced into the Po Valley. However, in 490 Odovacer was defeated again by Theoderic on the River Adda and his *comes domesticorum* Pierius was killed. He then returned to Ravenna, which fell under siege by Theoderic throughout the winter, forcing the price of wheat to rise to six *solidi* per *modius*. Though under siege, Odovacer did not give up. He made his son Thela Caesar and summoned allies from the Burgundians. Their king Gundobaudes, the Roman *patricius* from the 470s, led an army into Italy, attacking Liguria and taking large numbers of prisoners. And in July 491, Odovacer made a night sortie with a group of Heruls, but was defeated. While the blockade continued, the rest of Italy fell into Theoderic's hands, allowing him to send Festus (who had held the consulate in 472) to Constantinople, requesting the western imperial robes from Zeno. But it was not until Theoderic had assembled a fleet to blockade the city that Odovacer was finally starved into surrender. Theoderic entered the city on March 5, 493. Odovacer was promised a share in government, but was executed soon after his surrender. His son was arrested, and although he escaped from Gothic captivity, he soon died.

CONCLUSION

During the second half of the fifth century, the eastern Roman Empire was relatively stable. Despite the various political, military, religious, and economic problems, it was usually clear who the emperor was. And though there was plenty of disorder on the Danubian frontier, the borders of the eastern Empire changed little. In the west, it might be easier to tell the story of the last years of the Roman Empire through the career of the *magister militum* Ricimer rather than through the various emperors. After the death of Majorian in 461, there was little left of the western Empire. However, whereas the western Empire in the fourth century had been the only significant power in Europe, by the late fifth century it was only one of several powers. The settlements of barbarians and the loss of imperial territory to conquest leached away the military strength, though the succession of emperors after Majorian showed that the Empire could still carry on. Although Africa was not recaptured, despite the efforts of 460 and 468, the concept of a Roman Mediterranean was not yet dead, and Justinian was able to show that reviving it was not impossible. As important as the loss of western military power was the final separation of the aristocracy in the west from the Empire. In the early fifth century, there were enough imperial resources and enough imperial stability to make serving the emperor a viable career choice. But from the 450s onward, many of the other choices, including avoiding imperial politics and service altogether, became increasingly attractive. Thus problems in finding good officials, as well as in paying for less capable officials, began to cripple the Empire's ability to run itself.

FURTHER READING

The source material for this period is highly fragmentary, and there is no coherent narrative for either east or west written by a contemporary. This was not always the case, and detailed histories in the classicizing style were written in the east by the contemporaries Priscus, Malchus, Candidus, and Eustathius of Epiphania, all now preserved only in fragments. Although these generally avoid mentioning religious events, they are paralleled by a series of slightly later ecclesiastical histories, including those of Evagrius (using Zachariah of Mytilene), pseudo-Zachariah of Mytilene, and the fragmentary history of Theodore Lector. This lack of a connected history has often led to a reliance on Jordanes' *Getica*, written in the sixth century in Constantinople. This is difficult to use, in part because its author was not always well informed, in part because it filled gaps in the source material with a methodology based on favoring the Amal government of Theoderic in Italy. There is, however, much other material. There are many useful letters from emperors and Popes in the *Collectio Avellana*, other papal letters, proceedings of church councils, and some eastern laws included in the *Codex Justinianus*. The letter collections and poems of Sidonius Apollinaris and Epiphanius provide much detail for Gaul and Italy. There are numerous chronicles and there are many saints' lives such as those of Symeon the Stylite in Syria or Daniel the Stylite in Constantinople, those written by Cyril of Scythopolis for Palestina, or Eugippius' *Life of Severinus* and Ennodius' *Life of Epiphanius* for Noricum and Italy, respectively.

A good overview of the fifth century is provided by Maas, M., ed., *The Cambridge Companion to the Age of Attila* (Cambridge, 2014). For the reign of Leo, there are excellent recent treatments of politics and the sources in Croke, B., "Dynasty and Ethnicity: Emperor Leo I and the Eclipse of Aspar," *Chiron* 35 (2005), 147–203 and Wood, P., "Multiple Voices in Chronicle Sources: The Reign of Leo I (457–474) in Book Fourteen of Malalas," *Journal of Late Antiquity* 4 (2011), 298–314. For Zeno, see Kosinski, R., *The Emperor Zeno: Religion and Politics* (Cracow, 2010), Brooks, E. W., "The Emperor Zenon and the Isaurians," *English Historical Review* 8 (1893), 209–238, and Elton, H. W., "Illus and the Late Roman Aristocracy under Zeno," *Byzantion* 70 (2000), 393–407. On Christianity in the east, see Frend, W. H. C., *The Rise of the Monophysite Movement* (Cambridge, 1972), Gray, P., *The Defense of Chalcedon in the East (451–553)* (Leiden, 1979), and Wood, P., "*We have No King but Christ": Christian Political Thought in Greater Syria on the Eve of the Arab Conquest, 400–c.585* (Oxford, 2010).

For the west, good starting points include Gillett, A., "Rome, Ravenna, and the Last Western Emperors," *Papers of the British School at Rome* 69 (2001), 131–167 and Kulikowski, M., "Marcellinus of 'Dalmatia' and the Dissolution of the Fifth-Century Empire," *Byzantion* 72 (2002), 177–191. On the aristocratic environment of Gaul, see Harries, J., *Sidonius Apollinaris and the Fall of Rome, AD 407–485* (Oxford, 1994), Mathisen, R. W., *Roman Aristocrats in Barbarian Gaul* (Austin, 1993), and Teitler, H. C., "Un-Roman Activities in Late Antique Gaul: The Cases of Arvandus and Seronatus," in Drinkwater, J. F. and Elton, H. eds., *Fifth-Century Gaul: A Crisis of Identity?* (Cambridge, 1992), 309–317. A medieval perspective is provided by Halsall, G., *Barbarian Migrations and the Roman West, 376–568* (Cambridge, 2007).

On the significance of 476, Croke, B., "A.D. 476: The Manufacture of a Turning Point," *Chiron* 13 (1983), 81–119, is useful; see also the wide-ranging and provocative articles by Halsall, G., "Movers and Shakers: The Barbarians and the Fall of Rome," *Early Medieval Europe* 8 (1999), 131–145 and Heather, P. J., "The Huns and the End of the Roman Empire in Western Europe," *English Historical Review* 110 (1995), 4–41.

7

THE MILITARY SITUATION, 395–493

At the end of the fourth century, the Romans continued to face enemies in Europe, Persia, and along the southern and eastern shores of the Mediterranean. At this point, the Empire's strategic problems differed very little from those of the mid-third century. But by the end of the fifth century, the Empire's military situation had changed greatly. The disastrous defeat at Adrianople in 378 soon led to barbarians settling as independent kingdoms within the Empire. This loss of territory in the west, particularly the occupation of Africa by the Vandals in 429, led to a decline in military resources that ultimately doomed the western Empire. The decreasing money and manpower meant that in the west the Roman army was unable to provide security for the people of the Empire. The Rhine ceased to function as a defended barrier by the mid-fifth century, by which point Roman imperial authority was confined to southern Gaul, Italy, and areas where there was a Roman army. The western Empire collapsed twenty years later. In the east, the creation of a Hunnic confederation of the Danubian tribes under Attila's leadership led to challenges to Roman control of the Balkans. On the other hand, there was peace with Persia for most of the century, allowing eastern emperors to concentrate most of their attention on Balkan and western affairs. The territory and armies of the eastern Empire continued almost unchanged and, indeed, the Empire was able to reconquer Africa and Italy by the mid-sixth century. Understanding the numerous and complex political changes in this period is difficult because of the limited source material. There is very little informed writing about warfare, with the result that modern historians are often forced to rely on parallels from the better-known fourth and sixth centuries.

After the death of Theodosius I in 395, fifth-century emperors rarely commanded armies in the field, a distinct change in the style of imperial leadership. Some of this was chance. Both of Theodosius' sons were young in 395, as were their sons when they became emperors, but even as adults they did not lead armies. Other emperors, including men with military experience such as Leo, generally remained absent from the battlefield. Policy making, however, remained in the hands of the emperor advised by the consistory. The more sedentary nature of the emperor may have increased the number of civilian officials involved in discussions, but the consistory still included many men with military experience. Roman strategy continued to be mostly reactive. Choices were limited by available resources, making it rarely possible for either the eastern or western emperor to engage in offensive or defensive campaigning in more than one theater at once. Thus in 441, the Huns attacked the Balkans while an east Roman force was on its way to Africa. Theodosius II could not fight both wars at once and chose to abandon the African expedition. These choices made for military reasons often had political costs, as when the closer presence of Alaric in Italy forced Honorius to recognize the imperial challenger Constantine III in Gaul in 408. However, limited resources did not mean the Romans could not launch offensives or make strategic choices. An eastern army campaigned in Africa for four years between 431 and 434, and further eastern expeditions were sent against the Vandals in 441 and 468. As late as 461 in the west, Majorian led an expedition into Spain with plans to attack Africa, and Anthemius in 471 sent troops against Euric in Gaul.

TREATIES AND DIPLOMACY

The Romans continued to manage relationships with the barbarians by treaties. These were still seen as personal agreements, so that we often hear of attacks after the death of an emperor. Thus Hun attacks on the eastern Empire are recorded in 395 on Theodosius I's death and in 408 on Arcadius' death. More developed states tried to manage the process of changing rulers, and the Romans, Sasanids, and Vandals informed each other of accessions. At the same time, familiarity and weakness diminished the Roman ability to overawe barbarians with displays of military strength. Treaties could result in military alliances with Rome, the provision of allied troops, supplies of food, land, the taking or giving of hostages, and appointment to honorary Roman offices, though it may only be propaganda when the poet Claudian claimed that Alaric issued his Goths with arms from the *fabricae* of Illyricum in 398. Hostages from barbarian royal families usually lived at the imperial court, like Peter the Iberian and Theoderic the Amal at Constantinople. The Romans could also exchange hostages with barbarians, though these were never from the imperial household. They could, however, be aristocrats, like Aetius, who was a hostage with both Alaric's Goths and some Huns in the early fifth century.

The Romans tried to keep themselves as well informed as possible of events in the *barbaricum*. They did this by having spies beyond the borders, listening to rumors, and having regular contact with barbarian leaders and defectors. On his way into Hunnia in 449, Priscus saw what he was told was a captured spy who had been impaled on Attila's orders. However, with the creation of barbarian kingdoms within the western Empire the previously politically clear boundaries of Roman territory became blurred. Even within the new kingdoms, there were large numbers of Roman aristocrats, many of whom still had estates and family members living in Roman territory. This would have made it easier for emperors to discover what was happening among these peoples, but also brought challenges when it came to defining loyalties and borders.

CIVIL WAR AND REBELLION

During the fifth century, there were numerous internal challengers to imperial power in the West, though fewer in the east, mostly in the reign of Zeno. At the same time, rivalries between imperial officials in both parts of the Empire were occasionally mediated by armed conflict. Lastly, there were a number of occasions when eastern and western empires were in a state of cold war. In the west, during the second half of Honorius' reign there were several imperial challengers. Faced with a combination of Alaric's presence in the western Balkans, another Gothic invasion of Italy, led by Radagaisus, and a crossing of the Rhine in 406, Honorius' authority was sadly diminished. Over the next few years, a series of rival emperors began to appear in Britain (Marcus, Gratian), and then later in Gaul (Constantine III, Jovinus, and later Attalus), Italy (Attalus), Africa (Heraclianus, though he is not known to have acclaimed himself as emperor), and Spain (Maximus). Honorius in 408 chose to recognize Constantine III and in 410 Attalus, decisions that allowed him to concentrate on other problems. But once Honorius' reign was over, there were only two moments in western Roman history when there were two rival western emperors competing for power: in 423, when Theodosius II was faced with the dilemma of whether to support his cousin, the four-year-old Valentinian, against John; and in 474, when Nepos was sent by Leo against Glycerius. However, other occasions when emperors were created without the approval of the senior Augustus, at the accession of Marcian in 450, Majorian in 457, and Severus in 461, could have led to war between the two parts of the Empire. There were other moments of tension; relations between Honorius and Arcadius were difficult in the early years of their reigns, with Stilicho campaigning twice in the eastern Empire without authorization. Gildo's transfer of allegiance to the east in 398 brought an immediate response from the west in the form of an expeditionary force led by Gildo's brother Mascezel, though this might also have provoked an eastern military reaction. In the east, although Zeno faced challenges from Basiliscus, Marcian, and Leontius, he was eventually able to defeat them all. However, before his reign, no other fifth-century eastern emperor was challenged while on the throne, though there were some suspicions at the end of the reign of Theodosius II that his general Zeno was aiming at the throne.

While civil war was perhaps less frequent than in the fourth century, rebellions were more common. This partly reflects a diminution of imperial power, but the refusal of the majority of these rebels to declare themselves emperor suggests that it was seen as a less desirable position. These rebellions were frequently the result of rivalries between senior imperial officials rather than a rejection of imperial authority. Some of these rivalries were exacerbated by long terms in office, like those of Aspar, *magister militum praesentalis* in the east from 434 to 471, or Aetius, *magister militum* and patrician in the west from 433 to 454. These were exceptional cases, but it was common to hold the office of *magister militum* for a decade. In the east, the revolt of Tribigild and Gainas in 399 was a struggle for influence in Constantinople, while the western civil war between Aetius and Bonifatius, which led to the Battle of Ariminum in 433, was for influence over Valentinian III. Rebels could survive unmolested for some time if they seemed not to be a threat, as when the Emperor John ignored Bonifatius in Africa until he supported Valentinian III in 425.

When civil wars did occur, whether between emperors or against rebels, they were different from fighting barbarians. Since both forces had similar capacities, numbers and leadership were critical. The lack of Roman troops led to the frequent use of allied contingents. Examples include the Franks and Alamanni used by Constantine III, the Huns by John in 425, and Goths and Rugi by Zeno against Leontius. In the case of Zeno's war against Odovacer, no Roman troops were involved, only delegated Goths. Loyalties were often confused. In 410, Constantine III had been negotiating with Allobichus about deserting Honorius, and in 476 Zeno was able to detach both Armatus and Illus from loyalty to Basiliscus. Naval power was also important in these wars. Gainas attempted to fight his way across the Hellespont in 400, Heraclianus made a crossing from Africa to Italy in 413, and Italy was assaulted from the sea by Ardabur in 425. Finally, sieges were often critical; in the war against John, Aspar besieged Salona for four months in 424, while Anthemius was besieged in Rome for five months by Ricimer in 472.

Most of those defeated in internal conflicts were executed. In 422, Honorius celebrated his *tricennalia* by executing the Spanish imperial challenger Maximus and his general in the arena at Ravenna. After such executions, severed heads were often displayed over city gates, such as that of Leontius at Constantinople after his capture in 488, though when Basiliscus was deposed by Zeno, he and his family were starved to death in a cistern in Cappadocia. Other deposed emperors were luckier. Attalus on his second deposition in 415 had the fingers of his right hand cut off and was then exiled, and during the late fifth century Avitus and Glycerius were consecrated as bishops. Even senior supporters of defeated emperors could do well. After the defeat of John in 425, Aetius was able to negotiate a pardon for himself and other supporters of the defeated regime, but only because he had the support of a large number of mercenary Huns.

IMPERIAL RESOURCES

The financial basis of the Roman army collapsed in the fifth century in the western Empire as territory was lost, and by the end of Valentinian III's reign his income was probably half that of Honorius in 395. The east was far less affected by territorial losses. Since the army was by far the largest single area of state expenditure, it is unsurprising that contemporaries commented on its expense. Valentinian III in 444/445 lamented that

> nothing is so necessary for the defence as that the strength of a numerous army should be prepared for the exhausted circumstances and afflicted condition of the state … Neither for those who are bound by new oaths of military service nor even for the veteran army can those supplies seem to suffice that are delivered with the greatest difficulty by the exhausted taxpayers, and it seems that from that source the supplies that are necessary for food and clothing cannot be furnished (*Novellae of Valentinian* 15).

However, with no figures or good estimates for either the size of the army or the imperial revenues, it is difficult to assess how underfunded the army was. Nor should all contemporary comments be taken at face value. In 405, Synesius described the regiment of the *Balagritae* in Libya. "These men, before Cerealis had taken over the command of the province, were mounted bowmen; but when he took up his office, their horses were sold and they became only archers" (*Ep.* 131). Synesius may have been describing an army crippled by lack of finance, but he was also accusing Cerealis of corruption. Roman payments of gold to barbarians similarly resulted in much contemporary complaint. The maximum annual payment ever extracted by Attila was 2,100 pounds of gold, similar to the 2,000 pounds of gold that Symmachus paid for his son's praetorian games in 401. This sum would have paid the wages and rations of about twenty regiments of infantry, i.e., about the cost of maintaining any one of the four frontier ducates on the Danube. Much larger field armies were more expensive. And actually fighting wars, as opposed to merely feeding and paying soldiers in peacetime, was yet more expensive. According to Candidus, the 468 expedition against the Vandals cost 64,000 pounds of gold and 700,000 pounds of silver, in addition to some western financial contributions. This amount was roughly equal to two years of taxes from the eastern Empire. This was a particularly expensive operation, but suggests that buying peace was much cheaper than paying for military operations, despite the political cost. The process of supplying troops still ran through the office of the praetorian prefect, but officials were now assigned as praetorian prefects to expeditionary forces, such as when Pentadius was appointed to supply Theodosius' African expedition of 441.

As the three expeditions against the Vandals in 431, 441, and 468 show, the eastern Roman Empire continued to be able to raise large armies and to conduct difficult military operations throughout the fifth century. Nor should we be distracted by Priscus' emotive treatment of subsidies paid to the Huns into thinking that the eastern Empire was unable to afford an effective army. It was very different in the west, where from the reign of Honorius onward the amount of territory available and thus the tax revenue and manpower resources were slowly diminished. Already weaker at the end of Honorius' reign than at the beginning, western military resources and thus capacity continued to diminish during Valentinian's reign. By the 460s, the western Empire was able to conduct effective military operations only in and around Italy.

At the end of the fourth century, the Roman army was approximately half a million strong, though by the end of the fifth century there were far fewer troops. Recruiting before any major campaign was common, while in extreme situations such as Radagaisus' invasion of Italy in 405 slaves were offered freedom if they volunteered for military service. Finding men was always a problem, mostly because of an unwillingness to serve, not because of a demographic crisis. Much of the problems with recruiting came from a political process that favored the wealthy. A law of Honorius, issued in 412 when he was still involved in his war with Jovinus in Gaul, exempted most court officials, "for recruits must not be demanded from the resources of those whose virtue subjugates enemy captives for our triumphs" (*CT*

11.18.1). However, an eastern edict of 444 demanded recruits from most of these too, unless they came from Africa (*Novellae of Theodosius* 6.3). Other laws prohibited tied farmers (*coloni*) and town councilors from serving. This was good for keeping taxes coming in and for managing civic administration, but did deny the army a source of recruits. There were other restrictions too. The army had minimum height standards (5' 7" = 1.65 meters) (*CT* 7.13. 3), though it may be significant that this law was not repeated in the *Codex Justinianus*. And in addition to many men being less willing, others had become clergy or monks who were also exempt from service. Another group of men that emperors were keen to keep out of the army were heretics such as Manichees, rejected by Valentinian III in 445, following a law of Theodosius II in 438 that banned pagans, Jews, and Samaritans.

Despite the difficulties in raising men, Roman emperors were still able to field armies. These soldiers came from several sources. Military service was still theoretically hereditary, though this seems not to have been as rigorously enforced as in the fourth century. Thus we know of two fifth-century sons of soldiers, Marcian and Saba, who were not forced to join their fathers' regiments. There were annual levies of conscripts, including barbarians who had been settled within the Empire, often known as *laeti*. A 409 edict exempted some Sciri who had recently settled in Bithynia from providing recruits for the army for twenty years "because of a shortage of farm produce" (*CT* 5.6.3). Other defeated enemies could be recruited directly; after the Battle of Fiesole in 405, Stilicho took twelve thousand barbarians into service. And there were always volunteers from within and beyond the Empire. In the reign of Leo, Justin (who became emperor in 518), and his friends Zimarchus and Ditubistus from Dacia Mediterranea joined up to better themselves. Some volunteers from outside the Empire were like Sarus, a Gothic aristocrat who entered Roman service in the early fifth century because of his hostility to other Goths, others were ambitious men, like the brothers Onoulphus and Odovacer. Recruiting could take place on a larger scale too. The agreements that Leo and Zeno had with both Pannonian and Thracian Goths seem to be too formalized to be a relationship with independent powers as allies and yet were not as formal as the hiring of regiments of *foederati*. Assessing the proportions of these various sources of recruits is impossible with the evidence that we have. It is clear, however, that many troops, especially in European regiments, were recruited from outside the Empire. We are often told that men were Goths or Franks, but inferring ethnicity from names is difficult. In particular, many second-generation immigrants had names similar to men born outside the Empire but had spent their entire lives within the Empire.

The structure of the Roman army in 395 is recorded by the *Notitia Dignitatum*, a register of imperial positions that was updated for the west to the 420s, though in a nonsystematic fashion. At Theodosius' death, both eastern and western imperial (i.e., praesental) armies were nominally commanded by two equally ranked *magistri militum praesentales* (see Figure 17). In practice, in both parts of the Empire one general was always dominant. In the west during the reign of Valentinian II (375–392), Arbogast was so influential that his office of *magister peditum* took charge of all western military positions and was often known as "the patrician." Following Arbogast, Stilicho, Aetius, and Ricimer successively used this position to control all the armies of the western Empire down to the 470s. The army of the *magister peditum* was based in northern Italy, usually at Milan or Ravenna. The regional field army in Gaul often wintered in and around Trier until the prefecture capital was transferred to Arles ca. 402, but it continued to fight in the north. Several smaller field armies existed under *comites rei militaris* in Britain, Africa, Spain, Argentoratum, Italy, and western Illyricum. These had disappeared by midcentury, but the Gallic army continued to exist into the 460s under Aegidius and Syagrius, even surviving after imperial control of this part of Gaul was lost. New imperial armies could be created during civil wars, such as that of Constantine III drawn from troops in Britain and Gaul, though these were rapidly reintegrated into regional armies when these conflicts were over. In the east, the imperial army was based at Constantinople, the Thracian army at Marcianopolis, the Illyrian army first at Sirmium and then from 441 at Thessalonica, and the eastern army at Antioch. In Asia Minor, *comites* had been appointed for Pisidia, Pamphylia, and Lycaonia by the reign of Leo, while Isauria was commanded by a *comes* from the early fifth century. These changes were probably in response to problems with bandits. After he reorganized the Armenian provinces, Zeno added a *comes Armeniae* to manage the defense of the region.

The army, like the Empire, was a single organization split into two parts. Thus the fifth century saw continued transfers of both units and officers between east and west. In 409, six regiments were sent from Theodosius II to Honorius, while troops accompanied Anthemius and Nepos to the west in 467 and 474. Promotus was *comes Africae* before serving as *magister equitum* in Thrace in 386, and Chariobaudes was *dux Mesopotamiae* between 383 and 392 before becoming *magister militum per Gallias* in 408. And in 393, Varanes was in Constantinople before accompanying Theodosius I to Italy against Eugenius. After the campaign, he was given a western military position, and by 408 he was *magister peditum*, though he had returned in 409 to Constantinople, where he was appointed consul for 410. Other transfers were less formal, like that of Titus, whose military exploits in Gaul induced

Figure 17. Page from the *Notitia Dignitatum* showing the insignia of the eastern *magister militum praesentalis* and the shield patterns of his senior regiments, including the *Lanciarii seniores*, the *Ioviani iuniores*, and the *Herculiani iuniores* (Bodleian, MS. Canon. Misc. 378, fol. 145r, early fifteenth century).

Leo to invite him and his *bucellarii* to Constantinople and give him the rank of *comes*. Officers with border commands reported to the *magister militum* of their region. At the beginning of the fifth century, there were three commands in Britain, four in Gaul, eight along the Rhine and Danube, nine in the east and Egypt, and five in Africa. Regiments were sometimes transferred from the *limitanei* into the field armies as *pseudocomitatenses*. One such regiment was the Septimani, drawn from *Legio VII Gemina* in Spain, which served in the Italian field army in the early fifth century. Although the division of the Empire between two emperors meant that armies such as Julian's expedition against the Persians in 363 could no longer be raised, armies continued to be substantial. In 478, Zeno claimed to have thirty thousand infantry and eight thousand cavalry in the Thracian and imperial armies. However, many armies were smaller, such as the force of five thousand led by Mascezel to Africa in 398 or the thirty regiments (between fifteen thousand and thirty thousand men if at full strength) led by Stilicho against Radagaisus in 406.

By the sixth century, the Roman army was placing a greater tactical emphasis on cavalry than in the fourth century. However, except for small forces, armies usually had a mixture of foot and horse. Infantry continued to dominate armies numerically since they were cheaper and better suited to garrisons, sieges, and fighting in woods and mountains. Cavalry, though more expensive, provided greater battlefield flexibility when well trained. The *Notitia Dignitatum* at the start of the fifth century listed twice as many infantry units as cavalry units, and cavalry regiments were smaller than infantry regiments. Border commands had higher numbers of cavalry regiments proportionately than field armies, probably to facilitate patrolling and the pursuit of small groups of raiders. The field armies were the home of the cavalry regiments more focused on decisive actions in the battlefield, in particular cataphracts and the high-status *vexillationes palatinae*.

Officers in the field army regiments (*comitatenses*), the *scholae*, and legions and *vexillationes* of border troops received their commission from the *primicerius notariorum*, and their units were often described as "on the list" (*katalogoi*). The main difference between the border troops and field armies was in types of regiment and use, but physical standards, length of service, and tax benefits on retirement were similar. Border troops were scattered along the frontiers, with many small detachments in forts and outposts. Establishments were similar to the fourth century, though recorded strengths were often lower. Thus Mascezel's force in the 398 campaign against Gildo involved five thousand men from three *legiones palatinae* and three *auxilia palatina*; their establishment would have probably been 7,200. Field army regiments and border troop cohorts were commanded by tribunes, all other units by *praefecti*. Until the end of the fourth century, most regimental commanders had served as *protectores*, but by the early fifth century the cessation of imperial campaigning changed the *domestici* and *protectores* into palace officials. Unit commanders came from direct commission or after long service. Conon, conscripted in 444 into a regiment of Isaurians, became its tribune ca. 464 and remained in post until his death in 491. Many generals in the late fourth and fifth centuries had bodyguards, usually mounted, known as *bucellarii*. According to Olympiodorus, "in the days of Honorius, the name *bucellarius* was carried not only by Roman soldiers, but also by some Goths" (fr. 7.4). The term is not found in the fourth century, though the institution may have existed then. Such men would have had little impact on the army and probably saw little action in the field. They are not attested as being involved in any field battles in the fifth century. *Bucellarii* were few in number and we hear of no groups larger than two hundred to three hundred strong. They also served as a source for regimental commanders.

From the end of the fourth century, the *comitatenses* also included regiments known as *foederati*. Although this term has often been used loosely by both ancient and modern writers, at this date the terms referred to permanently established units of the Roman army, with ranks, pay, and equipment all regulated by the state. At their foundation, they were deliberately recruited from barbarians, hence the name, though they also included Romans. Most, if not all, of these regiments were cavalry, such as the Alans used by Stilicho in the 401–402 campaign or the Huns led by Olympius in 409. The corps of *foederati* was commanded by a *comes*, first attested in 422, while the regiments were commanded by tribunes. Regimental titles and sizes were similar to other field army regiments. Another group of elite cavalry regiments was the *scholae*, composed of five regiments in the west at the date of the *Notitia* and seven in the east. These fought less often than in the fourth century once emperors stopped leading armies, but did fight in Anastasius' Isaurian war (491–498). Palace security continued to be carried out by the *excubitores*, who also fought the Isaurians. The unit was commanded by the *comes excubitorum*, who reported directly to the emperor.

Roman armies were often supported by allies who fought in their own fashion. These could be hired for a particular campaign as mercenaries or summoned through treaty obligations. There were also some cases of genuine political collaboration, for example the decision by the Visigothic king Theoderic in 451 to fight with Aetius against the Huns in Gaul. Zeno sent Goths against Illus in 484. In some cases, allied leaders were given positions within the Roman military hierarchy, such as Theoderic Strabo, leader of large group of Goths, who was *magister militum praesentalis* in 473. As part of his agreement with the emperor, it was stipulated that "Theoderic should fight with the emperor against anyone he ordered, except only the Vandals" (Malchus fr.2). In the east, the Romans had semipermanent arrangements with a number of Saracen groups whose leaders were called phylarchs (*phylarchai*). Their combat power was small, but they were useful for scouting.

The late Roman navy consisted of several small fleets of oared galleys, with additional ships for supply and transport of troops. The same generals commanded fleets and armies. In 424, Ardabur commanded a combined arms operation against Italy, while Basiliscus first fought in Thrace and then later was in command of the naval expedition of 468 against the Vandals. In the west, there were major naval bases in the Mediterranean at Ravenna, Misenum, and Arles, as well as smaller bases along the Atlantic and North Sea coasts. In the east, the main base was at Constantinople, although there were other bases. Frontier commands included flotillas of river patrol boats. In 412, Moesia Secunda had one hundred light boats, while Scythia had 125 in addition to older boats used for transporting supplies.

THE ENEMIES OF THE EMPIRE

In 395, the Rhine and Upper Danube were secure frontiers. By the middle of the century, these were Roman borders in name only; all of Britain and Africa had been lost and large parts of Gaul and Spain. The western Empire in the fifth century thus saw almost continuous warfare, completely different from the frontier with Persia. Roman field armies continued to fight and often to win victories, but with the collapse of the Rhine frontier after 406 their role changed from supporting the border troops into one of campaigning against barbarians within the Empire. There was also change from defending all Romans against external enemies to defending the imperial system against challengers. The loss of Britain and northern Gaul exposed the coasts of Gaul and Spain to raiding from the sea, while the Vandal occupation of Africa meant that the southern coast of Europe, from Spain to Greece, suffered from Vandal raids. Defense against these was difficult since the length of the coastline and naval mobility made it hard to predict where raiders would strike. Because of these problems, Valentinian III in 440 permitted Romans to bear arms when the Vandal king Genseric was "reported to have led forth from the port of Carthage a large fleet whose sudden excursion and fortuitous depredation must be feared by all shores" (*Novellae of Valentinian* 9). Although often weakened, border troops continued to exist throughout the fifth century. Eugippius mentioned *limitanei* in Raetia and in Noricum Ripensis at Batavis and Favianis in the 450s. But these regiments were a lower priority for imperial resources than the field armies.

Roman armies in the west were rarely able to muster large forces, though they continued to have some successes. In 405, Radagaisus at the head of some Goths crossed the Alps into Italy, where he divided his forces into three groups, probably for ease of supply. One group besieged Florence, bringing it close to surrender before Stilicho arrived with the imperial army. Stilicho won a battle outside the town, then drove Radagaisus into the hills, where the Goths soon began to starve. When Radagaisus tried to break out, he was captured and executed. Leaderless, his men surrendered. It was a great triumph for the Romans and Stilicho justifiably made much of it. It was more common for the Romans to replace or supplement their forces with allies, as in the Visigothic campaigns in Spain against the Vandals and Alans in 416–418 or when defending against the Huns in 451. However, the use of allies was often necessary to stop them exploiting the absence of Roman forces fighting against other enemies. Thus during the 422 campaign against the Suevi in Spain, the Visigoths were used as allies rather than being left to their own devices in Gaul. In addition to direct confrontation in a field battle, there were other ways of achieving victory. Like Stilicho engaging Radagaisus, in 415–416 Constantius blockaded the Visigoths in Gaul. On some occasions, the Romans were even able to induce barbarians to fight each other, as in 414, when Paulinus of Pella persuaded the Alans in Gothic forces besieging Bazas in Gaul to defect. The result was the Goths lifting the siege. Similarly, in 469 in the Balkans, the Romans blockaded a force of Huns and Goths and then set the two groups against each other.

Although there was much campaigning, large field battles were rare. Stilicho was never able to defeat Alaric, with indecisive campaigns in Thessaly and the Peloponnese in Greece in 395–397, and indecisive battles at Verona and Pollentia in Italy in 402. There was a balance between the forces and abilities of these two leaders: Stilicho could not defeat Alaric, but Alaric could not defeat Stilicho. Fifty years later, Aetius, with the support of the Visigoths and some Franks, was unable to defeat Attila in 451 at the Catalaunian Plains and in 452 did not engage the Huns in Italy. These were the last major western imperial operations. After this, the fracturing of the western Empire led to the rapid collapse and disappearance of the western army. Majorian's campaign against Spain was on a small scale. A few years later, Odovacer's army was mostly Heruls, Sciri, and other barbarians, even though they were still led by *magistri militum* and units of *scholares* and *protectores* still existed at Rome, though in an atrophied condition. This army was organized enough to be defeated by Theoderic on the Isonzo and then fall back to fight again at Verona. However, the last twenty-five years of western imperial history was a desperate time to be a Roman general.

While the western defensive system in Europe had collapsed by the mid-fifth century, the changes in the east were more gradual. In Europe, the Danube remained the frontier of the Empire, though the defenses were often penetrated by both small groups of raiders and larger armies. When the western lynchpin of the Danubian defenses at Sirmium was lost in 441, Singidunum assumed this role. The conventional narrative attributes this collapse to the Huns. Their arrival north of the Danube in the late fourth century was certainly a shock to the inhabitants of the regions and to the Romans, yet nothing about the Huns was new militarily. Contemporaries were struck by their skill at mounted warfare, their archery, and their horses, but the Romans also praised Persian archery and their horses.

Until the 430s, there was no Hun unity but numerous Hunnic tribes with their own leaders. Only then was Attila able to forge a confederation, though his continued demands for the return of refugee aristocrats suggest it was always fragile. The composite nature of Hun armies meant that their style of warfare was little different from other armies on the Danube. Most troops were foot soldiers, and even though many aristocrats were mounted, the host could only move at the speed of the wagon trains and pack animals. Many of the Huns were mounted archers, but there is no evidence for strings of remounts for their stocky horses, much praised by Vegetius. Nor were Hun horses or any Hun military equipment adopted by the Romans, though by the sixth century the *Strategikon* mentions the Roman use of Bulgarian cloaks, Herulian swords, Slavic spears, and Gothic tunics and shoes. The Huns, unlike most other European barbarians, did have some skill at siege warfare, using siege engines at Naissus in 441 and sacking many cities, including Singidunum. These successes are an interesting contrast to events on the eastern frontier in the sixth century, when the Persians were unable to capture Amida, Edessa, and Dara easily, despite having a very strong siege train. Nor were the sixth- and seventh-century Avars able to capture Roman cities in the Balkans easily. Some of the Hun success in 441 may be the result of eastern Roman involvement in an expedition against the Vandals. Following six years of peace, the Huns attacked again in 447. Attila crossed the Danube, attacking Marcianopolis in Thrace, reaching Thermopylae, threatening Constantinople, and defeating Arnegisclus at the River Utus (Vit) in the province of Dacia Ripensis. This was one of the few battles fought between eastern Romans and the Huns, but we only know that it was very hard fought and that Arnegisclus died. Following negotiations, a demilitarized zone was created on the Roman bank of the Danube between Singidunum and Novae, and the subsidies were increased to 2,100 pounds of gold annually.

AN EMBASSY TO THE HUNS, 449

In 449, another Roman negotiating party left Constantinople to meet the Hun king Attila. There had been many similar embassies over the past two decades, but what makes this one significant is that one of its members, Priscus, wrote a detailed account. According to the Byzantine encyclopedia the *Suda*, "he wrote a history of Byzantium and affairs concerning Attila" (Pi.2301), suggesting that the account of the embassy was the high point of the work. Priscus' account survives only in fragments, which come from a tenth-century encyclopedia organized in books by topic; one of the books, concerning diplomacy between Romans and barbarians, survives intact. Priscus was an eyewitness, but he was also writing within the constraints of the historical genre. When he met a Roman who had been captured by the Huns at Viminacium, had won his freedom in battle, and was now living among the Huns, it provided an opportunity to write a rhetorical set piece in which the two debated the virtues of living under Roman and Hunnic rule. The Roman was real, but it is unlikely that the debate took place as recorded by Priscus.

As they left for Hunnic territory, the Roman envoy Maximinus and Priscus were unaware that the Romans had bribed a Hun envoy, Edeco, to kill Attila. The envoys traveled with Edeco and with Vigilas, the Roman interpreter who had offered the bribe. Priscus described their journey through the Balkans devastated by war, the crossing of the Danube in dugout canoes, and then their arrival at Attila's camp. Here the envoys were invited to an audience with the Hunnic king:

> We came to his tent which was surrounded by a ring of barbarian guards. When we were granted entrance, we saw Attila seated on a wooden chair. We halted a little before the throne and Maximinus advanced, greeted the barbarian, gave him the letters from the Emperor and said that the Emperor prayed that he and his followers were safe and well. He replied that the Romans would have what they wished for him (Priscus fr. 11.2, 171–178).

Then Attila forbade the Romans from buying anything from the Huns except food, while Edeco demanded that Vigilas bring him gold that had been promised for Attila's murder. While Vigilas returned to Roman territory for the gold, Priscus and Maximinus accompanied Attila as he moved north. At one point, they met one of Bleda's wives, giving her as a present "three silver bowls, red skins, pepper from India, dates and other dried fruits which the barbarians value because they are not native products" (fr. 11.2, 309–31). Eventually they came to a large village in which Attila's palace was said to be more spectacular than those elsewhere. It was constructed of timbers and smoothly planed boards and was surrounded by a wooden wall that was built with an eye not to security but to elegance (fr. 11.2, 358–361).

Priscus goes on to mention that Attila's compound had towers, unlike that of others in the village, and that there was a bathhouse made of imported stones by a Roman prisoner. While there is great excitement for us in reading a detailed eyewitness account, Priscus' audience would be contrasting this with the way in which they and the emperor lived.

After further meetings, including an audience with Attila's wife Hereka and a banquet with Attila, the envoys were dismissed and returned home. Nothing had come of the embassy, but this was unimportant, as it was intended to provide cover for Vigilas' mission. But when he returned to Attila's palace bearing the gold, Vigilas was arrested, discovering that Edeco was more loyal to Attila than had been thought. Priscus' account makes clear the high volume of diplomatic traffic, from both western and eastern Roman courts to Attila and vice versa. Another Roman embassy was now sent, led by Anatolius and Nomus:

> At first [Attila] negotiated arrogantly, but he was overwhelmed by the number of their gifts and mollified by their words of appeasement. He swore that he would keep the peace on the same terms, that he would withdraw from the Roman territory bordering the Danube, and that he would cease to press the matter of the fugitives with the Emperor provided the Romans did not again receive other fugitives who fled from him. He also freed Vigilas (Priscus, fr. 15.4).

These relations with Attila were very different from those with fourth-century barbarians on the Danube where the Romans were imposing peace. These were far closer to relationships with the Persians, i.e., between two equals. But it is important not to confuse the form of the negotiations with their weight. Even after exposing Vigilas' plot to assassinate him, Attila was forced to give ground in negotiations. When Marcian became emperor in 450, he refused to cooperate with Attila and pay the subsidies. Attila then chose not to attack the eastern Empire, perhaps because the 447 campaign had not been easy. Instead, he moved west, either to support the son of a deceased Frankish king against his brother or to campaign against the Goths in Gaul. The Hunnic ability to launch a campaign from the Middle Danube into central Gaul, over one thousand kilometers away, is impressive. Once in Gaul, Attila besieged but failed to capture Orleans. After this, there was an inconclusive battle at the Catalaunian Fields, near Troyes, by a Roman army led by the *patricius* and *magister utriusque militiae* Aetius, which included allied Visigoths, Burgundians, Franks, and Alans. In 452, Attila then attacked Italy. After a long siege, Aquileia fell to blockade, then Ticinum and Milan. The Roman army appears absent, but the Huns withdrew, hastened by problems finding food in a famine-struck landscape and by the outbreak of disease. Following Attila's death in 453, a rebellion by some of the subject peoples destroyed Hunnic dominance overnight. The impact of the Huns on the fifth century was great, but it was the result of Attila, not of a superior military system. With the destruction of the Hunnic Empire, the Danubian frontier became harder for the Romans to control. Raiding across the Lower Danube by Hunnic remnants, Goths, and Bulgars, and at the end of the century by Slavs, became common, and the river was now a political rather than a military border, with the defenses being confined mostly to cities and fortresses. Some security was provided by hiring one group of Goths in Thrace, but parts of Pannonia were lost to settlements by other Goths.

THE PERSIAN FRONTIER

Fifth-century Europe saw frequent warfare, but it was very different in the east. After the partition of Armenia in 387, there was a long period of peace between Rome and Persia, punctuated only by brief wars in 421 and 441. Both empires faced significant distractions in other areas. The Sasanids in particular began to pay much greater attention to their northern frontiers in the area of modern Afghanistan, where the Hephthalites were becoming a major problem, even killing King Peroz I in 484. The brevity of the two wars means that little is known about them. In 421, the new Persian king Bahram V declared war. Roman forces, led by Ardabur, first of all devastated Arzanene and then laid siege to Nisibis. After withdrawing from Nisibis on the approach of Bahram, Roman victory in a field battle led to peace. While little is known of the Roman forces, they included Areobindus holding an office possibly anachronistically described as the *comes foederatorum*, and the Persian army included the regiment of the Immortals. In 441, soon after the accession of Yazdgard II (438–457), there was another short war, mostly raiding by the Persians across the frontier from Nisibis. Theodosius' forces were already heavily committed in the west, and an expedition against Africa had to be recalled from Sicily because of a Hun attack. In both of these wars, Saracens attached to one or both armies, though their actions were of little military significance. The long period of peace in the fifth century came to an end in 502, with the eruption of a war in the reign of Anastasius. From then onward, Rome and Persia were at war almost continuously until the seventh century.

AFRICA

In the early fifth century, Africa was a secure zone for the Empire. This wealthy region produced large quantities of money and manpower while requiring few resources to defend it. It also provided the annual shipments of grain to Rome, important for feeding the city. Its attractions were well known, and Alaric in 410 had been hopeful of leaving Italy for Africa. The frontier to the south was always hard to control, being mostly urbanized and inhabited by nomads. Many of these groups would raid the Empire on occasion. Mostly they were a threat to the population of the countryside, but were rarely able to assault defended sites or to be successful against Roman troops. All of this changed with the crossing of the Vandals from Spain in 429. Initially, they met with little resistance, in part the result of the struggle between Bonifatius and Aetius. However, eastern reinforcements were soon sent to Carthage under Aspar in 431, who stayed there until 434. Peace was made in 435, but the Vandals broke it in 439 and occupied Carthage. The loss of Africa was, like the dominance of the Huns, a political issue. The Romans were not defeated in battle in 434 or in 441, but simply were unable or unwilling to allocate enough resources to Africa. The loss of Carthage then prompted a second expedition from the east in 441 that reached Sicily, but had to be abandoned when the Huns crossed the Danube. Majorian in turn planned an attack on Africa that was abandoned after reaching Spain, and a fourth attempt was made to reconquer Africa in 468. This was a joint force assembled from both parts of the Empire, although the majority was eastern, divided into the main expedient and two smaller supporting forces. One eastern fleet was commanded by Marcellinus, who sailed to Sardinia, capturing it from the Vandals. A second force, led by Heraclius, sailed from Constantinople to collect troops in Egypt before landing at Oea in Tripolitania. From here, Heraclius defeated a Vandal army and began marching toward Carthage. Meanwhile. the main expeditionary force under the command of Basiliscus, *magister militum* and Leo's brother-in-law, sailed from Constantinople. Basiliscus' reputation is poor, because of the failure of the expedition as well as his short-lived imperial reign. A fragment of the Suda, possibly derived from Priscus, describes him as "successful in battle but slow-witted and easily taken in by deceivers" (*Suda* B 163).

Basiliscus first defeated the Vandal fleet near Sicily. After this victory, he landed briefly on the island before crossing to land at Cap Bon, no more than 120 kilometers from Carthage. Procopius claims that if he had not hesitated but attacked Carthage immediately, he would have been successful. As Basiliscus was readying to march on Carthage, Geiseric built some fire ships. When the wind was right, he sent them against the Roman fleet and then followed up with the Vandal fleet. Most of the Roman fleet was destroyed, while the rest retired to Constantinople with Basiliscus. On hearing of the destruction of Basiliscus' fleet, Heraclius also retreated. This failure had significant consequences for the western Empire. However, the ability of Leo to assemble this force, then send it across the Mediterranean to land troops in Africa and supply them, is impressive. The personalities of the two commanders are also important. Basiliscus seems to have been a slow and deliberate man, whereas Geiseric was resilient in a difficult situation. As the successful Roman reconquest in 533 showed, different commanders could bring about very different outcomes.

ROMAN MILITARY EFFECTIVENESS IN THE FIFTH CENTURY

The effectiveness of Roman military activity in the fifth century can be assessed in several different ways. We know little about events at tactical and operational levels, so are often at risk of overinterpreting anecdotes. Where Roman infrastructure was intact, troops continued to be recruited and trained in a traditional fashion. But as this infrastructure crumbled in the west, there was an increasing reliance on hiring barbarians rather than training Romans. These allied contingents were more effective than poorly trained and led Roman troops, though not as effective as well-trained and supplied imperial armies. But as the imperial army dwindled, especially after the 450s, the western Empire began to rely on these men. At a strategic level, the western army was handicapped by a lack of resources. The failure of both western and eastern Roman Empires to defeat Alaric decisively at the start of the century led to a diminution of imperial resources and eventually to the collapse of the western Empire. This failure was not the result of any inherent weaknesses in the Roman defensive system; using the same army, Stilicho was able to win a significant victory against Radagaisus. Rather, the continued existence of the Goths should be attributed to Alaric's skill. In the east, there were sufficient resources to defend the Empire effectively. However, even when the army was able to defend the state, there were many areas where the local population suffered grievously, similar to all periods of Roman imperial history. The continued effectiveness of the Roman defensive system in the fifth century can be judged by its lack of development between 395 and 493. Despite the significant military problems, the Romans did not make great changes to their style of operations. The entry of the Vandals into Africa was the most significant event in the west; the Romans made great efforts to first of all defend and then to reoccupy Africa. In addition to the loss of African resources, Vandal construction of a fleet allowed their raiders to threaten the southern coast of Europe, forcing the Romans to place more resources in their fleet than had been required previously. The Rhine and Danube frontiers were also crumbling. Much to the chagrin of vocal taxpayers, the defensive system could not deliver permanent elimination of barbarians threatening the Empire. Roman strategy was adequate to defend the Empire from barbarian threats, but the resources to support the armies were not always available.

FURTHER READING

The primary sources for a military history of the fifth century are very fragmentary. The *Notitia Dignitatum* provides a starting point, though this document was an administrative one, much updated in an irregular fashion in the west. For an introduction, see Kulikowski, M., "The *Notitia Dignitatum* as a Historical Source," *Historia* 49 (2000), 358–377. There are very few detailed descriptions of either Roman or barbarian armies, focusing us to reconstruct based mostly on anecdotes and interpretations based on the better-known fourth and sixth centuries. A useful starting point is Maas, M., ed., *The Cambridge Companion to the Age of Attila* (Cambridge, 2014), Elton, H. W., *Warfare in Roman Europe, AD 350–425* (Oxford, 1996), the essays on the Late Empire in Sabin, P., van Wees, H., and Whitby, Michael, eds., *Cambridge History of Greek and Roman Warfare* (Cambridge, 2007), and Whitby, Michael, "The Army c.420–602," in Cameron, Averil, Ward-Perkins, B., and Whitby, Michael, eds., *Cambridge Ancient History* 14 (Cambridge, 2000), 286–314. There are some useful papers in the wide-ranging Lewin, A. and Pietrina, P., eds., *The Late Roman Army in the East from Diocletian to the Arab Conquest*, BAR S1717 (Oxford, 2007), Useful on policy is Blockley, R. C., *East Roman Foreign Policy* (Leeds, 1992). On naval warfare, see Charles, M., "Transporting the Troops in Late Antiquity: Naves Onerariae, Claudian and the Gildonic War," *Classical Journal* 100.3 (2005) 275–299, Charles, M., "Vegetius on Liburnae: Naval Terminology in the Late Roman Period," *Scripta Classica Israelica* 24 (2005) 181–193, and Charles, M., "Ramming the Enemy in Late Antiquity: Galleys in the Fifth Century A.D.," *Latomus* 69.2 (2010), 479–488.

On the Huns, Kelly, C., *The End of Empire: Attila the Hun and the Fall of Rome* (New York, 2008) provides a more nuanced perspective than Thompson, E. A., *Attila and the Huns*, rev. (London, 1995) or Kim, H. J., *The Huns, Rome and the Birth of Europe* (Cambridge, 2013). See also Lindner, R. P., "Nomadism, Horses and Huns," *Past and Present* 92 (1981), 1–19. On the Battle of the Catalaunian Plains, see Whately, C., "Jordanes, the Battle of the Catalaunian Plains, and Constantinople," *Dialogues d'histoire ancienne*, supplément 8 (2013), 65–78. Important for the source material is Maas, M., "Fugitives and Ethnography in Priscus of Panium," *Byzantine and Modern Greek Studies* 19 (1994), 146–160. On the Persians, see Greatrex, G., "The Two Fifth-Century Wars between Rome and Persia", *Florilegium* 12 (1993), 1–12,), Greatrex, G. and Lieu, S.N.C., *The Roman Eastern Frontier and the Persian Wars, AD 363–630* (London, 2002), and Whitby, Michael, "The Persian King at War," in Dabrowa, E., ed., *The Roman and Byzantine Army in the East*, (Krakow, 1994), 227–263.

8

THE LATE FIFTH AND EARLY SIXTH CENTURIES, 491–565

After the deposition of Odovacer, the Roman Empire returned to having only one emperor ruling from one capital, Constantinople. Thus, for many historians, 476 marks the beginning of the Byzantine world, one which continued as a Greek Empire until the final fall of the imperial city to the Turks in 1453. For others, it remains a Roman Empire. During this period, the initially complex military clashes and diplomacy with the western barbarian kingdoms under Anastasius were only somewhat simplified by Justinian's reconquest of Italy and Africa. Unlike the fifth century, however, hostilities with Persia began again to be a major issue for the Roman Empire, while control of the Balkans continued to be disputed with tribes north of the Danube.

The tensions between eastern and western church hierarchies exposed by the Council of Chalcedon continued throughout this period. Two separate themes can be detected. One was the battle for orthodoxy, a topic of great concern for bishops and for emperors seeking unity. Here, the innate complexities of the subject matter were exacerbated by the linguistic boundary between east and west. The limited capacity among western bishops to understand theological disputes in Greek might have been of less significance had westerners been as dissatisfied with Chalcedon as many easterners were. In the west, the replacement of a single imperial power with many regional powers had allowed the Pope to acquire great influence, and there was little opposition to the Chalcedonian formula, which was seen as being based on the Tome of Leo. In the east, on the other hand, there was widespread opposition to what was seen as a solution imposed by the emperor. The eastern opposition to the imperial will was tempered by the fact the majority of eastern bishops were prepared to accept that the emperor was the vicegerent of God, a theme that became more fully developed in imperial propaganda in the late sixth century. In this respect, secular and ecclesiastical hierarchies were well aligned, though there were always individuals, particularly among the monks, who had differing opinions about the role of the emperor. But in the west, the Pope believed he was not subject to the emperor. This stance worked poorly when Rome was part of the Ostrogothic kingdom, but once Rome was restored to imperial control in 540, it became even more awkward. Furthermore, though eastern bishops were mostly prepared to accept a statement that ignored Chalcedon for the sake of church unity, the Pope was not prepared to see Chalcedon or the Tome of Leo ignored.

ANASTASIUS (491–518)

When Zeno died on April 9, 491, he had no obvious heir since both his sons had died young. One possibility for the succession was his brother Longinus, described by Theophanes as "the leader of the whole Senate." He hoped to become emperor, and was supported by the *magister officiorum*, another Isaurian also named Longinus. But others in the capital had different views. A detailed account of what happened in the hours after Zeno's death is contained in the tenth-century *de Caeremoniis*, extracted from the work of the mid-sixth-century writer Peter the Patrician:

> When the divinely chosen Zeno had died the *archontes* [senior officer holders] and the senators and the bishop came together in the night during the sixth hour in the portico in front of the Great Triclinium … The *archontes* … told the divinely chosen Augusta Ariadne to go up to the Hippodrome to address the people.

When Ariadne addressed the crowd, she promised to discuss who would be emperor with the *archontes*, the Senate, and the army. The *de Caeremoniis* continues:

> At the end of her speech, the Augusta came down and the *archontes* followed her. And the Augusta went into the Augusteus, but the *archontes*, benches having been placed in front of the Delphax, sat down and they began to discuss what needed to be done. And many arguments rose up amongst them (1.92).

Although we do not know whether Longinus was present, the "many arguments" probably turned on whether he was acceptable as emperor. At length, the *praepositus sacri cubiculi*, Urbicius, proposed that Ariadne make the decision, presumably a proposal to break a deadlock. When Urbicius' proposal was accepted, the patriarch Euphemius was asked to approach

Ariadne. This suggests the lack of an established procedure as well as confirmation of the absence of Ariadne from the discussions up to this point.

The *archontes* acted swiftly. Zeno had died during the night of April 9, 491, Ariadne addressed the crowd on April 10, and Anastasius was acclaimed emperor on April 11. Anastasius was a sixty-one-year-old decurion of the silentiaries, originally from Dyrrachium in Epirus Nova. Tall and beardless, he was nicknamed Dikoros ("double-pupil") because of one black and one blue eye. Anastasius did not marry Ariadne until May 20, 491, six weeks after his accession, suggesting it was more important to have an emperor than a link to the previous regime. The rapid acclamation may have been intended to forestall any action by Longinus, who was exiled to the Thebaid in Egypt. However, an Isaurian rebellion soon began, led by the now ex-*magister officiorum* Longinus of Cardala, but his army was defeated at Cotiaeum in Phrygia Salutaris late in 491 or early in 492. This campaign did not produce an imperial challenger, perhaps because it was intended to place Zeno's brother on the throne and he was unavailable. Anastasius' army in this campaign was led by John the Hunchback and John the Scythian, who had also commanded in Zeno's war against Leontius. After their victory, the imperial forces pursued the rebels into the Taurus Mountains. Slowly, John the Scythian was able to capture the remaining rebel leaders, although the last of these did not fall into his hands until 498. The prisoners were executed, but not before some were taken to Constantinople to be paraded in triumph by Anastasius.

While his generals were pursuing the rebels into the Taurus, Anastasius was also securing power elsewhere. Although he may have initially gained some popularity because of his exiling of the Isaurians, he was by no means universally beloved, and there were riots in Constantinople in 491, 493, and 506. As early as 493, statues of Anastasius and Ariadne were even pulled down. We also hear of significant violence in the city between the supporters' clubs of the Green and Blue racing teams. Nor would edicts prohibiting mimes and wild beast fighting have made Anastasius popular. Anastasius had no legitimate children of his own, and though there was a son by a concubine, he died in a riot at the Brytae festival in 501. He was, however, well provided with nephews, Probus, Hypatius, and Pompeius, all three of whom held consulates and positions as *magister militum*, while his brother Paulus was also a consul. As well as being generous toward his family, Anastasius also lavished wealth on his birth city Dyrrachium.

After the Isaurian war, Anastasius conducted military operations in three main areas: the Balkans, Italy, and the east. As compared to the problems faced by Leo and Zeno, the departure of the Ostrogoths for Italy in 489 made defense of the Balkans easier. However, Pannonia Prima was still under

Gothic control, while Pannonia Secunda and the critical city of Sirmium were held by the Gepids. As well as defending against these enemies, the eastern Empire had to secure the Danube. We hear of the death of the *magister militum per Thracias* Julian at hands of the "Scythians" in 493 in Thrace and the defeat of the *magister militum per Illyricum* Aristus at the Tzurta, an unknown river in Thrace, by the Bulgars in 499. The sixth century also saw groups of Slavs start to cross the lower Danube to raid the eastern Balkans. This general insecurity, coupled with the recent problems caused by the presence of the Thracian and Pannonian Goths so close to Constantinople, led to the building of the Long Walls by Anastasius. This forty-five-kilometer defensive structure ran from the Black Sea to the Sea of Marmara, taking advantage of the location of Constantinople, cutting across the promontory about sixty-five kilometers west of the city. Although it was too long to garrison, it made defense of the city far easier.

In the east, peace with the Persians continued until 502. At this point, the Sasanid king Kavadh I (488–531) demanded money from Anastasius to help with the defense of the Caucasus. Anastasius refused. Kavadh then went to war, the first significant clash for over a century. This war revealed that the partition of Armenia in 387 had made it easier for the Persians to reach Roman territory in Asia Minor. Thus the third- and fourth-century wars with the Persians had been fought entirely in Mesopotamia, but from the fifth century, additional fronts were often opened in Armenia and in the Caucasus. The first Persian action in 502 was the invasion of Armenia. After swiftly capturing Theodosiopolis (Erzurum) in August, Kavadh then marched south through the eastern reaches of the Taurus Mountains to besiege Amida in early October. The city fell to a Persian assault in January 503, and, as in earlier centuries, many prisoners were deported to Persia.

Although taken by surprise, the Roman forces soon recovered and Theodosiopolis was recaptured late in 502 by Eugenius, the *dux Armeniae*. In the spring of 503, an expedition was sent to Mesopotamia under the command of the *magister militum per Orientem* Areobindus and the two *magistri militum in praesenti*, Patricius and Anastasius' nephew, Hypatius. Patricius and Hypatius besieged Amida while Areobindus campaigned farther south; after initial successes, he was pushed back and even briefly besieged in Edessa. Not surprisingly, command by three equally ranked generals did not work well; in 504, the *magister officiorum* Celer was appointed to overall command while Hypatius was recalled. Patricius again besieged Amida, Areobindus raided Persarmenia, and Celer plundered Mesopotamia. Now that the Romans were better led, they were able to gain the upper hand over the Persians. Amida surrendered in early 505, and in 506 the Romans and Persians negotiated a seven-year peace with no territory changing hands.

The Romans then built a fort at the village of Dara, a well-watered site close to Nisibis, making it a city called Anastasiopolis. This provided an effective forward base for Roman troops, replacing Amida, and subsequently became the base of the eastern field army.

The third major area of Anastasius' foreign policy was in Italy with Theoderic. Relations with Theoderic at the start of the reign were good, and in 497 Anastasius even confirmed Zeno's grant of the office of *magister militum*. Theoderic tried hard to appear Roman, minting gold and silver coinage in the name of Anastasius, while his laws were *edicta* like those issued by praetorian prefects, not *leges* normally issued by the emperor. Moreover, the Roman administrative structure was maintained, so Theoderic's first praetorian prefect of Italy was Liberius (493–500), who had also served Odovacer, and when he gained control of parts of southern Gaul in 510, he created a separate praetorian prefecture there. Other officials included a *magister officiorum*, *quaestor*, and *vicarius* of Rome, while provincial governors still held their Roman titles such as *consularis*, *corrector*, or *praeses*. Although there were numerous elements of administrative continuity, and the Roman nature of the kingdom is much praised by Cassiodorus and Ennodius, Italy was no longer part of the Roman Empire. Anastasius could not collect taxes or raise troops from it and was soon at war with Theoderic.

As Theoderic became more established, his relationships with the Romans deteriorated. A significant cause of tension was the attempt to gain control over the whole of Pannonia. A force led by the *comes* Pitzias captured Sirmium from the Gepids in 504. Anastasius may have seen this as an opportunity to recapture Sirmium, but it quickly became a war with the Ostrogoths and the Gepids. Sabinianus, *magister militum per Illyricum*, supported by a large number of allied Bulgars, was defeated by the Gepid Mundo and Pitzias in 505. After this, there was less fighting, though a Roman fleet of two hundred ships raided Italy in 508. Finally a peace treaty was made in 510 that recognized Theoderic's control of Dalmatia, Savia, and the western part of Pannonia Secunda, including Sirmium, but left to the Romans the eastern part of Pannonia Secunda and the fortress at Bassiana between Sirmium and Singidunum. Some Heruls were settled at Singidunum in 512, though an imperial expedition against them was required in 514. Mundo soon moved on to reappear in Roman service in the reign of Justinian.

ANASTASIUS AND THE CHURCH

In addition to these military challenges, Anastasius also faced significant ecclesiastical problems stemming from the Council of Chalcedon and the ongoing Acacian schism. At the start of his reign, he continued the moderate path of Zeno's *Henotikon*, but soon began to favor the anti-Chalcedonians. However, his inherited patriarch of Constantinople, Euphemius (490–496), in 492 had rejected the *Henotikon* by confirming Chalcedon and promised Pope Gelasius (492–496) to end the Acacian schism. Gelasius' aggression and Anastasius' leaning toward tolerating anti-Chalcedonians meant that the churches remained divided, while none of Gelasius' successors, Anastasius (496–498), Symmachus (498–514), or Hormisdas (514–523), could make any headway with the emperor either. In 496, Anastasius had Euphemius exiled to Euchaita, ostensibly on the grounds of Nestorianism, and replaced him with Macedonius (496–511). For over a decade, Macedonius was able to keep a balance between the pro- and anti-Chalcedonians, but the arrival of the powerful intellectual Severus of Sozopolis in Constantinople in 508 brought about change. Severus' anti-Chalcedonianism was opposed to the nascent neo-Chalcedonian ideas that used the 433 Formula of Reunion to bridge the discord opened by Chalcedon. Since Severus argued that the ideas expressed by Cyril of Alexandria in 433 were unclear, he hardened rather than closed the differences with the pro-Chalcedonians. Anastasius was thus trapped between Macedonius, with a pro-Chalcedonian perspective and the strongly anti-Chalcedonian perspective of Severus. With no clear way forward, he followed his own beliefs, but began to find greater resistance to his attempts to create religious unity within the Empire. Although in 510 he could persuade Flavianus of Antioch (500–512) to subscribe to the *Henotikon* and to renounce both Diodorus of Tarsus and Theodore of Mopsuestia, Flavianus would not reject Chalcedon (itself not mentioned in the *Henotikon*). Some of his bishops, however, were prepared to take a firmer line on Chalcedon, and, for example, Constantine of Seleucia in Isauria anathematized the council. When Flavianus complained to Anastasius about interference in church matters, he was angrily rebuked by the emperor. Anastasius also demanded that Macedonius reject Chalcedon, which he refused to do, and when the patriarch submitted a statement of faith to the emperor in 511, he was found to be Nestorian, exiled to Euchaita, and replaced by Timothy (511–517). Flavianus' beliefs soon failed to satisfy the emperor, so in 512 he too was removed and Severus was appointed as patriarch in his place. In Constantinople, Anastasius attempted to add the phrase, "who was crucified for us," to the Trisagion hymn. This phrase was viewed as being anti-Chalcedonian and led to riots in Constantinople in which pro-Chalcedonian protestors threw down statues of Anastasius, burned the house of Marinus the eastern praetorian prefect, and tried to make Areobindus, husband of Anicia Juliana, emperor. Wisely, Areobindus fled. Anastasius appeared in the

Hippodrome without his diadem, and calmed most of the crowd, though he subsequently set troops on the remaining rioters.

These actions caused one of the most significant challenges to Anastasius, the revolt of Vitalian. Vitalian, from Zaldaba in Moesia Secunda, had fought in the Persian war of 502–506 and was serving in Thrace in 513. Like many in Constantinople, Vitalian was concerned about Anastasius' revisions to the *Trisagion* as well as the depositions of Flavianus and Macedonius. At the same time, the *foederati* under his command were upset at Hypatius, *magister militum per Thracias* (probably not Anastasius' nephew), for allegedly depriving them of their payments (*annona*). When Vitalian revolted, Hypatius withdrew to Constantinople. Vitalian pursued him to the Hebdomon, only seven miles from the city itself, proclaiming his interest in justice for his troops and a desire to support the pro-Chalcedonian faith. He did not declare himself emperor. Anastasius sent Patricius, *magister militum in praesenti*, who arranged an audience for Vitalian's envoys to meet Anastasius. When Anastasius won them over by gifts, by promises that the supplies due to them would be sent, and by undertaking that the Pope would be allowed to settle the religious questions, Vitalian then began to return to Moesia Secunda. Anastasius replaced Hypatius as *magister militum per Thracias* with Cyril, but when fighting broke out, Cyril was murdered by Vitalian. Anastasius then sent a second army under Hypatius against Vitalian, but Hypatius was defeated and taken prisoner.

Vitalian in 514 returned to Constantinople and again opened negotiations with Anastasius. This time, Anastasius sent a senatorial delegation to Vitalian. He was appointed *magister militum per Thracias* and ransomed Hypatius for nine hundred pounds of gold. It was also agreed that a church council held with western bishops would be held at Heraclea in 515. Although Anastasius did write to Pope Hormisdas on the topic, the council did not meet. Nor did Anastasius keep his promise to restore a number of pro-Chalcedonian bishops. With Anastasius' failure to organize a council, Vitalian then returned to Constantinople a third time in 515 and occupied the area across the Golden Horn from the city. The imperial fleet was commanded by Marinus, eastern praetorian prefect. This was, according to Malalas, because the two *magistri militum in praesenti*, Patricius and John, were friends of Vitalian and feared accusations of treason if they were defeated. When Marinus defeated Vitalian's fleet at Constantinople, Vitalian retreated to Thrace. Some negotiations then occurred, with Anastasius appointing a new *magister militum per Thracias*. Nothing is heard of Vitalian for the next two years. Anastasius' tolerance suggests that he did not see Vitalian as a threat to the Empire. In this respect, his behavior was similar to other late fifth-century figures such as Anagastes, Marcellinus, and Aegidius who challenged imperial authority but did not declare themselves emperor.

By the last part of his reign, Anastasius finally seemed to have imposed order on the church. At the Synod of Tyre in 515, Severus of Antioch's argument that accepting the *Henotikon* required the rejection of Chalcedon was accepted by the patriarchs of Constantinople and Alexandria. This superficial eastern unity was, however, as fragile as that imposed by Constantine in the aftermath of Nicaea. The exact degree of compliance exacted from the fourth eastern patriarch, Elaias of Jerusalem, is unclear, but by later in 516 he too had been removed from office. Although his successor John (516–524) had been prepared to foreswear Chalcedon, when confronted by, according to Cyril of Scythopolis, ten thousand Palestinian monks, he thought better of it. The *dux Palestinae* also thought it too risky to intervene, even though Anastasius chose not to listen to their petition.

As well as resistance within the eastern Empire to the anti-Chalcedonians, the Pope continued to support the cause of the pro-Chalcedonians. Following the abortive negotiations over a council at Heraclea, an embassy composed of Ennodius, bishop of Ticinum, and Peregrinus, bishop of Misenum, was sent by Pope Hormisdas to Constantinople in 517. When Anastasius refused to allow the envoys entry to Constantinople and ordered them to return directly to Rome, the two contacted what the *Liber Pontificalis* called "orthodox monks" and used their help to spread Hormisdas' letters regarding orthodoxy. Numerous bishops sent the letters to the emperor, who then wrote to Hormisdas, outraged: "we are able to stand being insulted and ignored, but we cannot stand to be commanded" (*Collectio Avellana* 138).

Perhaps ironically, given his inability to manage his bishops, Anastasius has received great praise for his administration. Frequently cited is his leaving of a surplus in the treasury of 320,000 pounds of gold, despite having fought major wars in Isauria, against the Persians, and against Vitalian. Exactly how Anastasius himself contributed to this is more difficult to understand, and it may be that our source for the surplus, Procopius, was more interested in showing that Justinian was wasting money than in accuracy:

> This Justinian, when his uncle Justin took over the Empire, found the state well supplied with public money. For Anastasius had been both the most cautious and at the same time the most economical administrator of all Emperors, and fearing, as actually happened, that his future successor to the throne, finding himself short of funds, might perhaps take to plundering his subjects, he had filled all the treasuries to overflowing with gold before he completed the term of his life. All this money Justinian dissipated with all speed (Procopius, *Secret History* 19.4–6).

There were administrative reforms, but none of these seem to be significant enough to account for a surplus larger than that reported for any other emperor. The most noticeable change was the introduction of a new series of bronze coins that now had a fixed relationship to the gold *solidi*. Throughout the fifth century, the Roman state had minted only small quantities of bronze coinage, so this new coinage eased smaller-scale transactions. There were only three imperial mints, at Constantinople, Nicomedia, and Antioch, though, like Odovacer, Theoderic in Italy issued coinage in the name of Anastasius. In 498, the *collatio lustralis* was abolished, a popular decision. However, Malalas' claim that the loss of imperial income was made up from the *res privata* (and administered from a new suboffice known as the *patrimonium*) should be rejected. One factor that probably contributed to the efficiency of the administration was the fact that Celer was *magister officiorum* between 503 and 518, a long term of office. Another was the creation of the office of *vindex*, an imperial financial official in each city, reporting to the praetorian prefect. This could be seen as an extension of imperial power or as a reflection of the failure of city councils to provide effective government.

Ariadne died in 515, leaving Anastasius alone for his remaining years. He died on July 8, 518, aged ninety years and five months according to the *Chronicon Paschale*, and was buried in the Church of the Holy Apostles.

JUSTIN I (518–527)

Although Anastasius' death may have been a surprise, he was ninety and the ambitious would have been making plans for a while. A crowd soon assembled in the Hippodrome, demanding an emperor. "Long live the Senate! Senate of the Romans, *tu vincas*! We demand our Emperor, given by God, for the army; we demand our Emperor, given by God, for the Empire!" (*De Caeremoniis* 1.93). When compared to recent transfers of power in the west, the acclamation of his successor Justin on July 10, 518, appears trouble-free. It is only when we turn to the very detailed description in the *de Caeremoniis* (1.93) that Justin's difficulties become clear. This records that the consistory and the bishop of Constantinople met immediately after Anastasius' death. While they were discussing the situation in the Portico in front of the Great Triclinium, the *excubitores* acclaimed a certain John in the Hippodrome, though the assembled supporters' club of the Blues did not approve and began throwing stones. Then the *scholares* acclaimed the *magister militum* Patricius. Neither of these claims were well received by the consistory. As their discussions continued, violence flared between the *scholares* and the *excubitores*. The future emperor Justinian, at this point serving as a *candidatus*, rescued Patricius, leading to his name being put forward, though he declined. After this, a series of other names were then proposed to the *cubicularii* who were behind the ivory doors to the emperor's apartments and in control of the imperial regalia. The name of Justin, the *comes excubitorum*, was then put forward with the support of all the senators as well as the Blue and the Green supporters' clubs, though not before he had been punched in the mouth by a *scholarius*. This was a highly embarrassing detail for Justin and its preservation is significant. Clearly there was a tremendous amount of confusion in the palace.

Justin, having finally been given the imperial robes by the *cubicularii*, was crowned on July 10 in the Hippodrome by the patriarch John and acclaimed as emperor by the crowd. He was a Latin speaker from the village of Bederiana in the territory of Naissus in the province of Dacia Mediterranea, born ca. 450. Procopius describes how Justin came to the capital in the reign of Leo to seek his fortune, with a loaf of baked bread wrapped in his goat-hair cloak, and joined the *excubitores*. Justin fought at Cotiaeum in 491 as *comes rei militaris*, then became *comes excubitorum*, participated in the 502–506 war against the Persians, was present at the siege of Amida in 504, and fought in the battle against Vitalian in the Golden Horn in 515. His rise to imperial power, though hardly typical, shows the possibilities the Roman Empire provided to the ambitious and talented; Procopius' claim in the *Secret History* that Justin was illiterate and used a stencil to sign documents does not fit with his career. Justin had several nephews but no children of his own, despite his marriage to Euphemia.

Justin almost immediately replaced imperial support for the anti-Chalcedonians with aggressive pro-Chalcedonianism, bypassing the concil-iatory approach of Zeno's *Henotikon* and the early part of Anastasius' reign. However, Justin took a more rigorous approach to unity than earlier emperors, removing large numbers of anti-Chalcedonian bishops, most prominently Severus of Antioch, but also Philoxenus of Maboug; the *Chronicle* known as that of pseudo-Dionysius lists fifty-four bishops sent into exile, mostly to Alexandria or Constantinople. Monastic leaders suffered too; a gener-ation later, John of Ephesus mentions seeing monks from Cilicia, Isauria, and Cappadocia at Constantinople being given hospitality by Theodora. After this purge, all sees in the Empire had bishops who were at least nom-inally Chalcedonian. This massive exercise of imperial power changed the way that Chalcedon was discussed, moving discussion away from whether the dominant thought would be pro- or anti-Chalcedonian toward a new position where the problem was how to fit the anti-Chalcedonians into the Chalcedonian world.

Justin was thus able to resolve the Acacian schism. When envoys from the Pope reached Constantinople in March 519, they were met first by a delegation of Vitalian, Pompeius, and Justinian, then escorted into the city, where they were received by Justin and the entire Senate. No eastern church leader or his representatives had ever been so honored. Communion with Rome was restored. To celebrate, Justinian started building a basilica of Peter and Paul in the Palace of Hormisdas, while Justin made gifts to the church of Rome. Justin also started slowly replacing the supporters and relatives of Anastasius, especially his nephews Hypatius, currently *magister militum per Orientem*, and Pompeius, the *magister militum per Thracias*. Vitalian returned to Constantinople and was made *magister militum in praesenti* and consul in 520. However, in July 520 he was murdered in the imperial palace, with many later historians suggesting that Justinian was responsible. Whether he was or not, trusting Vitalian was clearly a risk and Justin would have been alert for even a rumor of treacherous behavior. Justin's aggressively pro-Chalcedonian approach weakened somewhat after Vitalian's death.

With the restoration of imperial ecclesiastical unity, Justin initially had good relationships with the Ostrogoths in Italy. King Theoderic, with no son of his own, had in 515 adopted a Spanish Goth, Eutharic, who married his daughter, Amalasuntha. Justin accepted Eutharic as western consul in 519, honored him by holding the eastern consulate himself in the same year, and adopted him as "son-at-arms" (*per arma*), a vague term. Then for 522, Justin did not nominate an eastern consul and instead allowed both slots to be filled by sons of Boethius, Theoderic's *magister officiorum* in 522. Soon afterward, the closer relationship began to deteriorate. When Eutharic died in 522, Theodoric appointed as heir his grandson Athalaric, the eight-year-old son of Eutharic and Amalasuntha. However, Justin did not recognize Athalaric in the way that he had recognized Eutharic. A senator Albinus had written to Justin in a way that made Theoderic suspect his loyalty; Boethius defended him and was imprisoned; he wrote the *Consolation of Philosophy* here, but was executed soon after. And then in 526, in response to a recent anti-Arian edict of Justin, Theoderic sent Pope John to Constantinople to request that churches be restored to Arians. This was the first visit by a Pope to Constantinople. Like the envoys sent in 519, John was well treated by Justin, who even acknowledged his precedence over the patriarch Epiphanius. Nonetheless, he did not rescind his edict, which made it clear that all heretics, as well as pagans, Jews, and Samaritans, continued to be excluded from government positions, although an exception was made for Goths among the *foederati*. For Theoderic, however, Justin's Edict and the Boethius affair were unpleasant reminders that, despite the independence of his kingdom, many in Italy were still strongly linked to the Roman Empire. Theoderic himself could manage these challenges to this legacy, but on his death in 526, he was succeeded by Athalaric (aged eight or ten), whose mother Amalasuntha ruled as regent.

In Africa, the new Vandal king Hilderic (523–530) had ceased to persecute Catholics, thus easing his relationship with Constantinople. In the Balkans, Slav and Bulgar raids continued. And natural disasters forced the repair of the walls of Edessa following a flood in 525 and of Antioch after a major earthquake in 526. There were no major administrative changes, though mints were recreated at Thessalonica and Cyzicus. In Constantinople, Anicia Juliana built a huge and elaborately decorated church of St. Polyeuctus in Constantinople, close to the Column of Marcian. Her son Olybrius, who had held the consulate in 491 and was the grandson of Anicius Olybrius, western emperor in 472, might have been considered a possible successor. This great church could easily be seen as challenge to Justin's family. Justin was probably concerned to avoid a succession like his own and, with Euphemia's death in 524, there was no hope of an accession like that of Anastasius. As the reign continued, the childless Justin made greater use of one of his nephews, Justinian. The Senate had already approached Justin about making Justinian a co-emperor, perhaps concerned that Anastasius' nephews were still highly visible. Justinian was thus in 524 appointed *nobilissimus* and then in 525 acclaimed as Caesar. Later in the sixth century, Procopius in the *Secret History* suggested that Justinian was behind every action taken by Justin, a view often followed by modern writers. This, however, fits poorly with both the primary sources and the substantial accomplishments of Justin himself.

At the end of the reign, war broke out with Persia, caused by rising tensions in the Caucasus. In Lazica, which had previously been heavily influenced by Persia, King Ztathius converted to Christianity, was baptized in Constantinople in 521/522, and was given a royal robe with an embroidered portrait of Justin. In Iberia, King Gourgenes ca. 524/525 asked for Roman protection, which led the Persian king Kavadh I to invade and thus to war with Rome. There was some skirmishing in Persarmenia and a failed assault on Nisibis, after which Anastasius' nephew Hypatius was reappointed as *magister militum per Orientem*. When Justin fell ill in 527, Justinian was raised to the rank of Augustus on April 1. Several issues of coins and a few laws attest to the joint rule. On August 1, 527, Justin died aged seventy-five or seventy-seven. He was the first eastern emperor since Constantine not to be buried in the Church of the Holy Apostles, but in the Monastery of Augusta, founded by his wife.

JUSTINIAN I (527–565)

Justinian was Justin's nephew, born Flavius Petrus Sabbatius Justinianus, a Latin speaker from the village of Tauresium in the territory of Scupi in the province of Dardania. Following his uncle, he came to Constantinople, where he served first as a *scholarius* and then as a *candidatus*. He was made patrician in 518, *magister militum praesentalis* in 520, and consul in 521. However, unlike Justin, he had not led troops in battle. Early in Justin's reign, Justinian was one of many possible heirs, until he was made Caesar in 525. The promotion ceremony took place inside the palace, rather than in public in the Hippodrome, attended only by the *silentium cum conventu*. Justinian was apparently Justin's favorite nephew, but there were others who might have been considered, including another nephew, Germanus, who had had military success as *magister militum per Thracias*. There was a need to be clear about the succession, since Anastasius' nephews Hypatius, Pompeius, and Probus were still alive, as was Olybrius, grandson of the western emperor of the same name, and might be considered by themselves or others as possible emperors. Although married to Theodora, the forty-five-year-old Justinian had no children of his own, though he made great use of relatives throughout his reign as commanders.

Lasting for thirty-eight years, Justinian's reign was one of the longest in Roman history, exceeded only by Augustus and Theodosius II. Justinian had great ambitions, but unusually had commensurate ability, energy, and a long life. Accounts of his reign are often dominated by the attempt to reconquer the western provinces, but these wars were only a part of his story. Justinian was a controversial figure even during his lifetime, as shown by Procopius' *Secret History*, a highly readable and highly prejudiced account that is at odds with many other sources for the period. Mostly because of the writings of Procopius, controversy over the emperor continues, and Justinian attracts almost as much modern attention as Constantine.

At the beginning of his reign, Justinian was faced with a war with Persia that was well under way. A first action was to upgrade the office of *comes Armeniae* to *magister militum per Armeniam* based at Theodosiopolis (Erzurum). The Persian offensive in 530 shows the effectiveness of this restructuring of Roman defenses. Their king Kavadh sent Mihran to attack Dara in Mesopotamia with fifty thousand troops, but he was defeated by the *magister militum per Orientem* Belisarius with twenty-five thousand men. At the same time, the *magister militum per Armeniam* Sittas defeated a second Persian force led by Mihr-Mihroe at Satala in Armenia. Campaigning continued on both fronts in 531, with Belisarius being defeated in a pitched battle at Callinicum and a failed Persian attempt on Martyropolis (Silvan). Belisarius was recalled to Constantinople and the whole of the eastern war was left under the command of Sittas. The war soon came to an end when Kavadh died late in 531 and was succeeded by Xusro I (531–579), allowing Justinian to negotiate the so-called Endless Peace, finally ratified in spring 532. The Persians received a lump payment of eleven thousand pounds of gold, nominally for the defense of the passes through the Caucasus, and the Romans agreed not to use Dara as a military base, though they refused a Persian request to destroy the city. The *dux Mesopotamiae* now used Constantia as his headquarters.

Although the history of Justinian's reign is dominated by military campaigning, this was far from being the only interest of the government at this point. In February 528, Justinian issued orders for a new compilation of laws to replace the outdated *Codex Theodosianus*. This was completed by 529; a second edition, the text which now exists, was completed in 534. The *Codex Justinianus* was a striking achievement, though the speed of compilation means that there are many minor errors. The project was led by the eastern praetorian prefect John the Cappadocian (533–540) and included the lawyer Tribonian. The *Codex Justinianus* incorporated material from two Diocletianic legal collections, the *Codex Gregorianus* and the *Codex Hermogenianus*, unlike the *Codex Theodosianus*, which reached back only as far as Constantine. It also included laws issued in Greek, increasingly common since the reign of Zeno. Tribonian led the team, which compiled the second edition of the *Codex Justinianus* and the *Digest*. This was a compilation of fifty books of Roman civil law in Latin made up of extracts from the earlier jurists Gaius, Papinian, Ulpian, Paulus, and Modestinus, a work completed in 533. There were two others works, the *Institutes*, a handbook of civil law for students also issued in 533, and the *Novellae*, a collection of imperial edicts issued after 534; these were almost entirely in Greek unless directed to officials in Italy, Illyricum, or Africa. With these projects, together known as the *Corpus Juris Civilis*, Roman law had been placed on a completely new footing.

Although the first three collections were anchored in the past, the *Novellae* show the changes taking place in the Empire. Like the reforms of Diocletian and Constantine, much of this was the regularization of existing practices, made visible by the sudden abundance of legal evidence in the *Codex Justinianus* and the *Novellae*. One program was regularizing provincial administration between 535 and 539, led by the eastern praetorian prefect John the Cappadocian. In Armenia, the existing province of Armenia Prima was split into Armenia Prima and Secunda, and with some Pontic cities added, Armenia Secunda was renamed Armenia Tertia. A new province, Armenia

Quarta, was created from territory beyond the Euphrates and governed from Martyropolis. Several new praetors were created to govern the provinces of Thrace (combining the roles of the *vicarius* of Thrace and of the Long Wall), Pisidia, Lycaonia, Paphlagonia, Helenopontus, and Cappadocia, in each case combining civil and military responsibilities into one role. At the same time, the majority of *vicarii* were abolished, but many provinces were grouped into pairs under *duces* with civil and military responsibilities who reported to the eastern praetorian prefect. In 548, the vicariate of Pontica was restored, exploiting the transprovincial powers of the *vicarii*. The authority of this position was greatly expanded over the earlier *vicarius*, since in addition to acting as a deputy of the praetorian prefect, it now included command of all troops in the diocese, as well as all diocesan officials belonging to the *comes rei privatae*, the *comes patrimonii*, and the *magister officiorum*.

As a result of these changes, the earlier separation of civil and military officials was far less clear. The role of bishops was also changing. This is often seen as an increase in the power of the church as a result of the collapse of local government via city councils. Justinian simply saw bishops as servants of the state, like governors and *duces*. Bishops thus routinely received imperial orders, for example requiring them to intervene against provincial governors accused of injustice and to read imperial laws to their congregations. A sixth-century inscription from Hadrianopolis in Paphlagonia shows an imperial communication regarding local security being presented to the bishop for his information. However, provincial governors were still responsible for approving projects paid for with imperial funds, even if bishops had the responsibility of doing public works. Civic government was thus more complicated. Justinian was, however, only regularizing the existing situation; earlier emperors had also been prepared to give orders directly to bishops regarding secular affairs and to imperial officials regarding church matters. *Curiales*, meanwhile, did not disappear from provincial management. Although the structures of provincial government were continuously changing, the principles of local officials working for an imperial aristocracy continued unchanged. So too did the importance of being able to petition the emperor and his officials. Thus Justinian noted in 536 that "every day, whether we are praying or looking after public affairs, we are approached by a crowd of Cappadocians who have suffered injustice, and among them there are many priests and the greatest number of women" (*Novella* 30.5) (see Figure 18).

There were numerous other changes. In 529, Justinian issued an edict that banned all casting of lots, though attempts to forecast the future had always attracted imperial suspicion. In addition, it specifically banned the teaching of philosophy and astronomy at Athens (Malalas 18.47). The city had a long

Figure 18. An imperial governor in a scene from the Rossano Gospels showing Christ before Pilate, sixth century. (Photo by DeAgostini/Getty Images)

tradition of studying philosophy, which in its late Roman form was a pagan activity and so, as in all other such centers, it was under constant challenge from Christians. Some of these, such as Alexandria, continued to teach Neoplatonic philosophy throughout Justinian's reign. In Athens, however, the philosophers soon left the city, traveling to Persia in the hope that they would be able to work there. From the late 530s, regular issues of *solidi* were accompanied by some issues of reduced-weight *solidi*. These were marked in terms of the number of carats (twenty, twenty-two, or twenty-three rather than the regular twenty-four) and so did not replace the regular coinage. The size of these issues, which continued down to the reign of Heraclius, is uncertain, and the only substantial hoard comes from outside the Empire, suggesting that they may have been mainly intended for use in imperial payments to barbarians. With the reconquest, additional mints were now required to produce coinage in the west. These were established at Carthage, somewhere in Sicily, Rome, Ravenna, and Carthago Nova, while in the east, in addition to the existing mints at Constantinople, Antioch, Cyzicus, Nicomedia, and Thessalonica, coins began to be struck at Alexandria and at Chersonesus. Finally, the importance of the consulate changed. Belisarius was consul for 535 and John the Cappadocian for 538, but there was no eastern consul for 536 or 537. The last few consuls were westerners, with Basilius holding the final magistracy in 541, though emperors continued to hold the consulate in their first year in office.

THE NIKA RIOT

Neoplatonism was of interest to few in the Empire, but chariot racing was one of the most popular pastimes. The races also provided one of the few moments when the emperor could be seen by large numbers of his people, while unlike processions and church services, race days provided an opportunity for more informal interaction. In January 532, seven members of the Blue and Green circus supporters' clubs in Constantinople had been found guilty of murder. Five were executed, but two, one each from the Blue and the Green club, were saved by the scaffold breaking. With the assistance of some monks from the monastery of St. Conon, the two lucky murderers took refuge in the church of St. Laurentius. At the races in the Hippodrome on January 13, the Blues and the Greens asked Justinian several times for the release of the prisoners, but their appeals were ignored. Then late in the day, the two clubs started to riot, using the shout "Nika," the Greek for "Conquer," as a rallying cry.

Faced with a Hippodrome full of rioters, Justinian abandoned the races and retreated to the Great Palace. When the rioters learned that the prisoners had been moved to the headquarters of the urban prefect, they set fire to the building and set the prisoners free. Although Justinian attempted the next day to restart the races, rioting continued and the Hippodrome was set on fire. The rioters now demanded that the emperor remove three unpopular senior officials, the eastern praetorian prefect John the Cappadocian, the urban prefect Eudaemon, and the *quaestor* Tribonian. Justinian dismissed the officials, but when rioting continued, he tried unsuccessfully to suppress the riots with the troops he had available. Up to this point, the riot was an urban matter, with no political overtones. This changed when the crowd acclaimed one of Anastasius' nephews, Probus, as emperor. Probus could not be found, suggesting he had no interest in challenging Justinian. The next day, troops under Belisarius summoned earlier from bases in Thrace arrived in the city and reached the palace. On Sunday, January 18, Justinian made another public appearance in the Hippodrome to the assembled crowds, appealing for order. His appeals were rejected, and the rioters acclaimed Hypatius, another nephew of Anastasius, as emperor. Hypatius, having consulted some senators, accepted the acclamation, went to the Hippodrome, and entered the *kathisma* (the imperial box) wearing imperial regalia. At this point, Justinian was faced with a similar situation to Zeno in 475 and Mauricius in 602. According to Procopius:

> Now those around the emperor were in council as to whether it would be better for them if they remained or if they took to flight in the ships. And many opinions were expressed favouring either course. And the Empress Theodora said these things: "... If, now, it is your wish to save yourself, O Emperor, there is nothing to it. For we have much money, and there is the sea, here the boats. However, consider whether it will not come about after you have been saved that you would gladly exchange that safety for death. But for me, I approve that ancient proverb that royalty is a good burial-shroud" (Procopius, *Wars* 1.24.32–37).

Justinian finally decided against flight and sent Belisarius and Narses against the rioters. Their troops remained loyal to the emperor and by the end of the day, thirty thousand lay dead in the Hippodrome. If these many people were really killed, it would have been 5 to 10 percent of the city's population. More importantly for Justinian, Hypatius was captured and executed and his body thrown into the Bosporus. Justinian seems to have taken the view that Hypatius was caught up in a situation beyond his control, since he asked the family to bury the body when it washed ashore. Although Hypatius' property was confiscated, it was later restored to his children. As for the deposed officials, John was back in office before the end of the year, and Tribonian was made *magister officiorum* in 533. Despite the horrendous scale of the slaughter, the riot itself was similar to other urban disturbances such as the Riot of the Statues in 387 and Theodosius' massacre at Thessalonica in 391. For the crowd to seek to acclaim another man emperor was not new either; in 512, a rioting crowd had pulled down statues of Anastasius and shouted for Areobindus as emperor. The scale of the slaughter was the result of Justinian's hesitancy to be harsh in the early phases of the riot. He learned his lesson: in

547 and 562, at riots between the Blue and Green clubs the *excubitores* were sent in immediately.

RELIGIOUS POLICY

The riot of 512 had been caused by the attempted modification of the Trisagion, a change interpreted by the people of Constantinople as being anti-Chalcedonian. Even though the problems caused by the Council of Chalcedon had been resolved by Justin as far as the west was concerned, it was clear to most eastern bishops and Justinian that the unity created by Justin's expelling all known anti-Chalcedonian bishops had only driven the problem underground, not solved it. Thus Justinian's accession in 527 was accompanied by the issuing of a fiercely Chalcedonian edict, but this was mostly intended to keep up good relations with the Pope. Although this edict suggested continuity with Justin's policy, Justinian's next actions were very different. In 532, various anti-Chalcedonian leaders, including Severus of Antioch, were invited to the palace. Severus initially refused to come, and these discussions were not productive. However, in 533 the emperor issued a Theopaschite edict, stressing that the Christ who suffered was one of the Trinity and thus emphasizing his human nature. This moderate document, taking the same approach as Zeno's *Henotikon* by avoiding mention of Chalcedon, was cautiously accepted throughout the Empire, though there were some extremists who rejected it.

Although Justinian was still hopeful of finding a way to bring the two lines of thought regarding Chalcedon together, most of the leaders of the anti-Chalcedonians had now abandoned attempts to change the definition of orthodoxy. Moreover, the anti-Chalcedonians had no unity, being already split between various leaders, including Severus of Antioch, who by 534 was living in Constantinople, and Julian of Halicarnassus, making it even more difficult for the emperor to attempt to impose order. Critically, one group of anti-Chalcedonian bishops led by Jacob Baradaeus and John of Tella began consecrating priests and bishops from the middle of the 520s. John of Ephesus was present at one of these occasions in 541, officiating with John of Hephaestus at Tralles in the upper room of a church that was simultaneously being used for services below (John of Ephesus, *Lives of the Eastern Saints* 25). These consecrations meant there were now two churches within the Empire. There had been multiple bishops on many occasions earlier, but these were usually confined to a single city in a time of a disputed succession. These challenges to the state also led to Jacob and John being hunted.

Justinian's attempts to unite with the anti-Chalcedonians also had an impact on his relationships with Chalcedonians. In 535, Anthimus, bishop of Trapezus (Trebizond), was elected as patriarch of Constantinople. Moving a bishop between sees (also known as translation) was in violation of Canon 15 of the Council of Nicaea, though at this point no one seemed particularly concerned. When elected, Anthimus had accepted the Council of Chalcedon. He was also well versed in contemporary theological subtleties, having been a participant in the discussions of 532–533 in Constantinople. However, the willingness of Anthimus to talk to Severus and his acceptance of Zeno's *Henotikon* was seen by some as evidence of anti-Chalcedonian beliefs. Thus Ephraim, patriarch of Antioch, sent letters with a certain Sergius to Pope Agapetus, while other delegations came directly to Justinian. Early in 536, Agapetus himself traveled to Constantinople, accompanied by Sergius and five Italian bishops, as well as a number of lower-ranking clergy, including Pelagius, who later became Pope. Agapetus was acting as an ambassador of the Ostrogothic king Theodahad, concerned that the Romans had already landed in Sicily and were known to have designs on the Ostrogothic kingdom.

Once Agapetus arrived in Constantinople, his ecclesiastical concerns took precedence over his ambassadorial duties when he refused to take communion with Anthimus. It is hard to see how any subject of the emperor who hoped to reconcile the warring parties over Chalcedon could have done anything better or differently than Anthimus. However, Agapetus' presence led almost inevitably to this confrontation. Justinian decided it was worth more to him to get the support of Agapetus for his operations in Italy and sacrificed Anthimus. Anthimus resigned. On March 13, Menas was elected to replace him and was then consecrated in the Great Church by Agapetus himself.

Having stirred up the Chalcedonian issue that Justinian was trying to resolve, Agapetus died in Constantinople on April 22, 536. The cost of even talking to the anti-Chalcedonians was now clear, while Severus was still intransigent. Justinian now ordered Menas to investigate Anthimus. There followed five meetings of the Home Synod, starting on May 2, whose proceedings have been preserved. The synod met in the Church of the Theotokos close to Hagia Sophia, which was still being rebuilt after the Nika riot. The main focus of the meetings was the accusations against Anthimus, condemned in the fourth session on May 21, though Severus was condemned in the final session. Like earlier patriarchs John Chrysostom and Nestorius, Anthimus saw no point in attending the meetings, and though strenuous efforts were made to find him, involving among others the historian Zachariah of Mytilene, they were fruitless. As in the synod of 448 that condemned Eutyches, this synod assembled the large numbers of bishops currently in Constantinople. At the first session on May 2, there were fifty-three bishops and eleven lower-ranking clergy. A year earlier, Justinian had required bishops not to be away from their sees for more than a year at a time, unless conducting imperial business, and if coming to Constantinople to report in to the emperor on arrival (*Novella* 6). Finally, in a statement by the emperor from August 13, 536, addressed to Menas, Justinian claimed that Anthimus was deposed by Agapetus, confirmed the synod's condemnation, and exiled him from the city. John of Ephesus later claimed that Anthimus was kept in secret in the palace by Theodora until her death in 548, at which point he was discovered and received hospitably by Justinian, though the history of pseudo-Zachariah of Mytilene is explicit that he left the city. This was derived from the work of the participant Zachariah of Mytilene and should be preferred to John's version.

THE RECONQUEST OF THE WEST

The term "reconquest" is often used to describe the western campaigns of Justinian. He was ambitious to restore the lost territories of the Empire in the west, though it is unclear whether the attack on Africa was seen as the first step in a planned program or whether each action was opportunistic. Justinian had no need to justify the wars to reoccupy Roman territory, but chose to do so, suggestive of a world in which others' opinions of Rome now mattered. Justinian chose to attack Vandal Africa first, perhaps because it seemed the easiest area to conquer. After the failure of Leo's 468 campaign against the Vandals, the eastern Romans negotiated a peace, while relations were eased further when Hilderic (523–530) stopped persecuting Catholics. When Hilderic lost his throne to his cousin Gelimer (530–534), Justinian used this as a pretext for war. The war was Justinian's decision, taken after listening to discussion in the consistory where the eastern praetorian prefect John the Cappadocian argued fiercely against his plan.

Belisarius set sail to Africa in 533 at the head of an army of sixteen thousand men. Even as the expedition was being readied, news of Roman preparations caused revolts against the Vandals in Tripolitania and Sardinia. The Romans were also helped by the readiness of Amalasuntha the Ostrogoth to allow the use of Syracuse in Sicily as a staging post. Belisarius landed in Africa, defeated the Vandals in a minor action at Ad Decimum, then occupied Carthage in September before winning a major victory at Tricamarum in December. The Vandal kingdom collapsed and Roman control was restored to the African provinces, as well as the Balearic Islands (previously part of the Spanish diocese), Corsica, and Sardinia (both earlier under Italy). Gelimer was sent to Constantinople, along with the royal treasury, the western imperial regalia that had been captured in 455, and the booty brought by Titus from Jerusalem in 70. When Belisarius returned to Constantinople in early 534, he was rewarded with the consulate for 535, and displayed the booty and defeated king in a triumphal procession. Gelimer was exiled to Galatia, and many of the other Vandal prisoners were conscripted and sent to fight in Persia.

Once occupied, the Roman administration of Africa had to be recreated. Restoring the fifth-century framework of cities and provinces was easy, but Africa was now given its own praetorian prefect based at Carthage in place of a *vicarius*. There was also a separate *magister militum per Africam* with a field army, as well as four *duces* who controlled the restored *limitanei*. At first, Solomon held both posts of *magister militum* and praetorian prefect, foreshadowing the later position of exarch, which combined them in one office, a practice occasionally repeated over the next two decades. The mint used by the Vandals continued to produce coinage. There was also a massive program of building and repair of defenses in which the walls of Carthage were restored. More complicated was the restoration of churches to Catholics. The Vandals, never numerous, disappeared as a people, while the emperor received a huge collection of estates, many of which had previously belonged to the western emperor.

Africa in the third and fourth centuries had served as a reservoir of men and manpower for the western Empire and only occasionally required intervention from Europe. In the sixth century, the reconquered area was far less profitable. Although various Moorish tribes had been relatively easy to keep under control when the Empire was intact, they were a far more serious problem for Justinian's overstretched forces; Solomon defeated some of them in two battles in 534 at Mammes and Bourgaon. There were also serious mutinies by the army in 536 (slowed by the return of Belisarius from Sicily and then suppressed by Germanus, Justinian's cousin) and 545–546, with the mutineers joined by Moors. The Moors were also dangerous in their own right, with a war being started in 544 with murder of eighty members of the tribe of the Leuathae at Leptis Magna. The Moors were able to defeat the Romans in the Battle of Cillium in 544, where Solomon was killed; at Thacia in 545; and Marta in 546. Justinian then appointed John Troglites as *magister militum per Africam*, who was victorious at the Fields of Cato in 548. Nonetheless, exports of African pottery and other goods, continued after the reconquest, while cities were given new fortifications or repaired and upgraded as at Carthage. Carthage also saw the construction of a maritime agora.

With Africa now under Roman control, Justinian's gaze turned to Italy. After the death of Theoderic's grandson Athalaric in 534, the imprisonment and then murder of his daughter Amalasuntha in 535 by King Theodahad (534–536) gave Justinian a justification to invade Italy, though it seems likely that the invasion would have proceeded without any *casus belli*. Justinian certainly ignored Theodahad's attempts to negotiate. His initial plan was for Belisarius to sail to Sicily while a second force under the *magister militum per Illyricum* Mundo was sent against Salona in Dalmatia to threaten the north and to open the Adriatic to the Roman fleet. He also encouraged the Franks, in particular King Theodebert, to attack the Po Valley, though the negotiations were unsuccessful. The Franks subsequently proved able to intervene in northern Italy, though against rather than for the Romans. Mundo was successful in occupying Dalmatia in 535, but was killed in a Gothic attack in 536 and a second Roman force was sent under Constantianus.

Belisarius meanwhile landed in Sicily in late 535 with around seven thousand men, swiftly restoring the island to Roman rule. This war was very different from North Africa, dragging on until the final Gothic collapse in 552 and defeat of the Franks in 554. At first, the campaign seemed to be easy, with Belisarius reaching Naples in early 536 before meeting with any opposition. Theodahad was replaced as king of the Ostrogoths by Vitigis (536–540), who then abandoned Rome. Having occupied Rome at the end of 536, Belisarius restored some of the church ornaments taken to Africa by the Vandals in 455. However, once Vitigis had assembled an army and the winter was over, he marched to confront Belisarius. The small size of the Roman army meant that Belisarius could not risk battle and instead withstood siege in Rome (537–538). The city, however, was too big to besiege effectively, and several groups of reinforcements reached Belisarius before Roman threats to Ravenna forced Vitigis to abandon the siege. In 538, a substantial Roman reinforcing army under Narses arrived in Picenum, probably sent by sea. This allowed Belisarius to enter the Po Valley, where he garrisoned Milan. The city was then recaptured in 539 by the Goths, who were reinforced by Burgundians sent by King Theodebert. Nonetheless, Roman negotiations began with the Goths. Belisarius was more optimistic of total victory than Justinian, who was prepared to make concessions for a more rapid peace. As the negotiations dragged on, the Goths offered to support Belisarius if he declared himself emperor. He used this as a pretext to enter Ravenna in 540, and then, suddenly, the Goths had lost control of their capital and the war was over. Italy was now reoccupied (except for Ticinum and Verona), though there were many loose ends to be tied up, in particular the recreation of a Roman administration. A start had been made in 537, when Sicily was given a praetor, the Italian Fidelius was appointed praetorian prefect of Italy, and a new *comes patrimonii* was appointed for Italy. Like Gelimer, Vitigis was well treated, also being given an estate in Asia Minor.

This is traditionally seen as the midpoint in Justinian's reign, before which it can generally be termed a success, after which everything became more difficult. This view can be symbolized by two natural events. Procopius in 536 noted that "during this year a most terrible sign occurred. For the sun gave forth its light without brightness ... and it seemed very much like the sun in eclipse, for the beams it shed were not clear" (Procopius, *Wars* 4.14.5). A Syriac Chronicle claimed that "the sun became dark and its darkness lasted for 18 months. Each day it shone for about four hours only, and still this light was only a feeble shadow ... the fruits did not ripen and the wine tasted like sour grapes" (Michael the Syrian 26). And there was a drought in Mesopotamia in 536, which, according to Marcellinus Comes, forced fifteen thousand Saracens to move from Persia to Euphratesia. Dendrochronological evidence for 536 shows very low levels of growth in northern Europe as well as in North and South America. The greater impact in the northern parts of the Empire in the literary sources suggests a volcanic eruption. Regardless of what caused this event, it was not mentioned by many sixth-century writers, and we thus need to be careful about overinterpreting it. In particular, none of the seventy-six *Novellae* from 536 to 539, several of which are concerned with provincial revenues, suggest any impact.

A second catastrophe was the plague of 541–542, described by the eyewitness Procopius as "a pestilence by which all humanity was close to being annihilated" (Procopius, *Wars* 2.22.1). Starting at Pelusium in Egypt in summer 541, by the following spring it had spread via shipping routes to Constantinople and Italy and then inland. By 543, it had spread across the whole Mediterranean from Persia to southern Gaul. The death toll, especially in large cities, was enormous, with mass graves being required to keep up with the fatalities, reported to have exceeded a thousand a day. So great were the fatalities that John of Ephesus (recycled by the *Chronicle of Zuqnin* in its entry for 543) recorded that he saw fields "in which grain was becoming white and stood erect, but there was no one to gather it in." Another historian, Evagrius, caught the plague but, like the emperor Justinian, survived. The plague recurred in Constantinople in 558, 573–574, and 599, with repeated outbreaks elsewhere.

Despite their horror, from the perspective of the state these events had little impact; subsequent problems in recruiting and raising taxes were not new problems. Although we have no reliable estimates of mortality, it is clear that this pandemic was not on the same scale as the fourteenth-century Black Death. Most deaths were among the urban poor, who paid few taxes and made up few of the recruits for the army, while most taxation was based on land, not on heads. Two *Novellae* from 543 and 544 blame various tradesmen, sailors, and agricultural workers for price rises. Yet despite the survival of large numbers of papyri detailing labor costs and property leases in Egypt, there is little difference in the costs between the early and late sixth century. Regardless of the impact of the dark event and the plague, dividing Justinian's reign into two parts is not the best way to analyze it. Its length makes it difficult to analyze without subdivisions, yet contemporaries seemed unaware of any major shifts in the middle.

Although the Romans had been successful in reoccupying much of Italy, the Goths still had a king in the Po Valley at Ticinum and also controlled Verona. In 542, in what should have been a mopping-up operation, the Romans attacked King Totila (541–552) but were defeated at Faventia. After this, the Romans lost the strategic initiative because they could not assemble a new field army; following the outbreak of the Persian war in 540, there were few reinforcements available until the end of conflict in Mesopotamia in 545. Naples was then lost to the Goths in 543. With the Persian war over, Justinian sent Belisarius back to Italy in 544, with a second army following in 545. Rome was besieged again (545–546) and fell when some Isaurians betrayed the city, though it was soon reoccupied in 547. After Belisarius was withdrawn again in 549, Rome was captured a third time in 550, then betrayed by troops who had not been paid. Totila now controlled most of Italy and was even able to ravage Sicily, laying siege to Syracuse. By this point, Roman possessions were reduced to Ravenna, Croton, and a few other cities mostly in Sicily. By 551, the Gothic fleet was also able to attack the west coast of Greece, plundering Corcyra, as well as occupying Corsica and Sardinia.

To replace Belisarius, Justinian sent his cousin Germanus, who recruited a large army in the Balkans. He also married Theoderic's granddaughter Matasuntha in a move which would have given many Goths a difficult political choice. Germanus, however, died at Serdica late in 550 and was replaced as commander for the Gothic war by Narses in 551. Narses was the *praepositus sacri cubiculi*, a eunuch. The only eunuch to have led Rome's armies before was Eutropius in 395, though Justinian had put Narses in charge of some troops in Italy in 538 and gave another eunuch, Scholasticus, a field command in 551. The direction of success in the Gothic war now changed again. First, late in 551, Totila's fleet met a Roman fleet at Sena Gallica near Ancona and was destroyed completely. Taking advantage of the lessening of intensity in the Persian war, Narses had added further troops to the army raised by Germanus, including allied Lombards, Heruls, and Gepids. Marching into

Ravenna in 552, he was able to challenge Totila directly in battle at Taginae near Sentinum (see Chapter 10). Totila died in the battle, and the reoccupation of Rome later that year and a second battle at Mons Lactarius in which his successor Teias died finished the major fighting. The Ostrogoths now collapsed as a state, and no further king appeared, though a few independent groups in the cities of Cumae and Centumcellae were still holding out. Although the Ostrogoths had been destroyed, other enemies still threatened Italy. An army of Franks and Alamanni, supposedly seventy-five thousand strong, led by the brothers Butilinus and Leutharis, entered the Po Valley in 553, then in 554 ravaged the length of Italy. When the army divided and Leutharis started to return to Gaul, Narses was able to destroy Butilinus' forces at Casilinum in Campania. The surrender of a Gothic force at Campsa in 555 marked the effective end of the war, though Verona and Brixia were not reoccupied until 562.

The imperial administration of Italy was now recreated fully. The measures of the Gothic kings before Totila were respected, but he was treated like a defeated imperial challenger and his acts were annulled. Land held by the Gothic church was transferred to the Roman church in Italy, while land held by the kings was transferred to the emperor. A series of four military border commands were established in northern Italy under the command of *magistri militum*. The corn dole was restored to Rome and a mint was established there, while Ravenna was restored as the capital of Italy. Here, the church of San Vitale was consecrated in 547 by Bishop Maximian, decorated with a series of spectacular mosaics showing the emperor and his wife (see Figure 19). Similar mosaics were also commissioned to decorate the Chalke in Constantinople. With Roman troops firmly in charge of Italy, popes now turned to secular authority to impose their will. Thus several letters from Pope Pelagius (556–561) were sent to Narses and to the *magister militum* John, requesting the arrest of Bishop Paulinus of Forum Sempronii (Fossombrone) in Flaminia et Picenum so that he could be brought before an ecclesiastical court.

This war had been long and hard, very different from the brevity of the African campaign. Behind the eventual military success lay the devastation of two decades of war. More difficult to restore, however, was a feeling of *Romanitas*. After 476, Italian aristocrats had come to terms with loyalties to Roman culture and barbarian secular power, but after Belisarius' landing in 535 they were caught in a situation resembling a civil war, trying to guess at who would ultimately be victorious. As the influence of impoverished aristocrats declined, bishops became more important. Thus according to an edict known as the Pragmatic Sanction of 554, Italian provincial governors were now chosen by the emperor from

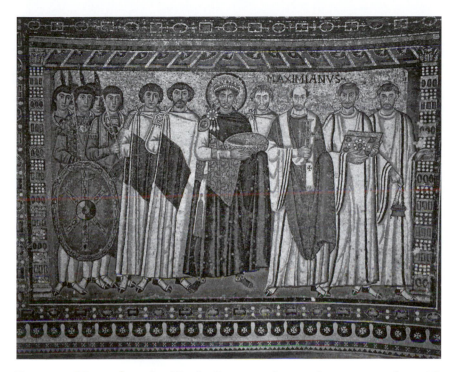

Figure 19. Mosaic from San Vitale, Ravenna, showing Justinian together with senior officials, the bishop of Ravenna, and his bodyguards.

a list of names provided by bishops and local aristocrats. At the same time, opportunities for Italians to become part of the imperial administration were reduced by the elimination of the imperial offices of *magister officiorum*, *quaestor*, and *comes rei privatae*. Under the Ostrogothic kings, these posts were usually held by members of Roman senatorial families such as Cassiodorus or Boethius, but now the only such imperial office left in Italy was the praetorian prefecture, though this was as often held by easterners as by Italians.

Even before the final Roman victory in Italy, Justinian sent Roman troops to land in Spain. In 551, a Visigothic aristocrat in Spain, Athanagild, had requested help from Justinian in his revolt against King Agila I (549–554). Justinian sent a force from Italy under the now aged Liberius (he had served Odovacer and Theoderic) as praetorian prefect of Italy. Athanagild's revolt was successful, though he may not have been expecting a small Roman province to be created on the Spanish coast and in the Baleares. This was administered by a *magister militum Spaniae* and a mint was established, though it struck only *tremisses*.

JUSTINIAN AND THE BALKANS

The Balkan wars of Justinian have often received less scholarly attention than those in Persia and Italy, probably because they do not form a distinct focus in Procopius' narrative. War in the Balkans can be divided into two major zones. The western regions around Sirmium, where Rome was faced by the Goths, Gepids, Heruls, and later the Avars, were managed by the *magister militum per Illyricum* based at Thessalonica. The lower Danubian region, where Rome was faced by more loosely structured Bulgars, Huns, Antae, and Slavs, was managed by the *magister militum per Thracias* based at Marcianopolis. During this period, no capable leaders or strong confederations emerged and neither region presented a major military threat to the Empire. In this respect, the period was very different from the mid-fifth or late sixth centuries, when the confederations of Huns and Avars were more dangerous. However, the Danube was no longer a secure frontier. Throughout this period, parties of barbarian raiders entered Roman territory in most years to plunder. Like previous emperors, Justinian continued to enhance the defenses of the Balkans with numerous fortifications being built or restored, including Thermopylae and Corinth. Justinian also founded a city at Justiniana Prima in the province of Dacia Mediterranea in 535, making it the capital of the prefecture of Illyricum and of the diocese of Dacia in place of Thessalonica. This change brought the base of the Illyrian army closer to Pannonia and Dalmatia. Justiniana Prima is usually identified as Caričin Grad, a fortified hilltop site with a central plan, a bishop's palace, and cathedral. Supplying the lower Danube was reorganized in 536 with the creation of the *quaestura exercitus*, which placed a *quaestor* over the Danubian provinces of Scythia and Moesia Secunda and the Mediterranean provinces of Caria, the (Aegean) Islands, and Cyprus. This reform compensated for the economic damage done to Thrace by the constant raids, but at the same time probably made better use of these provinces, shipping their supplies directly to the Danube.

Roman military activity in the western Balkans revolved around the region between Sirmium and Singidunum. In 527, Sirmium was under Gothic control. The Romans were able to persuade the Gepids and Heruls to attack the city, though this attack was defeated by the Ostrogoths under Vitigis (who was later king). After the death of Mundo in 536, a second Roman expedition under Constantinus had to be sent to recover Salona in Dalmatia and then to resist a Gothic attack in 537. At the same time, the Gepids captured Sirmium from the Ostrogoths and proceeded to hold it between 536 and 568. The Gepid control of Pannonia as Roman allies was shattered in 548 when they fell out with the Lombards, both groups sending envoys to Constantinople. Justinian decided to back the Lombards, resulting in a major Roman expedition in 549 led by Aratius, Constantianus, and Buzes. A second army was also sent under John, *magister militum per Illyricum*, with orders to move on to Italy once the campaign was completed. A third Roman army in 552, led by Justin (cousin of the future emperor) fought against the Slavs and Gepids.

The lower Danube frontier involved defending against raids by the Antae, Huns, Bulgars, and Slavs. In 529 and 530, Bulgar armies attacked Thrace, though soon after Chilbudius, *magister militum per Thracias*, was able to cross the Danube several times before being killed in a Slav ambush in 533. In 540, another army described by Procopius as Hunnic captured thirty-two fortresses in Illyricum and reached as far as the suburbs of Constantinople where, according to John of Ephesus, a fearful Justinian shut himself up in the palace. In 550, a Roman army led by Constantianus was defeated at Adrianople. In 559, another Kutrigur raid divided into three groups. One of these entered Greece but was stopped at Thermopylae, a second reached the Chersonese but was defeated in the field, and a third group marched on Constantinople. These were forced to retreat by Belisarius, who had been recalled from retirement.

In addition to armies and fortifications, the defensive system made considerable use of diplomacy. One way for the Romans to get in contact with the peoples north of the Danube was via the Crimea, where there was a small Roman garrison as well as two Roman cities, Chersonesus and Bosporus. In 528, King Grod of the Utigur Huns, who lived north of the Black Sea, came to Constantinople to be baptized. Grod came to a sticky end in a revolt following his decision to melt down the tribe's pagan religious items, and Roman control had to be reimposed by a small expedition. The Utigur Huns were encouraged to attack the Kutrigurs in 551, 557, and 559. The situation in the Balkans was poised to change, however, with the arrival of a new steppe people, the Avars, in 558. Their ruler Candich sent ambassadors to Justinian's court and fought against the Utigurs in the Ukraine. A second Avar embassy arrived in 562, representing the new Chagan Baian and asking for land in a Roman province. The full impact of the Avars, however, was not felt until the reign of Justin II (565–578).

Although in 532 Rome and Persia had made peace, King Xusro I made plans to attack Rome again following an Armenian revolt in 539. He was well aware of Roman commitments in Italy, even if it seems unlikely that the war itself was a direct result of Gothic appeals for help. In 540, Xusro invaded Syria, leading his army personally. Beroea and Antioch were stormed and sacked and many of the population deported, while two hundred pounds of gold was exacted from both Apamea and Edessa in exchange for not being sacked. Although a peace was made, it was deemed to be broken when Xusro attacked Dara unsuccessfully on his withdrawal. In 541, Belisarius and the *magister militum per Armeniam* Valerianus were sent to Mesopotamia, though they were unopposed since Xusro had chosen to operate in Lazica during this campaigning season. At the same time, the Persians had widened their range of operations by allying with the Laz king Gubazes and occupying Petra. Then in 542, Xusro returned to Mesopotamia, where he plundered Euphratesia and Osrhoene. In 543, the Roman forces from Mesopotamia and Armenia made an unsuccessful attempt on the Persarmenian city of Dvin. In 544, Xusro fought again in Mesopotamia and laid siege to Edessa unsuccessfully.

After 545, the war was confined to Lazica, where it lasted until 557. The Laz returned their allegiance to the Romans after it was discovered that Xusro had planned to have Gubazes assassinated. The new *magister militum per Armeniam* Dagistheus invaded Lazica in 548, though he was unable to recapture Petra. A Persian army invading in 549 was defeated at the River Hippis. In 550, Bessas replaced Dagistheus and in 551 captured Petra. Relationships between the Romans and their allies were not always easy, and Bessas was relieved after Gubazes wrote a letter of complaint to the emperor. When relations between the generals in Lazica and the king soured further in 555, Gubazes was assassinated by one of the Roman generals. Following an appeal from the Laz, Justinian sent Athanasius, a leading senator, to investigate, while at the same time sending Gubazes' brother Ztathius, who had been kept as a hostage in Constantinople to take up the position of king. Following the investigation, the Roman generals involved were executed. After some further Roman operations in 556, the war began to slow down and the so-called Fifty Years Peace was negotiated in 562 by Peter the Patrician and by Yazdgushnasp. The complete terms of this treaty are preserved by Menander (fr. 6.1), with the main feature being Roman annual payments of thirty thousand *solidi* to the Persians for fifty years in return for control of Lazica.

THE COURT OF JUSTINIAN

In 540, an Egyptian villager Apollos of Aphrodito came to Constantinople at a time when Justinian was deeply concerned with the Persian invasion of Syria. Apollos was trying to resolve a dispute about tax collection in his village in the territory of Antaeopolis in the province of the Thebaid. Although the emperor Leo had given the village the right to collect its own taxes (*autopragia*), Apollos claimed that imperial tax collectors were trying to collect the taxes themselves. The Augusta Theodora owned some estates in or near the village and it may be that this had emboldened Apollos to appeal to the emperor. The preserved material represents only Apollos' point of view. Despite Apollos' visit, the problem was not resolved to the villagers' satisfaction. Thus, in 548 Apollos' son Dioscurus wrote a petition to Justinian. He also wrote a report (*didaskalia*) to be sent to Theodora's estate manager. Since the original, complete with numerous signatures in different hands, was found in his archive in Egypt, it may never have been delivered, perhaps because Theodora died in 548. Although Dioscurus' petition to Justinian resulted in an imperial rescript ordering an investigation, the results were unsatisfactory to the villagers, so Dioscurus went to Constantinople himself in 550. This visit resulted in the curator of the divine household in 551 requesting the *dux Thebaidis* to investigate the new claim that taxes had been collected from the village but not deposited in the provincial treasury. The curator's office hoped to resolve this issue before it came to the attention of the emperor himself. This letter in a very ornate hand is preserved outside Dioscurus' archive (see Figure 20).

While in Constantinople, Dioscurus also conducted some other business, making an agreement with the *comes sacri consistorii* Palladius to investigate a separate dispute with Heraclius, son of Psaious, offering a share of the proceeds and reimbursement of expenses to Palladius to resolve. Although petitioners could deposit their petitions at the palace relatively easily, it was usually felt to be more effective if someone at the palace could ensure that it was considered. Dioscurus put some of his hopes in Domninus, *cancellarius* to an eastern praetorian prefect, by writing poems addressed to both Domninus and his son Paul. The closely connected poetic and political environment of Justinian's court can be seen in the *Cycle* of Agathias, which collects a number of epigrams written by others. One of these authors was Paul the *silentiarius*, who wrote about Damocharis, proconsul of Asia, probably in 551, who helped restore Smyrna after an earthquake. Damocharis wrote poetry himself, including a poem on Agathias' cat, a cat that had eaten Agathias' pet partridge. Agathias also wrote a history that continued Procopius' work, and Paul also wrote an epigram on Domninus in the reign of Justin II, when he renovated the lawcourts (*praetorium*) in Constantinople. In other connections to the same group, Dioscurus wrote a poem for another *silentiarius*, Dorotheus, and Paul exchanged poems with Agathias.

Justinian also continued also his attempts to create ecclesiastical unity, issuing an edict in 544, usually referred to as *The Three Chapters*, which attempted to reconcile the anti-Chalcedonians by condemning Theodoret of Cyrrhus, Ibas of Edessa, and Theodore of Mopsuestia. All three had been exonerated at the Council of Chalcedon in 451, though Justinian constructed

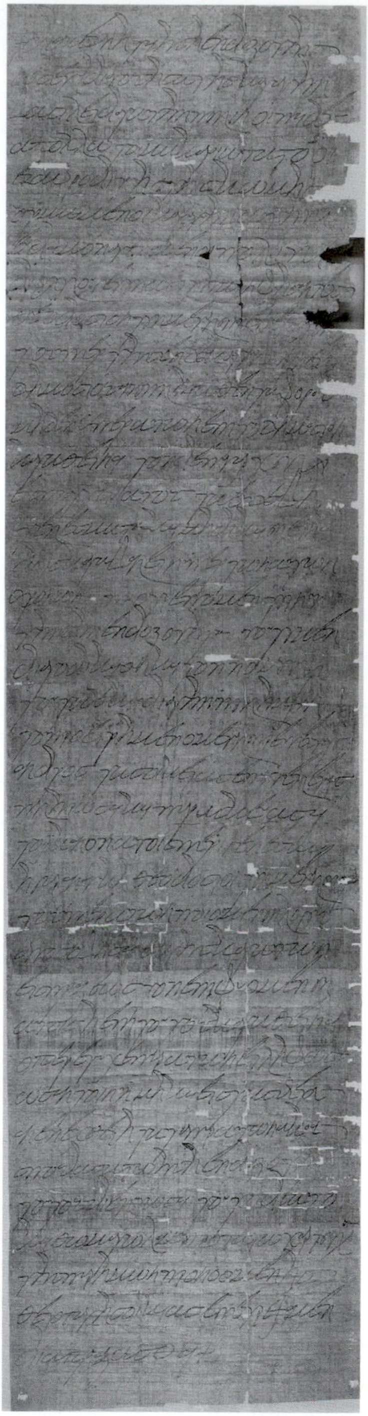

Figure 20. Letter from the curator of the divine household regarding Dioscurus' appeal. This papyrus from Hamburg (P.Hamb. 410) shows a script typical of the imperial chancery.

a revised narrative that claimed that this was not the case. This new narrative did much violence to the historical record, similar to an imperial investigation in Mopsuestia, which claimed that Theodore had been condemned by his home city and his name replaced in the bishop list by the perfectly orthodox Cyril of Alexandria. Understandably, Pope Vigilius of Rome (537–555) refused to accept the edict. During the Acacian schism, Zeno and Anastasius had accepted the recalcitrance of the Pope because he was out of reach in the Ostrogothic kingdom. But after the Roman reoccupation of Rome in 536, Vigilius was to discover that opposition to the emperor was more complex than any simplistic story of Ambrose and Theodosius I might suggest. After he had refused to endorse the emperor's view on *The Three Chapters*, Vigilius was arrested by the *scribo* Anthemus in 545, brought to Constantinople, and placed under house arrest. By 550, he was reluctantly prepared to condemn *The Three Chapters*. When the *comes* Diapoundaritses went to the Church of Sergius and Bacchus to summon him to the emperor, "Pope Vigilius went to the Holy sanctuary and the *comes* grasped him by the beard to remove him from there. The bishop held on to the column of the holy altar and the holy altar fell to ground" (Malalas 18.111). Despite being forced to submit, Vigilius soon reverted to his earlier position and excommunicated Menas, patriarch of Constantinople, in 551.

In May and June 553, Justinian summoned a church council to meet in Constantinople. This was attended by 168 bishops, including a handful of African bishops, some from Macedonia and Dacia, but none from Italy. The council condemned Theodoret and thus established a neo-Chalcedonian position. Vigilius, who in 550 had been forced to accept that the condemnation of *The Three Chapters* was not an attack on Chalcedon, now recanted. Justinian's council proceeded to condemn Vigilius. A year later, uncomfortable with the official record that showed his condemnation by 168 bishops, Vigilius decided in 554 that he was in error. Justinian had already shown that he was prepared to rewrite the historical record to condemn the authors of *The Three Chapters*. Now he did the same to protect his attempt to create church unity by having the proceedings of the council rewritten to show that Vigilius had in 553 condemned *The Three Chapters*. Vigilius in 555 was finally permitted to leave Constantinople, where he had lived under semi-arrest for ten years. Western and eastern churches were thus brought into alignment by Justinian, though there was widespread but low-level discontent in the west. Despite the attempts to reach out to the anti-Chalcedonians, the Council of Constantinople did little to resolve the problems in the east.

Justinian's wife Theodora has attracted much attention from historians, usually inspired by the spectacular invective provided by the *Secret History*. Although this picture is obviously exaggerated by Procopius' hostility to

Justinian, many details are still often believed. Theodora is always represented as being a supporter of the anti-Chalcedonians, though her minimal presence in the accounts of the Chalcedonians Malalas and Evagrius contrasts with the enthusiastic mentions of her in the works of the anti-Chalcedonian John of Ephesus. Her known acts, as opposed to imputed influence, were like those of other empresses: building churches and monasteries. There is little evidence for Theodora supporting an anti-Chalcedonian church, and acts such as providing sanctuary in the Palace of Hormisdas for anti-Chalcedonian monks expelled from Chalcedonian monasteries was an act of Christian kindness. Nor, despite her appearance at a meeting during the Nika riot, was Theodora part of the government. She is mentioned in only one of the ca. 160 preserved *Novellae* from Justinian's reign, in *Novella* 8 from 535, when she is named as one of the parties Justinian had consulted before issuing the law. Unlike many other empresses, coins were not minted in Theodora's name.

Justinian was a great collector of imperial victory titles. All emperors had a number of these, but Justinian seems to have made more of his successes than any emperor since the fourth century. After the victories in Africa, his full titles included the names Alamannicus, Gothicus, Francicus, Germanicus, Anticus, Alanicus, Vandalicus, and Africanus. Their use could irritate other monarchs, further evidence of how perceptions of Roman superiority had changed from the fourth to the sixth century. The Frankish king Theodebert was upset at Justinian's holding titles such as Francicus and Alamannicus "as though these peoples had all been enslaved by him" (Agathias 1.4.3).

The devastation following the Nika riot gave Justinian an opportunity for significant building in the heart of the city, especially with the burning down of Theodosius II's church of Hagia Sophia. Probably inspired by Anicia Juliana's construction of St. Polyeuctus, Justinian had a new and ambitious church built by the architects Anthemius of Tralles and Isidore of Miletus. This church still stands today, one of the few Roman buildings to survive intact almost 1,500 years after its construction. Any feelings of insecurity that Anicia Juliana's church might have provoked (and her husband Areobindus had been proposed as emperor during a circus riot in 512) would have been put to rest by this stunning achievement. Justinian and the patriarch Eutychius consecrated the Hagia Sophia on December 27, 537. The lavish marble decoration of this enormous building made it a very expensive undertaking while Justinian also regulated its staff (who also covered three associated churches) in an edict of 535, at a maximum of sixty presbyters, one hundred deacons, forty deaconesses, ninety subdeacons, one hundred readers, twenty-five singers, and one hundred doorkeepers (*Novella* 3).

In the same region, the Great Palace was refurbished. The Chalke, the main entrance to the Palace, opened into a courtyard decorated with colored marbles and mosaics showing Justinian's African victories. Other nearby structures included the subterranean Basilica Cistern (Yerebatan Sarayı) begun at the beginning of the reign and completed in 541. There was also a rebuilding of the Church of the Holy Apostles, with the addition of a second imperial mausoleum. Outside Constantinople, as well as the new city of Justiniana Prima, particularly important buildings included the Church of St. John at Ephesus and the Church of the Nativity in Bethlehem. Justinian also devoted much energy to restoring and repairing the defenses of the Empire. This program was enthusiastically described by Procopius in his *Buildings*, even though he often, as at Dara, attributed work to Justinian that had been carried out by Anastasius or Justin.

Although Procopius tried to suggest that Justinian was a monster, there was very little opposition to his reign. Apart from the Nika riot, there was only one imperial challenger, a certain Julian who was acclaimed as emperor during a Samaritan revolt in 529. Once defeated, his head was sent to Constantinople. A second Samaritan revolt took place in 556, leading to the death of the *consularis* of Palestina Prima, Stephanus, before its suppression. Similarly minor are the two plots known against Justinian. In 548, two Armenians, Artabanes and Arsaces, planned to murder the emperor and put Germanus on the throne. When they approached Germanus' son, he revealed the plot to Marcellus, the *comes excubitorum*. After the conspirators were arrested, there was a trial held before a *silentium cum conventu*. The plotters were treated well and Artabanes was soon pardoned and even given a military command. When Justinian was furious about the delay in the news to elevate Germanus reaching him, "the others cowed by fear remained silent, yielding to him by not opposing his wish; Marcellus alone, however, by speaking with plain directness succeeded in saving the man [Germanus]" (Procopius, *Wars* 7.32.48). In 562, another plot was made to assassinate Justinian, supposedly involving the retired general Belisarius. This was investigated by the Senate, and Belisarius was briefly imprisoned. Justinian had also treated John the Cappadocian generously in 541 when he removed him from office, possibly for plotting against the emperor, simply exiling John to Egypt.

When Justinian died in 565, he was aged eighty-three. He rarely left Constantinople, the only known occasions being late in the reign when he visited Selymbria in Thrace in 559 and in 564 Germia in Anatolia, where there was a church dedicated to the Archangel Michael. Analyses of his reign vary. Some are based heavily on Procopius' *Secret History*, and these tend to be negative. Others focus on the increased western commitments resulting from the Reconquest and, perhaps with a teleological perspective, are also negative. And for a few, Justinian's achievements in reigning long, governing well, and passing on an intact state to his successors rank very highly. He was a gentleman, being merciful to the various plotters, giving deposed kings estates, and even the treatment of the Nika riot seems to have escalated because of an initial reluctance to act harshly. With the end of the reign of Justinian, it is often easy for historians with their roots in the classical world to lose their way. The late sixth century can often feel strangely disconnected from the Roman Empire in a way that Justinian's reign does not. Such a temptation should be avoided, but it shows the success of Justinian in stamping his mark on history.

FURTHER READING

There are a large number of sources for the sixth century. The tradition of classicizing historians writing in Greek continued with Procopius, Agathias, and Menander. Procopius was born in Caesarea in Palestina, educated in Greek and Latin, and trained as a lawyer. In 527, he became the *assessor* of the general Belisarius and accompanied him on the eastern frontier between 527/528 and 531, then went to Constantinople in 532, where he witnessed the Nika riot, and served against the Vandals in Africa (533–536) and against the Goths in Italy (536–540). These experiences were recorded in his *Wars*, which covered Roman campaigns down to 554. Procopius also wrote the *Buildings*, a panegyrical account of Justinian's building activities, and the *Secret History*, a hostile account of his reign. Procopius' *Wars* were continued to 558 by Agathias of Myrina, a lawyer and poet. Agathias' work was in turn continued by Menander the Protector, who wrote a detailed history covering 558–582, now preserved only in fragments, the majority of which cover diplomacy. Marcellinus Comes wrote a Latin chronicle, while other histories are in Syriac, like those of pseudo-Joshua the Stylite, the *Ecclesiastical History* of John of Ephesus, and the heavily edited work of Zachariah of Mytilene. In Greek, later writers include Malalas, who wrote a chronicle focused on the city of Antioch, and Evagrius, who wrote an *Ecclesiastical History*, which continued to 594, though there were also other shorter Latin accounts such as that of the African priest Liberatus.

These histories provide a narrative core to which can be added details from a wide array of sources. There are significant collections of official documents, including a Latin version of the proceedings of the Council at Constantinople in 553, ceremonial guidelines contained in the *De Caeremoniis* (mostly extracted from the work of Peter the Patrician, Justinian's *magister officiorum*), and laws in the *Codex Justinianus*. There is plentiful material regarding ecclesiastical policy in various papal letters in the *Collectio Avellana*, and in Italy both Cassiodorus and Ennodius preserved material relevant to the Gothic court. The *Liber Pontificalis* contains lives of the Popes; from ca. 490 to 530, it was written by contemporaries and preserves a western and low-level ecclesiastical perspective on events. There are also numerous saints' lives, including a large Syriac collection by John of Ephesus and some very long and detailed lives by Cyril of Scythopolis. The copious *Letters of Severus of Antioch* give a good sense of what it meant to be patriarch in the early sixth century. There is much poetry, some like Paul the Silentiary's *Ekphrasis* (Description) on the building of Hagia Sophia being of more historical value than Corippus' epic poem in Latin concerning the campaigns by John Troglita against the Moors in Africa in 546–548. Nonreligious material in prose includes a history of the praetorian prefecture by John the Lydian and a large rhetorically driven *Dialogue on Political Science*, translated by Peter Bell in *Three Political Voices from the Age of Justinian* (Liverpool, 2010).

For a series of stimulating essays on various aspects of the period see Allen, P. and Jeffreys, E. M., eds., *The Sixth Century – End or Beginning?* (Brisbane 1996). For Anastasius, Haarer, F., *Anastasius I: Politics and Empire in the Late Roman World* (Cambridge, 2006), while Greatrex, G., *Rome and Persia at War, 502–532* (Leeds 1998) covers the military history in detail. On Justin, Vasiliev, A. A., *Justin I* (Cambridge, MA, 1950) presents a perspective minimising Justin's independence; for a convincing rebuttal, see Croke, B., "Justinian under Justin: Reconfiguring a Reign," *Byzantinische Zeitschrift* 100 (2007), 13–56.

For Justinian, the best introduction is Maas, M., ed., *The Cambridge Companion to the Age of Justinian* (Cambridge, 2005), with the best single monograph being Evans, J. A. S., *The Age of Justinian* (London, 1996). Justinian's reign is controversial, with some scholars seeing it as a heavily oppressive state, a view strongly expressed by Kaldellis, A., *Procopius of Caesarea: Tyranny, History and Philosophy at the End of Antiquity* (Philadelphia, 2004), Honoré, A., *Tribonian* (London, 1978), and Bell, P., *Social Conflict in the Age of Justinian* (Oxford, 2013). Also recommended are Arjava, A., "The Mystery Cloud of 536 CE in the Mediterranean Sources," *Dumbarton Oaks Papers* 59 (2005), 73–94, Cameron, A., *Circus Factions* (Oxford, 1976), Feissel, D. and I. Kaygusuz. "Un mandement impérial du VI siècle dans une inscription d'Hadrianoupolis d'Honoriade," *Travaux et Mémoires* 9 (1985), 397–419, Foss, C., "The Empress Theodora," *Byzantion* 72 (2002), 141–176, Greatrex, G., "The Nika Riot: A Reappraisal," *Journal of Hellenic Studies* 117 (1997), 60–86, Harrison, M., *A Temple for Byzantium* (London, 1989), Little, L. K., ed., *Plague and the End of Antiquity* (Cambridge, 2007), and Watts, E., "Justinian, Malalas, and the End of Athenian Philosophical Teaching in AD 529," *Journal of Roman Studies* 94 (2004), 168–182. For church politics, see Menze, V., *Justinian and the Making of the Syrian Orthodox Church* (Oxford, 2008), Wood, P., "*We Have No King but Christ": Christian Political Thought in Greater Syria on the Eve of the Arab Conquest (c.400–585)* (Oxford, 2011), as well as Millar, F. G. B., "Rome, Constantinople and the Near Eastern Church under Justinian: Two Synods of C.E. 536," *Journal of Roman Studies* 98 (2008), 62–82, Millar, F. G. B., "Linguistic Co-existence in Constantinople: Greek and Latin (and Syriac) in the Acts of the Synod of 536 C.E.," *Journal of Roman Studies* 99 (2009), 92–103, and Wickham, L. R., "Aspects of Clerical Life in the Early Byzantine Church in Two Scenes: Mopsuestia and Apamaea," *Journal of Ecclesiastical History* 46 (1995), 3–18.

On the Balkans, see Wozniak, F. E., "East Rome, Ravenna and Western Illyricum," *Historia* 30 (1981), 351–382, Curta, F., *The Making of the Slavs: History and Archaeology of the Lower Danube Region, c. 500–700 A.D.* (Cambridge, 2001), and Sarantis, A., *Justinian's Balkan Wars: Campaigns, Diplomacy and Development in Illyricum, Thrace and the Northern World, A.D. 527–65* (Cambridge, 2015).

For society in Italy, see Amory, P., *People and Identity in Ostrogothic Italy, 489–554* (Cambridge, 1997). For Egypt, McCoull, L., *Dioscurus of Aphrodito: His Work and His World* (Berkeley, 1988), Salomon, R., "A Papyrus from Constantinople (Hamburg Inv. No. 410)," *Journal of Egyptian Archaeology* 34 (1948), 98–108, Sarris, P., *Economy and Society in the Age of Justinian* (Cambridge, 2009), and Van Minnen, P., "Dioscurus and the Law," in MacDonald, A. A., et al., eds., *Learned Antiquity* (Louvain, 2003), 115–134.

9

THE LATE SIXTH CENTURY, 565–610

After Justinian's death in 565, the revenue from the Empire was mostly spent on maintaining the status quo. The reconquest of Africa and Italy had increased the military demands on the Empire without a corresponding increase in resources, although the need to defend Italy against the Lombards could not have been foreseen. Because the Empire did not have the resources to fight effectively in Italy, in the Balkans, and against Persia, concentrating significant forces in one region meant depriving other regions of resources, often precipitating further crises. This already difficult situation was made worse by the arrival of the Avars in the Balkans, with the Turks looming behind them. Nonetheless, by the end of the sixth century, the frontiers were in the same place as they were at Justinian's death, and Mauricius could feel confident of further success. This promising situation was then overturned when Phocas seized power in 602.

JUSTIN II (565–578)

At the death of Justinian in the Great Palace of Constantinople on November 14, 565, the only official present was Callinicus, the *praepositus sacri cubiculi* and *sacellarius*. He claimed that Justinian had named Justin, one of the emperor's three nephews, as his heir. Justin was certainly a convenient choice, being married to Sophia, a niece of Theodora, and he had held the office of *cura palatii* since 552. Another nephew, Marcian, might have been a contender, but he was in North Africa and thus far away. Justin rapidly entered the Great Palace, where the *excubitores* under their *comes* Tiberius provided security. Justinian's death was only announced after Justin was crowned by the patriarch John Scholasticus (565–577). On November

15, the new emperor appeared to the crowd in the Hippodrome as Augustus, and on November 16, his wife Sophia was acclaimed *Augusta*. This swift and decisive action headed off any possible response by another potential heir, also named Justin, the son of Justinian's cousin Germanus, who was currently serving on the Danube as *magister militum per Illyricum*. Evagrius records that the two Justins had made an agreement that whoever became emperor would continue to honor the other. However, the emperor did not keep this agreement, but removed his cousin from office and sent him to Alexandria, where he was soon executed. Justin and Sophia had no sons, but their daughter Arabia was married to Baduarius, who was soon made *cura palatii* and *patricius*, so marking him as a likely successor.

Justin was faced with several immediate problems. Although he claimed that "We found the treasury burdened with many debts and reduced to utter exhaustion," he was confident enough to cancel any taxes still unpaid from 560 or earlier (*Novella* 148 preface). In 566, two senators, Aetherius (who had been twice acquitted of plotting against Justinian) and Addaeus (urban prefect in 565), were executed after they were accused of planning to poison Justin. Both had earlier been accused of recommending the magician Masidies to Justinian (who had him burned to death) and were involved at the end of Justinian's reign in the exiling of Eutychius, patriarch of Constantinople, to Amasya in 565. Addaeus denied the plot to murder the emperor, but admitted to being guilty of the murder in 548 of the eastern praetorian prefect Theodotus. Justinian appears to have been able to accept such restlessness among his subordinates, but at the start of his reign Justin was far less secure on his throne. Justin was a generous distributor of relics, giving fragments of the True Cross to Pope John III (561–574) and to the Gallic nun Radegund of Poitiers. In the Great Palace, he built a new ceremonial dining room known as the Chrysotriklinos. Here, a portrait of Christ was placed above the emperor's throne, a firmer statement of the relationship between the Empire and Christianity than had existed before. Relics continued to be imported to Constantinople, like the Kamouliana, an icon of Christ from a village in Cappadocia. In 569, he extended Justinian's Pragmatic Sanction of 554, which gave responsibility to local bishops and aristocrats to recommend candidates for provincial governorships to the emperor to cover the whole Empire. Other laws were more pedestrian, such as a law of 572 dealing with the rights of Samaritans, still banned from military service, civil office, and teaching (*Novella* 144).

In terms of religious policy, he inherited an Empire that was still divided over Chalcedon, a division exacerbated by the rise during Justinian's reign of a parallel anti-Chalcedonian church with its own bishops. Justin began by attempting to reunite the churches, releasing the imprisoned anti-Chalcedonians and allowing the exiled bishops to return. In 566, he issued a statement of faith that retained *The Three Chapters* (i.e., the anathemas of Theodoret, Theodore, and Ibas), annulled any anathemas passed on Severus of Antioch, and made no explicit mention of Chalcedon. Like Zeno's *Henotikon*, his statement said nothing about Chalcedon, and though acceptable to the moderates it failed to satisfy the extremists of both beliefs. At the same time, the anti-Chalcedonian leader Jacob Baradaeus came to Constantinople for negotiations, although the prolonged discussion had no immediate results. Moreover, the emerging lack of anti-Chalcedonian unity meant that Jacob could not guarantee that any settlement that he negotiated would be accepted by others. The anti-Chalcedonians were already split between the followers of Severus and of Julian, but there now emerged Tritheists, concerned that the three elements of the Trinity were not sufficiently distinct within the formulation of God. Justin's position was considered at an imperially ordered council of anti-Chalcedonians at Callinicum in 567. Although this position was supported by Jacob Baradaeus and many priests and bishops, others, particularly the monks, refused to endorse it. With the failure of negotiation, Justin began persecuting the anti-Chalcedonians, targeting priests and bishops and purging monasteries. Two of the bishops consecrated by Jacob Baradaeus, Conon of Tarsus and Eugenius of Seleucia, were arrested and excommunicated in 569 and then sent to prison in Palestina in 571. Other bishops who had been appointed through normal processes were also deposed, including Patriarch Anastasius of Antioch in 570. In these persecutions, there was such close cooperation between the Constantinopolitan patriarch John Scholasticus (565–577) and the *quaestor* Anastasius that some anti-Chalcedonians even accused Anastasius of being a pagan. At the same time as the persecutions, a second imperial statement of faith, also known as the *Henotikon*, was issued in 571 that returned to the neo-Chalcedonian approach from the end of Justinian's reign.

Justin's foreign concerns can be divided into the Balkans, the west, and Persia. In the western Balkans, the Romans were faced with several major powers. North of the upper Danube in the Great Hungarian Plain were the Avars, led by the Chagan Baian. South and west of the Danube in Pannonia were the Lombards, led by Alboin. Finally, the Gepids, led by Cunimund, held the important Pannonian city of Sirmium as well as some of the Great Hungarian Plain and were in conflict with the Lombards. Within a week of his accession, Justin had received envoys from the Avars. They had first appeared to the Romans in the late 550s in the Danube basin. The Avar Chaganate was very similar to the Hunnic Empire and proved to be similarly short-lived. They received annual Roman subsidies during much of the late sixth century, producing a society that benefited more from threatening war than from waging it. During the frequent diplomacy with the Romans, the Chagan was especially concerned to receive gifts, which he then distributed to his followers. However, Justin refused to pay the subsidies that the Avars had received from the previous emperor; as with Marcian's firm treatment of the Huns in 450, there was no immediate reaction. At the same time, the Gepid king Cunimund appealed to Justin for help against the Lombards, promising in return to hand over Sirmium to the Romans. With the help of a Roman force led by Justin's son-in-law Baduarius, Cunimund defeated the Lombards, but then refused to hand over Sirmium. When the defeated Lombards turned to the Avars for assistance, Cunimund gave up Sirmium in 568 in return for more Roman help. Justin occupied Sirmium, but then left the Gepids to the mercy of the Lombards and Avars. The abandoned Gepids did not last long and after their defeat, Alboin turned Cunimund's head into a drinking cup and married his daughter Rosimunda.

Any Roman feelings of satisfaction with regaining control of Sirmium did not last long. In 568, Alboin led the Lombards out of Pannonia into northern Italy. This region was still recovering from three decades of fighting, and Roman forces had been run down after the end of the Gothic war in 554. There was thus little Roman resistance, and the Lombards quickly occupied the Po Valley, though Ticinum held out under siege for three years. The Lombards had little unity as a people, and Alboin was murdered in 573 in a failed revolt led by his wife Rosimunda, supposedly after she had been asked to drink from the cup made from her father's skull. After Alboin's successor Cleph was murdered in 574, the Lombard kingdom disintegrated. Some dukes remained in the Po Valley, but others drifted south with their retinues and founded dukedoms, the most successful being at Spoletum and Beneventum. Rome and Ravenna, however, remained under Roman control, as well as a thin strip between them, and there were additional Roman enclaves at Naples and in Liguria, Calabria, and Sicily. These cities were still part of the Empire, and even after the Lombard attacks Justin ordered grain to be sent to Rome from Egypt to relieve a famine. However, the Lombard occupation meant that the opportunities offered by the reconquest were lost. Instead of bringing resources into the Empire, Italy was draining them from it. In the Balkans, now that the Gepids had been destroyed and the Lombards had entered Italy, the Avars were left as the dominant power. They immediately attempted to expand their territory by trying to capture Sirmium in 568, wounding the *magister militum per Illyricum* Bonus in the battle. Bonus was then replaced by Tiberius, holding the combined position of *magister militum* for the imperial field army and *comes excubitorum*. At first, he won some successes, but after an Avar victory in 571 Justin made peace.

Elsewhere in the west, there were continuing difficulties. In Spain, the Roman provinces came under attack from the Visigothic king Leovigild (568–586), who captured Malaga, Asidona, and Cordoba between 569 and 571, but in 572 made peace. In Africa, the Moorish king Garmules led a major revolt in which the praetorian prefect Theodore was killed in 569, the *magister militum* Theoctistus was killed in 570, and his replacement Amabilis was killed in 571. After the *magister militum per Africam* Gennadius finally defeated Garmules in 578, he remained in Africa for the next twenty years. Although all of the western provinces were still part of the Empire, they were less of a priority for Justin than the Danubian and eastern frontiers, and resources were sent only when available, not when they were needed.

JUSTIN AND PERSIA

After peace was made with the Avars in 571, Justin turned his attention to the east. Although peace had been made with the Persians in 562, Suania in the Caucasus, north of Lazica, was disputed between Rome and Persia. Then in 572, Justin refused to pay the Persians the next payment required by the 562 treaty. There were various reasons for Justin's provocation of the Persians. When the Persians tried to erect a Zoroastrian fire temple at Dvin, a Christian city in Persarmenia, the Persarmenians, led by Vardan Maimikonian, revolted; killed the Persian *marzpan* stationed there; and sent his head to Justinian, *magister militum per Armeniam*, at Theodosiopolis in Mesopotamia. Justin could now claim to be acting on behalf of the Christian Persarmenians, who were soon joined in revolt by Iberia. There was also tension in Mesopotamia caused by conflict between Saracens allied to the two powers and fears following the Persian occupation of Himyar (Yemen) in 570. A final factor was the appearance of a new people on the steppes, the Turks, who were moving west from central Asia. The Turks came into contact with both Rome and Persia, but following the poisoning of a Turkish embassy by the Persians, in 568 their ruler Sizabulus sent envoys to Constantinople, making an alliance that lasted until 576. The Turks were so far from the Roman world that when Zemarchus was sent to them to negotiate in 569, he had to travel more than three thousand kilometers from the Crimea to reach Sizabulus. This distance meant they were useful to the Romans as a threat to the Persians and the Avars, but were not yet close enough to be a problem themselves.

Justin had good reasons to go to war with Persia, but there were equally good reasons not to fight. The list of current crises was long, and financially the Empire was still recovering from the costs of Justinian's wars. In particular, fighting in the east meant neglecting the Balkans and sacrificing Italy to the Lombards. Nonetheless, Justin chose to seize the opportunity offered by the Persarmenian revolt. In the decades that followed, the consequences of this decision became clear, though Justin probably did not expect the war to last for nineteen years. At first, the war against the surprised Persians went well for the Romans, led by the *magister militum per Orientem* Marcian, Justin's cousin, but when Marcian besieged Nisibis in 573, his failure to achieve rapid success led to his replacement by Theodore Tzirus and the abandonment of the siege. By this point, two Persian armies had been mobilized. One, under Adarmahan, ravaged Syria, sacking Apamea and plundering the suburbs of Antioch. The other, led by Xusro himself, besieged Dara, which fell after a five-month siege on November 15, 573. Prisoners and plunder were taken to Persia, and it was said that some of the prisoners were sent as gifts to the Turks.

When news of the fall of Dara arrived in Constantinople, the emperor lost his sanity. Justin II's illness was extremely debilitating, with moments where physical restraint was required to stop him harming himself and others. He assaulted his son-in-law Baduarius in a meeting of the *silentium*, and John of Ephesus recorded many disturbing stories before adding, "the whole senate and city, natives as well as foreigners, bear witness to the truth and exactness of our details: and that much besides happened, too unseemly to be recorded in writing" (*HE* 3.2). Justin continued to have lucid intervals until his death and was clearly aware that he was ill. John interpreted this as Justin's punishment by God for persecuting the anti-Chalcedonians, whereas Evagrius claimed that "he did not endure what had happened like a mortal" (5.11.1). There was no precedent for a Roman emperor suffering from mental illness and no hope of a swift resolution. In this unusual situation, his wife, the Augusta Sophia, suddenly became an important figure in the palace. This attracted hostility, with the contemporary historians John of Ephesus and Evagrius both portraying her in a hostile light, claiming that Sophia turned to a Jewish doctor, Timotheus, supposedly also a magician, for help. After a year in which the direction of the Empire was uncertain, Justin in one of his lucid spells appointed Tiberius as Caesar on December 7, 574.

JUSTIN II HANDS POWER OVER TO TIBERIUS

According to Evagrius, Tiberius was adopted as Justin's son and acclaimed as Caesar "at the prompting of Sophia" (5.13.1), but John of Ephesus records that "the whole Senate took counsel with the empress," and then "they chose and appointed Tiberius as Caesar" (*HE* 3.5). This involved passing over

Justin's son-in-law Baduarius, *comes stabuli* and, like Tiberius, with military experience. There was some tension between Justin and Baduarius, following a fight between them in the consistory, and this may be why he was not chosen. John of Ephesus then described how Justin,

> weeping, and with his words broken by tears and sobs, said, "O son Tiberius, come and take the kingdom of the wretched Justin, who has made God angry, so that he has rejected him, and cast him out of his royal estate while still living. Come, my son, enter upon your office, and displace him who has set his Creator at nought, that Creator who gave him the kingdom, from which his own eyes now see him rejected and fallen." And when he thus spoke with a loud voice in the presence of the many thousands assembled there, all who heard his words broke out into bitter weeping and loud sobs ... These words, and many more to the same effect, but which we have omitted because of their too great length, were spoken by the king ... and then he invested [Tiberius] with the insignia and dress and emblems of royalty (John of Ephesus, *HE* 3.5).

Despite the sadness, there was still the full-scale imperial ceremonial. Tiberius put on the imperial garments, was crowned by the patriarch John Scholasticus, and then distributed gifts. After the ceremonies, the hard work of ruling the Empire began.

Tiberius, born in a Latin-speaking region of Thrace, had been *comes excubitorum* in 565 before the death of Justinian and was instrumental in the accession of Justin II. He continued to hold this post until his promotion to Caesar in 574, fighting against the Avars in two campaigns. Immediately after his acclamation, Tiberius began ruling the Empire directly, although he consulted with Justin whenever the emperor's illness allowed. He rapidly earned a reputation for generosity, spending 7,200 pounds of gold in his first year as emperor, as well as remitting a portion of taxes and abolishing Justin's levy on holders of the bread tickets in Constantinople and his tax on the import of wine (in response to a petition). Differing interpretations of what imperial wealth was for are nicely shown by a supposed exchange between Sophia and Tiberius. When Sophia complained that "'all that we by great industry and care have gathered and stored up, you are scattering to the winds as with a fan', he said to her 'what you collected by iniquity and plunder and rapine I am doing my best that not a fragment of it may remain in my palace'" (John of Ephesus, *HE* 3.14). Since Sophia was determined to maintain her own position as Augusta and as wife of the emperor, it is not surprising that relations between her and Tiberius soon became difficult. As long as Justin was alive, Sophia refused to let Tiberius bring his wife, Ino, into the Great Palace, forcing her to live instead in the Palace of Hormisdas.

Contemporary claims that Sophia hoped to marry Tiberius or that she was conspiring with Justinian, the son of Germanus, to replace him may reflect popular gossip, but seem unlikely to have any basis in reality. Outside the palace, no one was in any doubt that Tiberius was now ruling the Empire.

In 575, Tiberius was able to organize a one-year peace with the Persians in Mesopotamia, but specifically excluding Armenia, in exchange for a payment of 45,000 *solidi*. Xusro may have been persuaded to make peace by a personal letter from Sophia, as claimed by Evagrius, but the diplomacy was conducted by the Roman envoys Zacharias and then Trajan in traditional fashion. Taking advantage of this lull, Tiberius began an extensive recruiting campaign, as well as conducting operations in the Caucasus. When the one-year peace treaty expired, a three-year extension was negotiated with the Romans making annual payments of 30,000 *solidi*. As the peace continued to exclude Armenia, in 575 the Persians under Xusro besieged Theodosiopolis and then captured Sebaste and Melitene. In response, the *magister militum per Orientem* Justinian (son of Germanus and brother of the Justin executed at Alexandria) pursued the Persians to Melitene, capturing many elephants, which were then taken to Constantinople and used for imperial displays. John of Ephesus described how they were trained to make the sign of the cross with their trunks in front of the emperor in the Hippodrome (*HE* 2.48). Justinian then continued operations in Hyrcania on the southern coast of the Caspian Sea, wintering there over 575. Following a further Persian offensive in Armenia in 577, Justinian was recalled, and Tiberius appointed the *comes excubitorum*, Mauricius, to serve as *magister militum per Orientem* in charge of the entire eastern front. In 578, shortly before the 575 peace treaty would have ended, both Romans and Persians were preparing for a resumption of hostilities. The Persians invaded Roman territory in Mesopotamia forty days before the end of the treaty, but Mauricius then counterattacked, capturing Singara.

Although Tiberius' priorities were Persia and the Balkans, there were attempts to reconquer the Lombard-occupied parts of Italy. In 576, Justin's son-in-law Baduarius fought against them, dying during the campaign. Then in 578, the Italian *patricius* Pamphronius came to Constantinople, asking for the emperor to send further troops. Tiberius had no men available, so gave Pamphronius three thousand pounds of gold, either to buy Lombard allies to fight against Persia or to induce Frankish leaders to fight against the Lombards. Both policies were well founded, as some Lombards were recruited to fight against the Persians and King Childebert, following several Lombard attacks on Francia, later entered Italy on behalf of Rome. Further trouble was brewing north of the Black Sea as the Turks drifted west. After Sizabulus' death, his successor Turxanthus accused the Romans of "having flattered and deluded all the tribes with your various speeches and your treacherous designs ... To lie is alien to a Turk and your emperor shall pay me the necessary penalty" (Menander fr. 19.1). They captured the city of Bosporus in the Crimea around 576, though the Romans retained control of the city of Chersonesus (Sevastopol). Tiberius spent little time on religious policies. When Eutychius, exiled in 565, restored as patriarch of Constantinople in 577, "daily visited him and incited him against the heretics, he at length answered 'trouble me about such things no more: I have as much as I can do with the wars I am engaged in'" (John of Ephesus, *HE* 3.21). Nonetheless, he did continue Justin's persecutions of the anti-Chalcedonians. There was now a reluctant acceptance in the east of two separate churches, one Chalcedonian, the other anti-Chalcedonian. Nonetheless, the inadequacies of Chalcedon as a doctrinal statement were also understood. Despite the differences, there were still real possibilities of forging a consensus between the pro- and anti-Chalcedonian factions.

TIBERIUS II (578–582)

In a final moment of service to the Empire, Justin proclaimed Tiberius as Augustus on September 26, 578. He died less than two weeks later on the night of October 4 and was buried in the Church of the Holy Apostles. Tiberius moved Ino into the Great Palace, acclaimed her Augusta, and renamed her Anastasia. Sophia was immediately forced to move into the Palace of the Sophianae, where she lived on into Mauricius' reign. Tiberius then remitted a year's taxation, but not the *annona militaris*, which brought immediate popularity, though at a cost in much-needed revenue.

Tiberius continued to focus most of his energy and resources on the Persian frontier, trying to manage the Balkans by diplomacy. In 578, he arranged for a large Avar force, described by Menander as sixty thousand cavalry, to be escorted from Pannonia through the Empire to the lower Danube, then ferried across the river to attack the Slavs. In 579, Tiberius paid a subsidy of eighty thousand *solidi* (ca. 1,100 pounds of gold) to the Avars for peace, though Baian then broke the treaty and made another attempt on Sirmium in 580. Tiberius at this point refused to surrender the city, claiming that "I would rather betroth to him one of my two daughters than willingly hand over the city of Sirmium" (Menander fr.25.2). The Avars began to blockade the city, and by 582, despite his rhetoric, Tiberius agreed to surrender Sirmium. Though he evacuated the population, he was forced to pay the three years' worth of subsidies unpaid since 579. Slavs also began to invade the Balkans, reaching Greece and Thrace. Raiding had been common from the mid-sixth century, but some Slavs were beginning to spend winters in Roman territory.

Meanwhile in the east, the new Persian king, Hormizd IV (579–590), refused to agree to a new peace treaty with the Romans. There was no significant campaigning in 579, but Mauricius followed up his earlier successes by ravaging Mesopotamia in 580. These campaigns also involved working with local Saracen leaders, including al-Mundhir, who visited Constantinople in 580 and was awarded the title *patricius*. Then in 581, Mauricius fought his way down the Euphrates as far as Ctesiphon, the first Roman army to reach the Persian capital since Julian in 363. Mauricius then withdrew because the Persian general Adarmahan attacked Osrhoene from Armenia, but defeated him in 582 at Constantia.

With growing confidence following the military recovery, Tiberius continued the persecutions of the anti-Chalcedonians. However, following the deaths of Jacob Baradaeus in 578 and of Paul of Antioch in 581, there were again some hopes of reconciling the supporters and opponents of Chalcedon. But Tiberius also had other religious problems to deal with at a local level. In 579, Anatolius, who was both *praeses* of Osrhoene and *vicarius* of the eastern praetorian prefect, was alleged to have attended a festival of the pagan god Zeus in Edessa. Following his arrest in the house of the bishop of Edessa, Anatolius was transported to Antioch for trial, and an imperial official by the name of Theophilus conducted an enquiry. At the trial, the Chalcedonian patriarch Gregory of Antioch was alleged to be a pagan and to have participated in human sacrifice. Following riots in Antioch, the case was transferred to Constantinople. The trial in front of the urban prefect Sebastianus took place in the Palace of Placidia, close to the Golden Horn. Here, the trial resulted in a light sentence, and there were accusations that Gregory had been acquitted through bribery. Outraged, the Constantinopolitan mob rioted and broke into the palace looking for the supposed pagans. Tiberius eventually appeased the rioters by dismissing Sebastianus, though he also summoned troops into the city. Once the rioters had dispersed, he summoned the Senate to review the records of the trial, after which Anatolius was condemned to the beasts.

In the summer of 582, Tiberius fell ill. With no son of his own, he turned to his most successful general, Mauricius, *magister militum per Orientem*, who was acclaimed Caesar on August 5, 582, and betrothed to his daughter Constantina. As his illness worsened, Tiberius crowned Mauricius as Augustus on August 13 and then died at the Hebdomon on August 14, being buried in the Church of the Holy Apostles.

MAURICIUS (582–602)

Mauricius was born at Arabissus (Afşin) in the province of Armenia Secunda in 539. Originally a notary, he had been made *comes excubitorum*, probably in 574, and then *magister militum per Orientem* in 577. From this point, he gained much military experience, even writing a clear and practical handbook for generals, the *Strategikon*. Mauricius eventually had nine children with Constantina, though none would be in a position to succeed him for some time.

At his accession, Mauricius was faced with significant financial problems, finding the treasuries empty, "as if swept by a broom" (John of Ephesus, *HE* 5.20). One response was an attempt to cut military expenditure, with Mauricius proposing to reduce pay by 25 percent in 588 and in 593, reducing military allowances and attempting to deny booty taken in battle to soldiers. However, shortages of money did not mean that there was no money. Mauricius spent lavishly on Arabissus, providing it with a new cathedral and other churches, a hospice, civic basilica, porticoes, and a city wall, and then repaired buildings here and at Antioch when both cities were struck by an earthquake in 588. In Constantinople, he continued several buildings started by Tiberius, including a bath at Blachernae and the Church of the Forty Martyrs. Most significantly, he added a large icon of Christ to the already crowded façade of the Chalke, festooned with statues of emperors, philosophers, and generals. Like Justin II's addition of a portrait of Christ over the throne in the Chrysotriklinos, this was a significant statement of the relationship of the Empire to Christianity. And like Justin, he was concerned about relics. In 594, his wife Constantina requested a relic of St. Paul, preferably the head, from Pope Gregory for a church in the palace. Gregory refused, though he was prepared to send her some of the chains of St. Peter (*Ep.* 4.30).

There were several administrative changes during Tiberius' reign. One was the creation of exarchates in Africa and Italy, replacing the *magister militum* and praetorian prefect with a single official who combined civil and military duties. In Africa, the first such figure was the previous *magister militum* Gennadius, in Italy Decius. *Magistri militum* continued to exist in these areas, but they were now subordinate to the exarch. At the end of his reign, the *Chronicon Paschale* mentions Constantine Lardys, an ex-praetorian prefect holding another newly attested office, that of *logothete*, head of a financial office. This is the first mention of this post, which like the emergence of the *sacellarius* is suggestive of significant change in the financial organization of the Empire.

Like Tiberius, Mauricius followed a strongly pro-Chalcedonian policy, though he was prepared to make some concessions. Persecution of anti-Chalcedonians continued, particularly by the emperor's nephew Domitianus, who had been appointed bishop of Melitene in 580. Extreme measures were sometimes taken, leading the chronicler Michael the Syrian to claim that four hundred monks who refused to reject anti-Chalcedonian ideas were executed at Edessa in Syria in 598. Conflict with the Pope flared again when the proceedings of the trial of Gregory of Antioch were sent to Rome. As he read these, Pelagius II (579–590) was outraged to discover the use of the title ecumenical (i.e., universal) by the patriarch of Constantinople, though this was by no means an innovation. Pelagius' anger over this issue was inherited by Pope Gregory (590–604).

Mauricius was more concerned to manage events in the west than Tiberius had been. Little is known of Africa, though Gennadius was promoted to exarch there, serving to at least 598. Rome was still hanging on to the province of Spania, and although Cordoba was lost in 584, Comentiolus in 589 repaired the walls at Carthago Nova. In Italy, the main problem was in keeping the Lombards under control. Mauricius paid the Frankish king Childebert fifty thousand *solidi* to attack them in 584. Although Childebert exacted tribute from the Lombards, the Lombards also recreated their monarchy and in 584 acclaimed Cleph's son Authari as king (584–590). Other Lombards deserted to the Romans, such as Droctulf (born a Suevian), who first occupied Brixellum and then led Roman troops, including a fleet, near Ravenna. These successes allowed Smaragdus, exarch of Italy, to negotiate a three-year peace with the Lombards in 585. Although central Italy was now mostly held by the Lombards, the strip connecting Rome and Ravenna remained in Roman hands. The Franks fought again against the Lombards in 587 and 588. With the arrival of a new exarch, Romanus, in 589, there were sustained Roman efforts, also aided by Frankish allies, to regain control of the Po Valley. Despite recapturing a number of cities, the lack of men and money meant Romanus was not able to challenge the Lombards in battle. The new Lombard king Agilulf (590–616) attacked Rome in 593, briefly laying siege to it. Gregory even negotiated his own truce with the Lombards, against Mauricius' wishes. After Romanus' death ca. 595, peace negotiations were finally completed by the exarch Callinicus in 598, though this lasted only until 601. During this period, Gregory's letters and other documents show the continuing functioning of the Roman state in Italy, including the maintenance of the imperial palace in Rome, though it also shows his continuous nudging of Roman officials and of his own representative in Constantinople. Thus in 596 Gregory wrote to Mauricius' wife, complaining that the governor of Sardinia was being bribed by pagans to overlook their activities. Gregory's letters also show the arrival of a certain Leontius in Sicily in 598, sent by the emperor to investigate accusations of corruption among recent imperial officials in the island. The difficulties of Italy at this period are well illustrated when he wrote to bishop Sebastianus of Sirmium:

> … most holy brother we are hardly able to describe what we suffer in this land from the person of your friend, the lord Romanus. Yet I may briefly say that his malice towards us has exceeded the swords of the Lombards; so that the enemies who kill us seem kinder than the governors of the republic who by their malice, pillage, and lies wear us out with anxiety (*Ep.* 5.42).

These problems were not confined to Italy, of course, and third-century Romans had said similar unkind things about their governors. And Gregory could also be a realist, aware that in Africa he had little influence and that the commands of the emperor were necessary to deal with the Donatists (*Ep.* 6.65), while in 598 we find him forwarding an imperial law to several bishops regarding restrictions on soldiers becoming priests or monks (*Ep.* 8.5).

In general, however, events in the west were a lower priority than the Danubian and eastern regions, where Mauricius sent the family members that he often used as generals, especially his brother Petrus and his brother-in-law Philippicus. In the Balkans, Mauricius was on the defensive in the first part of his reign. The Avars under the Chagan Baian had already forced Tiberius to surrender Sirmium in 582. Then in 583, they occupied Singidunum, the next major city to the east, and demanded an increase in their annual subsidy to one hundred thousand *solidi* before they returned the city to the Romans. As well as the Avars, there was also continued raiding by the Slavs. Mauricius himself led an army against the Slavs in 584, the first Roman emperor to lead troops for over a century. In 584 and 585, other generals won successes against the Slavs and recovered Roman prisoners. In 586, the Chagan led a raid along the Danube as far as Marcianopolis, capturing several cities, though he was pursued by an army under Comentiolus. An Avar attack on Thessalonica was also repulsed. Comentiolus was later replaced by John Mystacon, who won a victory against the Avars in 587 at Adrianople. In 588, Priscus was appointed *magister militum per Thracias*. The Slavs and Avars besieged Singidunum unsuccessfully, then advanced toward Constantinople, reaching Heraclea, where they briefly laid siege to Priscus' army before making peace with the Romans and withdrawing. There then followed a five-year lull in operations in the Balkans, allowing Mauricius to concentrate his resources on the east.

Although most of our information about the Balkans at this period concerns wars, it was still a region of Roman cities, governors, and bishops. In 593, a dispute between bishop Adrian of Thebes in Achaea and some of his clergy escalated when Adrian refused to accept the judgment of his metropolitan, John of Larissa. After this,

> John and Cosmas, deacons who had been deposed from their office, one for frailty of the body and the other for fraudulent dealing with ecclesiastical property, had sent a representation to our most pious emperors against [Adrian], with respect to financial matters and also criminal charges. [The emperors] in their commands sent to you [Bishop John of Justiniana Prima] desired you, that is with strict observance of law and canons, to take cognizance of the matter so as to pass a sentence firm in law as to the financial questions, but, as to the criminal charges, to report to their Clemency after a searching examination (Gregory, *Ep.* 3.7).

Following John's investigation, he deposed Adrian, who then traveled to Rome to appeal to Gregory. After Adrian's arrival, Gregory wrote to both John of Larissa and John of Justiniana Prima, though his outrage at Adrian's treatment does not fit well with his lack of investigation of the case, a striking difference between the attitudes of the Pope and the emperor (*Ep.* 3.6–7). And since we do not have any material laying out the opposing case, it is likely that both Johns would have told a different story.

In the east, Mauricius did not follow the offensive strategy he had used in 581 but was more conservative. The majority of the fighting was in Mesopotamia, where after a defeat by the Persians near Martyropolis, John Mystacon, *magister militum per Orientem*, was replaced in 584 by Philippicus, Mauricius' brother-in-law and *comes excubitorum*. Following much raiding by both sides, in 586 Philippicus won the Battle of Solachon near Dara; his officers included Heraclius, father of the later emperor. Philippicus was succeeded as *magister militum per Orientem* in 588 by Priscus, who had barely arrived when he was faced with a mutiny following Mauricius' attempt to reduce military allowances. Priscus was forced to leave the camp, and the portraits of Mauricius were torn down. The patriarch of Antioch, Gregory, was instrumental in persuading the mutineers to return to obedience. Philippicus was restored to command, but before he could return, some of the mutinous troops betrayed Martyropolis to the Persians. Other mutineers, however, under Germanus won a victory over the Persians near Martyropolis and then returned to loyalty to the emperor. Soon afterward, Philippicus was replaced by Comentiolus, who in 589 defeated the Persians in battle at Sisarbanon near Nisibis. A revolt in Armenia was also suppressed by other Roman troops under Domnentziolus. The successful progress of the war in Mesopotamia was then overtaken by political events in Persia. In 589, Suania was occupied by a Persian force under Bahram, who had earlier won a significant victory over the Turks. But when Bahram advanced on Lazica, he was defeated by a Roman force under Romanus. Bahram was dismissed but then successfully revolted against King Hormizd IV in 590 and executed him. However, after Bahram refused to accept Hormizd's son Xusro as king, Xusro fled to the Roman Empire. He and his retinue, including his wives and their children, were received at Circesium by the Roman garrison commander Probus. From here, Xusro wrote an appeal for Roman support to restore him to his throne. This was sent to Mauricius in Constantinople and accompanied by Probus' report on the situation. This package went first to Hierapolis, where Comentiolus, *magister militum per Orientem*, added his own assessment of the situation before forwarding it to the imperial city.

When the various despatches arrived in Constantinople, Mauricius read them with joy. Theophylact claims that his account preserves the appeal "word for word," which is quite possible as his source for this section of his history is John of Epiphania, who had served on an embassy to Persia after the restoration of Xusro. Orders were immediately sent to Comentiolus to treat Xusro as a king. He was thus entertained by various local notables. In Edessa, this was taken as an opportunity by two local aristocrats Ioannes and Marinus to compete over who could give the best banquet for the exiled king.

Xusro, when his appeal produced no immediate imperial response, then requested to travel to Constantinople himself. Following an exchange of messengers, this was forbidden by Mauricius. Finally, a formal embassy was sent by Xusro, which Mauricius received in the consistory. The Persian ambassadors offered the terms of ceding Martyropolis and Dara and the Persian claims to Armenia. As well as the usual officials, such meetings now normally included the patriarch, in this case John IV the Faster (585–592). Mauricius' choosing to receive the embassy was, in itself, significant.

We have differing versions of the meeting of the consistory. In the version preserved by John of Nikiu, the patriarch thought that Xusro had caused the death of his father King Hormizd and so spoke against him. In this version, Mauricius rejected the advice of both John the Faster and his officials ("all the magistrates and officers"; John of Nikiu 96.9–13). Sebeos' version has Mauricius summoning the Senate (*synkletos*), which also advised him to reject the appeal, on the basis that the Persians were impious and it would be better for Rome if they were weakened by the civil war. In this tradition too, Mauricius overruled his advisers (Sebeos chapter 2, p. 15). Like Justinian's decision to attack Africa, this was a moment of great personal leadership by Mauricius. Rather than avoiding a decision, he made a positive choice to support a fellow legitimate monarch against a rebel.

Following the meeting of the consistory, a letter was sent to Xusro with the emperor's decision, as well as news of his being assigned a

Roman bodyguard of one thousand men. In 591, Mauricius had replaced Comentiolus with Narses, who led a combined force of Roman troops and Persian exiles into Mesopotamia to restore Xusro. Having joined forces with John Mystacon, *magister militum per Armeniam*, Narses pushed farther east into Media and defeated Bahram at the Battle of Blarathon. Xusro II (590–628) now sat again on the Persian throne. The peace treaty restored Armenia and the eastern part of Mesopotamia, including Dara and Martyropolis, to Rome. After this, there was peace on the Persian frontier for the rest of the reign of Mauricius, allowing him to transfer troops to concentrate on the Danubian frontier.

With peace in the East and the arrival of reinforcements, Mauricius was able to begin restoring Roman control of the Balkans. In 593, the *magister militum per Thracias* Priscus began an offensive across the Danube against the Slavs. Roman forces used pontoon bridges to cross the Danube and ravage Slav territory, taking numerous prisoners and booty. However, his demand to give much of this plunder to the imperial family resulted in so much discontent that Priscus was unable to follow Mauricius' orders that the army winter across the Danube. Priscus was briefly replaced by Peter, who campaigned against the Slavs north of the Danube in 594, but he returned as *magister militum per Thracias* in 595 and again crossed the Danube. He then abandoned the Slavic war to recapture Singidunum from the Avars. After a short lull, hostilities with the Avars continued in 597, when they boldly attacked Tomi on the Black Sea coast, striking deep into Roman territory. The Avars were eventually forced to retreat rather than get caught between Priscus with the Thracian army and Comentiolus, leading elements of the imperial army from Constantinople, although they roughly handled the latter near Drizipera. Peace was then made with the Avars again, with Mauricius paying 120,000 *solidi* annually. In 599, the armies of Priscus and Comentiolus moved to Singidunum and from here crossed the Danube into Avar territory, winning four battles and taking prisoner 3,000 Avars, 8,000 Slavs, and 6,200 other barbarians (Theophylact 8.2–3). In 601, Peter replaced Priscus and fought against the Avars in the central Danubian region north of the Danube, then in 602, campaigned north of the Danube against the Slavs. These campaigns between 593 and 602, especially those across the Danube, show the strength of the Roman army, with the Avars and the Slavs rarely able to defeat them in the field. However, the limited Roman resources were mostly applied to the field armies, with a corresponding loss of control of the borders and much of the countryside. Despite the success of Roman strikes against the Slav homelands, there were still numerous groups of Slavs raiding south of the Danube. And despite Roman attacks on Singidunum, the ability of the Avars to move freely through the Balkans is striking, particularly when the Chagan arrived near Tomi in 597, having marched for several hundred kilometers through Roman territory.

Mauricius' reign is generally well treated by historians. Yet in antiquity, he was heavily criticized, and following a famine in 601 was stoned in Constantinople by the mob. According to Evagrius (5.19), he was "not easily accessible for petitions" by his subjects, though for Evagrius this was a virtue, and John of Ephesus thought that though petitioners reached him, he did not listen. He was generally thought to be greedy, and when news of his fall reached a monastery at Sykeon, near Anastasiopolis in central Anatolia, the monks rejoiced. Mauricius' will, made when he fell badly ill in 597, shows that the emperor still thought of the Empire as a Mediterranean power and had by no means given up on the west. Rather, as at Theodosius I's death in 395, the Empire was to be split between his sons, with Theodosius to succeed in the East and Tiberius in Rome.

THE ACCESSION OF PHOCAS

In November 602, Mauricius ordered his brother Peter's army to winter north of the Danube in Slavic territory. The army at first requested that Peter change the order, but when he insisted on it, they mutinied. At this point, there was no thought of overthrowing the emperor, until an embassy from the army, which included the centurion Phocas, went to Peter and was rebuffed. Only then was Phocas acclaimed as emperor, being raised on a shield in the camp. Peter fled to Constantinople, followed by the army under Phocas. Mauricius had few troops available, since most of the imperial army had already been detached to the Thracian army. He thus turned to the supporters clubs of the circus teams to defend the city. These only produced fifteen hundred Greens and nine hundred Blues.

As the army approached Constantinople, the rebel leaders wrote to Mauricius' son Theodosius, offering him the throne or, if he rejected it, offering it to his father-in-law, Germanus. Theodosius remained loyal to his father, but Germanus was thought to be interested. After surviving a difficult audience with Mauricius, he took refuge in Hagia Sophia. When Mauricius sent troops to drag Germanus from the church, riots started and the supporters' clubs abandoned the city walls. Then Mauricius lost his nerve; he abandoned the city on November 22 and fled to the church of St. Autonomus on the Asiatic side of the Bosporus. As news of Mauricius' flight spread, Germanus asked the leader of the Green circus supporters' club for the club's support. They refused, saying that "Germanus would never break from his support for the Blues." And now the army under Phocas arrived. When the Greens acclaimed Phocas, he summoned the Senate, the people, and the patriarch Cyriacus to join the army at the Hebdomon on November 23. Here he was acclaimed again by the army and then crowned by the patriarch. On November 25, Phocas entered the city, gave a donative to the troops, and acclaimed his wife Leontia as Augusta. He also swore an oath of orthodoxy administered by Cyriacus

With his loss of the capital, Mauricius' support drained rapidly away. Phocas sent soldiers who murdered him, together with his five sons, his brother Peter, Constantine Lardys, and Comentiolus, on November 27. Although Mauricius' son Theodosius was executed, a failure to deliver his head to Phocas allowed the rise of persistent rumors that he had escaped. Mauricius' widow and their three daughters survived by entering a convent, but the emperor was buried in the Church of St. Mamas at Constantinople. When faced with a similar situation in 475, Zeno had not delayed near Constantinople, but had fled to Isauria; Mauricius would have been wise to have done the same.

PHOCAS (602–610)

Following his seizure of the imperial throne, Phocas was acclaimed at the Hebdomon outside Constantinople on November 23, 602. His reign is usually seen as a disaster, partly the result of the propaganda of his successor Heraclius. Thus Theophylact, writing under Heraclius, described him as a barbarian half-breed, a cyclops, and a centaur (Theophylact, *Dialogue* 4); such opinions were certainly not voiced at the beginning of Phocas' reign. Pope Gregory, after welcoming the portraits of Phocas and Leontia in conjunction with the Senate, praised him as an instrument of God who lifted the "yoke of tribulation" from the necks of the people (*Ep.* 10.31). This is probably more reflective of Gregory's difficulties with Mauricius than of Phocas' intrinsic virtue.

Phocas was fifty-five when he became emperor, following a long military career culminating in the rank of centurion. Like most sixth-century emperors, he relied heavily on his family to help him rule, making his brother Domnitziolus *magister officiorum* at the start of the reign. Mauricius had made great use of relatives for generals, many of whom were soon removed. Comentiolus and Peter were executed in 602 and Philippicus and Germanus became priests. Priscus, however, away from the capital on a recruiting mission in Armenia, continued to serve and was soon made *comes excubitorum*. Not all those spared remained loyal, and in 605 the eastern praetorian prefect Theodore and another *illustris*, Elpidius, were executed, along with Athanasius, *comes sacrarum largitionum*, and Germanus the priest. As well as having problems with senior officials, Phocas seems always to have been short of money. The purity of his *solidi* dipped to 94.7 percent gold, whereas Mauricius' *solidi* were 97.2 percent pure, suggesting that there was something other than the constant warfare of the past century responsible. Another suggestion of a lack of popularity was a circus riot in Constantinople in 603, which resulted in a major fire along the Mese and the execution of John Crucis, leader of the Greens.

The most serious problem for Phocas came in 603, when Narses, *magister militum per Orientem* since 591, revolted and asked the Persian king Xusro for help. Phocas' first response was to use local forces under a certain Germanus to lay siege to Narses in Edessa, but these troops were soon defeated by the Persians at Constantia. Faced by an eastern field army in revolt and a Persian invasion, Phocas made a hurried peace with the Avars in 605, greatly increasing their subsidies. This allowed him to reverse Mauricius' concentration of effort on the Balkans and transfer large numbers of troops from the Danube to the eastern frontier. Under Leontius, the Romans soon captured Edessa. However, despite the reinforcements, Dara was lost in 604 after a nine-month siege and then Leontius was defeated by the Persians at Arzamon in 605. Phocas then replaced Leontius with his nephew Domnitziolus, who persuaded the rebellious Narses to surrender; he was promised his life and sent to Constantinople, where Phocas executed him.

In Italy, the problems posed by Lombards had begun to spread outside the peninsula. After King Agilulf (590–616) made peace with the Avars, both peoples began raiding Dalmatia. In 603, the Chagan even sent some Slavs to Italy who helped Agilulf capture Cremona and Mantua. The Italian exarch Smaragdus, who had been reappointed to a second term, then organized a peace with Agilulf that was repeatedly extended until 612. Smaragdus focused much of his attention on Ravenna and the north, often leaving Rome to the Pope, though he did erect a statue of Phocas in the Forum. Boniface IV (608–615) was, with imperial permission, even able to convert the Pantheon in Rome into a church.

Although Phocas was popular in Rome, there were further circus riots in Constantinople and rising political tension in the capital. Priscus, following his marriage to the emperor's daughter Domentzia in 607, now began to be honored with his portrait next to that of the emperor. Though this gesture of respect was traditional, Phocas was known to dislike it. This moved Priscus to encourage Heraclius, the exarch of Africa, to rebel against the emperor. Both had fought alongside Mauricius and were probably as distressed by Phocas' low social origin as the problems in the east. The continued sending of imperial officials to the west, and then the revolt of one and his return to seize power in Constantinople, shows continued imperial unity. When Heraclius revolted in 608, he sent a naval expedition under his son Heraclius to Constantinople via Sicily and a land expedition from Africa into Egypt under his nephew Nicetas. Once Nicetas reached Egypt, a long, violent struggle ensued, with the loyalists being led by the patriarch Theodore Scribon, later reinforced by troops from Mesopotamia under the *comes Orientis* Bonosus. The civil war in Egypt eventually came to an end when Heraclius' supporters achieved victory and Bonosus retreated to Constantinople. At the same time, this withdrawal of troops from Mesopotamia in 609 allowed the Persians to launch a successful campaign in 610, capturing the key Roman fortresses along the frontier and driving the Romans out of Armenia.

As the rebellion continued, the *exarch* Heraclius died in 610 and his son took over. Even before the younger Heraclius arrived by sea in Constantinople on October 5, several eastern mints had issued coins for him. Heraclius then won a naval battle against Phocas. Phocas had few resources to defend the city, mostly the circus supporters clubs and a few troops under Bonosus. He should also have had the *excubitores*, but Priscus betrayed Phocas and denied him their support. Phocas was soon brought before Heraclius and when the two met, said to Heraclius, "Will you be able to do better?" (John of Antioch fr.218.6). Heraclius supposedly kicked Phocas and beheaded him on the spot. Phocas' right arm and hand were then cut off and his corpse was disemboweled and then burned in the Forum of the Ox. His ashes were then scattered, and there was no imperial burial.

Heraclius had good reason to hope that he could do better than Phocas. The wars of Justinian's reign had made it clear that the Empire did not have the resources to fight effectively on multiple fronts, and the period of Justin's reign was particularly challenging, with the challenges in Italy and the Balkans being made worse by his decision to go to war with Persia in 572. However, twenty years later, after Mauricius' restoration of Xusro II, the Romans were in a different position, with friendly relations with Persia and dominance over Arzanene, Persarmenia, and Iberia. A decade of concentrating resources in the Balkans was bringing success when this was overturned by Phocas' seizure of power, but Heraclius could be confident that he could restore order rapidly.

FURTHER READING

There are several narratives available for this period. The secular classicizing historian Menander continued Agathias' *History* from 558 to 582, although his work is preserved mostly in fragments concerned with diplomacy. Menander's *History* was then continued by Theophylact for the period 582 to 602, a history that, unusually, is complete. There are several more elaborate chronicles, including Theophanes, John of Antioch, and John of Nikiu. John of Biclarum wrote a Latin chronicle covering 567–590. There are several *Ecclesiastical Histories*, including that of Evagrius, which covered 431 to 594, and the Syriac *Ecclesiastical History* by John of Ephesus, which covered 571 to 586. For events in Italy, Paul the Deacon is occasionally useful, though written in the eighth century, and for Gaul there is much in the work of Gregory of Tours.

In terms of nonhistorical works, Corippus wrote four books of Latin hexameters commemorating Justin II's accession. Both these poems and the *Chronicle* of John of Biclarum show the continuing use of Latin in the late sixth century, though for most daily purposes Greek was the preferred language. The emperor Mauricius wrote a *Strategikon*, which shows how the Roman army wished to fight and how it saw its enemies. There are several important saints' lives, including Eustratius' *Life of Eutychius*, the *Life of Theodore of Sykeon* in central Anatolia, and the *Miracles of St. Demetrius*, with an account of the sieges of Thessalonica. John of Ephesus wrote a long series of lives of holy men and women available in the *Patrologia Orientalis*. There is also the voluminous correspondence of Gregory (sometimes known as the Great), as well as of other popes and of Frankish rulers. Other documents include the *Pratum Sprituale* of John Moschus, a collection of anecdotes regarding holy men and women.

Despite the excellent source material, this period has attracted less scholarly attention than the reign of Justinian. On Justin II's reign, there is a series of excellent articles by Cameron, Averil, "The Early Religious Policies of Justin II," *Studies in Church History* 13 (1976), 51–67, "The Empress Sophia," *Byzantion* 45 (1975), 5–21, "The Artistic Patronage of Justin II," *Byzantion* 50 (1980), 62–84, and "An Emperor's Abdication," *Byzantinoslavica* 37 (1986), 161–167. For Mauricius' reign and campaigns, see Whitby, Michael, *The Emperor Maurice and His Historian: Theophylact Simocatta on Persian and Balkan Warfare* (Oxford, 1988). For Phocas, see Olster, D. M., *The Politics of Usurpation in the Seventh Century: Rhetoric and Revolution in Byzantium* (Amsterdam, 1993). For a positivist perspective on the role of women in imperial government, see Garland, L., *Byzantine Empresses: Women and Power in Byzantium, AD 527–1204* (London/New York, 1999). Religious matters are well discussed in Frend, W., *The Rise of the Monophysite Movement* (Cambridge, 1972), though the terminology is often dated, and in Wood, P., *"We Have No King but Christ": Christian Political Thought in Greater Syria on the Eve of the Arab Conquest, 400–c.585* (Oxford, 2010).

There are good studies of the northern barbarians, including Christie, N., *The Lombards* (Oxford, 1995), Curta, F., *The Making of the Slavs* (Cambridge, 2001), Vryonis, S., "The Evolution of Slav Society and the Slavic Invasions in Greece: The First Major Slavic Attack on Thessaloniki, AD 597," *Hesperia* 50 (1981), 378–390, and Wozniak, F. E., "Byzantine Diplomacy and the Lombard-Gepidic Wars," *Balkan Studies* 20 (1979), 139–158. For the Avars, see Pohl, W., "A Non-Roman Empire in Central Europe: the Avars," in Goetz, H.-W., Jarnut, J., and Pohl, W., eds., *Regna et Gentes. The Relationship between Late Antique and Early Medieval Peoples and Kingdoms in the Transformation of the Roman World*, (Leiden, 2003), 571–595. For events in Spain, see Wood, J., "Defending Byzantine Spain: Frontiers and Diplomacy," *Early Medieval Europe* 18 (2010), 292–319.

10

THE MILITARY SITUATION, 491–610

The Roman defensive system changed significantly in the century following the collapse of the Empire in the west. This reflected the required reorientation of the Roman world into one centered only on Constantinople rather than on the Mediterranean. It also reflected the change of the world into one where Rome was only one of many powers, not the largest power. Although there were clashes with the Ostrogoths in Italy and the Balkans, no coherent threat to Rome was posed by the various powers in the west. But with Justinian's reconquest of Italy and Africa in the 530s, large numbers of Roman troops were tied up here, straining the resources available for the Persian and Danubian frontiers, where there were significant threats to Roman security. However, the Empire continued to campaign effectively in the east, repeatedly crossing the Danube against the Avars and Slavs in the late sixth century. Despite numerous local successes, there were too many military commitments for the state. The sixth century, then, despite Justinian's success in reconquering much of the West, saw the Roman army constantly struggling to defend the population and tax revenues of the Empire.

RESOURCES

Foreign policy continued to be decided by the emperor in consultation with the consistory. As in the fifth century, the available resources were only sufficient to campaign effectively in one region. Yet at the beginning of the sixth century, defense of the Empire often required fighting simultaneous wars in the east and in the Balkans, while from Justinian's reign onward there were additional demands in Africa and Italy. Agathias writing in the reign of Justinian claimed that there were "now" 150,000 men to defend the whole Empire, whereas "previously" there were 645,000. Although Agathias disliked Justinian and had a rhetorical point to make, the Empire was certainly smaller in 527 than earlier. Justinian's reconquest added to the defensive responsibilities but did not increase imperial resources to the same extent. Our knowledge of the resources dedicated to various theaters is limited, but the largest commitment was clearly to the eastern frontier, followed by the Balkans. Procopius is explicit that when Belisarius was sent to Italy for the second time in 544, he had few troops because of the ongoing war against Persia (*Wars* 7.10.1). With these constant demands, supporting the campaigning field armies took priority over concern for the population and territory. The Danube may have been the limit of the area claimed by the Romans, but they were rarely able to use it as a military barrier. This led to an acceptance of the loss of Roman control of the countryside on many occasions, which reduced the state's ability to collect taxes as well as any commercial activity. In this environment, lawlessness flourished and bandits even ambushed an Avar embassy returning from Constantinople in 571.

These realities of Roman power were clearly understood by its enemies. Though there was no grand strategy of alliances between barbarians against Rome, once wars were started, Rome's enemies could ask each other for help, as in 539 when Vitigis sent envoys from Italy to the Persians or in 626 when the Avars and the Persians agreed to besiege Constantinople together. The Romans were thus concerned to minimize such cooperation by diplomatic means, making treaties with the surrounding barbarians. At their most effective, these relationships could cause barbarians to be set against barbarians, e.g., encouraging the Franks to attack the Lombards in 586 and 590 or in 578 transporting a force of Avars through Illyricum and then across the Danube to fight the Slavs. The barbarians might see these treaties differently. When the Avar Baian was negotiating with Justin II in 568, he was particularly concerned to receive the annual subsidies that the Romans had earlier sent to the Kutrigurs and Utigurs. Most of these treaties were negotiated by envoys traveling to and from the emperor in Constantinople; Corippus has left a description of the Avars at the court of Justin II in 565:

> But when the curtain was drawn aside and the inner part was revealed, and when the hall of the gilded building glittered and Tergazis the Avar looked up at the head of the emperor shining with the holy diadem, he lay down three times in adoration and remained fixed to the ground. The other Avars followed him in similar fear and fell on their faces and brushed the carpets with their long hair (Corippus, *In Praise of Justin II* 3.255–262).

These arrangements were managed by the Office of the Barbarians (*scrinia barbarorum*) reporting to the *magister officiorum*. In Italy, Belisarius in 537 claimed that he was unable to negotiate with the Goths himself, requiring them to send envoys to Justinian, but by the end of the sixth century, emperors seem to have been content to allow the exarch (or even the Pope) to negotiate on their behalf. While the envoys were traveling, a truce between the Romans and Goths was guaranteed by hostages. The most elaborate treaties were with the Persians, and Menander preserves the entire text of a treaty from 562. At the conclusion of these negotiations,

> the fifty-year peace treaty was written out in Persian and Greek, and the Greek copy was translated into the Persian language and the Persian into Greek. For the Romans the documents were confirmed by Peter, *magister officiorum*, Eusebius, and others; for the Persians by the Zikh Yesdegusnaph, the Surenas, and others. When the agreements had been written on both sides, they were placed side-by-side to ensure that the language corresponded (Menander fr 6.1).

As agreements such as these were being set up, they were guaranteed by hostages, as when John from Edessa was sent to Xusro I in 542. Procopius comments that when the negotiations failed, John could only be retrieved by paying a ransom. In Constantinople, ambassadors were received in the Consistorium in the Great Palace. This room was named after the emperor's advisory council, which could meet here or in smaller chambers, depending on whether meetings were ceremonial or administrative. Two of the great policy decisions of the period, Justinian's decision to reconquer the western Empire and Heraclius' decision to leave Constantinople and attack Persian territory, were taken by the emperor after meetings of the consistory. Other topics discussed in the consistory included Anastasius' decision to build a fortified city at Dara and Mauricius' decision to restore the Persian king Xusro II to power after he was deposed in 591. And after the Roman defeat at Callinicum by the Persians in 531, the commander Belisarius, *magister militum per Orientem*, was recalled to Constantinople. This followed an investigation carried out by Constantiolus, who was probably *dux Moesiae Secundae*. He traveled to the eastern frontier, questioned the participants, then reported back to the emperor (Malalas 18.60–61). Following his report, Belisarius was recalled to the capital and replaced as commander in the east by Mundo. This decision too was probably discussed in the consistory.

The ability of the consistory to make good decisions was dependent on the quality of the information it received. Getting good information about the west was becoming more difficult. Following the Vandal occupation of Africa, travel across the Mediterranean was more difficult, although as Belisarius' expedition arrived in Sicily in 533, Procopius mentions a household servant who had crossed from Carthage only three days earlier. Easterners visited the west less and thought of it as being only Africa and Italy. There was also a reduction in linguistic competence, with Latin being used far less in the east, though the continuing ability of Roman poets in Constantinople to write and perform in Latin suggests that the elite were still bilingual. In the West, knowledge of Greek became much less common. At the same time, the Empire's eastern horizons seem wider, with more attention being paid to Yemen and Axum (modern Ethiopia), as well as to the Crimea and the steppes beyond. The Romans continued to take efforts to find out what was happening around their Empire. When the African defenses were reconstituted in 534, Justinian wrote to Belisarius:

> We also order that your magnitude shall provide at the straits that are opposite Spain at a place called Septem as many soldiers as you decide, together with their tribune, a man of prudence and devoted to serving our Empire in all things, who can both guard the crossing itself and report to the *vir spectabilis dux* [of Mauritania] all things that happen in Spain, in Gaul and among the Franks, so that he himself [i.e., the *dux*] may refer these things to your magnitude (*CJ* 1.27.2.2).

As well as gathering information, the Romans also tried to limit the spread of information about their plans and capacities. Controlling information leakage was difficult, and the planning time required for major offensives meant that the 533 expedition against the Vandals was known about months ahead of its launch. This leakage of information could work in the Romans' favor, as in this case when the news caused revolts against the Vandals in Tripolitania and Sardinia. Since information was expected to leak, the Romans often planted it. In 556, Martinus at the siege of Phasis claimed to have reinforcements on the way, expecting the story to leak to the Persians. And in 588, the *magister militum per Thracias* Priscus was besieged at Heraclea by the Avars. After a seven-day siege, the Avars withdrew, misled by a planted message claiming that the Romans were launching an expedition against the Avar homeland. And even when good information was available, decisions made by the consistory could be overtaken by events. In the final stages of the first phase of the Gothic war, Justinian sent to Italy two envoys, Domnicus and Maximinus, with terms for the Gothic surrender. By the time they arrived, the terms offered appeared to Belisarius to be extraordinarily generous. It was at this point too that the Goths thought they could persuade Belisarius to become king of Italy. He remained loyal, although this did not stop him being accused in Constantinople of planning to betray the emperor.

Justinian may have had some suspicions of Belisarius, but sixth-century emperors had few direct internal challenges. Although Anastasius faced an Isaurian war led by Zeno's brother early in his reign and the revolt of Vitalian toward its end, neither Longinus nor Vitalian declared themselves emperor. Anastasius was, however, concerned about the risk of revolt by his generals. His initial strategy for the Persian war in 502 was to divide the Roman field forces under several commanders, and only when they proved that they could not work together were they replaced with a single unified command. Justinian's concerns about his generals were similar. In 551, for example, when the Slavs attacked Thrace,

> Justinian sent a very considerable army against them, which was led by a number of commanders including Constantianus, Aratius, Nazares, Justinus the son of Germanus, and John who they used to call the Glutton. But he placed in command of them all Scholasticus, one of the eunuchs of the palace (Procopius, *Wars* 7.40.34–35).

Justinian was challenged during the Nika riot in 532 and executed Anastasius' nephew Hypatius after the rioting mob had tried to acclaim him emperor. When the Thracian field army mutinied against Mauricius in 602, its leaders did not challenge the emperor at first. It was only when their demands were not met that the mutiny evolved into a claim on imperial power. However, after Phocas had plunged the Empire into a disastrous war with Persia, Heraclius the Elder started a civil war in 608. This led to the first battles between the Roman emperor and a rival since the reign of Anastasius.

Although the emperor was rarely challenged directly, there were several mutinies during the sixth century. The causes were mostly related to financial conditions. Some Isaurian troops betrayed Rome to the Goths in 549 because of a lack of pay. In Africa, a major mutiny started in 536, initially incited by desire for land among the soldiers, which lingered on until the mid-540s. In 588, there was a mutiny on the eastern frontier at Monocarton near Edessa, caused by a proposed change from cash allowances for equipment to issues in kind. And in 602, an order to the army to winter across the Danube led to a mutiny and the acclamation of Phocas. Though these events are well recorded, there seems to have been no greater tendency to mutiny than in other periods of Roman history. At other times, the army showed itself remarkably loyal to the emperor. During the Nika riot, Belisarius and Mundo led their troops against the population of Constantinople, supposedly massacring thirty thousand people in the Hippodrome. And in 624, Heraclius was confident enough in the loyalty of the imperial city and its garrison to leave his son there while he marched into the mountains of Armenia, not to return for four years.

This loyalty to the emperor was in part the product of a professional army and professional officer corps. Military ability was valued very highly, as shown by the emperor Mauricius' writing of the *Strategikon*, a military manual intended to give practical advice in plain language. Although some relatives of the reigning emperor such as Justinian in the reign of Justin I and Justin in the reign of Justinian held significant military ranks, they did not hold field commands, suggesting that they were not thought to have the skills needed. Other relatives were used extensively, such as Anastasius' nephew Hypatius, Justinian's cousin Germanus, and Mauricius' brother Petrus and brother-in-law Philippicus, all of whom had long careers. The majority of generals, however, were appointed after long service. The third- and fourth-century role of *protectores* as a "staff college" was not inherited by the *scribones*, though occasionally members were promoted to field rank. One of these was Comentiolus, who was a *scribo* in the Balkans in 583, led troops successfully in 584 against the Slavs, and then next year was promoted to *magister militum*. More common were men such as Rhecithangus, who served as *dux* in Syria in 541 and later served as a general in Lazica and Illyricum. Many generals had wide-ranging careers, such as Belisarius, who fought in Africa, the east, near Constantinople, and Italy, Comentiolus fought in the Balkans, Spain, and the east, and John Mystacon served in Thrace, Armenia, and Syria in the late sixth century. In extreme situations, armies could be commanded by men who were not professional soldiers. The eastern praetorian prefect Marinus was in charge of the troops opposing Vitalian in 515, and the Italian prefect Maximinus led troops to Italy in 542, though Procopius was critical of his performance, "for he was totally inexperienced in military matters and because of this was both timid and especially prone to delay" (*Wars* 7.6.12). The army sent to Italy in 552 was commanded by Narses, holding the office of *praepositus sacri cubiculi*, and another eunuch, Theodore Trithyrius, was first *sacellarius* before being promoted to *magister militum per Orientem* under Heraclius. At the end of the sixth century, we even find Mauricius himself commanding the defense of the Long Walls in 585, and Heraclius led his army throughout the Persian war.

For Mauricius and Heraclius to lead troops in the field suggests significant crises. After the failure of the western part of the Empire in the late fifth century, the frontiers to be defended from Constantinople grew longer, while the financial resources to carry out this task remained the same. This meant that the numerous problems faced in the late fifth century by the emperors Leo and Zeno only became more difficult. However, the Roman Empire was still wealthy, and with care, large sums of money could still be collected. In particular, Egypt functioned like Africa had in the third and fourth centuries, producing a huge quantity of men and money as well as feeding the capital, but requiring little for its own defense. Thus Procopius claimed that Anastasius had amassed 320,000 pounds of gold by the end of his reign, despite fighting a war with the Persians in 502–506. Justinian managed to spend this accumulated money rapidly on the Persian wars and his expeditions to the west. Once Africa was recaptured, the restored taxation system may have covered the costs of its defense, but the costs of fighting in Italy were probably never matched by tax revenues. This difficult situation changed dramatically at the start of the seventh century with the Persian war started by Phocas. In less than a decade, the Persian occupation of Syria, Palestina, and Egypt deprived the Empire of perhaps a third of its territory, but over half of its wealth. Although Heraclius was able to reoccupy these areas, the process of reconstruction had barely begun when the Arab wars started, and these territories were again soon lost to Roman control.

These revenues were managed by the praetorian prefects of the east and Illyricum and, after the reconquest, also by prefects in Africa and Italy. The accession donative of five *solidi* and a pound of silver was issued until at least the accession of Tiberius as Augustus in 578 and probably continued into the seventh century. Troops were still paid with donatives and allowances of food (*annona*) and fodder (*capitus*). An edict of 534, reestablishing the Roman administration of Africa, valued *annonae* at five *solidi*, whereas in the late fourth century they had been valued at four *solidi*; *capitus* remained valued at four *solidi* (*CJ* 1.27.1-2). Praetorian prefects generally managed the supply of border troops directly, but in 536, the way in which supplies were sent to the lower Danube was reorganized with the creation of the *quaestura exercitus*. This involved the appointment of a *quaestor* over the Danubian provinces of Scythia and Moesia Secunda and the Mediterranean provinces of Caria, the (Aegean) Islands, and Cyprus. Procopius asserted that Justinian took away the status of soldiers from the *limitanei* as well as their donatives, though like many of his claims in the *Secret History*, this is an exaggeration (*Secret History* 24.12–14). As in the fifth century, additional praetorian prefects were assigned directly to campaigning armies. Thus in 502, the praetorian prefect Apion was appointed to supply the army in Mesopotamia. "Since the bakers could not make enough bread, he gave orders for wheat to be supplied to all the households in Edessa and for them to make the military biscuit (*bucellatum*) at their own expense. On the first occasion, the Edessenes produced 630,000 *modii*'" (ca. 4,200 metric tons) (Pseudo-Joshua the Stylite 54). Procopius described the way in which prefects were supposed to prepare this *bucellatum*:

> The bread which soldiers ought to eat in camp must be baked twice in the oven, and be cooked so carefully as to last for a very long time and not spoil

in a short time; bread cooked in this way necessarily weighs less and for this reason, when such bread is distributed, the soldiers generally received as their portion one-fourth more than the usual weight (Procopius, *Wars* 3.13.15).

RECRUITING AND ORGANIZATION

As in earlier periods, troops were both conscripts and volunteers, though sons of soldiers were not normally required to serve. In sixth-century Egypt, there could be a waiting period before being able to join a regiment of *limitanei*, but field army service was less popular and recruiting was needed before major campaigns. Belisarius in 544 and Narses in 551 took strenuous measures before they went to Italy, while Tiberius recruited new contingents aggressively from the Balkans for his Persian war of 575, some of whom were named Tiberiani after himself. The biggest problem in recruiting was finding men in a hurry, not the inability to find men. Unlike earlier practice, many regimental commanders were drawn from the same area as their men, although field army regiments were still usually deployed away from their area of origin. Thus in the 530s, the Isaurians Conon and Ennes led an Isaurian regiment deployed in Italy and in 554 a Tzannic force in Lazica was led by the Tzannian Theodorus. This is similar to Belisarius' confidence in using Goths recruited from Thrace during the Italian campaigns against other Goths.

The regions most favored for recruiting were Isauria, Illyricum, Thrace, and Armenia. Although some regiments were named after their recruiting regions, not all the troops in a unit necessarily came from the area. When Procopius mentioned a regiment of Isaurians at the Battle of Callinicum in 531, he commented that these men were in fact Lycaonians (Procopius, *Wars* 1.18.38). We hear of *scribones* looking for recruits in Sicily in 591, when Pope Gregory advocated giving them presents to make them well disposed (*Ep.* 2.32), and Michael the Syrian mentions them dragging children from parents and confiscating horses, cattle, and chickens to raise an army against the Avars (10.21). Other recruits came from defeated enemies, some in large groups, such as the five regiments of *Iustinianivandali* created after Belisarius' African victory and sent to the Persian frontier. Here, they were soon joined by units formed from Gothic prisoners from Italy. At the same time, prisoners taken in Persia were sent to serve in Italy as the *equites Persoiustiniani*. Other recruits were individuals, such as the Suevian Droctulf, who fought for the Romans in Italy, Thrace, and Africa before being buried in Ravenna in the early seventh century. Another was the Armenian Artabanes, who caused the death of the *magister militum praesentalis* Sittas in 538–539 when fighting for the Persians, but later joined the Romans and was by 546 *magister militum per Africam*. Though he was later accused of plotting against Justinian, he was sent to Italy in 550.

Once they joined the army, most of these recruits served for twenty or more years. Just before the Battle of Nineveh in 627, Heraclius was able to talk to two soldiers who had mutinied against Mauricius in 602. That this was not a literary flourish is suggested by the legionary garrison at Syene in Egypt in the late sixth century, which included Flavius Comes, who served for at least twenty years, while at nearby Elephantine, Flavius Patermuthis had served for at least twenty-eight years between 585 and 613. These long enlistments maximized the impact of the Roman training system. Various drills for individuals, regiments, and armies were recommended by the late sixth-century *Strategikon*. That this was not just theory is shown by Narses in 554 training his army at Rome before campaigning against the Franks and Heraclius conducting training exercises in Cappadocia in 622. The fossilized Latin commands preserved in the *Strategikon* and Theophylact's account of the *taxiarchos* Alexander giving orders near Marcianopolis in 594, as well as the existence of military manuals, were other signs of a professional army.

The use of manpower from many areas, particularly in field armies, and many exotic names make the army sound as if it were heavily barbarized, though it is unlikely that it was more dependent on men born outside the Empire than in the fifth century. The frequent lack of soldiers often resulted in regular units being supported by allied forces, especially in Italy and the Balkans, though perhaps to a lesser degree than in the fifth-century west. In the confusion of the Roman occupation of Italy in the 530s, some Goths such as Pitzas defected to the Romans, though other Romans also defected to the Goths. Such defections were as often for financial as for political reasons. Some Isaurian soldiers betrayed Rome to the Goths in 547 because they had not been paid for a long time, while Pope Gregory in 591 complained that it was hard to get the men of the Theodosiaci to guard the walls of Rome for the same reason (*Ep.* 2.46). In some cases, allied leaders were given Roman positions, such as Cutzinas, who was a *magister militum* in North Africa in the late 540s, while in the east, Saracen tribal leaders were often appointed as *phylarchai*, mostly for patrolling and security duties. Many of these allies were hired on limited-term contracts. In Italy in 552, Narses paid off his 5,500 Lombards immediately after the Battle of Taginae because of their poor discipline (Procopius, *Wars* 8.33.2). Similarly, Agathias complained that a force of Sabiri had fought for both Romans and Persians in the Caucasus in 556:

> At the end of the campaign they were discharged by the Romans after they had received what was agreed upon. Whereupon they offered their services to the very people whom they had but recently been fighting [i.e., the Persians]. Some were the same men, some were different, but Sabiri they were all the same and they were sent from their people to serve as allies (Agathias 4.13.9).

Roman troops served in field armies or border regiments. Constantine's structure of regional field armies supported by a central imperial army remained intact until Heraclius' reign. At the end of the fifth century, there was an eastern army based at Antioch, an Illyrian army at Thessalonica, and a Thracian army at Marcianopolis. These were supported by the imperial army at Constantinople, sometimes known as "the great army" (*Oxyrhynchus Papyri* 56.3872). After the reign of Anastasius, it mostly acted as a training depot for troops who were then sent to other armies. This meant that it was often severely understrength, and when Constantinople was attacked by the Kutrigurs in 559, the regular troops had to be supplemented by volunteers and recalled veterans even though there were no significant hostilities elsewhere. In 528, Justinian divided the eastern army into two parts. The army under the *magister militum per Orientem* continued to be based at Antioch with responsibility for Mesopotamia, but a new post of *magister militum per Armeniam*, based at Theodosiopolis (Erzurum), was created with five subordinate Armenian ducates, the result of the Persians changing the focus of their campaigning to add Armenia and the Caucasus as theaters of war. Following Justinian's conquests in the west, he created further field armies in Africa at Carthage, in Italy at Ravenna, and in Spain at Carthago Nova. Under Mauricius, the *magistri militum* in Italy and Africa were upgraded to exarchs (first mentioned in 584 and 591 respectively) who had authority over their praetorian prefects. By the early seventh century, the two *magistri militum* of the imperial army had been formally replaced by a single commander, the *comes obsequii* (*Opsikion*).

These Roman field armies were often large enough to match the *Strategikon*'s ideal army of 24,000 infantry and 10,000 cavalry. The eastern field army, once reinforced from Constantinople, had 25,000 men at Dara in 530 and 20,000 men at Callinicum in 531. Belisarius led 16,000 troops from the imperial field army to Africa and 8,000 to Italy in 535. Narses led over 9,500 Romans and 8,500 barbarian allies at the Battle of Taginae in 552, and at Casilinum in 554 he also had 18,000 men. Armies in the Balkans were often of similar size. Larger forces were created by combining several field armies, so the army deployed under Celer in 502 was made up of 52,000 men from the eastern field army and the imperial army from Constantinople. In the same way, Mauricius' expedition to restore Xusro II in 591 was more than 60,000 strong, combining the eastern and Armenian field armies as well as various Persian allies.

As in the fifth century, field armies acted in support of commands of border troops led by *duces* (often upgraded to *magistri militum* by the late sixth century). These officers remained responsible to the *magister militum* of their region. Anastasius created a command of the Long Walls for the local defense of Constantinople led by a *vicarius* attached to the imperial army and supplied by a *vicarius* of the eastern praetorian prefect. These two *vicarii* were replaced in 535 by a single *praetor Thraciae* who combined their military and logistical duties. Justinian also added extra *duces* to the eastern army at Circesium in Mesopotamia and Palmyra in Phoenice Libanensis. Following the reconquest of Africa and Italy, other ducates were established in these regions.

The regiments of the field army were now generally known as *katalogoi* rather than *comitatenses*. Many earlier regiments continued to exist, so that we hear of the *Felices Theodosiaci* at Ravenna around 600, and the *Daci* at Rome and the *Bracchiati* at Constantinople at the end of the sixth century. These units were commanded by tribunes at the end of the fifth century, though by the late sixth century, these commanders were usually *comites*. During the sixth century, a series of new infantry regiments were created. These had regional names, e.g., Isaurians, Thracians, Tzannici, and Armenians, and were larger than the earlier units. One of these regiments, the Isaurians fought at Callinicum in 531. After being moved to Dalmatia, they were three thousand strong when they landed in Italy in 535 under the command of Ennes. They were then reinforced in 537 by three thousand more Isaurians before being split into two units in 538. New cavalry regiments were also formed, such as the Numidae Justiniani, the Iustinianipersae, and Iustinianivandali. Some of these regiments were large, such as the two thousand Heruls led by Visandus, Aluith, and Phanitheus in Italy in 538. The existing regiments of *foederati* had become an elite brigade under a *comes foederatorum* attached to the imperial army in Constantinople. Two further elite cavalry brigades, the *Bucellarii* and *Optimates*, were created in the late sixth century, probably in the reign of Tiberius, and also attached to the imperial army. These elite regiments supplemented the existing seven regiments of the *scholae palatinae* and were collectively commanded by the *comes domesticorum* and known as the *obsequii*. The *scholares* fought in Anastasius' Isaurian war (491–498), and though reinforced by a further four regiments raised by Justinian, they are not known to have campaigned after this. However, in 559 they helped to defend Constantinople against a Hunnic attack and in 615 rioted following an attempt to divert their rations to regular troops. Another guard regiment, the *excubitores*, fought during in Isauria under Anastasius, with Belisarius in Africa, and was still active in 610. These troops were supplemented by the cavalry bodyguards of some generals, usually known as *bucellarii*. Procopius claimed that Belisarius equipped seven thousand mounted bodyguards from his own resources in a panegyrical summary of Belisarius' achievements, though in the accounts of the armies that landed in Africa and Italy, he only said there were "many" bodyguards (Procopius, *Wars* 7.1.20). In 537, Belisarius had at least eight hundred bodyguards, while we hear elsewhere of Valerian with one thousand men and Narses with fewer than three hundred.

Like the *katalogoi*, the regiments of border troops often had continuous histories from the third century. One of these was the fifteenth *Bandon* of the *Illyriciani* in Palestina in the 630s, one of the numerous units of *Illyriciani* recorded here by the *Notitia Dignitatum* at the end of the fourth century. Regiments from the *katalogoi* were sometimes attached to border ducates while regiments were also transferred from border commands to field armies. Thus in 528, Cutzes and Buzes, the two *duces* in the province of Phoenice Libanensis, led some of their troops and a small force of field army troops against the Saracen Alamundarus. Two years later, Buzes fought at the Battle of Callinicum, and a later *dux Phoenices Libanensis*, Eiliphredas, commanded the left wing at the Battle of Solachon in 586. And in 594 the *magister militum per Thracias* Peter was so impressed with a regiment of border troops based at Asemus in Moesia Secunda (possibly the regiment of the *Praeventores* based there at the end of the fourth century; *Notitia Dignitatum Or.* 40.19) that he tried to incorporate them into his field army. Border troops might also be assigned to provincial governors, as Justinian explained in a *Novella* (103) of 536, so that riots could be kept in check.

Most of the Roman fleet was based in Constantinople, but there were also smaller flotillas on the Danube, in Lazica, and after the 530s in Italy. The partially decked ships of the late fifth century were replaced by dromons with two banks of oarsmen, sitting above and below a complete deck, with a lateen sail, two masts, and a spike ("spur") rather than a ram. Some were equipped with bolt-shooting artillery. These fleets could be substantial. Anastasius sent one hundred transports and one hundred warships carrying eight thousand men against Theoderic in Italy in 508, and Belisarius' fleet in 533 contained ninety-two warships carrying sixteen thousand men. However, they could only carry small numbers of horses, so Belisarius bought the majority of his horses in Sicily prior to landing in Africa rather than transporting them from Constantinople.

For almost three centuries, there was little change in the system of field armies created by Constantine. However, by the middle of the seventh century the enormous losses of territory in the east and in the Balkans had forced a significant change. The Illyrian field army seems to have disappeared by the end of the sixth century, but the *Opsikion* and eastern, Armenian, and Thracian field armies were reconstituted in Anatolia. The *Opsikion* was based around Constantinople and northwestern Anatolia, the eastern field army was in southeastern Anatolia as the *Anatolikon*, the Armenian field army in northeastern Anatolia as the *Armeniakon*, and the Thracian field army in southwestern Anatolia as the *Thrakesion*. This new system of organizing Roman armies into themes (*themata*) was one of the changes that marked the transition from the Late Roman Empire into the Byzantine era.

ENGAGING THE ENEMY

Commanders in the field had to make choices as to how to engage the enemy, but as in earlier periods, it was usually thought best to avoid battle. In the sixth century, cavalry were more important numerically and doctrinally than they had been in the fourth and fifth centuries. Procopius placed great emphasis on bow and lance armed cavalry, an ideal also aspired to by the *Strategikon*. Although cavalry able to fight hand-to-hand and at a distance were especially useful in low-intensity warfare, they could never replace infantry in field battles or operations in woods, swamps, and mountains. Mauricius, who admits that most cavalry regiments were proficient only with lances, thus recommended combined forces of infantry and cavalry. Some small forces were composed entirely of cavalry, as when Constantianus led ten thousand cavalry against the Gepids in 549 while the battle at Ad Decimum near Carthage in 533 was decided by cavalry alone, though there were infantry present. Commanders preferred harassing actions and delaying tactics that maximized Roman strengths in logistics and intelligence. This style of warfare was also well suited to an army that was often underresourced. The *Strategikon* included a chapter on the approaches appropriate for four groups of enemies, explaining that "not all people fight in one formation or in the same way so that it is not possible to treat them all in the same way" (Mauricius, *Strategikon* 11 preface). The four short essays on how to fight the Persians, Slavs and Antae, Huns and other Scythians, and Western barbarians contain many stereotypes, but they also fit well the attitudes and practices described by contemporaries. The named enemies provide a sense of whom the Romans saw as important militarily, saying nothing about the Caucasus, Africa, or the Saracens.

Whatever the type of operation, personal leadership by generals was still expected. We thus find Belisarius trapped outside Rome at the Salarian

Gate in 537 while leading a cavalry attack. Germanus, the officer leading the defense of the Long Walls in 559, was wounded leading a sortie against the Huns. And Bessas, aged seventy, was one of the first men up a siege ladder in the assault on the fortress of Petra in Lazica in 551. These sorts of heroics were, however, frowned on by the *Strategikon*, which argued that they were the role of the soldier, not of the general. Soldiers were rewarded for their bravery. Before Taginae, Narses paraded in front of his men, "holding in the air armbands, torques, and golden bridles on poles and displaying certain other incentives to bravery" (Procopius, *Wars* 8.31.9). Rewarding the right men was facilitated by the sort of recordkeeping shown in Agathias' account, based on an official report, of a night assault on the fortress of Tzacher in the Caucasus in 556. This preserves the exact order in which the infiltration team approached the fortress:

> Illus went in front of the men and led the way … Immediately after him came Ziper, the bodyguard of Marcellinus and after him Leontius son of Dabragezas and then in turn Theodorus, *taxiarchos* of the Tzanni (Agathias 4.18.1).

This sort of recordkeeping allowed men to feel appreciated and to be rewarded for their bravery. While good behavior was rewarded, poor behavior was punished, and discipline could be fierce. When a Roman soldier, a Thracian named Burcentius, was caught carrying letters to the Goths in 539, Belisarius turned him over to his comrades who burnt him alive, in accordance with the regulations specified in the *Strategikon*. And when information leaked like this, there were ways to compensate. In his approach march to Ariminum in 539, Belisarius divided his force into two land forces and a sea force, ordering the land force, "when they came close to the enemy should burn more fires than the strength of the army and thus make the enemy believe their numbers to be much greater than they actually were" (Procopius, *Wars* 6.16.23). The Romans also tried to find out such information, as when they questioned captured prisoners by torture before the Battle of Solachon in 586. At a tactical level, the *Strategikon* was concerned to mask numbers, suggesting that generals deploy units in varying depths and to deploy battle lines close together to make it difficult for enemy commanders to estimate numbers, even when they had interrogated prisoners.

EUROPE

For Europe, the *Strategikon* divided its enemies into westerners and Balkan peoples. The western enemies in the early sixth century were the Goths and

Vandals, with occasional contacts with Franks and Burgundians. Later in the sixth century, the Romans fought the Lombards in Italy and the Visigoths in Spain. All these armies were dominated by mostly unarmored infantry, supported by a few archers and aristocratic cavalry, armored men on unarmored horses. Procopius described the Franks who entered Italy in 539 as "having a few cavalry about their leader, these were the only ones armed with spears, but all the rest were infantry with no bows or spears but each had a sword, shield, and an axe" (Procopius, *Wars* 6.25.2–3). The western barbarians' skills in siege warfare were weak. When Belisarius was besieged in Rome in 537, the Goths constructed ladders and rams. They also built a siege tower to attack the Salarian Gate, but the oxen that drew it were unprotected and quickly shot by the Romans. The siege was abandoned after a year. In 552, near Mons Lactarius, the Goths deployed some *ballistae*. A sense of the difficulties such sieges posed for the Goths is given by Totila's demolishing part of the walls of Naples after capturing the city in 543 and removing the gates of Rome and making some attempts to demolish the walls in 546. Nonetheless, blockade could bring victories in sieges; Milan in 538 and Naples in 543 both fell to the Goths in this fashion. Such long sieges could strain limited logistical skills. This was particularly true of the Franks, whose armies in northern Italy in 539 and 554 both suffered severely from disease. When the Romans were attacking, they were generally content to blockade barbarians in fortifications and cities rather than conduct a full siege assault. They were, however, always prompt to take opportunities to infiltrate, with four hundred men led by Magnus and Ennes sneaking into Naples through an aqueduct in 536. And on some occasions, such as the siege of Cumae by Narses in 552–553, the Romans undermined the defenses by tunneling. Roman armies continued to deploy artillery such as the *ballistae* used at the siege of Rome in 536, although by the late sixth century, torsion engines had been supplemented or replaced by simpler and more powerful traction trebuchets.

Naval battles remained rare. Anastasius' navy was able to land raiders in Italy in 508 without interference from the Goths and the absence of the Vandal fleet allowed the Romans to land in Sicily and Africa in 533. The only major clash in the Gothic war was when fifty Roman ships defeated forty-seven Gothic ships at Sena Gallica in the Adriatic in 551. In this battle, the Gothic ships were unable to maneuver effectively, and thirty-nine of them were lost, clearly showing the results of Roman training. However, Roman naval superiority could not be taken for granted. Totila was able to ambush Roman supply fleets off Naples in 543 and off Rome in 546, while one of his commanders, Indulf, defeated a Roman fleet at Laureate in Dalmatia in 549.

In the Balkans, the Romans had enemies in both the upper Danubian (Illyrian) region and the lower Danubian (Thracian) region. Following the departure of the Ostrogoths to Italy, the major barbarian groups on the upper Danube at the end of the fifth century were the Gepids and Lombards, whose armies were similar to those of the Goths. There were also some Heruls and Huns. By the mid-sixth century, the Gepids had been destroyed, the Lombards had entered Italy, and the Avars dominated the upper Danube. They first appeared on the Danube in the 550s and by 582 were living on the Great Hungarian Plain and had occupied Sirmium. This city was the key to Roman defense of the upper Danube area in the fifth century, sitting close to the confluence of the Savus and Dravus rivers on the main Roman land route across the Balkans. Although Sirmium was lost to Roman control for most of the sixth century (except 568 to 582), the Romans retained control of the forts and cities just to the east of the city. The regional defenses were unable to stop the Avars moving through Roman territory, but they were able to channel their movement. The main responsibility for Roman defense of this area fell to the *magister militum per Illyricum* based at Thessalonica, though Salona was important for operations against Italy and Singidunum for operations against the Avars. However, with few troops available, Roman commanders were often forced to rely on fortifications and harassment more than challenging the enemy in battle.

Avar power was very similar to that of the Huns. It was based on a fragile confederation of subject peoples. The Avar were strongest in cavalry, especially horse archers. Some of their styles of equipment, such as tents and tunics, were soon adopted by the Romans as being better than their own styles. They had few effective infantry, though these were often provided by subjects, especially the Slavs. When Avar armies went into battle, they were noisy, being accustomed to "raise a wild cacophony and to howl and beat their drums, raising such a noise as to stun and terrify the Romans" (Menander fr. 12.3). But apart from such anecdotes, we know little about the Avars in battle, even though Theophylact described four battles won by Priscus across the Danube in 599. Like the Huns, the Avars had some ability at siege warfare, capturing Sirmium in 582 and later laying siege to Thessalonica and Constantinople. Theirs was a basic knowledge, heavily dependent on deserters, though sufficient for rams, tortoises, and traction trebuchets. At the siege of Thessalonica in 586, an eyewitness reported that the Avars

> prepared siege machines, iron battering rams, huge stonethrowers, and the
> so-called tortoises, onto which, along with the stonethrowers, they placed
> dry skins, again having devised so that they might not be harmed by fire or

boiling pitch. They nailed bloodied hides of newly slain oxen and camels onto these machines and they thus brought them up near to the wall. From the third day, and thereafter, they hurled stones, or rather mountains as they were in size, and the archers shot further, imitating the winter snowflakes, with the result that no one on the wall was able to emerge without danger and thus to see something outside (*Miracles of St. Demetrius*, 148–149).

The main barbarian groups on the lower Danube were Bulgars, Slavs, Antae, and various Hunnic groups including Kutrigurs and Utigurs. The armies of the Bulgars and Huns were similar to the Avars. Slav and Antae forces had more in common with barbarian armies in the west, mostly unarmored infantry equipped with spears, shields, bows, and javelins. Unlike western barbarians, however, they had few cavalry. Nor did they have much political unity, with the *Strategikon* commenting that "owing to their lack of government and their ill-feeling toward one another that are not acquainted with an order of battle (*taxis*)" (11.4). Thus the second book of the *Miracles of St. Demetrius* mentions several tribes, including the Drugubites, Sagudates, Belegesites, and Berzetes. Most of their threat to the Romans was from raiders who made little attempt to settle until the early seventh century. However, these raids were frequent and widespread, sometimes reaching Greece and Constantinople. The defense of this region was carried out by the *magister militum per Illyricum* based at Thessalonica and the *magister militum per Thracias* at Marcianopolis. As in Illyricum, Roman control beyond the cities and major roads was often weak. Thus in 551, some Slav raiders reached Adrianople in Thrace before being engaged by the Romans. Scholasticus was defeated in this battle and the Slavs then plundered up to the Long Walls outside Constantinople. When the Romans counterattacked the retreating Slavs, they recovered much of the plunder and many of the prisoners. Though such actions were effective at a strategic level, the personal cost to the inhabitants was often severe.

None of the barbarian peoples living along the Danube were particularly proficient with boats. Although they were often able to assemble boats, rafts, and canoes in sufficient numbers to cross rivers, these sorts of operations were always very vulnerable. Thus in 559, when a raiding force of Kutrigurs built reed boats to outflank the Long Walls near Constantinople, they were met by Germanus with a flotilla of oared galleys that destroyed them totally. Similarly, at the Avar siege of Constantinople in 626, when some Slavs tried to ferry a Persian force across the Bosporus, they were destroyed by the imperial fleet. Nor were the Slavs were particularly good at long sieges, in part because of their logistical weaknesses. But like the western barbarians, they were still able to capture cities by surprise and to improvise battering rams and scaling ladders. Topirus in the Thracian province of Rhodope fell in 550 when the Slavs lured away the garrison:

> The inhabitants of the city, deprived of the support of the soldiers, were at a great loss and began to defend themselves against the attackers according to the present circumstances. First, heating fiercely oil and pitch, they poured it on the besiegers and, all of them hurling stones against them, came close to repulsing the danger. But then the barbarians, having driven them back from the parapets by a multitude of arrows and having placed ladders against the wall, took the city by storm. They killed all 15,000 men straightaway, plundered all the wealth, and enslaved all the women and children (Procopius, *Wars* 7.38.15–18).

Against both Balkan peoples and western barbarians, field battles were less common than sieges and not always as well described. Most of these field battles had similar characteristics, although the closely packed and poorly armored Goths, Franks, and Slavs were especially vulnerable to Roman archery.

THE BATTLE OF TAGINAE, 552

The Battle of Taginae shows what could happen when everything went as hoped for the Romans. Narses was marching south from Ravenna passing Ariminum (Rimini) and following the Via Flaminia to Rome. Meanwhile, Totila at the head of the Gothic army had left Rome to oppose him. The two forces met at Taginae (Gualdo Tadino) in the Apennines. The same plain had supposedly seen a defeat by Camillus of some Gauls in the fourth century BC; from their tombs, the battle is also known as Busta Gallorum. The battle is recorded only by Procopius, who at this point in his *History* was reliant on accounts provided by others rather than writing from his own experiences.

The plain between the two camps was mostly flat, though there was a small hill on the Roman left wing. Narses occupied this with some infantry during the night and was able to defeat several Gothic attempts to occupy it the next day. The armies then deployed for battle. Totila, in the speech to his men presented by Procopius, stressed the diverse nature of Narses' army:

> The vast number of the enemy is worthy only to be despised, seeing that they present a collection of men from the greatest possible number of peoples. For an alliance which is patched together from many sources brings firm assurance of neither loyalty nor power, but being split up in nationality (*genesi*), it is similarly divided in its opinions (*Wars* 8.30.17).

Totila was in no hurry to start the fight, waiting for some two thousand additional troops who were on the way. After giving his speech, he first displayed various ornaments and decorations that the Goths could win if they were brave enough. Then he organized a single combat between a Goth named Coccas and one of Narses' bodyguards, an Armenian named Anzalas. The Roman won. And then Totila performed a personal display of arms, with various tricks, including wheeling his horse in circles and tossing his spear in the air and catching it again. These diversions bought enough time for the additional Goths to arrive.

As the armies deployed, the Roman left was commanded by Narses, the right by Valerian, both with large contingents of infantry archers forming a crescent, and in the center were the Heruls and Lombards. The Goths formed up in two lines, cavalry ahead of infantry. Totila had seen the Roman archers and, aware that his troops would suffer heavily if they engaged in prolonged missile combat, ordered them not to use their bows, but only their spears. In his thinking, he was acting in the same way as Romans were advised to do when faced with Persians, Huns, and Avars. As the Gothic cavalry advanced between the horns of the Roman crescent, they were exposed to the Roman arrow storm:

> The Goths lost many men and many horses in this event before engaging with the opposition, and only after they had experienced very heavy losses did they with difficulty finally reach the ranks of their enemy (Procopius, *Wars* 8.32.10).

In the subsequent hand-to-hand fighting, the Gothic cavalry were pushed back onto their infantry in confusion. The Goths soon broke, with some six thousand falling and many being taken prisoner. Totila was wounded in the retreat and died soon afterward.

Narses' victory was a triumph for the Roman system, though his plan was helped by Totila's readiness to charge into the teeth of the Roman defenses. This crescent-shaped formation was often used by Romans and, indeed, Agathias records Narses using it again at Casilinum against an army of Franks and Alamanni in 554. Its success depended on the Roman infantry being able to repel the Gothic charge. Most Roman generals thought infantry were effective on the defensive, and a generation later, the *Strategikon* advised commanders not to "throw many cavalry into infantry battles" (12.B.23.14). As for many barbarian armies in Europe, Totila's main hope of success in his first major field battle was the fierceness of this charge; when it failed, Roman equipment and training were enough to carry the day.

However, Roman technical superiority did not always result in military victory. Battle remained unpredictable, and the Romans were defeated by the Goths at Verona and Faventia in 542 and by Slavs at Adrianople in 551. The greatest problem faced by the Romans was the lack of troops, which had both strategic and operational consequences. Operationally, commanders often had to make choices that reflected their lack of resources: Belisarius was forced to blockade many Gothic forts and cities after 538, and the campaigns against the Avars in the 580s were dominated by sieges. Such shortages could result in conflicts between commanders, as between Narses and Belisarius in Italy in 540. Strategically, it was often possible for the Romans to generate superiority in the east or the Balkans, but the multiple demands on resources meant that a sustained effort was often difficult. This accounts for the frequent transfers of troops between the east and the Balkans in the sixth century. Nonetheless, despite the extra demands placed on the Empire by the reconquest, by the end of the sixth century the Empire had reasonable control of the Balkans and Africa.

AFRICA

Roman military activity in Africa during the sixth century can be divided into three phases: before, during, and after the Roman reconquest in 534. Before the reconquest, there was peace in the reigns of Anastasius and Justin, though Roman generals would have been concerned with the Vandal fleet that had been able to raid Greece during the fifth century. The Vandals sent an army in a fleet of 120 ships to Sardinia in 533, but its absence gave Belisarius an easy passage to Africa. Once he had landed, there were two field battles at Ad Decimum and Tricamarum. At Ad Decimum, the Vandals were initially successful in pushing the Roman cavalry back, but as they advanced in disorder, a Roman cavalry counterattack forced the Vandals from the battlefield. After this victory, Gelimer recalled the expeditionary force from Sardinia, though the Moors remained neutral. He then advanced on Carthage. Attempts to besiege the city and to persuade the Huns attached to Belisarius' army to defect failed. At Tricamarum, the reinforced Vandals engaged the Romans who had deployed as a line of cavalry in front of a line of infantry. After a series of short sharp cavalry attacks, the battle became general and the Vandals were routed. Although there are few details in Procopius' accounts, the Vandal army appears to have been similar to those of the Franks and Goths.

Following the defeat of the Vandals, a new Roman defensive system had to be created. Two edicts of 534, directed to Belisarius and to the praetorian prefect of Africa, lay out the administrative arrangements for the region (CJ 1.27.1–2). A *magister militum per Africam* was created, though this post was sometimes combined with the praetorian prefect of Africa, foreshadowing the permanent combination of the two as the exarch of Africa by the end of the sixth century. In addition to field army troops commanded by the *magister militum*, a network of border troops under four *duces* (in Tripolitania, Byzacium, Numidia, and Mauritania) and a ducate in Sardinia was established to protect against raids. Existing fortifications were repaired and new ones built.

The focus of this defensive system was the large number of African tribes, often described by the Romans as Moors, a term including the tribes of the Frexi, Laguatan, Leuathae, and Austuriani. They were lightly equipped, and Solomon in a speech to his troops before the Battle of Mammes in 534 claimed that

> most of them have no armour, and those who have shields, small ones which are not well made, holding them up are not able to turn aside what strikes against them. And after they have thrown those two small spears, if they do not accomplish anything, automatically they turn to flight (Procopius, *Wars* 4.11.26–27).

Their light cavalry were particularly good, but they had only simple siege skills and logistical systems. Immediately after the reconquest, the Romans won several victories, including Mammes, where the Moors deployed their camels in a deep circle and fought from around and between them, similar to the Gothic wagon laager. After the Roman cavalry were upset by the smell of the camels, the position was carried by an infantry assault. The Moors could be a difficult enemy to pin down. In 544, the Roman murder of a group of envoys from the Leuathae started a war that lasted for four years. This confederation was able to defeat the Romans at Cillium in 544, at Thacia in 545, and at Marta in 546. Justinian then appointed John Troglita as *magister militum per Africam*. His exploits were later commemorated in the epic poem the *Johannid* by Corippus, a rare survival of a widespread type of literature, which described his victory at the Fields of Cato in 548.

PERSIA

War on the Persian frontier was very different from Europe and Africa. The long period of peace in the fifth century was followed by a prolonged period in which war with Persia was the norm rather than the exception. Anastasius fought against the Persians in 502–506, followed by Justinian's first war, 530–532, closed by the Endless Peace. Hostilities restarted in 540, though after 545 they were confined to Lazica until 557. Finally, the Fifty Years Peace was negotiated in 561. Justin, Tiberius, and Mauricius were involved in fighting between 572 and 591. After a decade of peace, war began again in 602 and continued until the final defeat of the Persians in 628.

Persian resources in money and manpower were similar to those of the Romans. Thus in 530, they had fifty thousand men in Mesopotamia and thirty thousand in Armenia, in 556 sixty thousand in Lazica, and in 591 forty thousand in Mesopotamia. Persian kings often commanded their armies in person, as with Kavadh I at Amida in 502 and Xusro I at Dara in 573, though they often sent out supporting forces under other generals. During the reign of Xusro I (531–579), there was a series of military reforms, replacing the previous single military commander (*Eran-spahbad*) with four regional commanders (*spahbad*), and efforts were made to establish a standing force. However, the core of Persian armies was always their heavy cavalry, provided by a feudal aristocracy. These supported the elite royal cavalry regiment known as the Immortals. These troops were mostly mailed lancers, though there were numerous archers among them. The majority of troops in Persian armies were unarmored spearmen, supported by mercenary or allied contingents of infantry (the Daylami from the mountainous area south of the Caspian Sea are often mentioned) and light cavalry (Turks and Huns). Elephants were occasionally used on the battlefield as at Blarathon in 591 but were often deployed in sieges as at Edessa in 544 and Archaeopolis in 551. As in earlier periods, these forces were well managed, with some written material regarding warfare being preserved in Arabic sources. Like the Romans, Persian forces usually made camps surrounded by ditches that could also be lined with caltrops. At the Battle of Solachon in 586, the Romans had attempted to force the Persians to fight at a disadvantage by their control of the approaches to the River Arzamon. This plan was stymied when the Persians created a train of camels loaded with water skins. When the Romans captured the fortress of Petra in 551, they found "a vast quantity of grain and of cured meat as well as all other provisions which were indeed sufficient to keep all the besieged adequately supplied for five years. But the Persians had not, as it happened, stored wine there other than sour wine, but they had brought in an ample supply of beans" (Procopius, *Wars* 8.12.18–19). And in 556, Nachoragan crossed a river in Lazica with a pontoon bridge at night to attack the city of Phasis. The Persian army was thus a fully professional force, well able to challenge the Romans with every hope of success.

When campaigning against the Romans, Persian objectives were slightly different from those of the Romans. Although both empires were concerned to capture territory, the Persians were interested in taking prisoners and deporting them to Persia, as Xusro I did with many of his prisoners from Antioch in 540. They were also prepared to spare Roman cities in return for the payment of tribute. Thus also in 540, Xusro extracted five hundred pounds of gold from the Romans. The fighting took place in several different theaters, the Caucasus (mostly involving the Lazi), central Anatolia (also known as Armenia), and Mesopotamia (mainly direct conflict between Rome and Persia). Allies often played important roles, especially in Lazica and Armenia. The campaigns in Mesopotamia involved large armies that moved on predictable routes, mostly in the area of the upper Tigris. The foundation and fortification of Dara by Anastasius were particularly important here, and the city was the site of major operations in 530 and 573. Sieges and field battles attempting to lift sieges thus dominated these campaigns. Persian siege technology included mounds, rams, and mines; siege towers and artillery were used less often. They also made use of chemical weapons, such as the fire pots containing sulfur and bitumen at Petra in 550–551. These techniques could prove effective quickly, and at Jerusalem in 614 the siege lasted for only twenty-one days. On other occasions, as at Dara in 573, sieges could drag on for months.

THE SIEGE OF AMIDA, 502

Amida was another long siege. When war broke out between the Persians and Romans in 502, the Persians swiftly captured Theodosiopolis (Erzurum) then crossed the Taurus Mountains to Amida, arriving outside the city on October 5. We are well informed about the events of the next three months, with separate accounts by pseudo-Joshua the Stylite, pseudo-Zachariah of Mytilene, and Procopius, the last two making different use of a common source. Amida (Diyarbakır) was a city with strong defenses, recently rebuilt by Constantius II. It sat on a large basalt outcrop, making mining a difficult proposition. It fell to the Persians in 359 in a siege where the historian Ammianus was present, but the city was returned to Roman control when peace was made in 363. In 502, there were few Roman troops in the city, which had to be defended by its population, including many of the local monks. The Roman defense was led by Cyrus, the *praeses* of Mesopotamia.

The initial Persian attack can be divided into two phases. In the first phase, the Persians began to build a siege mound. Various local raw materials were used to build the mound, including the monastery of Mar John. As the sector to be attacked was identified to the Romans, they built additional courses on the wall opposite, increasing its height. Once the mound was close enough to the wall, the Persians then brought up a battering ram. This did not penetrate the wall, but it did cause the collapse of the additional courses. At the same time, the Romans cut a hole through the city wall to countermine the siege mound; tunneling under the mound, as the Romans did at Dura Europus, was impossible because of the basalt. After the Romans fired their mine, the mound collapsed. In the second phase, the Persians repaired the mound and covered the assault ramp with a quilted cloth that they kept damp in order to defeat Roman incendiary weapons. Nonetheless, Roman artillery did much damage, including hitting the Persian ram. One of the Roman engines was a monster known as "The Striker," which could supposedly hurl boulders weighing over 150 kilograms.

After three months with little progress, the Persians were close to giving up the siege. The Persian king Kavadh I opened negotiations with the Romans, requesting money to leave the city. In reply, the Romans demanded the cost of the food the Persians had taken from the surrounding villages to feed their troops. Then a small party of Persians were able to infiltrate a tower one night through a stream that led into the city. They took over this tower, but then came under rapid Roman counterattack. When the Persians did this in 359, the Romans repulsed them. But this time, as the news of the Persian penetration of the Roman defenses spread, Cyrus came rushing up, his staff lighting the way with torches. It was a sad civilian blunder: the group were peppered with arrows shot from the dark, and Cyrus was wounded. In the morning, the Persians still held the tower, and now the troops outside launched an assault with scaling ladders. The fighting was very fierce, and some Persians fled rather than assault the wall; they were cut down by their comrades, aware of the Persian king standing nearby. Once over the wall, it was only a matter of time before the Persians could open the city's gates.

Field battles between Romans and Persians were also hard fought. Both armies tended to draw up in a similar fashion. At the Battle of Callinicum, fought against the Persians on April 18, 531, Belisarius led Roman forces totaling twenty thousand. He was able to anchor his left flank, composed of infantry, on the Euphrates, while his center was composed of cavalry. The right wing was held by some allied Saracen cavalry. The Persian commander Azarethes deployed similarly, close to the river with his allied Saracen cavalry guarding his left flank. But the armies were not identical. Callinicum began with an exchange of archery, with Procopius commenting on the speed of the Persian arrow shot. This is confirmed by Mauricius' advice in the *Strategikon* to attack rapidly, "for any delay in closing with the enemy means that their steady rate of shot will enable them to discharge more missiles against our soldiers and horses" (*Strategikon* 11.1.59–63). At Callinicum, when a Persian attack broke through the Saracen cavalry on the Roman right flank, many Romans fled, but the infantry by the river formed a shield wall to which other Romans, including Belisarius, retreated. Despite repeated charges, the Persians were unable to break the formation, and the Romans were able to use their archery effectively. The battle continued until the evening, and then the Romans conceded the field to the Persians. Another difference is seen at an engagement before the Battle of Blarathon in 591, where Narses commanded a combined force of Romans and Persians. Although "the Romans were directed to the engagement in disciplined silence and without noise, Narses was angry with the [Persian] generals Bindoes and Sarames who were unable to calm their barbarian forces into untroubled quiet" (Theophylact 5.9.6).

Beyond the major clashes in Mesopotamia, central Anatolia, and the Caucasus, Rome and Persia could fight by proxy. During the sixth century, both empires came into contact with the Turks. Initially, the Turks were so far away from the heartlands of both empires that their only contact was as expeditionary forces, first used by the Persians as allies against the Hephthalites, but later fighting for the Romans. Other Turks, however, were hostile to Rome, and there were Turkish attacks on the Crimean cities of Chersonesus and Bosporus from the late 570s. Along the eastern frontier from Mesopotamia to the Red Sea were, according to Menander in the sixth century, "myriads of Saracen tribes" (fr. 9.1). These tribes possessed little political unity though exceptional leaders could form dangerous confederations. Employing Saracens to keep the peace was a sensible strategy for the Romans, perhaps most useful in ensuring that these peoples did not instead fight for the Persians. Around 528, Justinian "put in command of as many tribes (*phylais*) as possible Arethas son of Gabalas, who ruled over the Saracens of Arabia" (Procopius, *Wars* 1.17.47). Arethas and his family were relatively successful, as was Alamundarus, who fought for the Persians in the first half of the sixth century. Since their power was personal and rarely spanned more than a generation, the use by some historians of Ghassanid for Rome's allies and Lakhmids for Persia's allies gives an exaggerated sense of their longevity. With their lack of fixed assets and great mobility, Saracen raiders could be hard to pin down. At the end of the fifth century, Theophanes mentions Romanus, *dux* in Palestina, defeating Ogarus, the son of Arethas, but failing to catch Ogarus' brother Badicharimus. These sorts of attacks were mostly nuisances, very different from the wars of Rome and Persia. When Alamundarus claimed in 529 that "he was not breaking the treaty between the Persians and the Romans since neither had included him in it," Procopius then adds, "and this was true. For no mention of Saracens was ever made in treaties on the grounds that they were included under the names of Persians and Romans" (Procopius, *Wars* 2.1.4–5). A later Roman–Persian treaty of 562 acknowledged Alamundarus' position by stipulating that Saracens allied to both states were covered (Menander fr. 6.1). Nor did contemporaries think much of their military skills, Procopius claiming that "the Saracens are by their nature incapable of attacking a wall, and the

weakest kind of fortification, even one put together with mud-brick, is sufficient to check their assault" (*Buildings* 2.9.4).

Although the Saracens of the sixth century were a nuisance to the Roman
state, they were not significant enough to be mentioned by Mauricius in
the *Strategikon*. The sixth century and the defeat of Persia by Heraclius had
shown that the Roman army was a formidable professional force. The changes
from the army of the fourth and fifth centuries were part of the evolution
of the Roman army, not a dramatic change. The structure established by
Constantine of professional infantry regiments supported by cavalry fighting
in regional field armies continued. At the same time, the performance of the
army in terms of battlefield success was high, as shown by Priscus' successes
against the Avars in 599. Where the Roman army failed was in gaining a sufficient share of the state's resources to carry out its tasks effectively. Then, in
the seventh century, the Saracens were able to defeat a Roman field army at
the Yarmuk and a Persian army at Qadisiyya. After these victories, they then
proceeded to occupy North Africa, Egypt, Syria, and Mesopotamia. These
Saracen armies were no different in terms of men, organization, tactics, or
equipment from the armies of the sixth century, but they were very differently motivated. Against the exhausted Roman and Persian empires, that
was enough.

FURTHER READING

Although the classicizing histories of Procopius, Agathias, and Theophylact provide a
narrative, we have no memoirs or works written by serving soldiers or commanders,
even if Procopius occasionally gives us a snapshot of their discussions. For a good survey,
see Greatrex, G., "Perceptions of Procopius in Recent Scholarship," *Histos* 8 (2014),
76–121. For the later sixth century, see Whitby, M., *The Emperor Maurice and His
Historian: Theophylact Simocatta on Persian and Balkan Warfare* (Oxford, 1988).

Mauricius' *Strategikon* was written in the late sixth century to provide advice to
generals about organization and equipment, and about operations and tactics. There are
a large number of relevant papyri from Egypt and the Levant, with an especially important collection from Syene and some useful material from Nessana. There are some useful
inscriptions, though not as many as in the fourth and fifth centuries. Another interesting
group of inscriptions is a group of Anastasian military laws from Libya, Lycia, and Arabia
that show that military terminology was now almost entirely Greek.

Overviews are provided by Elton, H. W., "Army and Battle in the Age of Justinian,"
in Erdkamp, P., ed., *A Companion to the Roman Army* (Oxford, 2007), 532–550, Haldon,
J. F., *Warfare, State and Society in the Byzantine World, 565–1204* (London, 1999), and
Whitby, Michael, "The Army c.420–602," *Cambridge Ancient History* 14 (Cambridge,
2000), 286–314.

For particular campaigns, see Greatrex, G., *Rome and Persia at War, 502–532* (Leeds,
1998), Rance, P., "Narses and the Battle of Taginae (Busta Gallorum) 552: Procopius and

Sixth-Century Warfare," *Historia* 54 (2005), 424–472, Sarantis, A., "War and Diplomacy in Pannonia and the North-west Balkans during the Reign of Justinian: The Gepid Threat and Imperial Responses," *Dumbarton Oaks Papers* 63 (2009), 15–40, and Sarantis, A., "Military Encounters in the Northern Balkans from Anastasius to Justinian," in Sarantis, A. and Christie, N., eds., *War and Warfare in Late Antiquity: Current Perspectives (Late Antique Archaeology 8.2)* (Leiden 2013), 759–808.

On Roman equipment, see Chevedden, P. E., "The Invention of the Counterweight Trebuchet: A Study in Cultural Diffusion," *Dumbarton Oaks Papers* 54 (2000), 71–116, Coulston, J. C., "Later Roman Armour, 3rd–6th Centuries AD," *Journal of Roman Military Equipment Studies* 1 (1990) 139–160, and Haldon, J. F., "Some Aspects of Byzantine Military Technology from the Sixth to the Tenth Centuries," *Byzantine and Modern Greek Studies* 1 (1975), 11–47. On fortifications and sieges, see Crow, J. and Croke, B., "Procopius and Dara," *Journal of Roman Studies* 73 (1983), 143–159, and Petersen, L. I. R., *Siege Warfare and Military Organization in the Successor States (400–800 AD): Byzantium, the West and Islam* (Leiden, 2013).

On organizational matters, see Casey, P. J., "Justinian, the *limitanei*, and Arab–Byzantine Relations in the Sixth Century," *Journal of Roman Archaeology* 9 (1996) 214–222, Greatrex, G., "Dukes of the Eastern Frontier," in Salway, B. and Drinkwater, J. F., eds., *Wolf Liebeschuetz Reflected* (London, 2007), 87–98, and Haldon, J. F., *Byzantine Praetorians* (Bonn, 1984).

On tactics, see Rance, P., "The *Fulcum*, the Late Roman and Byzantine *testudo*: The Germanization of Late Roman Tactics?" *Greek, Roman, and Byzantine Studies* 44 (2004), 265–326, Rance, P., "Simulacra Pugnae: The Literary and Historical Tradition of Mock Battles in the Roman and Early Byzantine Army," *Greek, Roman, and Byzantine Studies* 41 (2000), 223–276, and Rance, P., "Elephants in Warfare in Late Antiquity," *Acta Antiqua Academiae Scientiarum Hungaricae* 43 (2003), 355–384, and Trombley, F. R., "The Operational Methods of the Late Roman Army in the Persian War of 572–591," in Lewin, A. and Pietrina, P., eds., *The Late Roman Army in the East from Diocletian to the Arab Conquest, BAR S1717* (Oxford, 2007), 321–356.

On manpower and recruitment, see Whitby, Michael, "Recruitment in Roman Armies from Justinian to Heraclius (ca. 565–615)," in Cameron, Averil, ed., *The Byzantine and Early Islamic Near East 3: States, Resources and Armies* (Princeton, 1995), 61–124, Keenan, J. G., "Evidence for the Byzantine Army in the Syene Papyri," *Bulletin of the American Society of Papyrologists* 27 (1990), 139–150, Parnell, D. A., "A Prosopographical Approach to Justinian's Army," *Medieval Prosopography* 27 (2012), 1–75, Parnell, D. A., "The Careers of Justinian's Generals," *Journal of Medieval Military History* 10 (2012), 1–16, Sarantis, A., "The Justinianic Herules: From Allied Barbarians to Roman Provincials," in F. Curta, ed., *Neglected Barbarians* (Turnhout, 2011), 361–402, and Teall, J., "The Barbarians in Justinian's Armies," *Speculum* 40 (1965), 294–322.

On the Persians, see Rubin, Z., "The Reforms of Khusro Annushirwan," in Cameron, Averil, ed., *The Byzantine and Early Islamic Near East 3: States, Resources and Armies* (Princeton, 1995), 227–298, and Inostrancev, C. A., "The Sasanian Military Theory," translated by Bagdanov, L., *K.R. Cama Oriental Institute* 7 (1926), 7–52.

II

THE REIGN OF HERACLIUS, 610–641

When Heraclius seized power from Phocas in 610, the eastern frontier of the Roman Empire was in a disastrous state. It got worse as Antioch fell to the Persians in 611, Jerusalem in 614, and Alexandria in 619. By 626, Constantinople itself was besieged by a combined force of Avars and Persians. In this extreme situation, Heraclius led an army into Persia and defeated the Sasanids at Nineveh in 627. The triumphant emperor then personally restored the fragments of the True Cross to Jerusalem in 630. But from this high point, the exhaustion of two decades of war allowed the newly emergent Islamic forces to win major victories against the Romans at the Yarmuk in 636 and against the Persians at Qadisiyya in 637. For Rome, these defeats were followed by the loss of their control of Africa, Egypt, Syria, and part of Anatolia. This dramatic string of military defeats marked the end of the ancient world, but understanding what happened and why is one of the greatest challenges of studying the Late Roman Empire.

Following the execution of Phocas, the thirty-five-year-old Heraclius was acclaimed as Augustus on October 7, 610, and crowned in the Great Palace in the Church of St. Stephen by the patriarch Sergius. Heraclius was the son of Heraclius, one of Mauricius' generals who had served on the eastern frontier and was then exarch in Africa. Heraclius himself is not known to have held any imperial posts before his participation in his father's coup. On his coronation day, he married Eudocia, daughter of an African aristocrat, who was then acclaimed Augusta. Eudocia gave birth to two children: Epiphania (born 611), acclaimed Augusta in 612; and Heraclius Constantinus (born 612), who was acclaimed Augustus on January 22, 613. Eudocia died four months after Constantinus' birth, and Heraclius rapidly remarried, this time to his niece Martina. When the patriarch Sergius asked Heraclius to abandon the incestuous marriage, the emperor refused. Nonetheless, emperor and patriarch continued to work together well. This marriage produced five sons (two disabled) and two daughters.

According to Theophanes, there were so many problems at the beginning of Heraclius' reign that "he was at a loss as to what to do" (*AM* 6103). This is an accurate description of the challenges faced by Heraclius, though it could be applied to almost every Roman emperor. The most prominent challenges were military, but these were linked to significant financial problems, the result of the continuous campaigning in the reign of Mauricius and Phocas. By the early seventh century, much of the responsibility for military finance fell on the *sacellarius*. First attested in the reign of Zeno, this official was part of the imperial bedchamber (*cubiculum*) and thus usually a eunuch. He was originally in physical charge of the emperor's personal wealth; *sacellarius* literally means "the man with the sack." Since the reign of Justinian, *sacellarii* had been involved in various financial matters, in particular paying troops. This frequent association with the army brought *sacellarii* into great prominence and sometimes even to field commands. Under Heraclius, the *sacellarius* Theodore Trithyrius was assigned a second office in 634, *magister militum per Orientem*, to lead troops in Syria. This role was part of the transition of the emperor's household into a department of the imperial government with an increased use of the *cubiculum* in place of the *res privata*. However, our ability to trace such developments becomes extremely limited in the seventh century, with the virtual disappearance of the tradition of issuing laws. Only four *Novellae* of Heraclius survive, all dealing with ecclesiastical matters but showing the continuity of the imperial practice of restating and revising existing laws. Under Phocas and Heraclius, the mint structure of the Empire was simplified drastically, with the closing of numerous mints. Some of these were lost as the Persians conquered their territory, but when recaptured they were not reestablished. By 630, there were only two mints in the east, at Constantinople and at Alexandria, and two in the west in the exarchates of Ravenna and Carthage.

Although Heraclius' reign was dominated by military events, the Roman Empire continued to function as it always had. A minor event at the start of the reign shows this clearly. After one of the *candidati*, a certain Butilinus, had sent his slaves to murder a neighbor, the dead man's mother went to Constantinople. Here, she supposedly caught hold of the bridle of Heraclius' horse and showed the emperor the bloody garment her son had worn. No action was taken at this point, but when Butilinus later appeared in the hippodrome, he was arrested, tried, and executed. Although the historian Nicephorus tells this story in the style of a saint's life, it is a powerful indication of what Romans still expected from the emperors.

The area of greatest concern for Heraclius was Persia, but there were commitments in Spain, North Africa, Italy, the Balkans, and the Caucasus. By the end of the sixth century, the efforts of Mauricius had brought the Balkans into some sort of order, but the subsequent withdrawals of troops by Phocas to fight in the east allowed the Avars to cause significant problems again. During the first few years of Heraclius' reign, groups of Slavs raided widely in the Balkans, reaching into Greece in large numbers and capturing Salona, Serdica, and Naissus. Thessalonica, packed with refugees, was besieged twice by the Slavs in the early years of the reign. Many of the Slav raiders had now extended a pattern of wintering in the Balkans to one of settling there, part of the erosion of Roman control of the countryside.

In Italy, Roman control was concentrated on Rome and Ravenna, coexisting uneasily with the Lombards. The distance from Constantinople and the minimal resources allocated meant that this region often appears detached from the Empire. There was a change from Mauricius' attempts to reconquer Italy; exarchs now followed a policy of accommodation, accepting the Lombards rather than trying to destroy them. Acting as exarch was also difficult because of the tensions of working with the Pope, simultaneously a Roman official and leader of the western church, but resident in Rome rather than Ravenna. After the exarch John revolted in 616, he was assassinated, and the eunuch Eleutherius was sent to succeed him. However, in 619, Eleutherius also revolted, declaring himself emperor at Ravenna, but he was soon killed by troops loyal to Heraclius at Luceoli in Umbria and his head sent to Constantinople. The next recorded exarch was Isaac (625–643), an Armenian who had served in Heraclius' Persian campaigns. His major concern was relationships with the Lombards, more significant when the pro-Roman king Adaloaldus (616–626) was succeeded first by Arioaldus (626–636) and then Rothari (636–652), both of whom were more hostile to the Romans. Nonetheless, Isaac was able to reduce the annual payments to the Lombards for peace from three hundred pounds of gold to two hundred pounds. Pope Honorius I (625–638) was an active builder in Rome, but we also find him handling pay for imperial troops and giving instructions to the *magister militum* Anatolius regarding a soldier under his command at Salernum, near Naples. Handling imperial finance was a mixed blessing, and in 638 Isaac ordered troops who had not received their pay to occupy the Lateran in Rome. Isaac later visited Rome, staying in the imperial palace, and organized sending a portion of the stored treasure to Heraclius. Since the Pope was handling payment for some troops, the distress expressed at Isaac's actions in the *Liber Pontificalis* may not be entirely justified.

Africa, including Corsica and Sardinia, continued to be administered by an exarch based at Carthage, with a subordinate *magister militum per Africam* and a praetorian prefect. We thus find a letter from Honorius in 627 asking Gregorius, African praetorian prefect, to punish the *praeses* of Sardinia, Theodorus, who had prevented some clergy in Cagliari from going to Rome to appeal to the Pope and had instead sent them to Africa. We know even less about the small Roman enclave in Spain ruled from Carthago Nova. The last Roman cities here were captured by the Visigoths in the reigns of the kings Sisebut (612–620) and Suintila (621–631). At this point, the senior Roman official was a patrician named Caesarius, but he is known only from his correspondence with Sisebut, not from Roman sources.

DEFENDING AGAINST THE PERSIANS

Events in the east are far better known. At first, the change in emperor from Phocas to Heraclius had little immediate impact on the war against Persia. Phocas' brother Comentiolus was in charge of the eastern armies, and though there were some negotiations with Heraclius, he was soon assassinated. In 611, the Sasanids occupied Antioch for the first time since 540 and entered Cappadocia. Then at Caesarea in Cappadocia they were met by a Roman army commanded by Heraclius, the first Roman emperor since Theodosius I to lead a Roman army in the field for a prolonged campaign. Several of his predecessors, including Justin I and Mauricius, had had extensive military experience, but with minor exceptions did not command in the field when they became emperor. Heraclius was far more active and spent much of the first two decades of his reign on the back of a horse. Faced with a well-led Roman army, the Persians withdrew from Cappadocia into Armenia, giving Heraclius a breathing space to reorganize his senior officers. Priscus was replaced as *comes excubitorum* by Heraclius' cousin Nicetas. To keep Priscus from seizing the throne (he was married to Phocas' daughter), he was tonsured and sent to a monastery at Chora in Constantinople. Heraclius then appointed Theodore, his brother, as *cura palatii*, and Philippicus, Mauricius' brother-in-law, as *magister militum per Orientem*.

With this reorganized force, in 613 Heraclius began to counterattack the Persians. Philippicus campaigned in Armenia, but Heraclius was defeated near Antioch. The Persians then crossed the Amanus Mountains and defeated the emperor again at Alexandria-ad-Issum in Cilicia, after which they occupied Tarsus. Heraclius and Philippicus both retreated across the Taurus Mountains into Cappadocia. When the emperor returned to Constantinople, the Sasanids split their forces into two, Shahin campaigning in Anatolia and Shahrbaraz fighting in Syria. Shahrbaraz occupied Damascus in late 613 and after a siege of about three weeks captured Jerusalem in 614. The shock that this sent through the Empire was comparable to that felt when Rome was sacked by the Goths in 410. Roman resistance in this area was led by Heraclius' cousin, the *praefectus Augustalis* Nicetas, who at least managed to save two relics, the lance that pierced Christ's side and the sponge used to offer sour wine to Christ on the cross; both these were then sent to Constantinople. However, thirty-five thousand Romans, including the patriarch Zacharias, were deported to Babylon along with the fragments of the True Cross. Other inhabitants of the city were massacred or fled to Egypt. The monk Antiochus Strategius was an eyewitness to the occupation and was one of those marched to Babylon before he escaped. He claimed that 66,509 Romans were killed when the city fell.

Then in 615, Shahin reached Chalcedon, from where he could look across the Bosporus at Constantinople and Europe, a view no Persian commander had seen since Xerxes in 480 BC. There were some negotiations with Heraclius, who even sent gifts to Shahin, but they were unsuccessful and the military situation continued to deteriorate. In 617, the Persians attacked Cyprus, and in 619 Shahrbaraz occupied Egypt, overcoming Nicetas. By now, the Roman defensive system in the east was in tatters. As Alexandria fell, there were accusations of plots and treachery, and the patriarch John the Almsgiver fled to his native Cyprus.

The Persians had thus won control of the Levant and then Egypt, perhaps a third of the territory of the Empire but by far the richest part. The impact of these losses can be seen in several ways. In 615, a new silver coin called a hexagram was issued based on loans from church treasures. These coins were then used, according to the *Chronicon Paschale*, to pay imperial officials "at half the old rate." The Roman monetary system since the third century was based mainly on gold and bronze, which had allowed silver to become the dominant means of decorating churches. When the silver was stripped from Edessa's more than thirty churches in 622, it totaled 112,000 pounds. According to Theophanes, "after taking the money of the holy churches in the form of a loan, being held down by difficulties, [Heraclius] also took the *polykandela* [light fixture] of the Great Church as well as other serving vessels and struck large numbers of *nomismata* and *miliarisia*," i.e., gold and silver coins (Theophanes, *AM* 6113). This suggests real desperation; when Constantine had confiscated temple treasuries in the early fourth century, this was an antipagan action, not from military need. And unlike the earlier Persian occupations of Antioch in 260 and 540, the Sasanids began to administer the conquered territory, imposing governors of their own, such as Cyrus, a local appointed to administer Edessa. As the Persians advanced, the headquarters of the eastern Roman army, together with the apparatus of government, was forced back into Anatolia. In 611, a new mint was set up at Seleucia in Isauria to pay the imperial field armies. Seleucia was not secure for long, and the mint was at first moved farther inland to Isaura in 617 and then closed in 618 when the Persians occupied Isauria. With the loss of Egypt and its rich corn-producing provinces, the traditional free bread distribution in Constantinople was first changed to a subsidy and then canceled altogether. And then there was another outbreak of plague in 619 as the Persians occupied Ancyra. It is around this point that

> despondency and despair overcame the emperor and so he decided to go to Libya … When some of the citizens became aware of these things, they tried to prevent them as much as they were able. Indeed, the patriarch, inviting him to the church, bound him there by an oath that he would not by any means abandon the Imperial city (Nicephorus 8).

Heraclius now, instead of giving up or heading west, embarked on one of the riskiest ventures ever undertaken by a Roman emperor. He left Constantinople on April 5, 622, and began concentrating troops in Armenia. After much training and some inconclusive fighting against Shahrbaraz in Cilicia, Heraclius returned to Constantinople late in the year, confident in his plan to take the war to the Persians. Before he could begin, it was critical to make peace with the Avars so as to free up resources for the Persian war, similar to earlier actions of Tiberius and Mauricius. Thus Heraclius arranged to meet the Avar Chagan at Heraclea in Thrace in June 623. In what the Romans described as barbarian treachery and what the Avars probably called seizing an opportunity, the Chagan ambushed the emperor, captured the imperial baggage, and forced Heraclius to flee to Constantinople. The Avars then penetrated the Long Walls and ravaged the outskirts of Constantinople, taking large numbers of prisoners. Despite the ambush, the Avars had little hope of successfully besieging the imperial city and Heraclius was still able to negotiate peace. The terms were not good, with the emperor being forced to turn over his illegitimate son John Atalarichus and his nephew Stephen as hostages, as well as making a payment of two hundred thousand *solidi* (about 2,800 pounds of gold). However, the peace achieved its immediate objective by freeing Roman troops who could be used against the Persians.

It was thus in March 624 that Heraclius returned to Cappadocia to begin his Persian offensive. He had an ambitious and risky plan, to fight his way through Armenia into Persia, rejecting the usual Roman preference for campaigning in Mesopotamia and instead exploiting the lessons learned by Narses and John Mystacon in 591. This required Heraclius to leave Constantinople for several years, putting much faith in the Avars to keep their treaty. Although third- and fourth-century Roman emperors had often governed from remote areas, there was little recent experience of governing the Empire from the road. Heraclius left his twelve-year-old son Heraclius Constantine at home in the care of the regent Bonus, *magister officiorum* and *patricius*, but he did take his wife Martina. He marched east through Satala and Theodosiopolis and then headed southeast through the Zagros Mountains to Canzacon near Takht-i Suleiman. Persian troops led by King Xusro II withdrew hastily, but Heraclius was unable to exploit his success and withdrew to winter in Albania. In 625, there were a series of inclusive maneuverings in the Transcaucasus, then in 626 Heraclius marched south from Albania through Armenia to Mesopotamia and reached Samosata. Here he met Shahrbaraz, who had by now returned from Egypt. Crossing the Euphrates, Heraclius then withdrew to Cilicia via Germanicia, followed by Shahrbaraz. In March, he fought a successful battle at Adana, which allowed him to retreat north to Cappadocia and then on to Lazica, while sending his brother Theodore against Shahin. But when Heraclius went to Lazica, Shahrbaraz marched west against Constantinople. The Persians dared to ignore Heraclius since their negotiations with the Avar Chagan had persuaded him to break the treaty of 623. The two enemy armies soon both reached the Bosporus and laid siege to the imperial city.

THE SIEGE OF CONSTANTINOPLE, 626

After the foundation of the Roman Republic, the capital of the Roman Empire had been attacked by barbarians only once, by the Gauls in 390 BC. Constantinople had been threatened by various barbarian tribes before, but none of these had developed into a siege. The city's defenses, the walls built by Theodosius II, were spectacular. The main wall was twelve meters high with ninety-six towers. In front of this was a forewall, 8.5 meters high, with ninety-six towers in the intervals between the main wall's towers. And then in front of this was a moat about twenty meters wide and ten meters deep. There were also a series of seawalls surrounding the city. These were formidable defenses, provided the ca. 5.7 kilometers of land walls could be garrisoned effectively.

The Romans had plenty of warning as Persians and Avars approached. Riots took place in mid-May as the city authorities decreased the bread rations in preparation for the siege. The Roman defense of the city was led by the *magister officiorum* Bonus, though the patriarch Sergius also played a prominent role. Heraclius had left a large garrison, including twelve thousand cavalry and a force of Armenians, while Sergius enlisted the Virgin Mary and placed icons at all the gates. Shahrbaraz arrived at Chalcedon in mid-June. The first Avars arrived outside the city on June 29, 626, then the Chagan arrived a month later on July 29, at the head of a confederation of Avars, Slavs, and other transdanubian peoples. The Persian army was highly capable at siege warfare, but it was in Asia and unable to cross because of the strong Roman fleet. The siege thus began with a series of Avar assaults against the Theodosian walls. It was a spectacular sight, with huge numbers of Slavs supported by twelve siege towers and by stone throwers (*petrariai*). But such a series of assaults was exactly what the defenses were designed to resist, Moreover, the defenders were well motivated, with Sergius appearing on the walls himself, and well supplied because of their control of the sea. After three days of fighting, there was a pause for negotiations. The Persians had sent three officers across the Bosporus to appear at the negotiations with the Chagan, but the Romans caught them on their return. One was executed immediately, then his head was hung from the neck of another Persian whose hands were cut off; he was then sent back to the Chagan. The third prisoner was taken by boat to Chalcedon, executed in front of the Persians, and his head thrown on land. This broke the rules of diplomacy, but faced by two hostile armies, the Romans felt that they had no choice but to attempt to break the will of the enemy.

After a few more days, the Chagan tried to reinforce his army with some Persians, perhaps hoping to get some engineering assistance for the assault on the walls. After collecting together a group of small boats, he sent them to Chalcedon to collect the Persian troops. This improvised flotilla was intercepted on its return by the galleys of the Roman fleet. Not surprisingly, it was destroyed. With this failure, the Chagan lifted the siege and retired from the city on August 8.

HERACLIUS' DEFEAT OF THE PERSIANS

The tide of the war now began to turn for Heraclius. Shahrbaraz and Shahin both returned to Persia, and with rumors that Shahrbaraz was to be executed, he rebelled against King Xusro. In Lazica, Heraclius allied with the Turkish leader Jebu Xak'an (Yabghu) before settling down to besiege the Iberian capital at Tblisi. After Tblisi was captured, he massacred many of the defenders. Then the rebellion of Shahrbaraz allowed Heraclius to strike into Persia again, repeating the approach he had used in 624 and 625. In autumn 627, in conjunction with his Turkish allies, Heraclius crossed the

Zagros Mountains into Mesopotamia, then defeated the Persians at Nineveh on December 12. No Roman emperor had reached this far into Persia since Julian's campaign in 363. Heraclius continued to advance, now facing little Persian opposition, and occupied the royal palace at Dastagerd, where he recovered three hundred Roman military standards that the Persians had been captured over the centuries. He then withdrew to Canzacon, where he was isolated by the winter snows.

Faced with Shahrbaraz' rebellion and with his armies obviously unable to challenge the Romans on the battlefield, the Persian king Xusro was deposed in a coup launched by his son Kavadh II on February 24, 628. Kavadh soon made peace with Heraclius, but died before the end of the year and was succeeded by his young son Ardasir III (628–630). The Romans were in a good position with a victorious army in a weakly led Persia, but Persian troops were still occupying Syria and Egypt. In July 629, Heraclius and Shahrbaraz met at Arabissus in Armenia Secunda, and the emperor promised to support to the Persian general's rebellion. In return, Shahrbaraz gave up any claims to conquered territory and agreed to evacuate the Persian forces still in these areas and to restore the borders to where they were in 591. He also agreed to return of the fragments of the True Cross taken by the Persians in 614. Shahrbaraz then marched on Ctesiphon, murdered Ardasir, and crowned himself king. Shahrbaraz's reign lasted less than two months, after which a series of civil wars left Persia weakened and internally focused. For Rome, this was a great triumph in which after four centuries of warfare it was clear that Rome was the greater power. The historian Theophylact, probably writing after the Roman victory, had asked rhetorically, "what happiness would events bring to the Romans, if the Persians were deprived of power and pass their power to another people?" (Theophylact 4.13.13). The Empire would soon find out (see Figure 21).

As the *comitatus* marched south to Palestina, it would have attracted petitioners. Al-Tabari records an unlikely story about Harith al-Ghassani waiting to meet the emperor at Damascus when he received a letter for Heraclius from Mohammed. More certainly, at Tiberias in Palestina Secunda the emperor was approached by some local Christians who accused a Jew named Benjamin of oppressing them, a fact confirmed by Heraclius' questioning (Theophanes *AM* 6120).

When Heraclius arrived at Jerusalem, this was the first visit to the city by a Christian emperor. The return of the fragments of the True Cross prompted the writing of a panegyrical poem by George of Pisidia and a hymn by the future patriarch Sophronius as well as marking the end of the *Chronicon Paschale*. Sebeos' *Armenian History* suggests that emotions ran high:

Figure 21. Presentation of David to King Saul, silver plate from Cyprus from 629 to 630 (Metropolitan Museum, New York).

> There was no little joy on that day as they entered Jerusalem. [There was] the sound of weeping and wailing; their tears flowed from the awesome fervour of the emotion of their hearts and from the rending of the entrails of the king [Heraclius], the princes, all the troops, and the inhabitants of the city. No one was able to sing the Lord's chants from the fearful and agonizing emotion of the king and the whole multitude (Sebeos 41).

Despite George of Pisidia's triumphant comparison of Heraclius to Christ entering Jerusalem on Palm Sunday, he also described other less palatable events. The worst was Heraclius' ordering a massacre of Jews at Jerusalem and banning of Jews from living within a three-mile radius of the city, the final result of the events at Tiberias and the rumors of Jewish collaboration with the Persians in 614.

REBUILDING THE ROMAN EMPIRE

After the euphoria of the victory at Nineveh, the Persian withdrawal from Roman territory in Egypt and Syria, and the restoration of the True Cross to Jerusalem, the hard work of rebuilding Roman administration now followed. The succession was assured when the emperor's son Heraclius (Heraclonas) was acclaimed as Caesar in 630. But it was more important that Egypt and Syria had been under Persian control for over a decade. This was not long enough for memories of Roman administration to have faded, but it would have taken a substantial effort to fill all the administrative positions that had been allowed to lapse over this period. There would also have been numerous cases of properties lost or gained in controversial circumstances, while events such as the sack of Jerusalem and the accompanying massacres would have left many questions about who owned what. The measures taken would probably have been similar to those followed when Africa and Italy returned to Roman rule under Justinian. Tangled tales from Alexandrian papyri show squabbles over property complicated by first the Persians and then later the Arab occupations of the city. These sorts of problems make clear the need for extraordinary measures, such as the appointment of Cyrus as both patriarch (ca. 631–642) and *praefectus Augustalis*, acting as the head of civil government in Alexandria.

Once the war with Persia was over, Heraclius turned his attention to religious unity. In 634, he ordered all Jews within the Empire to be baptized as Christians. Although the ability of the state to follow through on this was soon limited by the Arab wars, enough conversions were carried out to prompt the writing of *The Indoctrination of Jacob the Recently Baptised (Doctrina Jacobi nuper baptizati)*. This was a dialogue set in Carthage in 634, but written later in Palestina after the Arab attacks had begun. Heraclius was able to make a renewed attempt to resolve the divisions caused by Chalcedon. His attempt at reconciliation between the pro- and anti-Chalcedonian churches was through monoenergism. This tried to bypass the Chalcedonian focus on the nature of Christ by stating that there was only a single energy in Christ, an energy that was divino-human (*theandrike*). By moving the dispute away from the controversial grounds of the fifth century, monoenergism worked well as a compromise and was generally accepted in the east, especially given its steering by the moderate Sergius of Constantinople (610–638). Heraclius was also able to gain some support from a meeting with the anti-Chalcedonian patriarch of Antioch, Athanasius, at Hierapolis in 629/630 and his attendance at a synod at Theodosiopolis (Erzurum) in 631/633. But like all earlier moderate attempts to forge consensus, monoenergism too ran afoul of more extreme opinion. In particular, Sophronius was a well-educated Palestinian monk who had concerns that some of the language that Sergius had used to define a monoenergistic Christ was Apollinarian. Apollinarianism was a fourth-century heresy claiming that Christ had a human body and a divine mind. Although he raised these concerns with Sergius, Sophronius was able, with some qualifications, to accept monoenergism, as did the majority of eastern bishops. Then in 634 Sergius wrote to Pope Honorius, describing how successful the monoenergistic approach had been in the eastern Empire, but scrupulously including Sophronius' concerns. Honorius' reply addressed these concerns, but fatally did so by replacing the concept of a single energy with that of a single will, a doctrine known as monotheletism. The tenuous religious compromise that Heraclius had erected now began to collapse. Soon after Sophronius had written to Sergius, he was elected as patriarch of Jerusalem (634–638). And now faced with Honorius' introduction of the concept of Christ's single will, rather than a single energy, he had had enough. There was a tradition of new patriarchs declaring their faith in a synodical letter to other patriarchs on their accession. In his devastating *Synodical Letter* in 634, Sophronius rejected monoenergism, the basis of the church unity that seemed to be willingly accepted through much of the Roman world. Sergius refused to accept the letter, but the damage had been done. Any hopes that Heraclius may have had of retrieving the situation were then shattered by the rise of Islam.

THE ARAB WARS OF HERACLIUS

The wars with the Arabs brought the ancient world to an end, invoking the most severe external crisis faced by the Roman state since the Second Punic War in the third century BC. The Roman Empire barely survived and by the end of the seventh century was radically different from what had existed before. The sudden emergence of a military threat from the Syrian and Palestinian deserts was a surprise to both the Romans and the Persians. It is also one of the most difficult problems for historians of the Roman Empire to explain. From the 630s, the Romans were repeatedly defeated by Arab armies, and yet these armies, which had not presented significant threats to Rome in the fifth and sixth centuries, were smaller, more poorly equipped, and untrained. The exhaustion caused by the Persian wars is part of the story, but much of the reason for the Roman defeats must be attributed to the new factor of Islam. To mark the change, the term "Arabs" is now used in place of "Saracens."

By the early seventh century, the Romans were comfortable with how they were handling the Levantine frontier. There was a need for regular patrolling and police work against bandits, but garrisons, alliances with the local Arabs, and a thin scatter of forts kept the peace. Romans writing in the late sixth century or early seventh century, such as Theophylact Simocatta, were unaware of anything momentous in the Arabian desert. Mauricius' *Strategikon* included chapters on how to fight various enemies of the Roman state, but had nothing to say about the Arabs, while in the *Spiritual Meadow*, written by John Moschus around 600, Arabs were generally portrayed as bandits, not as a power that might overturn the Empire. The shock of the Islamic assault was thus the result of rapid change in Arabia, not of Roman ignorance of the region.

Like the barbarians faced by the Romans elsewhere, these groups had no central places, standing armies, or royal authority, even though some extended families such as the Nasrids and Jafnids were prominent. The Arab groups close to the Romans and Persians were for the most part nonagricultural societies. Movable goods, especially cash and livestock, were the basis of wealth, not land. By the seventh century, there were developed forms of writing, mostly used for poetry. There were more heavily structured Arab societies in Yemen, but this was so far away from the Roman Empire that there was only occasional diplomatic contact.

Roman sources tell us what the Romans knew about the region, but to explain the rise of Islam, we must use Arab sources. Modern historians vary greatly in their assessment of the reliability of this material based on oral traditions written down over a century after the events described. Many of these sources contradict each other, some of the material is clearly fabulous, and on many occasions it does not fit well with the Roman sources. The challenges can be seen with the life of Mohammed, for which there is no contemporary source in Arabic or any other language. The earliest large body of written material for his life is the Koran, not written at one moment, but traditionally assembled from oral material by the first Caliph Abu Bakr (632–634) in a process only completed by the third Caliph Uthman (644–656). The Koranic material is usually supplemented by biographies of Mohammed, of which the earliest was the mid-eighth-century *Sirat al-Nabi* of Ibn Ishaq. Since he was writing over a century later, it was unlikely that Ibn Ishaq talked to anyone who had known Mohammed, though he was working in an environment in which tales of Mohammed were still being told. This was also a period of rapid political change. Researchers in other societies have found that oral tradition is often revised to match political reality, and it would be naïve not to consider whether this might have happened to some of the Arabic material. Even though Ibn Ishaq and most later writers record the *isnad* (chain of transmission) of the stories they were telling, this does not provide any certainty that the stories were not adjusted for each generation. Moreover, Ibn Ishaq's original text is now lost and is available only in a version revised in the ninth century by Ibn Hisham, who deleted material that he thought was extraneous. There were other writers who covered the period before the death of Mohammed, including al-Waqidi (d. 823) and al-Tabari (d. 923), whose work covered the whole period of the conquests. As well as using a version of Ibn Ishaq's history that predated Ibn Hisham's revisions, al-Tabari used numerous other sources, but for the early period these too could only have been oral. Assessing the validity of this early material is complicated by numerous passages that Nöldeke, the first modern translator of al-Tabari's work, omitted from his 1879 translation. These include a description of Ya'fur, nephew of Tubba', a Yemeni king in the reign of the Persian king Kavadh I (488–531). Ya'fur first visited Constantinople, where the population promised to pay tribute, and then went on to Rome, which he besieged unsuccessfully. The inclusion of such passages suggests that some historians had a highly optimistic view of an Arab past.

Nonetheless, there is a unity to the material that is consistent with Roman sources and gives a good sense of Arab society in the late sixth and early seventh centuries. Mohammed was born ca. 570 to the Banu Hashim branch of the Quraysh tribe of Arabs in the small town of Mecca, over 1,200 kilometers from the Mediterranean. Affiliation by people rather than place remained an important feature of Arab society, similar to other barbarians around the Roman Empire and very different from the urban or regional identifiers used by Romans. Like many Arabs, Mohammed's early life included herding, trading, and raiding. In the 590s, he married a rich widow and trader Khadija, giving him some financial security. From about 610, Mohammed began to receive the revelations recorded in the Koran from a divine messenger that he later identified as Gabriel. His public preaching proved to be socially divisive since it was monotheistic rather than henotheistic. Like Christianity, it required abandoning previously held beliefs about other gods. Mohammed's ideas provoked opposition, but he was well supported within the Banu Hashim by his uncle Abu Talib, head of the clan. However, after Abu Talib and Khadija both died in 619, Mohammed moved to Medina in 622 in what subsequently became known as the Hijra (migration). This was in response to an appeal from his supporters there, showing that his teachings were beginning to gather support. Mohammed recaptured Mecca by 630, though he continued to live in Medina. In 632, he made the Hajj (Great Pilgrimage) to Mecca and then returned to Medina, where he died. The remarkable character of these events and their dependence on the person of Mohammed himself suggest that the Romans had not missed any major changes in Arab society in the sixth century.

As in the sixth century, the seventh century saw frequent skirmishes between the Romans and Arabs along the edge of the desert. At Mu'ta in Palestina Tertia, perhaps in 629, a certain Theodore defeated a group of raiders (Theophanes, *AM* 6123) in a battle described by both Theophanes and al-Waqidi. At first glance, this suggests an event recorded by Roman and non-Roman sources. However, the Arabic material is either based on or shares a common source with Theophanes, who himself used a Syriac chronicle in this section. For both this and subsequent events, the Roman sources are thin. On the other hand, the Arabic sources are highly detailed, listing many participants in the campaigns and providing precise dates. Yet it is impossible to begin to tackle the problems posed by the Arabic sources without a comprehensive series of modern editions and commentaries. The version of the conquest presented here is thus highly interpretative and no more likely to be correct than the majority of other versions.

Political unity among the Arabs was forged by military success. After the death of Mohammed in 632, Abu Bakr was the first Caliph (literally "successor," but a term coming to mean the leader of the Islamic community) (632–634), followed by Umar (634–644). The raids on Roman territory that had occurred in the late 620s continued, though attacks on Persia also began, led by Khalid b. al-Walid. Then in 634, with the return of Khalid b. al-Walid from Mesopotamia, the Arabs began to occupy Roman cities, including Bostra and Damascus. The Christmas sermon preached by Sophronius in Jerusalem in 634 claimed that these Arab attacks were a surprise, though his descriptions differ little from the way in which other Roman writers had traditionally described barbarians. Then over the next few years, four battles were fought between the Romans and the Arabs, at Ajnadayn, Fahl (Pella), Marj al-Suffar, and Yarmuk, but even the sequence of these is uncertain. The tradition recorded by Ibn Ishaq in the eighth century records the capture of Bostra, the defeat of al-Qubuqular (i.e., the *cubicularius*, perhaps Theodore Trithyrius) at Ajnadayn, then the Battle of Fahl, then Marj al-Suffar, the siege of Damascus in 635, and finally the Battle of Yarmuk in 636. It is impossible to relate this to the Roman sources, which record the defeat of Heraclius' brother Theodore in 634 and his replacement by Baanes and the *sacellarius* Theodore Trithyrius, jointly holding the position of *magister militum per Orientem*. Regardless of the sequence of events, it was soon clear that these attacks were more than a passing menace by raiders. Damascus was supposedly besieged by the Arabs for six months before the city fell. The scale of the threat had changed from that posed by various Arab tribes in the fifth and sixth centuries. This was recognized by the Romans with Heraclius' dispatch of a field army in 636, the first time that a Roman field army had been sent to campaign against the Arabs.

THE BATTLE OF THE YARMUK, 636

The Battle of the Yarmuk was the decisive battle between the Romans and the Arabs. The sources are very poor indeed. No detailed Roman account survives; the Arab sources are all considerably later and often cannot be reconciled with each other or the Roman sources. Reconstructing the battle is thus a highly speculative process.

The Roman forces were commanded by the *magister militum per Orientem* Baanes, an experienced Armenian soldier who had fought at Nineveh in 627 under Heraclius, and a eunuch, Theodore Trithyrius, who was recorded in Arab and Syriac sources as the *sacellarius* rather than by his name. The core of the Roman force was the eastern field army, reinforced by garrisons from Antioch and Aleppo. Later non-Roman sources mention some Arabs led by Jabala ibn al-Ayham and some Armenians led by Jarajah. The Arab sources describe the Roman army in ethnic terms, similar to the third-century Persian vision of the Roman Empire as recorded in Sapor's great inscription. There are no numbers preserved in Roman sources for this force, though a number in the range of ten thousand to twenty thousand is more likely than the one hundred thousand suggested by al-Tabari in the ninth century. The approach of this large Roman army forced the dispersed Arabs to unite. We have very little reliable information about the number of Arabs present or from which tribes, though when written records begin to appear, many claimed that their ancestors were present. Al-Tabari suggested twenty-four thousand men. The two armies met near where the Yarmuk River flowed into the River Jordan near the Sea of Galilee in the province of Palestina Secunda.

The state of the source material is such that even a sketchy narrative such as this is highly tendentious, in particular the sequence of events and the intervals between them. The battle opened well for the Romans, who pushed the Arabs back to their camp. This led to some desperate fighting in which some of the Arab women took part. Then something went wrong for the Romans as the Arabs broke part of the Roman line and forced them into a wadi. As the Romans tried to break out of the wadi, they were slaughtered. The defeat at the wadi and the breakout may be two separate battles, since al-Tabari has a month-long interval between the first clashes and the breakout from the wadi. Regardless of the details, the battle ended in a severe defeat for the Romans, with many troops being killed, including Theodore and Baanes.

The Romans had lost numerous battles before, though not even Adrianople led directly to such a dramatic change in the Empire. The strength of the Empire was still, despite the challenges of the sixth century, considerable, surviving the loss of Syria and Egypt, seeing off the joint Avar–Persian attack on Constantinople in 626, and then conquering Persia. The effort required to win these confrontations was immense, and even after the victory at Nineveh, the Empire would need decades to recover and rebuild both its finances and its confidence. The series of defeats in Syria at the hands of the Arabs could not be overturned because the exhausted Roman state was unable to send a second field army. This marked one of the differences between the Yarmuk and many other disasters that had afflicted the Romans. Even after Adrianople, the Romans still had enough troops to continue to fight, but in Syria, once the Romans had been defeated in the field and were unable to counterattack, other factors became relevant. The most important was the separation of the local aristocracy from the imperial aristocracy. This gap was not new but was a characteristic of the Empire that had continued to widen since the third century. However, the years of the Persian occupation had increased this separation, so that when the Battle of the Yarmuk was lost, it was probably seen by many as the defeat of a foreign Empire, rather than their own Empire. For some, the association of Chalcedonianism with the state also contributed to this feeling of detachment. In addition to these internal factors, there was Islam, which united and motivated the Arabs in a new way. The Roman state eventually found answers to this challenge, but it took time to develop them. The importance of Islam is also suggested by developments in Persia. The Persians had not suffered as badly as the Romans during Heraclius' wars. The civil wars following Heraclius' victory, however, had left them politically divided, leading to a swift political collapse after their defeat by the Arabs at the battle of Qadisiyya in 637.

After the Yarmuk, the Roman abandonment of Syria soon followed. In some cases, Roman officials made peace for themselves with the Arabs, such as John Cateas, governor of Osrhoene, who agreed to pay the Arabs if they did not cross the Euphrates into his province. Heraclius recalled him and sent him into exile. Following the occupation of Syria, other losses of Roman territory to the Arabs followed rapidly while raids began to penetrate deep into the Empire. In 640, there were Arab attacks on Armenia, and we even hear of a raid by Mu'awiya on Euchaita in central Anatolia in 640. The loss of Egypt soon followed in 641, though there was little resistance and in Alexandria Patriarch Cyrus negotiated peace with the Arabs, though this resulted in his recall and exile. The rapid disintegration of the east was similar to the rapid losses of territory in the west in the fifth century, but unlike that situation, the emperor in the east retained enough military power that he could continue to rule.

At the same time as the Romans were losing control of Syria and Egypt, Heraclius was attempting to manage other problems. There were continuing military problems on other frontiers. In the Balkans, the Avars were regrouping, though their failure at Constantinople had weakened their confederation and at least one tribe, the Ounogoundouroi Huns, rebelled. They were led by King Koubratos, who had been a child hostage in Constantinople when he was baptized in 619. When Koubratos made peace with the Romans, he received the honor of patricius. In Italy, the exarch Isaac confiscated much of the Papal treasury to pay his troops in 638, as well as sending some of this treasure to Heraclius. Little is known of Africa or Spain. With all these challenges and defeats, confidence in Heraclius' leadership had been weakened. In 637, Heraclius' illegitimate son John Atalarichus was involved in an unsuccessful plot to replace the emperor together with Theodore, *magister officiorum* and Heraclius' nephew, and an Armenian noble David Saharuni. Heraclius may have decided that he could afford to lose an heir since he had several other male children. Atalarichus and Theodore were mutilated and exiled to an island in the Sea of Marmara, while David was arrested but escaped. Soon afterward, the succession was confirmed with the acclamation on July 4, 638, of the twenty-three-year-old Heraclius (Heraclonas) as Augustus and his younger brothers David and Marinus as Caesars.

In addition to the secular problems, Heraclius' attempts to resolve the problems caused by Chalcedon had also foundered following Sophronius' *Synodical Letter*. Nonetheless, emperor, patriarch, and Pope still stood together behind monotheletism, reinforced in an edict of 638. This was the so-called *Ekthesis* (Statement), a justification of monotheletism issued in the name of Heraclius but written by Sergius. All was in vain, and a decade later Heraclius' successors abandoned the attempt to reconcile the churches. Less than fifteen years after the humiliation of Persia and the triumphal visit to Jerusalem, Heraclius' Empire was on the verge of collapse.

Heraclius, probably sad and tired, died on February 11, 641, after a reign of thirty years, four months, and six days. He was buried at the Church of the Holy Apostles in Constantinople in a sarcophagus of white marble. Of his predecessors as Roman emperor, only four, Augustus, Constantine I, Theodosius II, and Justinian I, had ruled for longer. Heraclius' will left the Empire to his two adult sons from his second marriage, Heraclius Constantine and Heraclius II (Heraclonas), but it was a daunting legacy. The Arabs continued to gain territory from the Romans, so that by the end of the seventh century all of North Africa was in their hands. This process was one of continued struggle, so that the Romans recaptured Alexandria in 645, but lost it again in 646, while Carthage fell in 696, was recaptured by the Romans in 697, and then lost again in 698. At the same time, Constantinople itself began to be attacked, with Arab raids on the Bosporus in 653–654 and sieges of Constantinople in 674–678 and 717–718. The certainties of the sixth century, of the two lamps of the Romans and Persians illuminating the world, were now long gone and were replaced with a new task for the Christian emperor of opposing the forces of Islam.

Assessing the reign of Heraclius involves making judgments about whether the Roman state should have been able to surmount the challenges posed by the Persians and by the Arabs. Heraclius can thus be seen as the savior of the Roman state or as a man struggling uselessly against the tides of history. Despite his defeat of the Persians, in what was the most successful campaign against them since the reign of Trajan in the early second century AD, Heraclius' reign is characterized by military failure. Yet the rise of Islam took the whole of the Mediterranean by surprise. Christianity had taken several centuries to change the face of the Roman Empire, whereas Islam shattered the fabric of the Empire in less than a century. The rise of Islam brought about the most significant political, cultural, and religious changes in Europe since the Roman unification of the Mediterranean in the second century BC.

FURTHER READING

The sources for events in the seventh century are disparate and incomplete, and present numerous difficulties in interpretation. There are Greek narratives by Nicephorus and Theophanes, both dating from the early ninth century, but based on earlier material. Nicephorus' *Breviarium* provides a highly condensed account of events between 602 and 769, but one that is so compressed that it does not mention the Battle of the Yarmuk. Theophanes was a contemporary of Nicephorus, whose chronicle, despite numerous problems, remains the foundation for seventh-century chronology. The basis of his narrative was a Greek translation of a Syriac chronicle also used by Dionysius of Tel-Mahre. For events down to 628, especially those taking place in Constantinople, the *Chronicon Paschale* is useful. This originally covered history from Adam down to Easter 630, only a few weeks after Heraclius had returned the True Cross to Jerusalem. The description of the fall of Jerusalem is most easily accessible in Conybeare, F. C., "Antiochus Strategos' Account of the Sack of Jerusalem in A. D. 614," *English Historical Review* 25 (1910), 502–517. Histories in other languages are also useful, including the Latin *History of the Lombards* by Paul the Deacon. Dionysius of Tel-Mahre wrote a history in Syriac covering 582–842. This work is now lost, but material from it was incorporated into other Syriac chronicles, including the *Chronicle of Michael the Syrian*. The *History* attributed to Sebeos, written in the 660s in Armenian, covered the period between 572 and Sebeos' own day and is unusual in its use of Persian documents. Lastly, the *Chronicle* of Bishop John of Nikiu was written in Greek in late seventh-century Egypt but is now only available in an Ethiopian translation of an Arabic translation, so its text sometimes poses problems.

These narrative sources can be supplemented by a number of other works. George of Pisidia wrote several panegyrical poems in praise of Heraclius, the patriarch Sergius, and Bonus the Patrician. There are some saints' lives, mostly in Greek, including the *Life of Theodore of Sykeon*, documenting central Anatolia in the late sixth and early seventh century, Leontius' *Life of John the Almsgiver*, covering Alexandria in the early seventh century, and the *Life of Anastasius the Persian: The Indoctrination of Jacob the Recently Baptised* covers events around the occupation of Jerusalem; see Dagron, G., and Déroche, V., "Juifs et chrétiens dans l'Orient du VIIe siècle," *Travaux et Mémoires* 11 (1991), 17–248 for the text and French translation. Other ecclesiastical material and a good introduction are contained in Allen, P., ed., *Sophronius of Jerusalem and Seventh-Century Heresy: The Synodical Letter and Other Documents* (Oxford, 2009). There are useful collections of papal letters, in particular the voluminous correspondence of Gregory the Great (590–604). Papyri include an archive from Nessana, Kraemer, C. J., ed., *Excavations at Nessana 3: Non-Literary Papyri* (Princeton, 1960), but few inscriptions and laws, just a few novels of Heraclius. And finally, there is a large body of Arabic material, but historians are often uncertain as to the best way to approach this. Recent introductions include Donner, F., *Muhammad and the Believers: At the Origins of Islam* (Cambridge, MA, 2010) and Hoyland, R., *Seeing Islam as Others Saw It* (Princeton, 1997).

For the reign of Heraclius, the best modern introduction is Kaegi, W. E., *Heraclius, Emperor of Byzantium* (Cambridge, 2003) or the papers in Reinink, G. J. and Stolte, B. H., eds., *The Reign of Heraclius (610–641): Crisis and Confrontation* (Leuven, 2002). Howard-Johnston, J. D., *East Rome, Sasanian Persia and the End of Antiquity* (Aldershot, 2006) includes the critical article "Heraclius' Persian Campaigns and the Revival of the Eastern Roman Empire," *War in History* 6 (1999), 1–44, which is used as the basis of the chronology followed here. See also Howard-Johnston, J., *Witnesses to a World Crisis: Historians and Histories of the Middle East in the Seventh Century* (Oxford, 2010). A wider perspective comes from Haldon, J. F., *Byzantium in the Seventh Century* (Cambridge, 1990). Greatrex, G. and Lieu, S. N. C., *The Roman Eastern Frontier and the Persian Wars AD 363–628* (London, 2002) provide easy access to the sources in translation. For the Arab wars of the seventh century, two monographs provide very different perspectives, Donner, F., *The Early Islamic Conquests* (Princeton, 1981) and Kaegi, W. E., *Byzantium and the Early Islamic Conquests* (Cambridge, 1995). For events in Italy from the Roman perspective, a good introduction is Brown, T. S., *Gentlemen and Officers* (Edinburgh, 1984), but see also Moorhead, J., *Gregory the Great* (London, 2005). For the impact of the successive occupations of Egypt, Schiller, A. A., "The Budge Papyrus of Columbia University," *Journal of the Egyptian Research Centre in Egypt* 7 (1970), 29–118.

CONCLUSION

The history of the Roman Empire from the third to the seventh century AD is defined by the relationship of the emperors to their aristocracy. The late Roman Empire was the period of an imperial aristocracy that assisted the emperor in managing a pan-Mediterranean Empire. Before the mid-third century, emperors ruled by using local aristocrats, whose hierarchy was based on landed wealth rather than on imperial service. And after the mid-seventh century, the imperial aristocracy was defined solely by opposition to Islam and the struggle for control of the Balkans and Anatolia. As long as the Empire could reward a sufficiently large number of aristocrats, it could survive local setbacks and even the loss of significant territory. The fifth-century loss of western territories and resources changed the size of the Empire, but did not destroy it or force change to its way of operating. Nor did the Arab conquests of the seventh century cause the collapse of the Roman Empire, though they did force substantial change.

Christianity was an important part of the story of the Empire. However, the mechanics of ruling the Roman Empire changed little as it became Christianized. The critical factors of ruling through consensus, the power of law, and the right to appeal all existed long before the conversion of the Empire to Christianity. The centralization of the Empire around its rulers generated the need for professionalism. Throughout the Late Roman Empire, government was by the emperor, though in response to reports, petitions, and appeals. The quality of imperial rule was high, though this did not stop contemporaries from criticizing emperors. But Christianity did divert many men and much money into the church as it changed the social and cultural world, and many of the talented church leaders might have been brilliant governors or generals. Christianity also brought a major new challenge to emperors, that of attempting to forge religious unity. The repeated failure of emperors to create a lasting consensus was probably inevitable, the result of a divided Greek east with a powerful emperor interacting with a unified Latin west; a clear understanding of the political pressures and theological subtleties consistently evaded all parties.

The Late Roman Empire did not die. It survived numerous military, ecclesiastical, and financial crises. The fall of Africa to the Vandals caused the collapse of the western parts of the Empire, while the Arab conquests brought about the loss of Syria and Egypt, restricting the state to Anatolia and the Balkans. These defeats were ultimately the result of the divergence of the interests of the state and of the Roman aristocracy. The uniting of these interests had created the Roman Republic and driven it across the Mediterranean. And they would again be reunited in the smaller Roman Empire of the late seventh century as it struggled for survival. But between these two periods, there stood a flourishing Late Roman Empire characterized by diversity, good government, and hard-working emperors.

GLOSSARY

Note on plurals: The plural forms of Greek and Latin words usually involve a change in the final letters. These are indicated in parentheses after the singular form.

Acclamation, the ceremony by which a Roman emperor was accepted by the army, the Senate, and the people.

Akoimetoi, the monks of a monastery in Constantinople whose prayers continued throughout day and night, hence the name, which means "sleepless ones." They had a tendency to religious extremism.

Adventus, literally "the arrival," the name given for the ceremony of arrival for an emperor at a city.

Advocatus, lawyer.

Agens (agentes) in rebus, a low-ranking imperial official with miscellaneous duties, often sent out from the imperial court to investigate problems.

Agri deserti, land that was taxed at a lower rate because at one point it had been abandoned.

Annona, either the process of collecting taxation in the form of goods or a ration allowance for a Roman soldier.

Archimandrite, head of a monastery.

Artaba, an Egyptian measure of wheat and other dry goods, ca. 25 kilograms.

Assessor, legal secretary.

Augustus (Augusti), the Roman emperor. There were often several Augusti at the same time, making up the imperial college, which acted jointly in most matters.

Aureus (*aurei*), gold coin, issued at 60 or 70 to the pound; replaced by *solidi* in the reign of Constantine.

Aurum coronarium, a gold crown given to the emperor on his accession by each city in the Empire.

Aurum oblaticum, payment in gold by individual senators to the emperor on his accession.

Biarchus, military rank approximately equal to corporal.

Caesar (*Caesares*), Roman emperor, usually appointed by an Augustus and subordinate to him.

Candidatus (*candidati*), member of the imperial bodyguard, drawn from the *scholae.*

Cataphract, fully armored cavalry soldier on an armored horse.

Chalke, the main entrance to the Great Palace in Constantinople, named after the bronze roof tiles or the bronze-plated gates.

collatio glebalis, tax introduced by Constantine paid by senators on landholdings.

collatio lustralis, informally known as the *chrysargyron,* this was a very unpopular tax imposed by Constantine and levied every five years on merchants and craftsmen. It was abolished by Anastasius.

Comes (*comites*), literally a companion, used as both an honorary title and as an office; sometimes translated as count.

Comes excubitorum, officer in command of the excubitores, a regiment of guard infantry.

Comes foederatorum, from the fifth or sixth centuries, an officer in command of several elite cavalry regiments.

Comes Orientis, official in charge of the diocese of Oriens.

Comes patrimonii, from the reign of Anastasius, the official in charge of imperial estates.

Comes rei militaris, senior military officer with either territorial or field army responsibilities.

Comes rei privatae, replacing the *rationalis rei privatae,* the imperial official in charge of the income from emperor's personal holdings, including gifts and bequests.

Comes sacrarum largitionum, replacing the *rationalis rei summae,* the imperial official in charge of the income from the Roman Empire.

Comitatus, those accompanying the emperor, usually the imperial court and the army.

Comitatenses, soldiers or regiments of Roman field armies.

Comitiva, geographical area of authority of a *comes.*

Consistory, the imperial advisory council, with all members except the emperor standing.

Consul (consules), honorary position held by two magistrates annually (from Constantine's reign onward, one in the east, one in the west); years were named after the consuls. The institution faded in the reign of Justinian.

Consularis, governor of a Roman province.

Corrector, governor of a Roman province.

cubicularius (cubicularii), literally a member of the bedroom staff of the emperor or empress, used for any member of the close household, often a eunuch.

Cura Palatii, originally an official who managed the imperial palace, but from the reign of Justinian a title often given to men close to the emperor.

Curialis, town councilor.

Cursus publicus, imperial post service, responsible for an empire-wide network of couriers on carts and horses.

Decennalia, ten-year anniversary of an imperial accession.

Decurion, member of a city council.

Diocese, one of twelve territorial subdivisions of the Roman Empire, administered by a *vicarius* reporting to a praetorian prefect and containing a varying number of provinces, usually between six and twelve.

Donative, gift of money to the army on imperial accessions and anniversaries.

Drachma, silver coin used in the Greek east. There were several variations, but the most common, the Attic drachma, was the equivalent of a denarius.

Dux (duces), military official in charge of a frontier province or group of provinces.

Exarch, late sixth-century official in Africa and in Italy combining roles of *magister militum* and praetorian prefect.

Fabrica, imperial workshop for the production of arms and armor for the army.

Indiction, fifteen-year cycle starting from AD 312. Initially financial, but soon became used for dating purposes.

Iugerum (iugera), Roman measure of land, covering an area 280 × 120 feet, ca. 0.25 hectares.

Iugum, tax unit of land made up of a variable number of *iugera.*

Kathisma, the imperial box in the Hippodrome at Constantinople. It was connected to the Great Palace by a spiral staircase known as the Snail.

Katholikos, terms used for patriarchs of Armenia, Persarmenia, and Georgia.

Limitanei, category of troops deployed on the borders of the Empire, as opposed to in field armies.

Logothete, financial manager.

Magister militum, magister utriusque militiae, a post introduced by Constantine for the officers commanding Roman field armies.

Magister officiorum, master of the offices, a post introduced by Constantine for the manager of the *scholarii,* the *agentes in rebus,* and several other imperial bureaus.

Marzpan, governor of a province of the Persian Empire, sometimes called satraps by the Romans.

Modius, measure of dry goods, ca. 6.7 kilograms.

Novella, a new, i.e., just issued, imperial law.

Patriarch, archbishop of Alexandria, Antioch, Constantinople, and, from 451, Jerusalem. The term patriarch is used here for consistency, but they were often referred to as bishops or archbishops by contemporaries.

Patricius, honor given to high-ranking Romans. In the fifth-century west, there was usually only one *patricius,* though in the east there were often several. Also used as a personal name.

Persarmenia, name given to the eastern part of Armenia after the partition of 387. Its chief city was Dvin.

Phylarch, tribal leader, usually of Arab allies, working for the Romans.

Pope, bishop of Rome. The term Pope is used throughout this work, though it was not in general use until the fifth or sixth century.

Praefectus Augustalis, the imperial official in charge of the diocese of Egypt (established in the reign of Valens), equivalent to a *vicarius.*

Praefectus vigilum, imperial official in charge of the night watch of Rome.

Praeses, governor of a Roman province.

Praetorian prefect, in the third century, commander of troops and in charge of justice and the levying of supplies usually reporting to an emperor. From the reign of Constantine, prefects lost their military duties, and by the mid-fourth century they were assigned to one of four geographical areas.

Princeps Senatus, the first man of the Senate, an honorary position in both eastern and western Senates.

Province, smallest unit of imperial administration, made up of a number of cities under the authority of a governor.

Pseudocomitatenses, regiments of limitanei (border troops) temporarily transferred to the *comitatenses* (field army troops).

Quaestor, imperial official responsible for drafting legislation.

Quinquennalia, five-year anniversary of an imperial accession.

Res privata, the private possessions of the Empire.

Res summa, the possessions of the Roman state, e.g., land captured in war.

Sacellarius, the emperor's personal treasurer, though by the middle of the sixth century this official was responsible for many financial matters.

Schola, regiment of guard cavalry.

Scholarius (scholarii), member of a regiment of guard cavalry.

Scribo (scribones), imperial bodyguards often entrusted with special missions, attested from the reign of Justinian onward.

Senate, the city council of Rome, composed of office holders and their descendants, later duplicated at Constantinople. Senators were important, but neither Senate had any role in governing the Late Roman Empire.

Silentiarius, ushers in the imperial palace, first attested in the fourth century.

Silentium, term often used for the consistory in the sixth century. Sometimes this body met with the Senate, in which case it was the *silentium cum conventu.*

Siliqua, silver coin worth 1/24th of a *solidus,*

solidus (solidi), gold coin introduced by Constantine minted at 72 to the pound. This remained the standard coin of imperial payment through the Late Roman Empire. Also known as a *nomisma.*

Tremissis, a gold coin worth one-third of a *solidus.*

Tricennalia, thirty-year anniversary of an imperial accession.

Vexillatio (vexillationes), a cavalry regiment named after its standard (*vexillum*).

Vicarius, imperial official responsible for a diocese, reporting to a praetorian prefect.

Vicennalia, twenty-year anniversary of an imperial accession.

Vota, public vows for the welfare of the state and the Empire, usually expressed in terms of five and ten years.

PRIMARY SOURCES

This is intended primarily as a guide for students to explore the primary sources cited in the text. The focus is thus on accessible English translations rather than on scholarly editions of the texts. References are made to printed editions, although many of the older and ecclesiastical texts are available online. Numbering systems chosen are for the ease of use of Anglophone students, thus the *Latin Panegyrics* are numbered in accordance with the edition of Nixon and Rodgers. Most entries are also accompanied by some secondary reading. Translations are from the cited sources; Greek and Latin are often modified, Syriac and Armenian are not.

Acta Maximiliani, ed. and tr. Musurillo, H., *The Acts of the Christian Martyrs* (Oxford, 1972)

Acts of Chalcedon, tr. Price, R. M. and Gaddis, M., *The Acts of the Council of Chalcedon* (Liverpool, 2005)

Acts of Council of Constantinople 553, tr. Price, R., *The Acts of the Council of Constantinople of 553* (Liverpool, 2009)

Acts of Second Ephesus, tr. Perry, S. G. F., *The Second Synod of Ephesus* (Dartford, 1881). See also Millar, F., "The Syriac Acts of the Second Council of Ephesus (449)," in *Chalcedon in Context: Church Councils 400–700*, eds. Price, R. M. and Whitby, Mary. (Liverpool, 2009), 45–69

Agathias, tr. Frendo, J. D., *Agathias: The Histories* (New York, 1975)

Ambrose, tr. Liebeschuetz, J. H. W. G., ed., *Ambrose of Milan* (Liverpool, 2005); see also McLynn, N. P., *Ambrose of Milan* (Berkeley, 1994)

Ammianus, tr. Hamilton, W., *Ammianus Marcellinus: The Late Roman Empire* (Harmondsworth, 1986), though this omits some passages; for entire text and translation, Rolfe, W., *Ammianus Marcellinus* (Cambridge, MA, 1935–1939); see also Matthews, J. F., *The Roman Empire of Ammianus* (London, 1989)

Anonymus, *de Rebus Bellicis*, ed. and tr. Thompson, E. A., *A Roman Reformer and Inventor* (Oxford, 1952)

Anonymus Valesianus, *Pars Posterior* in Rolfe, W., *Ammianus Marcellinus*, vol. 3 (Cambridge, MA, 1939)

Athanasius, tr. Robertson, A., *Select Writings and Letters of Athanasius, Bishop of Alexandria, Nicene and Post Nicene Fathers*, second series, vol. 4 (London, 1892); see also Barnes, T. D., *Athanasius and Constantius* (Cambridge, MA, 1993)

Augustine, tr. Baxter, H. B., *Augustine: Select Letters* (Cambridge, MA, 1930); see also O'Donnell, J. J., *Augustine: A New Biography* (New York, 2006)

Aurelius Victor, tr. Bird, H. W., *de Caesaribus* (Liverpool, 1994)

Candidus, tr. Blockley, R. C., *The Fragmentary Classicising Historians of Later Roman Empire*, vol. 2 (Liverpool, 1981)

Cassiodorus, *Chronicle*, no English translation currently available; see Heather, P. J., "Cassiodorus and the Rise of the Amals: Genealogy and the Goths under Hun Domination," *Journal of Roman Studies* 79 (1989), 103–128

Cedrenus, no translation currently available, Greek text in Bekker, I., *Georgius Cedrenus, Compendium Historiarum, CSHB* 33–34,(Bonn, 1838–1839)

Chronicle of Zuqnin, tr. Harrak, A., *The Chronicle of Zuqnin*, Parts III and IV (Toronto, 1999)

Claudian, tr. Platnauer, M., *Claudian* (Cambridge, MA 1922); see also Cameron, Alan, *Claudian* (Oxford, 1970)

Codex Justinianus, tr. Blume, F. W. in Frier, B. W., ed., *The Codex of Justinian* (Cambridge, 2016)

Codex Theodosianus, tr. Pharr, C., *The Theodosian Code* (Princeton, 1952); see also Matthews, J. F., *Laying Down the Law* (New Haven, 2000)

Collectio Avellana, no complete translation, though many of the documents are translated in Coleman-Norton, P. R., *Roman State and Christian Church*, 3 vols. (London, 1966); see also Cooper, K. and Hillner, J., eds., *Religion, Dynasty, and Patronage in Early Christian Rome, 300–900* (Cambridge, 2007)

Corippus, *In Praise of Justin II*, tr. and ed., Cameron, Averil, *Flavius Cresconius Corippus, In laudem Iustini. Augusti minoris* (London, 1976)

De caeremoniis, tr. Moffat. A. and Tall, M., *The Book of Ceremonies* (Sydney, 2013)

Dexippus, no English translation currently available; see Millar, F., "P. Herennius Dexippus: The Greek World and the Third-Century Invasions," *Journal of Roman Studies* 59 (1969), 12–29

Digest, tr. Watson, A., *The Digest of Justinian* (Philadelphia, 1985)

Ennodius, *Life of Epiphanius*, tr. Cook, G. M., *The Life of Saint Epiphanius by Ennodius* (Washington, 1942); see also Kennell, S. A. H., *Magnus Felix Ennodius: A Gentleman of the Church* (Ann Arbor, 2000)

Eugippius, *Life of Severinus*, tr. Robinson, G. W., *The Life of St. Severinus* (Cambridge, MA, 1914); see also Thompson, E. A., *Romans and Barbarians* (Madison, 1982), 113–136

Eunapius, *History*, tr. Blockley, R. C., *The Fragmentary Classicising Historians of Later Roman Empire*, vol. 2 (Liverpool, 1981); *Lives of the Sophists*, tr. Wright, W. C., *Philostratus and Eunapius, Lives of the Sophists* (Cambridge, MA, 1921)

Eusebius, *Ecclesiastical History*, tr. Lake, K. and Oulton, J. E. L., *Eusebius, Ecclesiastical History*, 2 vols. (Cambridge, MA, 1926–1932); *Life of Constantine*, tr. Cameron, Averil and Hall, S. G., *Eusebius, Life of Constantine* (Oxford, 1999); *Martyrs of Palestine*, tr. McGiffert, A. C. and Richardson, E. C., *Eusebius Pamphilius, Nicene and Post Nicene Fathers*, second series, vol. 1 (London, 1890); *Tricennial Oration, in Praise of Constantine*, tr. Drake, H. A., *In Praise of Constantine: A Historical Study and New Translation of Eusebius' Tricennial Orations* (Berkeley, 1976); see also Barnes, T. D., *Constantine and Eusebius* (Cambridge, MA, 1993)

Eutropius, *Breviarium*, tr. Bird, H. W., *Eutropius Breviarium* (Liverpool, 1993)

Evagrius, tr. Whitby, Michael, *The Ecclesiastical History of Evagrius Scholasticus* (Liverpool, 2000)

George of Pisidia, no translation currently available

Gregory Nazianzus, *de vita sua*, tr. Meehan, D. M., *Three Poems* (Washington DC, 1987); see also Daley, B., *Gregory of Nazianzus* (London, 2006)

Gregory of Nyssa, *de Deitate Filii et Spiritus Sancti*, no English translation currently available; see also Meredith, A., *Gregory of Nyssa* (London, 1993)

Gregory Thaumaturgus, *Canonical Letter* in Heather, P. J. and Matthews, J. F., *The Goths in the Fourth Century* (Liverpool, 1991)

Gregory the Great, *Letters*, tr. Martyn, John R. C., *The Letters of Gregory the Great* (Toronto, 2004)

***Historia Augusta*,** tr. Magie, D., *Historia Augusta*, 3 vols. (Cambridge, MA, 1921–1932)

Iamblichus, *de Mysteriis*, tr. Clarke, E. C., et al., *Iamblichus, de Mysteriis* (Atlanta, 2003)

Jerome, *Letters*, tr. Wright, F. A., *Jerome, Select Letters* (Cambridge, 1933); ***Preface to Commentary on Ezekiel*,** tr. Fremantle, W. H., *Jerome: the principal works of St. Jerome, Nicene and Post Nicene Fathers*, second series, vol. 6 (London, 1893); see also Rebenich, S., *Jerome* (London, 2002)

John Chrysostom, *Homilies on the Statues, Homily on Eutropius*, tr. Stephens, W. R. W., *St. Chrysostom, Nicene and Post Nicene Fathers*, first series, vol. 9 (London, 1889); see also Liebeschuetz, J. H. W. G., *Barbarians and Bishops* (Oxford, 1990) and Mayer, W. and Allen, P., *John Chrysostom* (London, 1990)

John of Antioch, tr. Gordon, C. D., *The Age of Attila: Fifth Century Byzantium and the Barbarians*, revised by D. Potter (Ann Arbor, 2013)

John of Ephesus, *Ecclesiastical History*, the only English translation is the inadequate version of Payne Smith, R., *The Third Part of the Ecclesiastical History of John Bishop of Ephesus* (Oxford, 1860); see also van Ginkel, J. J., *John of Ephesus: A Monophysite Historian in Sixth-Century Byzantium* (Groningen, 1995); *Lives of the Eastern Saints*, tr. Brooks, E. W., in *Patrologia Orientalis*, vols. 17–19; see also Harvey, S. A., *Asceticism and Society in Crisis: John of Ephesus and the Lives of the Eastern Saints* (Berkeley, 1990)

John of Nikiu, tr. Charles, J. H., *The Chronicle of John, Coptic Bishop of Nikiu* (London, 1916)

Joshua the Stylite, tr. Trombley, F. and Watt, J. W., *The Chronicle of Pseudo-Joshua the Stylite* (Liverpool, 2000)

Julian, *Letters*, tr. Wright, W. C., *Julian*, vol. 3 (Cambridge, MA, 1923)

Lactantius, *dmp*, ed. and tr. Creed, J. L., *Lactantius, De Mortibus Persecutorum* (Oxford, 1984)

***Latin Panegyrics*,** tr. Nixon, C. E. V. and Rodgers, B. S., *In Praise of Later Roman Emperors: The Panegyrici Latini* (Berkeley, 1995)

Leo, *Letters*, selected letters tr. Feltoe, C. L., *Leo the Great, Gregory the Great, Nicene and Post Nicene Fathers*, second series, vol. 12 (London, 1894)

Libanius, tr. Norman, A. F., *Selected Orations*, 2 vols., *Autobiography and Selected Letters*, 2 vols. (Cambridge, MA, 1969–1992); see also van Hoof, L., ed., *Libanius: A Critical Introduction* (Cambridge, 2014)

***Liber Pontificalis*,** tr. Davis, R., *The Book of Pontiffs (Liber Pontificalis)* (Liverpool, 2000)

***Life of Daniel the Stylite*,** tr. Dawes, E. and Baynes, N. H., *Three Byzantine Saints* (Oxford, 1948); see also Lane Fox, R., "The Life of Daniel," in Edwards, M. J. and Swain, S., eds., *Portraits: Biographical Representation in the Greek and Latin Literature of the Early Empire* (Oxford, 1997), 175–225

Malalas, tr. Jeffreys, E. et al., *The Chronicle of John Malalas* (Melbourne, 1986); see also Jeffreys, E. et al., *Studies in John Malalas* (Sydney, 1990)

Malchus, tr. Blockley, R. C., *The Fragmentary Classicising Historians of Later Roman Empire*, vol. 2 (Liverpool, 1981)

Marcellinus Comes, tr. Croke, B., *The Chronicle of Marcellinus* (Sydney, 1995); see also Croke, B., *Count Marcellinus and his Chronicle* (Oxford, 2001)

Mauricius, Strategikon, tr. Dennis, G. T., *Maurice's Strategikon* (Philadelphia, 1984); see also Rance, P., *The Roman Art of War in Late Antiquity: The Strategikon of the Emperor Maurice. A Translation with Commentary and Textual Studies* (Aldershot, forthcoming)

Menander, tr. Blockley, R. C., *The History of Menander the Guardsman* (Leeds, 1985)

Michael the Syrian, tr. (French), Chabot, J.-B., *Chronique de Michel le Syrien Patriarche Jacobite d'Antioche (1166–1199)*, 4 vols. (Paris, 1899)

Miracles of St. Demetrius, tr. (French), Lemerle, P., *Les plus anciens recueils des miracles de saint Démétrius et la pénétration des Slaves dans les Balkans* (Paris, 1979–1981)

Nestorius, *The Bazaar of Heraclides*, tr. Driver, G. W. and Hodgson, L. (Oxford, 1925); see also Wessel, S., *Cyril of Alexandria and the Nestorian Controversy* (Oxford, 2005)

Nicephorus, ed. and tr. Mango, C., *Nikephoros Patriarch of Constantinople: Short History* (Washington, DC, 1990)

Notitia Dignitatum, no good translation and commentary currently available, ed. Seeck. O., *Notitia Dignitatum* (Berlin, 1876); see also Brennan, P., "A User's Guide to the *Notitia Dignitatum*: The Case of the *dux Armeniae*," *Antichthon* 32 (1998), 34–49

Novellae, Theodosius II, Valentinian III, Majorian, Marcian, Severus, and Anthemius, tr. Pharr, C., *The Theodosian Code* (Princeton, 1952); **Justinian, Justin** II, tr. Miller, D., in Sarris, P., ed., *The Novels of Justinian* (Cambridge, forthcoming).

Olympiodorus, tr. Blockley, R. C., *The Fragmentary Classicising Historians of Later Roman Empire*, vol. 2 (Liverpool, 1981)

Optatus, tr. Edwards, M., *Optatus: Against the Donatists* (Liverpool, 1997)

Origo Constantini, tr. Lieu, S. N. C. and Montserrat, D., *From Constantine to Julian: Pagan and Byzantine Views* (London, 1996).

Orosius, tr. Fear, A. T., *Orosius. Seven Books of History against the Pagans* (Liverpool, 2010)

Oxyrhynchus *Papyri*, ed. and tr. Grenfell, B. P. et al., *The Oxyrhynchus Papyri*, (London, 1898–current)

P. Abinn., ed. and tr. Bell, H. I. et al., *The Abinnaeus Archive* (Oxford, 1962)

P. Beatty Panop., ed., Skeatt, T. C., ed., *Papyri from Panopolis* (Dublin, 1964)

Paul the Silentiary, tr. Bell, P., *Three Political Voices from the Age of Justinian* (Liverpool, 2010).

Peter the Patrician, tr. Banchich, T., *The Lost History of Peter the Patrician* (London, 2015)

Photius, *Bibliotheca*, partial tr. Freese, J. H., *The Library of Photius* (London, 1920); see also Wilson, N. G., *Photius: The Bibliotheca* (London, 1994)

Porphyry, *Life of Plotinus*, tr. Edwards, M. J., *Neoplatonic Saints: The Lives of Plotinus and Proclus by Their Students* (Liverpool, 2000)

Priscus, tr. Blockley, R. C., *The Fragmentary Classicising Historians of Later Roman Empire*, vol. 2 (Liverpool, 1981); see also Maas, M., "Fugitives and Ethnography in Priscus of Panium," *Byzantine and Modern Greek Studies* 19 (1995), 146–160

Procopius, *Wars, Buildings, Secret History*, tr. Dewing, H. B., *Procopius*, 7 vols. (Boston, MA, 1914–1940); see also Kaldellis, A., *Procopius of Caesarea: Tyranny, History and Philosophy at the End of Antiquity* (Philadelphia, 2004)

Sapur Inscription, tr. Frye, R. N., *The History of Ancient Iran* (Munich, 1984); often referred to as the *Res Gestae Divis Saporis*

Sebeos, tr., Thomson, R. W., *The Armenian History Attributed to Sebeos* (Liverpool, 1999)

Sidonius Apollinaris, *Ep.*, tr. Anderson, W. B., *Sidonius Apollinaris*, 2 vols. (Cambridge, MA, 1936–1965); see also Harries, J., *Sidonius Apollinaris and the Fall of Rome* (Oxford, 1994)

Socrates, tr. Zenos, A. C., *Socrates and Sozomenus, Ecclesiastical Histories, Nicene and Post Nicene Fathers*, second series, vol. 2 (London, 1890); see also Urbainczyk, T., *Socrates of Constantinople: Historian of Church and State* (Ann Arbor, 1997)

Sozomen, tr. Hartranft, D., *Socrates and Sozomenus, Ecclesiastical Histories, Nicene and Post Nicene Fathers*, second series, vol. 2 (London, 1890)

Suda, www.stoa.org/sol/

Symmachus, *Relationes*, tr. Barrow, R. H., *Prefect and Emperor: The Relationes of Symmachus, A.D. 384* (Oxford, 1973)

Synesius, *Letters*, tr. Fitzgerald, A., *The Letters of Synesius of Cyrene* (Oxford, 1926); ***de regno***, tr. Fitzgerald, A., *Essays and Hymns of Synesius* (Oxford, 1930); see also Cameron, A. and Long, J., *Barbarians and Politics at the Court of Arcadius* (Berkeley, 1993).

Syro-Roman lawbook, tr. Vööbus, A., *The Syro-Roman Lawbook* (Stockholm, 1983)

Themistius, tr. Heather, P. J. and Moncur, D., *Politics, Philosophy and Empire in the Fourth Century: Themistius' Select Orations* (Liverpool, 2001); see also Vanderspoel, J., *Themistius and the Imperial Court* (Ann Arbor, 1995)

Theodoret, ***Eccleiastical History***, tr. Jackson, B., *Theodoret, Jerome, Gennadius, & Rufinus: Historical Writings, Nicene and Post Nicene Fathers*, second series, vol. 3 (London, 1892); ***Curatio***, tr., Halton, T., *A Cure of Pagan Maladies* (Mahwah, NJ, 2013); ***Eranistes***, tr. Ettlinger, G. H., ***Theodoret, Eranistes*** (Oxford, 1975); see also Urbainczyk, T., *Theodoret of Cyrrhus: The Bishop and the Holy Man* (Ann Arbor, 2002)

Theophanes, tr. Mango, C. and Scott, R., *The Chronicle of Theophanes Confessor* (Oxford, 1997)

Theophylact, tr. Whitby, Mary and Whitby, Michael, *The History of Theophylact Simocatta* (Oxford, 1986)

Vegetius, tr. Milner, N. P., *Vegetius, Epitome of Military Science* (Liverpool, 1997)

Zachariah of Mytilene, tr. Phenix, R. R. and Horn, C. B., *The Chronicle of Pseudo-Zachariah Rhetor* (Liverpool, 2011)

Zonaras, partial tr. Banchich, T. and Lane, E., *The History of Zonaras* (London, 2009)

Zosimus, tr. Ridley, R. T., *Zosimus: New History* (Sydney, 1982)

INDEX

Roman emperors (*Augusti*) in bold